PURITY COOK BOOK

Foreword

The *Purity Cook Book* is a Canadian classic, part of the cooking tradition that I grew up with and that I'm glad so many more can now enjoy in this reprint of original Purity recipes.

When I was growing up, my mother didn't own many cookbooks, but the few she had were much-loved and much-used. One of those was the original *Purity Cook Book*. It became, and has remained, a favourite of mine.

I recall thinking, as I leafed through the pages of recipes so many years ago, that I had surely discovered one of the most wonderful cookbooks in the world! It had *everything*: dozens of cakes, cookies and pies galore, baked desserts and breads, soups, so many main dishes, cheese and egg specialties, salads and vegetables, even canning, preserving and freezing tips, directions and recipes. When my mother wasn't available, this was the book I turned to for ideas and guidance.

Those who know about my sweet tooth won't be surprised to learn that the first section of the cookbook that I explored was the "sweets" section! But eventually, I prepared and served recipes from every section of the *Purity Cook Book*. The delicious results explained why my mother liked the cookbook so much!

To this day, I'm grateful for what I learned about cooking from the tried-and-true recipes in my *Purity Cook Book*. And to have them available again through this reprint of the original recipe book will be welcome news for everyone who appreciates the tradition of home style cooking and baking.

The *Purity Cook Book* brings back a lot of memories of good food and good times. May the recipes in this edition help you create many memorable meals to share and enjoy with your family and friends.

Jean Paré

Jean Paré, author
Company's Coming cookbooks

Copyright © 2001 Historical Notes by Elizabeth Driver
Copyright © 2001 by Whitecap Books

Fifteenth Printing, 2006
16th Printing, 2007
17th Printing, 2007
First published in 1967 by Purity Flour, Maple Leaf Mills Limited
Purity is a licensed trademark of Robin Hood Multifoods Inc.

Printed in Canada

Canadian Cataloguing in Publication Data

Main entry under title:

The all new Purity cook book

Includes index.
ISBN 1-55285-183-4
ISBN 978-1-55285-183-8

1. Cookery.
TX715.6.A535 2001   641.5   C00-911185-9

> **Please note that the ingredients, methods
> and cooking times listed in this book are
> consistent with the kitchen appliances and
> techniques that were in use in 1967.
> Current equipment and supplies may pro-
> duce different results that are inconsistent
> with contemporary food safety theories.**

How to Measure

The importance of measuring accurately cannot be over-emphasized. Variability in
measurements will lead to variability in the finished product.

Flour: A "Dry Measuring Cup", NOT a liquid measuring cup, should be used to
measure flour and similar dry ingredients. A dry measuring cup has a
completely smooth, flat top rim, no pouring lip and provides exactly one cup
when filled to the top. Fill the dry measuring cup with flour until it is
heaped above the top. Level the top by lightly scraping the excess away with
the straight edge of a knife or spatula. DO NOT BANG OR TAP THE CUP OR
PRESS THE FLOUR DOWN AT ANY TIME WHILE MEASURING. The $^1/_2$ cup, $^1/_3$ cup
and $^1/_4$ cup dry measures should be used in the same way. Where a recipe calls for a tablespoon
or teaspoon of flour or other dry ingredient it should be similarly levelled off
with a spatula or knife.

TO CONVERT FLOUR MEASURES TO WEIGHTS

1 cup Pre-Sifted PURITY All-Purpose Flour	= 150 grams	= $5^1/_3$ ounces
1 tablespoon Pre-Sifted PURITY All-Purpose Flour	= $9^1/_2$ grams	= $^1/_3$ ounce

Contents

SEE ALSO ALPHABETICAL INDEX AT BACK OF BOOK

TABLE OF EQUIVALENTS

All recipes in this book are based on standard measuring spoons, standard 8-ounce measuring cup and the Imperial quart (5 cups).

All Measurements are Level

1 tablespoon	=	3 teaspoons
1 cup	=	16 tablespoons
1 quart (Imperial)	=	5 cups
1 quart	=	2 pints
1 gallon	=	4 quarts
½ cup	=	8 tablespoons
⅓ cup	=	5⅓ tablespoons
¼ cup	=	4 tablespoons
1 fluid ounce	=	2 tablespoons
1 pound	=	16 ounces (dry measure)

APPROXIMATE EQUIVALENT WEIGHTS

Butter and margarine	1 pound	=	2 cups
Cheese, shredded	1 pound	=	4 cups
Chocolate	1 ounce	=	1 square
Coconut, shredded	1 pound	=	6 cups
Corn Meal	1 pound	=	3 cups
Currants	1 pound	=	3 cups
Dates, pitted	1 pound	=	2½ cups
Flour, All-Purpose	1 pound	=	3 cups
Marshmallows	½ pound	=	32 large or 5 cups miniature
Mustard, dry	1 ounce	=	4 tablespoons
Nuts, shelled:			
Almonds	1 pound	=	3⅓ cups
Peanuts	1 pound	=	3 cups
Pecans	1 pound	=	4 cups
Walnuts	1 pound	=	4 cups
Raisins	1 pound	=	3 cups
Rice, uncooked, regular	1 pound	=	2 cups
Sugar:			
Brown, lightly-packed	1 pound	=	2¾ cups
Granulated	1 pound	=	2¼ cups
Icing, sifted	1 pound	=	3⅔ cups

SUBSTITUTIONS

Chocolate: 1 square = 3 tablespoons cocoa plus 1 teaspoon shortening

Flour: ⅞ cup All-Purpose = 1 cup Cake and Pastry

Sour Milk: 1 cup = 1 tablespoon lemon juice *or* vinegar plus milk to make 1 cup

THINGS TO REMEMBER

Buttermilk and sour milk may be used interchangeably.

The term "sugar" refers to regular granulated sugar.

Lightly-packed brown sugar will just hold its shape when turned from the measuring cup. Do not pack down firmly.

Icing sugar is sometimes referred to as confectioner's sugar; fruit sugar as powdered sugar or fine granulated.

THE ART OF BREAD-MAKING

Most of us remember the bread grandmother used to bake in her cosy kitchen. Fragrant, golden loaves—crusty, tender and delicious. Home bread-baking is not as common today, and that is a pity, because it is such a pleasant task and surprisingly easy.

There are just two essentials for successful bread-making:

*Select your ingredients with care.
Master a few simple skills.*

First, those all-important ingredients:

HARD WHEAT FLOUR is the most important basic ingredient because it contains the necessary proteins to make gluten, which gives bread its "elastic" quality. This enables the dough to hold the gas produced by the yeast and thus expand or "rise". It is essential that flour be uniform in protein content—and this is why, at PURITY, we employ protein-testing and quality-controls to assure you a reliable, uniform flour. PURITY All-Purpose Flour is *Pre-Sifted*, so it is not necessary for you to sift it before measuring.

YEAST is a tiny living plant which grows very quickly under proper conditions, producing carbon dioxide gas which makes the dough rise. It may be purchased in two forms, active dry yeast which is in tiny brown pellets, and compressed fresh yeast in cake form. Since the active dry yeast keeps longer and does not require refrigeration it is the more widely used and recipes in this book call for it.

NOTE:

To substitute fresh yeast for active dry yeast, use one yeast cake for each envelope of dry yeast. Do not sweeten the lukewarm water—just crumble yeast cake into the specified amount of lukewarm water, let stand 10 minutes and stir.

SUGAR is food for the yeast, helping it to produce carbon dioxide gas. It also improves the flavour of bread and helps give a golden brown crust.

SALT acts as a control for the yeast action and brings out the flavour of bread and rolls.

SHORTENING makes the dough easier to handle, gives that all-important tenderness and helps to improve the flavour and keeping qualities of the bread or rolls.

LIQUID binds together the other ingredients and is usually milk or water. Bread and rolls made with milk have a soft grain and white crumb, while water gives a crisper crust and less fine grain. All liquids should be lukewarm when used and fresh milk must be scalded so that it will not interfere with the yeast action.

Now, for those all-important skills . . .

THE BASIC METHODS

There are three ways in which yeast doughs may be combined:

1. BATTER METHOD: The ingredients are blended to form a batter which is not kneaded. Usually only one rising is required. A light open texture is characteristic of this type of yeast bread.

2. SPONGE METHOD: This is the oldest way to make yeast doughs. The yeast is combined with lukewarm water, sugar and flour to make a batter. This is allowed to rise until it is bubbly and resembles a sponge. The remaining flour and other ingredients are added and the dough is kneaded and finished in the same way as for the Straight Dough Method.

3. STRAIGHT DOUGH METHOD: This is now the most common way to combine yeast doughs. The softened yeast is added to the liquid, sugar, salt and shortening. Flour is then added to make a soft but not sticky dough which can be kneaded. Most of the yeast recipes in this cook book are prepared by the Straight Dough Method.

Following are the . . .

BASIC STEPS

These will help you to see the basic pattern to follow when making any type of yeast recipe by the "straight dough" method:

1. Assemble all necessary ingredients and utensils.

2. Combine the hot liquid with the shortening, sugar and salt. Cool to lukewarm.

3. Prepare the yeast and allow it to stand for 10 minutes. Add to the lukewarm liquid. If eggs are used, add them now.

4. Add half of the *Pre-Sifted* PURITY All-Purpose Flour, beat until smooth. Add remaining *Pre-Sifted* PURITY All-Purpose Flour and work in well.

5. Knead the dough until smooth and elastic (5 to 10 minutes).

6. Let the dough rise until doubled in bulk (from 1 to 1½ hours).

7. Punch down the risen dough. Divide it and shape into smooth balls; cover and let rest for 15 minutes.

8. Shape dough into loaves, rolls, etc., as directed.

9. Let rise in the pans until doubled in bulk (from ¾ to 1¼ hours).

10. Bake as directed.

Mouth-watering crusty home-made bread is easy to make (see following pages)

POINTERS FOR THE BREAD-MAKER

KNEADING THE DOUGH

Kneading develops the gluten ("elastic" quality) and evenly distributes the air bubbles. First, form the dough into a flattened ball; then fold dough over towards yourself.

Now, with the heels of your hands, push the dough away from you. Give a quarter turn and repeat this action with a rhythmic motion until the dough becomes smooth and satiny.

FIRST RISING

Temperature is important as yeast works best at about 80°. Grease top of the dough and cover to prevent drying. Set the dough in a warm place which is free from direct heat or cool drafts.

Allow dough for white bread or rolls to rise until doubled in bulk. To test, press two fingers into the dough and withdraw quickly. If they leave a deep impression the dough has risen enough. Allow dough for dark bread to rise only until about 1½ times in bulk.

SHAPING THE LOAVES

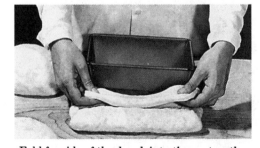

Press or roll the ball of dough into a rectangle measuring about 8″ wide by 10″ long. Press out all large air bubbles.

Fold far side of the dough into the centre; then the near side to the centre; press out any trapped air bubbles. Seal well by pressing seam firmly with fingers.

SHAPING THE LOAVES (Continued)

Stretch the dough slightly to make it uniform in size, then fold the ends in to meet the centre. Press out any air bubbles. Seal seams firmly with the fingers.

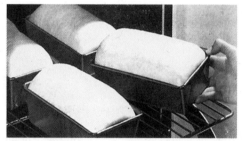

Fold the dough again and seal the edges carefully by pinching together with the fingers. The shaped loaves may now be placed in greased 8½″ x 4½″ bread pans.

SECOND RISING:

Loaves should be placed in the greased pans with folded side down; grease the tops to prevent drying. Cover and allow dough to stand in a warm place which is free from direct heat or cool drafts.

OVEN-READY:

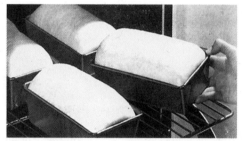

When completely raised, the dough for white bread should fill the pan with the centre rounded slightly above the edge. A gentle touch of the fingers leaves a slight impression when the loaves are oven-ready.

TEST FOR DONENESS:

Bake bread in a hot oven—400° to 425°. Bread is done when the crust is an even golden brown and the loaves lift free from the pan and sound hollow when tapped on the bottom.

COOL THE LOAVES:

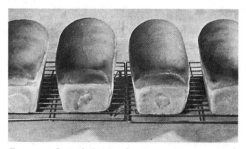

Remove bread from the pans as soon as it comes from the oven. Place loaves on a rack to cool. When thoroughly cooled, store in a well-ventilated bread box. For a soft crust, brush warm loaves with butter or margarine.

1   *White Bread*

Yield: 4 loaves (use 8½″ x 4½″ bread pans).

Scald

    2 cups milk

Pour into a large bowl and add

    ¼ cup sugar
    4 teaspoons salt
    ¼ cup shortening
    1 cup water

Stir until the shortening melts. Cool to lukewarm.

Meanwhile, dissolve

    2 teaspoons sugar

in

    1 cup lukewarm water

Over this, sprinkle

    2 packages active dry yeast*

Let stand for 10 minutes. (Keep at a temperature of about 80°.) Then stir briskly with a fork.

Add softened yeast to the lukewarm milk mixture. Stir.

Beat in

    5 cups *Pre-Sifted* PURITY
    All-Purpose Flour

Then add another

    4½ to 5 cups *Pre-Sifted* PURITY
    All-Purpose Flour

Work in last of the flour with a rotating motion of the hand. Turn dough onto a lightly floured board and knead for 8 to 10 minutes.

Shape into a smooth ball.

Place dough in a lightly greased bowl; grease top slightly. Cover and let rise until doubled in bulk—about 1½ hours— keep dough in a warm place (80° is ideal).

Punch down the risen dough and turn onto a lightly floured board. Cut into four equal pieces and form each into a smooth ball. Cover and let rest for 15 minutes.

Shape each ball of dough into a loaf. Place in greased pans and grease the tops. Cover and let rise until doubled in bulk (about 1¼ hours).

Bake in preheated 425° oven for 30 to 35 minutes.

VARIATION:

(a)   *Cracked Wheat Bread*

Prepare as for White Bread, substituting 3 cups PURITY Cracked Wheat for 3 cups of the *Pre-Sifted* PURITY All-Purpose Flour.

The cracked wheat should be added with the first addition of the flour.

2   *Rye Bread*

Yield: 4 loaves (use 8½″ x 4½″ bread pans).

Prepare this light Rye Bread by following the directions for White Bread (recipe No. 1), substituting 4 cups light rye flour and 1 cup *Pre-Sifted* PURITY All-Purpose Flour for the first 5 cups *Pre-Sifted* PURITY All-Purpose Flour.

Since it is important not to over-ferment rye bread, allow the dough to rise only until 1½ times its original volume. Therefore, the first rising will take about 1 hour and the bread should be allowed to rise in the pans for about 45 minutes before baking.

Bake in preheated 425° oven for 30 to 35 minutes.

VARIATION:

(a)   *Rye and Caraway Bread*

Add 1 tablespoon caraway seeds when adding rye flour in above recipe.

3   *Whole Wheat Bread*

Yield: 4 loaves (use 8½″ x 4½″ bread pans).

Scald

    1½ cups milk

Pour into a large bowl and add

    ½ cup lightly-packed brown sugar
    2 tablespoons salt
    ½ cup shortening

Stir until shortening melts.

Add

    2¼ cups lukewarm water

Cool this mixture until lukewarm.

Meanwhile, dissolve

    2 teaspoons sugar

in

    1 cup lukewarm water

Over this, sprinkle

    2 packages active dry yeast*

Let stand for 10 minutes. (Keep at a temperature of about 80°.) Then stir briskly with a fork.

Add softened yeast to lukewarm milk mixture. Stir.

Gradually beat in

    6 cups whole wheat flour

To use fresh yeast see "Note" page 6.

Add

**6 to 6½ cups *Pre-Sifted* PURITY
All-Purpose Flour**

Work in last of the flour with a rotating motion of the hand.

Turn dough onto a lightly floured board and knead for 8 to 10 minutes. Shape into a smooth ball.

Place dough in a lightly greased bowl; grease the top slightly. Cover and let rise until almost doubled in bulk—about 1¼ hours—keep the dough in a warm place (80° is ideal).

Punch down the risen dough and turn onto a lightly floured board. Cut into four equal pieces and form each into a smooth ball. Cover and let rest for 15 minutes.

Shape each ball of dough into a loaf. Place in the greased pans and grease the tops. Cover and let rise for 1 hour or until almost doubled in bulk.

Bake in preheated 400° oven for 30 to 35 minutes.

VARIATION:

(a) Molasses Whole Wheat Bread

Prepare as for Whole Wheat Bread, but substitute ½ cup light molasses for the ½ cup lightly-packed brown sugar. Decrease the lukewarm water to 2 cups.

4 Porridge Bread

Yield: 4 loaves (use 8½″ x 4½″ bread pans).
Pour

3 cups boiling water

over

**2 cups rolled oats
¼ cup shortening**

Stir until shortening is melted and let stand for about 20 minutes, stirring occasionally.

Meanwhile, dissolve

2 teaspoons sugar

in

1 cup lukewarm water

Over this, sprinkle

2 packages active dry yeast*

Let stand for 10 minutes. (Keep at a temperature of about 80°.) Then stir briskly with a fork.

Add to the partially cooled rolled oat mixture

**⅔ cup light molasses
4 teaspoons salt**

Cool to lukewarm.

Add softened yeast to the lukewarm rolled oat mixture. Stir.

Beat in

**2½ cups *Pre-Sifted* PURITY
All-Purpose Flour**

Then add another

**5½ to 6 cups *Pre-Sifted* PURITY
All-Purpose Flour**

Work in last of the flour with a rotating motion of the hand.

Turn dough onto a lightly floured board and knead for 8 to 10 minutes. Shape into a smooth ball.

Place dough in a lightly greased bowl; grease top slightly. Cover and let rise until almost doubled in bulk—about 1¼ hours—keep the dough in a warm place (80° is ideal).

Punch down the risen dough and turn onto a lightly floured board. Cut into four equal pieces and form each into a smooth ball. Cover and let rest for 15 minutes.

Shape each ball of dough into a loaf. Place in the greased pans and grease the tops. Cover and let rise for 1 hour or until almost doubled in bulk.

Bake in preheated 400° oven for 30 to 35 minutes.

5 Purity Easy Loaf

(Makes four 8½ x 4½-inch loaves)

Scald

2¾ cups milk

Pour into a large bowl and add

**¼ cup granulated sugar
2 tablespoons salt
⅓ cup shortening**

Stir until shortening melts. Cool to lukewarm.

Meanwhile, dissolve

1 tablespoon sugar

in

1½ cups warm water

Over this, sprinkle

3 envelopes active dry yeast*

Let stand for 10 minutes. (Keep at a temperature of about 100°F.) Then stir briskly with a fork. Add softened yeast to lukewarm milk mixture. Stir.

To use fresh yeast see "Note" page 6.

Beat in

4 cups *Pre-Sifted* PURITY
All-Purpose Flour

Beat vigorously by hand or with electric mixer.

Then gradually add an additional

6½ to 7 cups *Pre-Sifted* PURITY
All-Purpose Flour

Work in last of flour with a rotating motion of the hand. Turn dough onto a lightly floured surface and knead 8 to 10 minutes. Shape into a smooth ball, cover with wax paper and a cloth dampened with hot water, and let rest for 20 minutes. Divide in four. Roll out each portion, pressing out any large bubbles. Fold over and roll up tightly, shaping into loaves. Place in greased 8½" x 4½" loaf pans. Cover with oiled wax paper and a damp cloth and let rise.

Refrigerator Rising—Place pans of dough in refrigerator for 2 to 24 hours. Let loaves stand at room temperature for 20 minutes before baking.

Quick Rising—Let pans of dough rise at room temperature for about 1¼ hours.

Bake in preheated 400° oven for 30 to 35 minutes.

To keep a yeast dough at a uniform 80° temperature, place bowl in a pan of lukewarm water.

6   Bread Rolls

Yield: 16 rolls.

Roll one ball of the rested bread dough into a cylindrical shape about 1½" in diameter. Cut into 16 equal pieces. Shape each into a ball and arrange in a greased 8" or 9" square pan. Brush with melted butter or margarine. Cover. Let white and cracked wheat rolls rise until doubled in bulk (about 1¼ hours); rolled oat rolls should rise until almost doubled in bulk (about 1 hour); and rye rolls until 1½ times their original size (about 45 minutes). Bake in preheated 425° oven for about 25 minutes.

If your family is a small one you may wish to make only two loaves of bread at one time. We have thought of you when testing our recipes and so most of the bread recipes in this book are easily divided in two. Prepare the dough as for a full recipe; let rise and bake as directed.

7   Cheese Bread

Yield: 2 loaves (use 8½" x 4½" bread pans).
Scald

1 cup milk

Pour into a large bowl and add

2 tablespoons sugar
2 teaspoons salt
1 tablespoon shortening
½ cup water

Stir until shortening melts. Cool to lukewarm. Meanwhile, dissolve

1 teaspoon sugar

in

½ cup lukewarm water

Over this, sprinkle

1 package active dry yeast*

Let stand for 10 minutes. (Keep at a temperature of about 80°.) Then stir briskly with a fork.

Add softened yeast to the lukewarm milk mixture. Stir.

Beat in

2 cups *Pre-Sifted* PURITY
All-Purpose Flour
1 cup shredded Cheddar cheese

Now add another

2½ to 3 cups *Pre-Sifted* PURITY
All-Purpose Flour

Work in last of the flour with a rotating motion of the hand. Turn dough onto a lightly floured board and knead for 5 to 7 minutes. Shape into a smooth ball.

Place dough in a lightly greased bowl; grease top slightly.

Cover and let rise until doubled in bulk—about 1 hour. Keep dough in a warm place (80° is ideal).

Punch down the risen dough and turn onto a lightly floured board. Cut into two equal pieces and form each into a smooth ball. Cover and let rest for 15 minutes.

Shape each ball of dough into a loaf. Place in greased pans and grease the tops. Cover and let rise until doubled in bulk (about 45 minutes).

Bake in preheated 400° oven for 25 to 30 minutes.

---

*To use fresh yeast see "Note" page 6.

If using bulk active dry yeast, remember that 1 tablespoon is equal to the contents of one package active dry yeast or to one cake of compressed yeast.

8 Raisin Bread

Yield: 2 loaves (use 8½″ x 4½″ bread pans).

Scald

1½ cups milk

Mix together

¼ cup sugar
1 tablespoon salt
1 teaspoon cinnamon

Pour milk into a large bowl and add sugar mixture and

2 tablespoons sugar
¼ cup shortening

Stir. Cool to lukewarm.

Meanwhile, dissolve

1 teaspoon sugar

in

½ cup lukewarm water

Over this, sprinkle

1 package active dry yeast*

Let stand for 10 minutes. (Keep at a temperature of about 80°.)

Then stir briskly with a fork.

Add softened yeast to the lukewarm milk mixture. Stir.

Beat in

2½ cups *Pre-Sifted* PURITY All-Purpose Flour
1½ cups raisins

Then add another

2½ to 3 cups *Pre-Sifted* PURITY All-Purpose Flour

Work in last of flour with a rotating motion of the hand. Turn dough onto a lightly floured board and knead for about 5 minutes. Shape into a smooth ball. Try to prevent the raisins from protruding through the top of the dough as this will cause loss of the gases and poor rising.

Place dough in a lightly greased bowl; grease top slightly. Cover and let rise until doubled in bulk—1 to 1¼ hours. Keep dough in a warm place (80° is ideal).

Punch down the risen dough and turn onto a lightly floured board. Cut into two equal pieces and form each into a smooth ball. Cover and let rest for 15 minutes.

Shape each ball of dough into a loaf. Place in greased pans and grease the tops. Cover and let rise until almost doubled in bulk (about 1 hour).

Bake in preheated 400° oven for 30 to 35 minutes.

VARIATION:

(a) Fruit Bread

Prepare as for Raisin Bread, but replace the 1½ cups raisins with ½ cup glacé cherries, halved, ½ cup mixed candied peel and ½ cup raisins. Flour the fruit before adding it to the sponge.

THINGS TO DO WITH BREAD

9 Toast Cups

Remove crusts from thinly sliced bread and brush with melted butter or margarine. Press each slice into a large muffin cup. Bake in preheated 375° oven for 12 to 15 minutes or until golden. Use as you would patty shells.

10 Croustades (Toast Cases)

Cut unsliced bread into 2″ thick slices and remove the crusts. Cut into squares, oblongs or rounds of the desired size. Remove part of the bread from the centre of each, leaving a wall of bread which is about ⅜″ thick. Brush with melted butter or margarine and place on a baking sheet. Bake in preheated 375° oven for 12 to 15 minutes or until golden brown. Use as you would patty shells.

11 Cinnamon Toast

(a) Combine 1 teaspoon cinnamon and ¼ cup sugar. Sprinkle generously over hot buttered toast.

(b) Cream together 2 tablespoons butter or margarine, ¼ cup lightly-packed brown sugar and 1 teaspoon cinnamon. Spread over hot toast and place under broiler until bubbly.

12 Melba Toast

Cut day-old bread into ⅛″ slices. Remove crusts if you like. Cut into desired shapes and place on a baking sheet. Dry slowly in a 300° oven until crisp and golden brown—about 20 minutes.

*To use fresh yeast see "Note" page 6.

13 Orange Toast

Combine ⅓ cup sifted icing sugar, 2 teaspoons grated orange rind and 1 tablespoon orange juice. Spread over hot buttered toast.

14 Savoury French Bread

Slash French bread at about 1″ intervals *almost* through to the bottom crust.
Spread cut edges with one of the following:
(a) A mixture of ½ cup soft butter or margarine and ½ teaspoon garlic powder.
(b) A mixture of ½ cup butter or margarine and 2 tablespoons each of minced onion and finely chopped chives.
(c) About ½ cup of a tangy cheese spread. Sprinkle top with grated cheese, if desired.
Wrap loaf in aluminum foil. Heat in a pre-heated 375° oven for about 15 minutes, and then open the foil and heat for another 5 minutes.
Serve hot.

SWEET ROLLS

15 Basic Sweet Rolls

Yield: 2 to 3 dozen rolls.
Scald
   1½ cups milk
Pour into a large bowl and add
   ¼ cup sugar
   2 teaspoons salt
   ¼ cup shortening
Stir until shortening melts.
Cool to lukewarm.
Meanwhile, dissolve
   1 teaspoon sugar
in
   ½ cup lukewarm water
Over this, sprinkle
   1 package active dry yeast*
Let stand for 10 minutes. (Keep at a temperature of about 80°.) Then stir with a fork.
Add to lukewarm milk mixture
   Softened yeast
   1 well-beaten egg
Stir well.
Beat in
   3 cups *Pre-Sifted* PURITY All-Purpose Flour

Then add another
   2 to 2½ cups *Pre-Sifted* PURITY All-Purpose Flour

Work in last of the flour with a rotating motion of the hand.

Turn dough onto a lightly floured board and knead until smooth and elastic (about 5 minutes). Shape into a smooth ball.

Place dough in a lightly greased bowl; grease the top slightly. Cover and let rise until doubled in bulk—about 1½ hours—keep the dough in a warm place (80° is ideal).

Punch down the risen dough and turn onto a lightly floured board. Divide into four equal pieces and form each into a smooth ball.

Cover and let rest for 10 minutes.

Shape into desired type of rolls following the illustrations on pages 16 to 17.

Cover the shaped rolls and let rise until doubled in bulk—from ¾ to 1 hour.

Bake in preheated 375° oven as directed for each type of roll.

16 Refrigerator Rolls

Yield: 1½ to 2 dozen rolls.
Scald
   ¾ cup milk
   ¼ cup sugar
   1 teaspoon salt
   ¼ cup shortening
Pour into a bowl. Cool to lukewarm.
Meanwhile, dissolve
   1 teaspoon sugar
in
   ½ cup lukewarm water
Over this, sprinkle
   1 package active dry yeast*
Let stand for 10 minutes. (Keep at a temperature of about 80°.) Then stir briskly with a fork.
Add to lukewarm milk mixture
   Softened yeast
   1 well-beaten egg
Beat in
   2 cups *Pre-Sifted* PURITY All-Purpose Flour

*To use fresh yeast see "Note" page 6.

Then, thoroughly blend in
**1½ to 2 cups *Pre-Sifted* PURITY
All-Purpose Flour**
Brush with soft butter or shortening.

Cover the bowl tightly with aluminum foil or two layers of waxed paper; place a damp cloth over this and tie securely. Place dough in refrigerator (45° is ideal). Allow to rise for at least four hours. Cut off required amount of dough; knead for 5 minutes on a lightly floured board.

Shape into desired type of rolls, following the instructions given on pages 16 to 17. (If using all the dough at one time, divide into two balls before shaping.)

Cover the shaped rolls and let rise for 1½ hours or until doubled in bulk. Keep at a temperature of about 80°.

Bake in preheated 375° oven as directed for each type of roll.

NOTE: This dough may be kept refrigerated for 2 or 3 days. Also, the shaped rolls may be kept in the refrigerator for several hours and then removed about 2 hours before needed, allowed to rise and baked.

Refrigerator Dough: Cold retards the action of the yeast until the rolls are needed. A refrigerator dough has a special proportion of sugar and salt so that the action of the yeast will be extended over several days.

17 *Crusty French Rolls*

Yield: 2 dozen rolls.

Dissolve
1 teaspoon sugar
in
½ cup lukewarm water
Over this, sprinkle
1 package active dry yeast*

Let stand for 10 minutes. (Keep at a temperature of about 80°.) Then stir briskly with a fork.

Combine
**¾ cup lukewarm water
1 tablespoon sugar
1 teaspoon salt
2 tablespoons melted shortening**
Add
**Softened yeast
2 stiffly-beaten egg whites**
Mix thoroughly.

Add
**3 to 3½ cups *Pre-Sifted* PURITY
All-Purpose Flour**

Work in last of the flour with a rotating motion of the hand.

Turn dough onto a lightly floured board and knead for 7 to 8 minutes. Shape into a smooth ball.

Place dough in a lightly greased bowl; grease top slightly. Cover and let rise until doubled in bulk—about 1½ hours—keep the dough in a warm place (80° is ideal).

Punch down and allow to rise a second time until doubled in bulk (about 45 minutes).

Punch down after second rising; knead for 1 minute on a lightly floured board. Let dough rest for 10 minutes. Cut dough into 24 pieces; shape into round buns and place, well apart, on a greased baking sheet.

Cover and let rise until doubled in bulk (about 45 minutes).

Bake in preheated 450° oven for 18 to 20 minutes.

NOTE: For extra crustiness place a large flat pan of boiling water on the bottom of the oven during baking.

18 *Cinnamon Rolls*

Yield: 2 dozen rolls.

Prepare Basic Sweet Roll recipe No. 15.

Allow to rise until doubled in bulk; punch down and divide into 2 smooth balls. Cover and let rest for 10 minutes.

Roll each ball to an 8″ x 12″ rectangle. Brush with melted butter or margarine.

Combine
**1 cup lightly-packed brown sugar
1½ teaspoons cinnamon
½ cup raisins**

Sprinkle this mixture over the two rectangles of dough.

Starting from longer side, roll each up like a jelly roll; seal.

Cut the rolls into 1″ pieces and place in large greased muffin cups, cut side down. Brush the tops with milk.

Cover and let rise until doubled in bulk—about 45 minutes. Keep at a temperature of about 80°.

Bake in preheated 375° oven for about 25 minutes.

Remove from pans at once to prevent sticking.

To use fresh yeast see "Note" page 6.

19   *Pan Rolls*

Step 1: After dough has been punched down and allowed to rest for 10 minutes, roll each piece of dough into a cylindrical shape about 1½″ in diameter. Cut each into 8 equal pieces.

Step 2: Shape each piece of dough into a ball. Place 16 balls, almost touching, in a greased 8″ or 9″ square pan. Brush with melted butter or margarine. Cover and let rise (see recipe No. 15 or No. 16). Bake in preheated 375° oven for 25 to 30 minutes.

20   *Cloverleaf Rolls*

Step 1: After dough has been punched down and allowed to rest for 10 minutes, roll each piece of dough into a cylindrical shape about 1½″ in diameter and cut each into 8 equal pieces.

Step 2: Cut each piece of dough in three and form into balls. Brush with melted butter or margarine. Place three in each section of medium-size greased muffin cups. Cover and let rise (see recipe No. 15 or No. 16). Bake for 18 to 20 minutes in preheated 375° oven.

21   *Parkerhouse Rolls*

Step 1: After dough has been punched down and allowed to rest for 10 minutes, roll each piece of dough to ¼″ thickness. Cut into rounds with a floured 2½″ or 3″ cutter.

Step 2: Crease each round with back of a knife, just off-centre; brush with melted butter or margarine. Fold over with wider half on top, pressing edges together. Place on a greased baking sheet, brush with melted butter or margarine. Cover and let rise (see recipe No. 15 or No. 16). Bake in preheated 375° oven for 18 to 20 minutes.

22 *Crescents*

Step 1: After dough has been punched down and allowed to rest for 10 minutes, roll into rounds which are about 8″ in diameter. Brush with melted butter or margarine. Cut each round into 8 pie-shaped wedges.

Step 2: Starting from wide end, roll up each wedge and place on a greased baking sheet. Curve slightly to form a crescent, tucking ends under. Brush with melted butter or margarine. Cover and let rise (see recipe No. 15 or No. 16). Bake for 18 to 20 minutes in preheated 375° oven.

23 *Bowknots*

Step 1: After dough has been punched down and allowed to rest for 10 minutes, roll each piece of dough into rectangles which are ¾″ thick and 6″ wide. Cut each rectangle into strips, 6″ long and ¾″ wide. Roll each strip slightly before "tying".

Step 2: Tie each strip into a knot. Place on a greased baking sheet. Brush with melted butter or margarine. Cover and let rise (see recipe No. 15 or No. 16). Bake in preheated 375° oven for 18 to 20 minutes.

24 *Fan Tans*

Step 1: After dough has been punched down and allowed to rest for 10 minutes, roll each piece of dough into a rectangle measuring 9″ x 5″. Brush with melted butter or margarine. Cut each rectangle into five 1″ strips.

Step 2: Place strips in piles of five, buttered side up. Cut each pile into six 1½″ pieces. Place, cut side down, in greased muffin cups. Cover and let rise (see recipe No. 15 or No. 16). Bake in preheated 375° oven for 18 to 20 minutes.

25 Hot Cross Buns

Yield: 18 to 20 buns.

Scald
> 1 cup milk

Pour into a large bowl and add
> ⅔ cup sugar
> 2 teaspoons salt
> ⅓ cup butter

Stir until butter melts.

Cool to lukewarm.

Meanwhile, dissolve
> 1 teaspoon sugar

in
> ½ cup lukewarm water

Over this, sprinkle
> 1 package active dry yeast*

Let stand for 10 minutes. (Keep at a temperature of about 80°.) Then stir briskly with a fork.

Add softened yeast to the lukewarm milk mixture. Stir.

Then add
> 1 slightly beaten egg
> 1 egg yolk
> 1 teaspoon cinnamon
> ½ teaspoon allspice
> ¼ teaspoon nutmeg

Beat in
> 2½ cups *Pre-Sifted* PURITY
>   All-Purpose Flour
> ⅔ cup raisins or currants

Then add another
> 2½ to 3 cups *Pre-Sifted* PURITY
>   All-Purpose Flour

Work in last of the flour with a rotating motion of the hand.

Turn onto a lightly floured board and knead until smooth and elastic (about 5 minutes). Shape into a smooth ball.

Place dough in a lightly greased bowl; grease the top slightly. Cover and let rise until doubled in bulk—about 1 hour—keep the dough in a warm place (80° is ideal).

Punch down the risen dough and turn onto a lightly floured board. Divide into two equal pieces and shape each into a smooth ball. Cover and let rest for 10 minutes.

Divide each ball of dough into 9 pieces and shape each into a flattened bun. Arrange on greased baking sheets, 2″ apart.

Cover and let rise until doubled in bulk (about 45 minutes).

Combine
> 1 slightly-beaten egg white
> 1 tablespoon water

Brush risen buns with the egg white mixture.

Slash the top of each bun in the form of a cross.

Bake in preheated 400° oven for 15 to 18 minutes.

GLAZE:

Combine
> ¾ cup sifted icing sugar
> 1 tablespoon hot milk
> ¼ teaspoon vanilla

Drizzle over hot buns following the crevices.

26 Batter Rolls

Yield: 16 to 18 rolls.

Scald
> 1½ cups milk

Pour into a bowl and add
> ¼ cup sugar
> 2 teaspoons salt
> ¼ cup shortening

Stir until shortening melts.

Cool to lukewarm.

Meanwhile, dissolve
> 1 teaspoon sugar

in
> ½ cup lukewarm water

Over this, sprinkle
> 1 package active dry yeast*

Let stand for 10 minutes. (Keep at a temperature of about 80°.) Then stir briskly with a fork.

Add softened yeast to the lukewarm milk mixture. Stir.

Beat in
> 2¾ cups *Pre-Sifted* PURITY
>   All-Purpose Flour

Beat vigorously by hand or with electric mixer.

Beat in with a spoon an additional
> ½ cup *Pre-Sifted* PURITY
>   All-Purpose Flour

Cover and let rise until light and bubbly—about 40 minutes—keep dough in a warm place (80° is ideal).

Stir down the risen dough and let stand for 10 minutes.

Fill greased muffin cups ¾ full of dough.

Bake in preheated 375° oven for 20 to 25 minutes.

*To use fresh yeast see "Note" page 6.

Reheat rolls by one of these methods:

(a) *Place rolls in a moistened bag and heat in a 350° oven for about 10 minutes.*

(b) *Sprinkle rolls very lightly with water and then wrap in aluminum foil. Heat for about 10 minutes in a 350° oven or on a rack in an electric frying pan heated to this temperature.*

(c) *Heat rolls in a bun warmer or in the top of a double boiler over hot water.*

SWEET BREADS

Basic Sweet Dough

27

Scald
>**1 cup milk**

Pour into a bowl and add
>**⅓ cup sugar**
>**2 teaspoons salt**
>**½ cup shortening**

Stir until shortening melts. Cool to lukewarm.

Meanwhile, dissolve
>**1 teaspoon sugar**

in
>**½ cup lukewarm water**

Over this, sprinkle
>**1 package active dry yeast***

Let stand for 10 minutes. (Keep at a temperature of about 80°.) Then stir briskly with a fork.

Add to lukewarm milk mixture
>**Softened yeast**
>**1 well-beaten egg**

Stir well.

Beat in
>**2 cups *Pre-Sifted* PURITY All-Purpose Flour**

Then add another
>**2½ to 3 cups *Pre-Sifted* PURITY All-Purpose Flour**

Work in last of flour with a rotating motion of the hand.

Turn dough onto a lightly floured board and knead for 5 minutes or until smooth and elastic. Shape into a smooth ball.

Place dough in a lightly greased bowl; grease the top slightly. Cover and let rise until doubled in bulk (about 1½ hours). Keep the dough at a temperature of about 80°.

Punch down the risen dough and turn onto a lightly floured board. Divide into two equal pieces and form each into a smooth ball.

Cover and let rest for 10 minutes.

Use each portion of dough to prepare one of these sweet dough variations:

Hungarian Coffee Ring   Swedish Tea Ring
Pecan Loaf   Pecan Cinnamon Buns
Bohemian Hoska   Jam Blossoms

Recipes for these will be found on the following pages.

---

28   *Hungarian Coffee Ring*
(Use ½ Basic Sweet Dough recipe No. 27)

Yield: 1 coffee ring.

Prepare the Basic Sweet Dough as directed. Using the palm of the hand, roll one ball of the rested dough into a rope which is 20″ long. Cut into 20 equal pieces and form into balls. Dip the balls in melted butter or margarine. Then roll them in a mixture of
>**⅓ cup sugar**
>**1 teaspoon cinnamon**

Place the coated balls in a greased 9″ tube pan so they barely touch.

Sprinkle with
>**¼ cup chopped nuts**

Place maraschino cherries and raisins in the crevices between the balls. (Use about ¼ cup of each; halve the cherries if you wish.)

Cover and let rise until doubled in bulk (about 1½ hours). Keep at a temperature of about 80°.

Bake in preheated 375° oven for 30 to 35 minutes.

Invert at once on a serving plate. Break apart to serve.

---

29   *Pecan Loaf*
(Use ½ Basic Sweet Dough recipe No. 27)

Yield: 1 loaf.

Prepare the Basic Sweet Dough as directed. Roll one ball of the rested dough to an 8″ x 10″ rectangle.

---

*To use fresh yeast see "Note" page 6.

Brush with

1 tablespoon melted butter *or* margarine

Sprinkle with a mixture of

½ cup lightly-packed brown sugar
½ teaspoon cinnamon

Roll up like a jelly roll, starting from the shorter side.

Place in a greased 8½″ x 4½″ loaf pan.

Sprinkle with

¼ cup chopped pecans

Cover and let rise until doubled in bulk (about 45 minutes).

Bake in preheated 400° oven for 25 to 30 minutes.

GLAZE:

Combine

½ cup sifted icing sugar
2 teaspoons milk
⅛ teaspoon vanilla

Spread over partially cooled loaf.

30   *Bohemian Hoska*

(Use ½ Basic Sweet Dough recipe No. 27)

Yield: 1 braid.

Prepare the Basic Sweet Dough as directed. Divide one ball of the rested dough into 9 equal portions. Using the palm of the hand, roll each piece of dough into a rope which is about ½″ in diameter.

Loosely braid 4 of these ropes of dough. Place on a greased baking sheet.

Then braid 3 more ropes and place on top of the first braid.

Twist the remaining 2 ropes together and place on top. Pinch the ends together and tuck them under.

Cover and let rise until doubled in bulk (about 45 minutes). Keep at a temperature of about 80°.

Bake in preheated 375° oven for 30 to 35 minutes.

GLAZE:

Combine

¾ cup sifted icing sugar
1 tablespoon milk
¼ teaspoon vanilla

Spread over warm loaf.

Sprinkle with

¼ cup chopped nuts

31   *Swedish Tea Ring*

(Use ½ Basic Sweet Dough recipe No. 27)

Yield: 1 tea ring.

Step 1: Roll one ball of dough to a 9″ x 16″ rectangle. Brush with 1 tablespoon melted butter or margarine to within ½″ of edges. Sprinkle with a mixture of ¼ cup lightly-packed brown sugar, ⅓ cup chopped nuts, ⅓ cup raisins, ½ teaspoon cinnamon and ¼ teaspoon nutmeg. Roll up like a jelly roll starting at longer side.

Step 2: Seal edges firmly and place on a greased baking sheet bringing ends together to form a ring. Dampen and seal these ends carefully. Slash with scissors ¾ of the way through the dough in 1″ slices. Turn each slice carefully on its side.

Step 3: Cover and let rise until doubled in bulk (about 45 minutes). Bake in preheated 375° oven for about 25 minutes. Partially cool the ring. Drizzle with a mixture of ¾ cup sifted icing sugar, 1 tablespoon milk and ¼ teaspoon almond extract.

32 Pecan Cinnamon Buns
(Use ½ Basic Sweet Dough recipe No. 27)

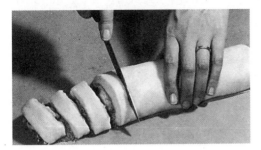

Yield: 12 buns.

Step 1: Roll one ball of dough to a 9″ x 12″ rectangle. Brush with 1 tablespoon melted butter or margarine. Sprinkle with a mixture of ¼ cup granulated sugar, 1 teaspoon cinnamon and ½ cup chopped pecans. Roll up like a jelly roll starting at longer side. Cut into twelve 1″ slices.

Step 2: Combine ¼ cup melted butter or margarine and ½ cup lightly-packed brown sugar. Spread in the bottom of an 8″ or 9″ square pan. Dot with pecan halves. Place slices, cut side down, in the prepared pan.

Step 3: Cover and let rise until doubled in bulk (about 45 minutes). Bake in preheated 375° oven for 25 to 30 minutes. Invert at once on a serving plate.

33 Jam Blossoms
(Use ½ Basic Sweet Dough recipe No. 27)

Yield: 8 blossoms.

Step 1: Roll one ball of dough to a 12″ circle. Place a custard cup in the centre and cut 24 slashes radiating from it. It is best to mark the divisions carefully before you actually begin to cut.

Step 2: For each "blossom", braid three strips together and curve towards the centre. There will be eight blossoms in all. Place on a greased baking sheet. Brush with melted butter or margarine. Cover and let rise until doubled in bulk (about 45 minutes).

Step 3: Place a teaspoon of jam in the centre of each blossom and in the centre of the ring. Bake in preheated 375° oven for about 25 minutes or until nicely browned.

34   Orange Sweet Dough

Prepare as for the Basic Sweet Dough (recipe No. 27), reducing scalded milk to ¾ cup.

Add 2 teaspoons finely grated orange rind and ¼ cup orange juice when adding the softened yeast and beaten egg. Prepare the dough as directed. Punch down the risen dough and divide in two equal portions; form into smooth balls and cover.

Let rest for 10 minutes.

Use each portion of the Orange Dough to prepare one of these variations:

> Orange Swirls
> Orange Braid
> Bubble Loaf

35   Orange Swirls
(Use ½ Orange Sweet Dough recipe No. 34)

Yield: 12 swirls.

Prepare the Orange Sweet Dough as directed.

Roll one ball of the rested dough to a 9" x 12" rectangle.

Brush with
> **1 tablespoon melted butter or margarine**

Sprinkle with a mixture of
> **¼ cup sugar**
> **1 tablespoon finely grated orange rind**

Roll up like a jelly roll, starting at the longer side. Cut into twelve 1" slices.

Combine
> **½ cup sugar**
> **2 tablespoons melted butter or margarine**
> **2 tablespoons orange juice**

Divide this mixture among 12 greased medium-sized muffin cups.

Place the swirls, cut side down, in the prepared muffin cups.

Cover and let rise until doubled in bulk (about 45 minutes). Keep at a temperature of about 80°.

Bake in preheated 375° oven for 20 to 22 minutes. Remove from pans immediately.

Most Sweet Breads are best when served warm, right from the oven. To reheat, wrap in aluminum foil and place in a preheated 350° oven for 10 to 15 minutes.

36   Orange Braid
(Use ½ Orange Sweet Dough recipe No. 34)

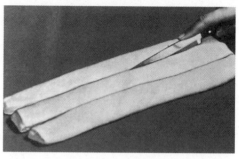

Yield: 1 braid.

Step 1: Roll one ball of orange dough to a 5" x 12" rectangle and cut lengthwise into three even strips. Roll each strip slightly to round the edges.

Step 2: Place strips on a greased baking sheet and braid together. Seal the ends well by pressing lightly, but firmly, with the fingers. Brush with melted butter or margarine. Cover and let rise until doubled in bulk (about 45 minutes).

Step 3: Bake in preheated 375° oven for 25 to 30 minutes. Ice when partly cool with a mixture of ¾ cup sifted icing sugar, 1 teaspoon grated orange rind and 1 tablespoon orange juice. Slice for serving.

Try this delicious Swedish Tea Ring (Recipe No. 31)

37 Bubble Loaf

(Use ½ Orange Sweet Dough recipe No. 34)

Yield: 1 loaf.

Prepare the Orange Sweet Dough as directed.
Divide one ball of the rested dough into 16 pieces and form into balls. Place 8 of these in the bottom of a greased 8½″ x 4½″ loaf pan.
Brush with melted butter or margarine.

Combine

¼ cup sugar
⅛ teaspoon mace
1 teaspoon finely grated lemon rind

Sprinkle half of this mixture over the balls of dough in the pan.

Place remaining balls of dough on top of first layer. Brush with melted butter or margarine and sprinkle with remaining sugar mixture.

Cover and let rise until doubled in bulk (about 45 minutes). Keep at a temperature of about 80°.

Bake in preheated 350° oven for 35 to 40 minutes.

Slice or break apart for serving.

38 Italian Cheese Ring

Yield: 1 ring.

Dissolve

1 teaspoon sugar

in

½ cup lukewarm water

Over this, sprinkle

1 package active dry yeast*

Let stand for 10 minutes. (Keep at a temperature of about 80°.) Stir briskly with a fork.

Cream

¼ cup soft shortening

Beat in

2 eggs
½ cup cold mashed potatoes
2 tablespoons milk
1½ teaspoons salt
¼ teaspoon oregano
¼ cup commercially grated Cheddar cheese
¼ cup grated Parmesan cheese

Add softened yeast and blend well.

Add about

2½ cups *Pre-Sifted* PURITY All-Purpose Flour

Work in last of flour with a rotating motion of the hand.

Turn dough onto a lightly floured board and knead for 5 minutes. Form dough into a ball and place in a greased bowl. Grease the top slightly.

Cover and let rise until doubled in bulk — about 1½ hours. Keep at a temperature of about 80°.

Punch down the risen dough and form into a ball. Cover and let rest for 10 minutes.

Using the palm of the hand, form into a roll which is about 20″ long. Place in a greased 9″ tube pan, sealing the ends together. Grease the top.

Cover and let rise until doubled in bulk (about 45 minutes).

Bake in preheated 375° oven for 25 to 30 minutes.

Brush hot loaf with melted butter or margarine and sprinkle with grated cheese.

39 Challah

Yield: 1 braid.

Dissolve

1 teaspoon sugar

in

½ cup lukewarm water

Over this, sprinkle

1 package active dry yeast*

Let stand for 10 minutes. (Keep at a temperature of about 80°.) Then stir briskly with a fork.

Add to the softened yeast

½ cup lukewarm water
1 tablespoon sugar
2 tablespoons vegetable oil
2 teaspoons salt
2 beaten eggs
1 slightly-beaten egg white

Then add

4 to 4½ cups *Pre-Sifted* PURITY All-Purpose Flour

Work in last of flour with a rotating motion of the hand. Turn dough onto a lightly floured board and knead for 5 minutes. Form dough into a ball and place in an oiled bowl.

Cover and let rise until doubled in bulk — about 1½ hours. Keep at a temperature of about 80°.

Punch down the risen dough and divide into 6 equal pieces. Shape into smooth balls. Cover and let rest for 10 minutes.

*To use fresh yeast see "Note" page 6.

Using the palm of the hand, shape each ball of dough into a rope which is about 12″ long. Twist the ropes together in pairs. Now place on an oiled baking sheet and braid the three twists into one large braid. Pinch the ends together well. Brush with oil.

Cover and let rise until doubled in bulk (about 45 minutes).

Mix together
    1 egg yolk
    2 tablespoons water

Brush the braid with this mixture.

Bake in preheated 400° oven for 30 to 35 minutes.

40   *Sally Lunn*

Yield: 2 small loaves.

Scald
    ¾ cup milk

Pour into a large bowl and add
    2 tablespoons sugar
    3 tablespoons butter *or* margarine
    1½ teaspoons salt

Stir until butter melts. Cool to lukewarm.

Meanwhile, dissolve
    1 teaspoon sugar
in
    ½ cup lukewarm water

Over this, sprinkle
    1 package active dry yeast*

Let stand for 10 minutes. (Keep at a temperature of about 80°.) Then stir briskly with a fork.

Add to the lukewarm milk mixture
    Softened yeast
    2 beaten eggs

Stir well.

Beat in
    3 cups *Pre-Sifted* PURITY All-Purpose Flour

Beat for 1 minute.

Cover and let rise until light and bubbly (about 1 hour). Keep at a temperature of about 80°.

Stir down the risen dough and divide between 2 greased one-pound coffee cans.

Cover and let rise for about 45 minutes. (Dough will just about fill the cans when risen, so be careful the tea towel does not stick to the top.)

Bake in preheated 375° oven for 25 to 35 minutes.

41   *Swedish Limpa*

Yield: 1 loaf.

Combine in a saucepan
    ¾ cup water
    ⅓ cup lightly-packed brown sugar
    2 tablespoons shortening
    2 teaspoons salt
    2 teaspoons grated orange rind

Heat until shortening melts. Cool to lukewarm.

Meanwhile, dissolve
    1 teaspoon sugar
in
    ½ cup lukewarm water

Over this, sprinkle
    1 package active dry yeast*

Let stand for 10 minutes. (Keep at a temperature of about 80°.) Then stir briskly with a fork.

Add softened yeast to the lukewarm liquid mixture.

Stir in
    1 cup *Pre-Sifted* PURITY All-Purpose Flour
    1¼ cups light rye flour

Beat well.

Then add another
    1 to 1½ cups *Pre-Sifted* PURITY All-Purpose Flour

Work in last of the flour with a rotating motion of the hand.

Turn onto a lightly floured board and knead for 5 minutes. Form dough into a ball and place in a greased bowl. Grease the top slightly.

Cover and let rise until approximately 1½ times its original volume (about 1¼ hours). Keep at a temperature of about 80°.

Punch down the risen dough and form into a smooth ball. Cover and let rest for 10 minutes.

Shape into a cylinder which is about 14″ long.

Taper the ends slightly, using the palms of the hands. Place on a greased baking sheet and slash 4 or 5 times across the top. Grease slightly.

Cover and let rise until almost doubled in bulk (about 45 minutes).

Bake in preheated 375° oven for 30 to 35 minutes.

_____

To use fresh yeast see "Note" page 6.

Quick Breads

BISCUITS

A tea biscuit dough should be soft but not sticky. A little kneading improves the quality of the biscuits, but should be done with a gentle touch as too much handling tends to make them tough.

42 BASIC RECIPE

Preheat oven to 450°.

Blend or sift together
- **2 cups *Pre-Sifted* PURITY All-Purpose Flour**
- **4 teaspoons baking powder**
- **1 teaspoon salt**

Cut in finely
- **⅓ cup shortening**

Add
- **¾ cup plus 2 tablespoons milk**

Stir with a fork to make a soft dough.

Tea Biscuits

Turn dough onto a lightly floured surface and knead gently 8 to 10 times. Roll or pat to desired thickness, (biscuits will be doubled in height when baked). Cut out with a floured cutter.

Place biscuits on an ungreased baking sheet, close together for soft-sided biscuits or about 1″ apart for crusty-sided biscuits.

Bake in preheated 450° oven for 12 to 15 minutes.

Yield: 18 to 20 — 1¾″ biscuits.

VARIATIONS:

(a) *Parkerhouse Biscuits*

Roll Basic Tea Biscuit dough (recipe No. 42) to a 9″ square and cut out with a floured 3″ cutter. Brush top of biscuits with melted butter or margarine, crease just off centre with a knife and fold over with larger half on top. Place on an ungreased baking sheet. Bake in preheated 450° oven for 10 to 12 minutes.

Yield: 9 biscuits.

(b) *Cloverleaf Biscuits*

Roll Basic Tea Biscuit dough (recipe No. 42) to ½″ thickness and cut into 30 pieces. Slightly round the pieces of dough. Grease medium-sized muffin cups and place 3 balls of dough in each cup. Brush with melted butter or margarine. Bake in preheated 450° oven for 12 to 15 minutes.

Yield: 10 biscuits.

(c) *Tea Biscuit Hors D'oeuvres*

Roll Basic Tea Biscuit dough (recipe No. 42) to ¼″ thickness. Cut into desired size and shape, using a floured cutter. Brush half of the biscuits with melted butter or margarine. Spread buttered biscuits with one of the following:

> Grated cheese
> Sausage meat
> Devilled ham
> Thick jam or marmalade

Press plain biscuits on top and brush with milk.

Place on an ungreased baking sheet. Bake in preheated 450° oven for 10 to 12 minutes.

Yield: 18 to 24 hors d'oeuvres.

(d) *Parsley Biscuits*

Prepare Basic Tea Biscuit recipe No. 42, adding 2 tablespoons freshly chopped parsley or 2 teaspoons parsley flakes to the dry ingredients. Bake as for Basic Tea Biscuits.

(e)   Salad Sticks

Prepare Basic Tea Biscuit dough (recipe No. 42), adding 1 teaspoon celery salt to the dry ingredients. Roll dough to a 9″ x 12″ rectangle. Brush with melted butter or margarine and sprinkle with 2 teaspoons celery seeds. Cut into strips which are about ⅓″ wide and 4″ long.

Place on an ungreased baking sheet and bake in preheated 450° oven for 8 to 10 minutes.

Yield: 7 dozen sticks.

(f)   Savoury Biscuits

Prepare Basic Tea Biscuit recipe No. 42, adding ⅛ teaspoon sage and ¼ teaspoon each of thyme and summer savoury to the dry ingredients. Bake as for Basic Tea Biscuits.

(g)   Cheese Biscuits

Prepare Basic Tea Biscuit recipe No. 42, adding ¾ cup shredded Cheddar cheese to the dry ingredients. Bake as for Basic Tea Biscuits.

(h)   Orange or Lemon Sweethearts

Prepare Basic Tea Biscuit recipe No. 42. Arrange biscuits on an ungreased baking sheet. Combine the grated rind and strained juice of one lemon or one orange. Dip small sugar cubes into the juice mixture and then press, point down, into the centre of each unbaked biscuit. Bake as for Basic Tea Biscuits.

43   Drop Biscuits

Preheat oven to 450°.

Blend or sift together
  1¾ cups *Pre-Sifted* **PURITY All-Purpose Flour**
  4 teaspoons baking powder
  1 teaspoon salt

Cut in finely
  ⅓ cup shortening

Add
  1 cup milk

Stir to make a drop batter.

Drop from a spoon onto a greased baking sheet. Bake in preheated 450° oven for 12 to 15 minutes.

Yield: 12 to 14 medium-sized biscuits.

VARIATION:

(a)   Fruit Drop Biscuits

Prepare Drop Biscuit recipe No. 43, adding ½ cup raisins, currants or chopped dates to the dry ingredients. Bake as for Drop Biscuits.

44   Butterscotch Pinwheels

Preheat oven to 450°.

Cream until soft
  ⅓ cup butter *or* **margarine**
Gradually blend in
  ⅔ cup lightly-packed brown sugar
Set aside.

Blend or sift together
  1¾ cups *Pre-Sifted* **PURITY All-Purpose Flour**
  2 tablespoons granulated sugar
  4 teaspoons baking powder
  1 teaspoon salt

Cut in finely
  ⅓ cup shortening

Add
  ¾ cup milk

Stir with a fork to make a soft dough.

Turn dough onto a lightly floured surface and knead gently 8 to 10 times. Roll to a 9″ square.

Spread rolled dough with brown sugar mixture. Roll up as for a jelly roll. Seal edges.

Cut into twelve ¾″ thick slices and arrange, cut side down, in greased medium-sized muffin cups.

Bake in preheated 450° oven for 12 to 15 minutes. Remove from pan immediately.

Yield: 12 pinwheels.

VARIATION:

(a)   Caramel Pecan Buns

Cream together
  3 tablespoons butter *or* **margarine**
  6 tablespoons brown sugar

Spread mixture in the bottoms of 12 medium-sized muffin cups. Place 2 or 3 pecan halves in each.

Prepare Butterscotch Pinwheels as directed above and place, cut side down, in the prepared muffin cups.

Bake in preheated 450° oven for 12 to 15 minutes. Remove from pan immediately.

45   Cheese Pinwheels

Preheat oven to 450°.

Prepare Basic Tea Biscuit recipe No. 42 and roll to a 9″ square. Brush with melted butter or margarine. Sprinkle with 1 cup shredded Cheddar cheese. Roll up as for a jelly roll; seal the edges.

Cut into twelve ¾″ thick slices. Place in greased medium-sized muffin cups or close together on a greased baking sheet. Bake in preheated 450° oven for 12 to 15 minutes.

Yield: 12 pinwheels.

46   Scones

Preheat oven to 450°.

Blend or sift together
- **1¾ cups Pre-Sifted PURITY All-Purpose Flour**
- **2 tablespoons sugar**
- **4 teaspoons baking powder**
- **½ teaspoon salt**

Cut in finely
- **⅓ cup shortening**

Add
- **½ cup currants or raisins**

Combine
- **1 well-beaten egg**
- **½ cup milk**

Add to dry ingredients and stir lightly with a fork to make a soft dough. Turn dough onto a lightly floured surface and knead gently 8 to 10 times.

Divide dough into two parts; roll each into a 6″ circle. Place on a lightly greased baking sheet. Brush with milk and sprinkle with sugar. Score each into quarters.

Bake in preheated 450° oven for 10 to 12 minutes.

Yield: 8 scones.

47   Buttermilk Biscuits

Preheat oven to 450°.

Blend or sift together
- **2 cups Pre-Sifted PURITY All-Purpose Flour**
- **4 teaspoons baking powder**
- **¼ teaspoon baking soda**
- **1 teaspoon salt**

Cut in finely
- **⅓ cup shortening**

Add
- **¾ cup plus 2 tablespoons buttermilk or sour milk**

Stir with a fork to make a soft dough.

Turn dough onto a lightly floured surface. Knead gently 8 to 10 times. Roll or pat to desired thickness, (biscuits will be doubled in height when baked). Cut out with a floured cutter. Place on an ungreased baking sheet, close together for soft-sided biscuits or about 1″ apart for crusty-sided biscuits.

Bake in preheated 450° oven for 12 to 15 minutes.

Yield: 18 to 20—1¾″ biscuits.

To serve day-old tea biscuits or muffins, split, butter and toast them, or wrap in foil and heat in a 400° oven for about 10 minutes.

48   Sour Cream Biscuits

Preheat oven to 450°.

Blend or sift together
- **1¾ cups Pre-Sifted PURITY All-Purpose Flour**
- **3 teaspoons baking powder**
- **¼ teaspoon baking soda**
- **1 teaspoon salt**

Cut in finely
- **¼ cup shortening**

Add
- **½ cup commercial sour cream**
- **½ cup milk**

Stir with a fork to make a soft dough.

Turn dough onto a lightly floured surface and knead gently 8 to 10 times. Roll or pat to desired thickness, (biscuits will be doubled in height when baked). Cut out with a floured cutter.

Place biscuits on an ungreased baking sheet, close together for soft-sided biscuits or about 1″ apart for crusty-sided biscuits.

Bake in preheated 450° oven for 10 to 12 minutes.

Yield: 16 to 18—1¾″ biscuits.

MUFFINS

The secret of a good muffin is in the mixing. Stir the batter until the flour just disappears. The batter should be lumpy. Overmixing causes tunnels and a tough texture.

49 BASIC RECIPE *Plain Muffins*

Preheat oven to 400°.

Blend or sift together
   2 cups *Pre-Sifted* PURITY All-Purpose Flour
   ¼ cup sugar
   3½ teaspoons baking powder
   ½ teaspoon salt

Make a well in centre of the dry ingredients.

Combine and add
   1 beaten egg
   1 cup milk
   ¼ cup vegetable oil *or* melted shortening

Stir only until combined. (The batter should be lumpy.) Fill greased muffin cups two-thirds full.

Bake in preheated 400° oven for 20 to 25 minutes.

Yield: 10 medium-sized muffins.

VARIATIONS:

(a) *Sugar-Topped Muffins*

Prepare and bake Plain Muffins (recipe No. 49). Dip tops of the hot muffins in melted butter or margarine, and then in a mixture of ½ cup sugar and 1 teaspoon cinnamon.

(b) *Fruit Muffins*

Prepare Plain Muffins (recipe No. 49), adding 1 cup raisins, currants or chopped dates to the dry ingredients. Bake as for Plain Muffins.

(c) *Blueberry Muffins*

Prepare Plain Muffins (recipe No. 49), folding ¾ cup fresh blueberries into the batter. Bake as for Plain Muffins.

50 *Banana Muffins*

Preheat oven to 400°.

Blend or sift together
   2 cups *Pre-Sifted* PURITY All-Purpose Flour
   ¼ cup sugar
   4 teaspoons baking powder
   ½ teaspoon salt

Make a well in centre of the dry ingredients.

Combine and add
   1 beaten egg
   ⅔ cup milk
   1 cup well-mashed banana
   2 tablespoons vegetable oil *or* melted shortening

Stir only until combined. (The batter should be lumpy.) Fill greased muffin cups two-thirds full.

Bake in preheated 400° oven for 20 to 25 minutes.

Yield: 10 medium-sized muffins.

Muffins may be baked in paper baking cups, placed in ungreased muffin cups. Remove the papers before serving.

51 *Apple Spice Muffins*

Preheat oven to 400°.

Blend or sift together
   2 cups *Pre-Sifted* PURITY All-Purpose Flour
   ¼ cup sugar
   3½ teaspoons baking powder
   ¾ teaspoon salt
   1 teaspoon cinnamon
   ¼ teaspoon nutmeg

Stir in
   ¾ cup finely chopped peeled apple

Make a well in centre of the dry ingredients.

Combine and add
   1 beaten egg
   1 cup milk
   ¼ cup vegetable oil *or* melted shortening

Stir only until combined. (The batter should be lumpy.) Fill greased muffin cups two-thirds full. Bake in preheated 400° oven for 20 to 25 minutes.

Yield: 10 medium-sized muffins.

52   Honey Muffins

Preheat oven to 400°.

Blend or sift together

> **2 cups *Pre-Sifted* PURITY
> All-Purpose Flour**
> **3½ teaspoons baking powder**
> **½ teaspoon salt**

Make a well in centre of dry ingredients.

Combine and add

> **1 beaten egg**
> **¾ cup milk**
> **½ cup liquid honey**
> **3 tablespoons melted butter *or*
> margarine**

Stir only until combined. (The batter should be lumpy.) Fill greased muffin cups two-thirds full. Bake in preheated 400° oven for 20 to 25 minutes.

Yield: 10 medium-sized muffins

To keep muffins hot for serving, loosen them and tilt slightly in the pans. Place them in a warm oven until needed.

53   Corn Meal Muffins

Preheat oven to 400°.

Blend or sift together

> **1 cup *Pre-Sifted* PURITY
> All-Purpose Flour**
> **¼ cup sugar**
> **3½ teaspoons baking powder**
> **¾ teaspoon salt**

Blend in

> **1 cup PURITY Corn Meal**

Make a well in centre of dry ingredients.

Combine and add

> **1 beaten egg**
> **1 cup milk**
> **¼ cup vegetable oil *or* melted
> shortening**

Stir only until combined. (The batter should be lumpy.) Fill greased muffin cups two-thirds full. Bake in preheated 400° oven for 20 to 25 minutes.

Yield: 10 medium-sized muffins.

54   Bran Muffins

Preheat oven to 400°.

Blend or sift together

> **1 cup *Pre-Sifted* PURITY
> All-Purpose Flour**
> **2 teaspoons baking powder**
> **½ teaspoon baking soda**
> **¾ teaspoon salt**

Blend in

> **1½ cups bran**
> **⅓ cup lightly-packed brown sugar**
> **½ cup raisins *or* chopped dates**

Make a well in centre of dry ingredients.

Combine and add

> **1 beaten egg**
> **1 cup sour milk**
> **2 tablespoons vegetable oil *or*
> melted shortening**

Stir only until combined. (Batter should be lumpy.) Fill greased muffin cups two-thirds full. Bake in preheated 400° oven for 20 to 25 minutes.

Yield: 12 medium-sized muffins

TEA BREADS

Allow a tea bread batter to stand in the pan for about 20 minutes before baking. This will prevent cracking along the top of the loaf.

55   Nut Bread

Preheat oven to 350°.

Blend or sift together

> **2 cups *Pre-Sifted* PURITY
> All-Purpose Flour**
> **¾ cup sugar**
> **4 teaspoons baking powder**
> **1 teaspoon salt**

Add

> **1 cup finely chopped walnuts**

Make a well in the centre.

Combine and add

> **1 beaten egg**
> **1 cup milk**
> **2 tablespoons vegetable oil *or*
> melted shortening**

Blend only until combined.

Pour into a greased 9" x 5" loaf pan. Let stand for 20 minutes. Bake in preheated 350° oven for 50 to 60 minutes.

56 Apricot Tea Bread

Preheat oven to 350°.

Soak in warm water for ½ hour
¾ cup dried apricots

Combine
¼ cup orange juice
½ cup boiling water

Cool to lukewarm.

Grind
Soaked, drained apricots
Peel from ½ orange
⅓ cup raisins

Blend or sift together
1¾ cups *Pre-Sifted* PURITY All-Purpose Flour
¾ cup sugar
1½ teaspoons baking powder
¼ teaspoon baking soda
½ teaspoon salt

Add
Ground fruit

Combine to coat the fruit. Make a well in the centre.

Add
1 beaten egg
Orange juice and water mixture
2 tablespoons vegetable oil *or* melted shortening

Mix only until combined.

Pour into a greased 9″ x 5″ loaf pan. Let stand for 20 minutes. Bake in preheated 350° oven for 50 to 60 minutes.

Many tea bread loaves will slice more easily the second day, and the flavour often improves as well. This is especially true when the loaves contain dried fruit.

57 Banana Bread

Preheat oven to 350°.

Blend or sift together
1¾ cups *Pre-Sifted* PURITY All-Purpose Flour
2 teaspoons baking powder
¼ teaspoon baking soda
½ teaspoon salt

Cream
⅓ cup shortening

Gradually beat in
⅔ cup sugar

Add
2 well-beaten eggs

Combine well.

Add dry ingredients alternately with
1 cup well-mashed banana

Beat until combined after each addition.

Pour into a greased 9″ x 5″ loaf pan. Let stand for 20 minutes. Bake in preheated 350° oven for 50 to 55 minutes.

VARIATION:

(a) Banana Nut Bread

Add ½ cup chopped walnuts to the dry ingredients in the above recipe.

Tea breads freeze well. See Freezing Section page 206 for details.

58 Corn Bread (*Johnny Cake*)

Preheat oven to 375°.

Blend or sift together
⅞ cup *Pre-Sifted* PURITY All-Purpose Flour
¼ cup sugar
4 teaspoons baking powder
½ teaspoon salt

Blend in
1 cup PURITY Corn Meal

Make a well in centre of dry ingredients.

Combine and add
1 beaten egg
1 cup milk
¼ cup melted butter *or* margarine

Stir until combined.

Pour into a greased 8″ square cake pan. Bake in preheated 375° oven for 25 to 30 minutes. Serve warm.

VARIATIONS:

(a) Apple Corn Bread

Prepare Corn Bread batter as directed above; cover with a layer of peeled apple slices; sprinkle with a mixture of
2 tablespoons sugar
1 teaspoon cinnamon

Bake as directed.

(b) Bacon Corn Bread

Fry ¼ pound bacon until crisp. Crumble into small pieces.

Add to dry ingredients in Corn Bread recipe above.

Bake as directed.

59 Cherry Bread

Preheat oven to 350°.

Cream
  ¼ cup shortening
  1 cup lightly-packed brown sugar
Add
  1 beaten egg

Beat well.

Blend or sift together
  2 cups *Pre-Sifted* PURITY
  All-Purpose Flour
  2 teaspoons baking powder
  ½ teaspoon salt
Combine
  ⅔ cup milk
  ⅓ cup syrup from red maraschino
  cherries

Add dry ingredients to creamed mixture alternately with milk mixture. Combine after each addition but do not beat.

Carefully fold in
  ½ cup drained red maraschino
  cherries, quartered
  ½ cup chopped walnuts

Pour into a greased 9″ x 5″ loaf pan. Let stand for 20 minutes. Bake in preheated 350° oven for 55 to 65 minutes.

60 Orange Bread

Preheat oven to 350°.

Grind the peel of 2 oranges. Place in a saucepan and add just enough cold water to cover the peel. Bring to a boil, remove from heat and drain off the water. Repeat this procedure twice more.

Add to drained peel
  ⅔ cup sugar

Place over low heat until sugar melts. Set aside.

Cream
  2 tablespoons shortening
  ¼ cup sugar
Add
  1 beaten egg

Beat thoroughly.

Blend or sift together
  2 cups *Pre-Sifted* PURITY
  All-Purpose Flour
  3 teaspoons baking powder
  ½ teaspoon salt

Add to creamed mixture alternately with
  ⅓ cup milk
  ⅓ cup orange juice
Mix only until blended.

Fold in
  Peel mixture

Turn into a greased 9″ x 5″ loaf pan. Let stand for 20 minutes. Bake in preheated 350° oven for 50 to 60 minutes.

61 Raisin Brown Bread

Blend or sift together
  1 cup *Pre-Sifted* PURITY
  All-Purpose Flour
  2½ teaspoons baking soda
  1 teaspoon salt
Blend in
  3 cups whole wheat flour
  1 cup raisins

Make a well in centre of dry ingredients.

Add
  2½ cups sour milk
  1 cup molasses
Combine thoroughly.

Divide batter among 4 greased 20-ounce cans. Cover each with aluminum foil and tie in place.

Steam for 1 hour.

Serve warm or cold.

Yield: 4 small breads.

62 Raisin and Nut Loaf

Preheat oven to 350°.

Blend or sift together
  2 cups *Pre-Sifted* PURITY
  All-Purpose Flour
  1 teaspoon baking soda
  ½ teaspoon salt
Add
  1 cup lightly-packed brown sugar
  1 cup raisins
  ½ cup chopped walnuts

Make a well in the centre.

Combine and add
  1 beaten egg
  1 cup sour milk
  2 tablespoons vegetable oil *or*
  melted shortening

Stir until well combined but do not beat.

Pour into a greased 9″ x 5″ loaf pan. Let stand for 20 minutes. Bake in preheated 350° oven for 55 to 65 minutes.

63 Date and Nut Loaf

Preheat oven to 350°.

Pour
  3/4 cup boiling water
over
  2 cups chopped dates
  1 teaspoon baking soda

Let stand until cool.

Cream
  2 tablespoons shortening
  3/4 cup sugar
Add
  1 beaten egg
  1 teaspoon vanilla

Beat until well combined.

Add
  Date mixture
  1 3/4 cups *Pre-Sifted* PURITY
  All-Purpose Flour
  1/2 teaspoon salt
  1/2 cup chopped walnuts

Stir only until combined.

Pour into a greased 9″ x 5″ loaf pan. Let stand for 20 minutes. Bake in preheated 350° oven for 60 to 70 minutes.

64 Lemon Loaf

Preheat oven to 350°.

Cream
  1/2 cup shortening
  1 cup sugar
Add
  2 eggs

Beat until light and fluffy.

Blend or sift together
  1 1/2 cups *Pre-Sifted* PURITY
  All-Purpose Flour
  2 teaspoons baking powder
  1/2 teaspoon salt
Add
  1/2 cup chopped walnuts
  2 teaspoons grated lemon rind

Add dry ingredients to creamed mixture alternately with
  1/2 cup milk

Pour batter into a greased 9″ x 5″ loaf pan. Let stand for 20 minutes.

Bake in preheated 350° oven for 60 to 70 minutes.

GLAZE:

When baked, remove from pan and slowly pour over the top a mixture of
  1/4 cup sugar
  2 tablespoons lemon juice

Cool, cover and let stand for 24 hours before serving.

65 Boston Brown Bread

Blend or sift together
  1/2 cup *Pre-Sifted* PURITY
  All-Purpose Flour
  1 1/2 teaspoons baking soda
  1 teaspoon salt
Blend in
  1 cup whole wheat flour
  1 cup PURITY Corn Meal

Make a well in centre of dry ingredients.
Add
  2 cups sour milk
  1/2 cup light molasses

Mix thoroughly.

Divide batter among 3 greased 20-ounce cans.

Cover with aluminum foil and tie in place.

Steam for 1 to 1 1/4 hours.

Serve hot, with baked beans.

Yield: 3 steamed breads.

NOTE: This bread may be reheated by steaming for about 20 minutes.

66 Cheese Bread

Preheat oven to 350°.

Blend or sift together
  2 cups *Pre-Sifted* PURITY
  All-Purpose Flour
  4 teaspoons baking powder
  1 1/2 teaspoons salt
Stir in
  1 cup shredded mild Cheddar
  cheese

Make a well in centre of dry ingredients.
Combine and add
  2 beaten eggs
  1 cup milk
  1/4 cup vegetable oil *or* melted
  shortening

Blend only until combined.

Pour into a greased 9″ x 5″ loaf pan. Let stand for 20 minutes. Bake in preheated 350° oven for 50 to 60 minutes.

"This loaf is especially good when served warm."

67 *Raisin Bran Bread*

Preheat oven to 350°.
Combine
  1 cup milk
  ¼ cup molasses
Add
  ⅓ cup bran
  1 beaten egg
Blend or sift together
  **1½ cups *Pre-Sifted* PURITY
    All-Purpose Flour**
  ⅓ cup sugar
  2 teaspoons baking powder
  ¾ teaspoon baking soda
  1 teaspoon salt
Add to milk mixture.
Stir in
  1 cup chopped walnuts *or* Brazil nuts
  1 cup raisins
  **3 tablespoons vegetable oil *or*
    melted shortening**
Do not over mix.
Pour into a greased 9″ x 5″ loaf pan. Let
stand for 20 minutes. Bake in preheated 350°
oven for 50 to 60 minutes.

68 *Pineapple Cheese Bread*

Preheat oven to 350°.

Blend or sift together
  **2 cups *Pre-Sifted* PURITY
    All-Purpose Flour**
  ¾ cup sugar
  3 teaspoons baking powder
  ½ teaspoon baking soda
  1 teaspoon salt

Combine
  1 cup crushed pineapple, undrained
  1 beaten egg
  **2 tablespoons vegetable oil *or*
    melted shortening**

Add to dry ingredients and combine until
moistened.

Fold in
  **½ cup shredded mild Cheddar
    cheese**
  ½ cup chopped walnuts

Pour into a greased 9″ x 5″ loaf pan. Let
stand for 20 minutes. Bake in preheated 350°
oven for 55 to 65 minutes.

COFFEE CAKES
Coffee Cakes are usually best when served warm, with butter.

69 *Raisin Spice Coffee Cake*

Preheat oven to 375°.
Cream together
  ½ cup shortening
  ⅔ cup sugar
Add
  2 eggs
Beat well.
Blend or sift together
  **1¾ cups *Pre-Sifted* PURITY
    All-Purpose Flour**
  3 teaspoons baking powder
  ½ teaspoon salt
  ½ teaspoon cinnamon
  ¼ teaspoon ginger
  ⅛ teaspoon mace
Add
  ½ cup raisins
Add to creamed mixture, alternately with
  ¾ cup milk
Stir until well combined.
Turn batter into a greased 8″ square cake pan.

Combine thoroughly
  **2 tablespoons melted butter *or*
    margarine**
  2 tablespoons sugar
  ½ teaspoon cinnamon
  **⅓ cup *Pre-Sifted* PURITY
    All-Purpose Flour**
  2 tablespoons chopped nuts
Spread evenly over the batter.
Bake in preheated 375° oven for 35 to 40
minutes.
Serve warm, with butter.

70 *Pineapple Crunch Coffee Cake*

Preheat oven to 400°.

CRUMB MIXTURE:

Blend together
  **½ cup *Pre-Sifted* PURITY
    All-Purpose Flour**
  ¼ cup brown sugar
  1 teaspoon cinnamon

Cut in until mixture is crumbly
¼ cup butter *or* margarine
Add
½ cup chopped walnuts
Set aside.
Drain
1 (10-ounce) can crushed pineapple (or about 1¼ cups)

CAKE BATTER:
Blend or sift together
1½ cups *Pre-Sifted* PURITY All-Purpose Flour
½ cup sugar
2 teaspoons baking powder
½ teaspoon salt
Make a well in centre of dry ingredients.
Combine and add
1 beaten egg
⅓ cup milk
⅓ cup syrup from crushed pineapple
3 tablespoons vegetable oil *or* melted shortening
Stir until well combined.
Spread half of batter in a greased 8″ square cake pan.
Sprinkle with one-half the crumb mixture and then spread with the drained crushed pineapple (about ¾ cup).
Spread remaining batter over the pineapple. Top with other half of the crumb mixture.
Bake in preheated 400° oven for 25 to 30 minutes.
Serve warm.

Coffee Cakes freeze very successfully. See Freezing Section page 206 for details.

71   Date Filled Coffee Cake

Preheat oven to 425°.
Blend or sift together
1½ cups *Pre-Sifted* PURITY All-Purpose Flour
⅓ cup granulated sugar
1½ teaspoons baking powder
½ teaspoon salt
Cut in
¼ cup shortening
Make a well in the centre.
Add
1 beaten egg
⅔ cup milk
Mix until well combined.
Spread half of batter in a greased 8″ square

cake pan. Cover with date filling made by combining
½ cup lightly-packed brown sugar
1 tablespoon *Pre-Sifted* PURITY All-Purpose Flour
¼ cup chopped walnuts
½ cup chopped dates
¼ cup melted butter *or* margarine
Spread remaining batter evenly over the top.
Sprinkle with
¼ cup chopped walnuts
Bake in preheated 425° oven for 25 to 30 minutes.
Serve warm.

72   Sally Lunn

Preheat oven to 400°.
Cream together
½ cup shortening
½ cup sugar
Add
1 teaspoon lemon juice
2 unbeaten eggs
Beat until light and fluffy.
Blend or sift together
1½ cups *Pre-Sifted* PURITY All-Purpose Flour
2¼ teaspoons baking powder
¾ teaspoon salt
Add to creamed mixture, alternately with
¾ cup milk
Mix well after each addition.
Pour batter into a greased 9″ round cake pan which is at least 1½″ deep.
Sprinkle with a mixture of
⅓ cup sugar
⅛ teaspoon nutmeg
1 tablespoon grated lemon rind
1 tablespoon melted butter *or* margarine
Bake in preheated 400° oven for 25 to 30 minutes.
Cut into wedges and serve while warm.

73   Streusel Coffee Cake

Preheat oven to 375°.
Cream together
⅓ cup shortening
½ cup granulated sugar
Add
1 egg

Beat well.

Blend or sift together

    1½ cups *Pre-Sifted* PURITY
        All-Purpose Flour
    2 teaspoons baking powder
    ½ teaspoon salt

Add to creamed mixture alternately with

    ¾ cup milk

Spread batter in a greased 8″ or 9″ square cake pan.

Thoroughly combine

    ½ cup lightly-packed brown sugar
    2 tablespoons *Pre-Sifted* PURITY
        All-Purpose Flour
    1 teaspoon cinnamon
    ½ cup chopped walnuts
    3 tablespoons melted butter *or*
        margarine

Sprinkle this mixture over the batter.

Bake in preheated 375° oven for 30 to 35 minutes.

Serve warm.

————————

To reheat Coffee Cakes, wrap in aluminum foil and place in a 350° oven for about 15 minutes.

74   Cinnamon Coffee Cake

Preheat oven to 350°.

Blend or sift together

    2½ cups *Pre-Sifted* PURITY
        All-Purpose Flour
    2½ teaspoons baking powder
    ½ teaspoon baking soda
    ½ teaspoon salt
    2 teaspoons cinnamon

Blend in

    2 cups lightly-packed brown sugar

Cut in finely

    ½ cup shortening

Reserve ½ cup of this mixture to use for topping. Make a well in centre of remaining flour mixture.

Add

    2 beaten eggs
    ¾ cup buttermilk

Mix until well combined.

Divide batter between 2 greased 8″ or 9″ round layer cake pans. Sprinkle topping mixture over these. Bake in preheated 350° oven for 35 to 40 minutes.

Cut into wedges and serve while warm.

POPOVERS

75   Purity Popovers

Preheat oven to 450°.

Pour ½ teaspoon vegetable oil or melted shortening in each of 8 medium-sized muffin cups, cast-iron popover pans or pyrex custard cups. Place pans in the oven to heat while making the batter.

Blend or sift together

    1 cup *Pre-Sifted* PURITY
        All-Purpose Flour
    ¼ teaspoon salt

Gradually add

    1 cup milk

Beat until smooth.

Beat until thick and light

    2 eggs

Add to flour mixture, along with

    1 tablespoon melted butter *or*
        margarine

Beat the mixture for 2 minutes, using a rotary beater.

Divide the batter among the 8 heated pans.

Bake in preheated 450° oven for 20 minutes.

Then lower the temperature to 350° and bake for another 20 minutes. Remove from the pans and cut a small hole in the side of each popover to allow steam to escape.

Serve immediately with roast beef; as a main dish filled with creamed chicken, meat or vegetables; or as a dessert with maple syrup or filled with fruit and topped with whipped cream.

Yield: 8 popovers.

VARIATION:

(a)   Yorkshire Pudding

Preheat oven to 450°.

Place about 1½ tablespoons roast beef drippings or vegetable oil in an 8″ square pyrex cake pan. Heat pan in the oven while preparing Popover batter as directed above. Pour batter into heated dish and bake 20 minutes at 450°, then lower temperature to 350° and bake for another 20 minutes. Cut into squares and serve immediately with roast beef.

Yield: 9 servings.

PANCAKES AND WAFFLES

76 BASIC RECIPE · *Pancakes*

Blend or sift together
  **1½ cups *Pre-Sifted* PURITY
    All-Purpose Flour
  1 to 2 tablespoons sugar
  3 teaspoons baking powder
  ½ teaspoon salt**
Combine
  **1 beaten egg
  1¾ cups milk
  2 tablespoons vegetable oil *or*
    melted shortening**

Add liquids to the dry ingredients. Beat only until combined.

Heat a heavy grill or frying pan to 380° (drops of cold water will dance across it).

Grease lightly with unsalted fat.

Use about ¼ cup batter for each 4″ pancake.

Bake until edge of pancake begins to dry and lose its gloss. Turn and bake until golden brown.

Serve hot, with butter and syrup.

Yield: About 12—4″ pancakes.

NOTE: If batter thickens, add a little more milk.

VARIATIONS:

(a)   Corn Pancakes
Prepare Pancake batter as directed in recipe No. 76, adding ½ teaspoon celery salt to the dry ingredients.
Fold in 1 cup drained whole kernel corn. Bake as for plain pancakes.
Serve with butter and molasses.

(b)   Main Dish Pancakes
Prepare Pancake batter as directed in recipe No. 76.
Fold in ¾ cup finely chopped ham, wieners or luncheon meat. Bake as for plain pancakes.
Serve with syrup or a raisin sauce.

(c)   Filled Pancakes
Combine 1 cup finely chopped cooked ham and 1 cup commercial sour cream. Set aside.
Prepare and bake Pancakes as directed in recipe No. 76. Spread each hot pancake with about 3 tablespoons of the sour cream mixture; fold over. Serve at once.

(d)   Blueberry Pancakes
Prepare Pancake batter as directed in recipe No. 76. Fold in ¾ cup fresh blueberries. Bake as for plain pancakes.

(e)   Dessert Pancakes
Prepare Pancake batter as directed in recipe No. 76, increasing sugar to ¼ cup. Use about 2 or 3 tablespoons of batter for each pancake and bake as for plain pancakes. Keep hot.
To serve, spread with jam, apple sauce or a cream filling. Roll up and sprinkle with icing sugar.

77   *Corn Meal Pancakes*

Blend or sift together
  **1 cup *Pre-Sifted* PURITY
    All-Purpose Flour
  1 tablespoon sugar
  3 teaspoons baking powder
  ½ teaspoon salt**
Blend in
  ½ cup PURITY Corn Meal
Combine
  **2 beaten egg yolks
  2 cups milk
  2 tablespoons vegetable oil *or*
    melted shortening**

Add liquids to dry ingredients and beat only until combined.

Beat until stiff, but not dry
  2 egg whites

Fold into pancake batter.

Heat a heavy grill or frying pan to 380° (drops of cold water will dance across it). Grease lightly with unsalted fat.

Use about ¼ cup batter for each 4″ pancake.

Bake until edge of pancake begins to dry and lose its gloss. Turn and bake until golden brown.

Serve hot, with butter and syrup.

Yield: About 18—4″ pancakes.

Modern grills are often treated so that greasing is unnecessary. Follow manufacturer's directions when using these.

78 Pancake Dessert Supreme

Blend or sift together
- **¾ cup *Pre-Sifted* PURITY All-Purpose Flour**
- **2 tablespoons sugar**
- **1½ teaspoons baking powder**
- **¼ teaspoon salt**

Combine
- **1 beaten egg**
- **¾ cup milk**
- **1 tablespoon melted butter *or* margarine**

Add liquids to the dry ingredients. Beat only until combined.

Heat a heavy grill or frying pan to 380° (drops of cold water will dance across it). Grease lightly with unsalted fat.

Use about ¼ cup batter for each pancake.

Bake until edge of pancake begins to dry and lose its gloss. Turn and bake until golden brown.

Keep hot while preparing the Raisin Sauce.

RAISIN SAUCE:

Melt over low heat
- **¾ cup butter *or* margarine**

Stir in
- **½ cup raisins**
- **½ teaspoon cinnamon**
- **½ cup finely chopped walnuts**

Add and mix lightly
- **1 cup sugar**

Remove from the heat at once (sugar should not dissolve).

To serve: Tear hot pancakes into bite-sized pieces and fold them into the Raisin Sauce.

Serve at once, plain or with whipped cream or ice cream.

Yield: 5 to 6 servings.

79 Buttermilk Pancakes

Blend or sift together
- **1½ cups *Pre-Sifted* PURITY All-Purpose Flour**
- **1 to 2 tablespoons sugar**
- **1 teaspoon baking powder**
- **½ teaspoon baking soda**
- **½ teaspoon salt**

Combine
- **1 beaten egg**
- **1¾ cups buttermilk**
- **2 tablespoons vegetable oil *or* melted shortening**

Add liquids to dry ingredients. Beat only until combined.

Heat a heavy grill or frying pan to 380° (drops of cold water will dance across it). Grease lightly with unsalted fat.

Use about ¼ cup batter for each 4″ pancake.

Bake until edge of pancake begins to dry and lose its gloss. Turn and bake until golden brown.

Serve hot, with butter and syrup.

Yield: About 12—4″ pancakes.

To keep pancakes hot, place between folds of a towel in a warm oven, or separately on a baking sheet. Do not stack pancakes while keeping them hot, as this causes sogginess.

80 Waffles

Blend or sift together
- **1½ cups *Pre-Sifted* PURITY All-Purpose Flour**
- **2 tablespoons sugar**
- **3 teaspoons baking powder**
- **½ teaspoon salt**

Combine
- **2 beaten eggs**
- **1½ cups milk**
- **¼ cup melted butter *or* margarine**

Add liquids to dry ingredients. Beat just until smooth.

Heat waffle iron as directed by the manufacturer. Pour batter into hot waffle iron. (About 1 cup of batter for a 9″ square iron, about ½ cup for a 7″ round iron.)

Bake until the waffle stops steaming.

Serve hot, with butter and syrup.

Yield: 3—9″ waffles, or 6—7″ waffles.

VARIATION:

(a) Buttermilk Waffles

Prepare Waffle recipe No. 80 as directed, but reduce baking powder to 1 teaspoon and add ½ teaspoon baking soda. Replace milk with buttermilk or sour milk.

Cakes

THINGS TO REMEMBER WHEN MAKING CAKES

A successful cake is the proof of one's baking skill, so it is most important to follow recipe directions *exactly*. Use the ingredients suggested in the recipe and have them at room temperature. *Never double a cake recipe as you will not get proper beating and blending of ingredients.*

You may "sift" or "blend" together the dry ingredients. If blending, be sure to do it thoroughly.

For best results, add the dry ingredients one-third at a time, and the liquid one-half at a time. Start and end with the dry ingredients and simply stir to combine the batter. *Do not beat* as this may result in a coarse, tough cake.

Use the size of pan recommended in the recipe. The batter should about half fill the pan and should be spread evenly.

Grease cake pans on bottoms only, using unsalted shortening or vegetable oil. Line with waxed paper cut to fit; or add about one teaspoon flour and shake to coat the bottom. Discard excess flour.

A cake is baked if the top springs back when pressed with the finger tips or when a cake tester, inserted in the centre, comes out clean.

Let a cake stand in the pan for about ten minutes and then remove from the pan and cool on a rack.

THE ART OF CAKE MAKING

81   Basic White Cake

Preheat oven to 350°.
Grease an 8″ or 9″ square cake pan or two 8″ round layer pans. Line the bottom with waxed paper or dust lightly with flour.
Cream
  ⅓ cup shortening
Gradually blend in
  1 cup sugar
Beat until light and fluffy.
Add
  1 egg
  1 teaspoon vanilla
Beat until well combined.

Blend or sift together
  1½ cups *Pre-Sifted* PURITY
  All-Purpose Flour

  2 teaspoons baking powder

  ½ teaspoon salt

Add dry ingredients to the creamed mixture, alternately with

  1 cup milk

Combine after each addition.

Pour batter into prepared pan.

Bake in preheated 350° oven—45 to 50 minutes for a square cake, 30 to 35 minutes for a layer cake.

VARIATIONS:

(a)   Spice Cake

Prepare as above, adding 1 teaspoon cinnamon, ½ teaspoon ginger, ½ teaspoon nutmeg and ¼ teaspoon allspice to the dry ingredients.

(b)   Maple Nut Cake

Prepare as for Basic White Cake, replacing the vanilla with ½ teaspoon maple flavouring. Fold ½ cup finely chopped walnuts into the batter.

(c)   Marble Cake

Prepare the Basic White Cake as directed. Divide the batter into two portions. To one portion add a mixture of 1 square unsweetened chocolate, melted, 2 teaspoons sugar, ⅛ teaspoon baking soda and 2 teaspoons hot water. Leave second portion of the batter plain. Drop alternate spoonfuls of the two batters into prepared pan. Swirl for a marbled effect. Bake as directed.

82 Three Egg Cake

Preheat oven to 350°.

Grease two 8″ or 9″ round layer cake pans. Line the bottoms with waxed paper or dust lightly with flour.

Cream
   ¾ cup shortening

Gradually blend in
   1½ cups sugar

Beat until light and fluffy.

Add
   3 well-beaten eggs
   1½ teaspoons vanilla

Beat until well combined.

Blend or sift together
   2½ cups *Pre-Sifted* PURITY
      All-Purpose Flour
   3½ teaspoons baking powder
   ¾ teaspoon salt

Add dry ingredients to creamed mixture, alternately with
   1½ cups milk

Combine after each addition.

Divide batter between two pans.

Bake in preheated 350° oven for 30 to 35 minutes.

83 Cream Cake

Preheat oven to 350°.

Grease a 9″ square cake pan or two 8″ round layer pans. Line the bottom with waxed paper or dust lightly with flour.

Beat until *very* thick (use a small bowl)
   2 eggs

Gradually beat in
   ¾ cup sugar
   1 teaspoon vanilla

Then transfer to a larger bowl.

Blend or sift together
   1½ cups *Pre-Sifted* PURITY
      All-Purpose Flour
   2 teaspoons baking powder
   ½ teaspoon salt

Add to egg mixture, alternately with
   1 cup whipping cream, unbeaten

Combine after each addition.

Pour batter into prepared pan.

Bake in preheated 350° oven—40 to 45 minutes for a square cake, 30 to 35 minutes for a layer cake.

84 Golden Butter Cake

Preheat oven to 350°.

Grease an 8″ square cake pan. Line the bottom with waxed paper or dust lightly with flour.

Cream thoroughly
   ½ cup butter

Gradually blend in
   1 cup sugar
   2 eggs
   1 teaspoon vanilla

Beat well.

Blend or sift together
   1⅔ cups *Pre-Sifted* PURITY
      All-Purpose Flour
   1½ teaspoons baking powder
   ½ teaspoon salt

Add dry ingredients to creamed mixture, alternately with
   ¾ cup milk

Blend well after each addition.

Pour into prepared pan.

Bake in preheated 350° oven—50 to 55 minutes.

Vary the flavour of a cake by changing the flavouring extract. For example, substitute maple flavouring for vanilla.

85 One Bowl Cake

Preheat oven to 350°.

Use a regular electric mixer.

Grease two 8″ or 9″ round layer cake pans. Line the bottoms with waxed paper or dust lightly with flour.

Blend or sift together
   2¾ cups *Pre-Sifted* PURITY
      All-Purpose Flour
   1½ cups sugar
   3½ teaspoons baking powder
   1 teaspoon salt

Add
   ½ cup shortening
   1 cup milk

Beat for 2 minutes.

When entertaining make this lovely Orange Chiffon Cake (Recipe No. 102 (a)

Then add
> ½ cup milk
> 2 eggs
> 1 teaspoon vanilla

Beat for 2 minutes.

Divide batter between prepared pans.

Bake in preheated 350° oven for 30 to 35 minutes.

Cake batter may be baked as cup cakes. Fill paper cups or liners (set in muffin cups) about ⅔ full. Bake at 400° for 18 to 20 minutes. A batter containing 2 cups flour will yield approximately 1½ dozen medium-sized cup cakes.

86   Cocoa Cake

Preheat oven to 350°.

Grease a 9″ square cake pan or two 8″ round layer pans. Line the bottom with waxed paper.

Cream
> ½ cup shortening

Gradually blend in
> 1 cup sugar

Beat until light and fluffy.

Add
> 2 well-beaten eggs
> 1 teaspoon vanilla

Beat until well combined.

Blend or sift together
> 1½ cups *Pre-Sifted* PURITY All-Purpose Flour
> ½ cup cocoa
> 2½ teaspoons baking powder
> ½ teaspoon salt

Add dry ingredients to the creamed mixture, alternately with
> 1 cup milk

Combine well after each addition.

Pour batter into prepared pan.

Bake in preheated 350° oven—45 to 50 minutes for a square cake, 30 to 35 minutes for a layer cake.

VARIATION:

(a)   Mocha Cake

Prepare as above, reducing the vanilla to ½ teaspoon. Add 2 teaspoons instant coffee powder and 1 teaspoon cinnamon to the dry ingredients.

87   Devil's Food Cake

Preheat oven to 350°.

Grease two 8″ or 9″ round layer cake pans. Line the bottoms with waxed paper.

Cream
> ½ cup shortening

Gradually blend in
> 1½ cups lightly-packed brown sugar

Beat until light and fluffy.

Add
> 2 well-beaten eggs
> ½ teaspoon vanilla

Beat until well combined.

Blend in
> 2 squares unsweetened chocolate, melted

Blend or sift together
> 1½ cups *Pre-Sifted* PURITY All-Purpose Flour
> 1¼ teaspoons baking soda
> ¾ teaspoon salt

Add dry ingredients to creamed mixture, alternately with
> 1 cup plus 2 tablespoons milk

Combine well after each addition.

Divide batter between prepared pans.

Bake in preheated 350° oven for 30 to 35 minutes.

Shiny metal pans give even browning and heat distribution. Discard those old darkened pans! When using heat-proof glass pans, reduce oven temperature 25°.

88   Chocolate Cake

Preheat oven to 325°.

Grease a 9″ square cake pan or two 8″ round layer pans. Line the bottom with waxed paper.

Cream
> ½ cup shortening

Gradually blend in
> 1 cup sugar

Beat until light and fluffy.

Add
> 2 well-beaten eggs

Beat until well combined.

Then blend in
> 2 squares unsweetened chocolate, melted
> ½ teaspoon vanilla

Blend or sift together
- **1½ cups *Pre-Sifted* PURITY All-Purpose Flour**
- **¾ teaspoon baking soda**
- **½ teaspoon salt**

Add to creamed mixture, alternately with
- **1 cup sour milk**

Blend well after each addition.

Pour batter into prepared pan.

Bake in preheated 325° oven—45 to 50 minutes for a square cake, 30 to 35 minutes for a layer cake.

89   Marble Cake

Preheat oven to 350°.

Grease a 9″ square cake pan or two 8″ round layer cake pans. Line the bottom with waxed paper.

Cream
- **½ cup shortening**

Gradually blend in
- **¼ cup sugar**

Beat until light and fluffy.

Add
- **2 well-beaten eggs**
- **1 teaspoon vanilla**

Beat until well combined.

Blend or sift together
- **2¼ cups *Pre-Sifted* PURITY All-Purpose Flour**
- **2½ teaspoons baking powder**
- **¾ teaspoon salt**

Add dry ingredients to creamed mixture, alternately with
- **1⅓ cups milk**

Combine well after each addition.

Divide batter into three equal portions.

To one portion, add
- **⅛ teaspoon cinnamon**
- **⅛ teaspoon cloves**

To second portion, add a mixture of
- **½ square unsweetened chocolate, melted**
- **⅛ teaspoon baking soda**
- **1 teaspoon sugar**
- **1 teaspoon hot water**

Leave third portion plain.

Drop alternate spoonfuls of batter into prepared pan. Swirl to give a marbled effect. Bake in preheated 350° oven for 40 to 50 minutes.

90   Nut Cake

Preheat oven to 350°.

Grease a 9″ square cake pan or two 8″ round layer pans. Line the bottom with waxed paper or dust lightly with flour.

Cream
- **½ cup shortening**

Gradually blend in
- **1¼ cups sugar**

Beat until light and fluffy.

Add
- **2 eggs**
- **1 teaspoon vanilla**

Beat thoroughly.

Blend or sift together
- **2¼ cups *Pre-Sifted* PURITY All-Purpose Flour**
- **2½ teaspoons baking powder**
- **¾ teaspoon salt**

Add dry ingredients to creamed mixture, alternately with
- **1⅓ cups milk**

Combine after each addition.

Then fold in
- **1 cup chopped walnuts**

Pour batter into prepared pan.

Bake in preheated 350° oven—45 to 50 minutes for a square cake, 35 to 40 minutes for a layer cake.

When using an electric mixer for cakes, add the eggs, unbeaten, and cream well with the shortening and sugar.

91   Mocha Nut Cake

Preheat oven to 350°.

Grease two 8″ or 9″ round layer cake pans. Line the bottoms with waxed paper.

Cream thoroughly
- **½ cup butter**

Gradually blend in
- **1½ cups sugar**

Beat until light and fluffy.

Add
- **3 egg yolks**

Beat thoroughly.

Then blend in
- **2 squares unsweetened chocolate, melted**

Blend or sift together
  **1¾ cups *Pre-Sifted* PURITY
    All-Purpose Flour
  3 teaspoons baking powder
  ¼ teaspoon salt**
Add dry ingredients to creamed mixture,
alternately with
  **1 cup milk
  ¼ cup cold strong coffee**
Combine after each addition.
Add
  1 cup chopped walnuts, floured
Beat until stiff but not dry
  3 egg whites
Fold into cake batter.
Divide batter between prepared pans.
Bake in preheated 350° oven for 30 to 35
minutes.

————————

*The term shortening in cake recipes refers only to
emulsified shortenings. Do not use lard.*

92   Apple Spice Cake

Preheat oven to 350°.
Grease an 8″ or 9″ square cake pan. Line the
bottom with waxed paper or dust lightly with
flour.
Cream
  ½ cup shortening
Gradually blend in
  1 cup lightly-packed brown sugar
Beat until light and fluffy.
Add
  1 egg
Beat thoroughly.
Blend or sift together
  **2 cups *Pre-Sifted* PURITY
    All-Purpose Flour
  2½ teaspoons baking powder
  ½ teaspoon salt
  1 teaspoon cinnamon
  ½ teaspoon nutmeg**
Add dry ingredients to creamed mixture,
alternately with a mixture of
  **⅔ cup canned applesauce (sweetened)
  ½ cup milk**
Blend after each addition.
Turn into prepared pan.
Bake in preheated 350° oven for 30 to 40
minutes.

93   Orange Cake

Preheat oven to 350°.
Grease an 8″ square cake pan and line the
bottom with waxed paper or dust lightly with
flour.
Cream
  ½ cup butter
Gradually beat in
  1 cup sugar
Then add
  2 egg yolks
Beat until thick and lemon coloured.
Add
  1 tablespoon grated orange rind
Blend or sift together
  **1½ cups *Pre-Sifted* PURITY
    All-Purpose Flour
  2 teaspoons baking powder
  ¼ teaspoon salt**
Add dry ingredients to creamed mixture,
alternately with
  **⅓ cup orange juice
  ⅓ cup water**
Combine after each addition.
Beat until stiff but not dry
  2 egg whites
Carefully fold into cake batter.
Pour into prepared pan.
Bake in preheated 350° oven—45 to 50 minutes
for a square cake, 30 to 35 minutes for a layer
cake.

94   Banana Cake

Preheat oven to 350°.
Grease a 9″ square cake pan or two 8″ round
layer pans. Line the bottom with waxed paper
or dust lightly with flour.
Cream
  ½ cup shortening
Gradually blend in
  1 cup sugar
Beat until light and fluffy.
Add
  1 well-beaten egg
Beat until well combined.
Blend in
  **1 cup mashed ripe bananas
  1 teaspoon vanilla**

Blend or sift together
**1¾ cups *Pre-Sifted* PURITY
All-Purpose Flour
1½ teaspoons baking powder
½ teaspoon baking soda
½ teaspoon salt**
Add dry ingredients to banana mixture, alternately with
½ cup buttermilk or sour milk
Blend after each addition.
Pour batter into prepared pan.
Bake in preheated 350° oven—50 to 55 minutes for a square cake, 30 to 35 minutes for a layer cake.

95 *Coconut Meringue Cake*

Preheat oven to 325°.
Grease a 9″ square cake pan and dust lightly with flour.
Cream
¼ cup shortening
Gradually blend in
½ cup sugar
Beat until light and fluffy.
Add
2 well-beaten egg yolks
Beat until well combined.
Blend in
1 tablespoon grated orange rind
Blend or sift together
**1 cup *Pre-Sifted* PURITY
All-Purpose Flour
2 teaspoons baking powder
¼ teaspoon salt**
Add dry ingredients to creamed mixture, alternately with
½ cup milk
Blend after each addition.
Pour batter into prepared pan.
TOPPING:
Beat to soft peaks
2 egg whites
Gradually beat in
½ cup sugar
Then fold in
1 cup coconut
Spread carefully over cake batter.
Bake in preheated 325° oven for about 45 minutes.

96 *Date Specialty Cake*

Preheat oven to 350°.

Grease a 9-inch square cake pan and line the bottom with waxed paper or dust lightly with flour.
In a saucepan combine
**1½ cups chopped dates
1 cup water**
Cook uncovered over medium heat until soft. Cool.
Sift together
**1⅔ cups *Pre-Sifted* PURITY
All-Purpose Flour
½ teaspoon salt
2½ teaspoons baking powder
¼ teaspoon baking soda**
Cream
**½ cup butter
1 cup lightly-packed brown sugar**
Blend in, beating until light and fluffy
**2 eggs
1 teaspoon vanilla**
Stir dry ingredients into creamed mixture alternately with
⅔ cup milk
Make 3 dry and 2 liquid additions, combining lightly after each.
Then fold in the date mixture and
½ cup chopped walnuts
Turn into prepared pan.
Bake in preheated 350° oven for 40 to 45 minutes, or until cake springs back when lightly touched.

97 *Crumb Cake*

Preheat oven to 350°.
Grease a 9″ square cake pan and dust lightly with flour.
Cream
¾ cup butter
Gradually blend in
1 cup sugar
Beat until light and fluffy.
Blend or sift together
**1¾ cups *Pre-Sifted* PURITY
All-Purpose Flour
1 teaspoon cinnamon
¼ teaspoon nutmeg
¼ teaspoon cloves
¼ teaspoon salt**
Add dry ingredients to creamed mixture and blend with electric mixer or with a pastry blender until mixture resembles corn meal.
Measure and reserve 1 cup of this mixture to use for crumb topping.

Blend into remainder
  1 teaspoon baking soda
Add and beat smooth (2 minutes)
  2 eggs
  ¼ cup buttermilk or sour milk
Add and beat 1 minute
  ½ cup buttermilk or sour milk
Pour batter into prepared pan. Sprinkle crumb mixture over top and press down lightly.
Bake in preheated 350° oven for 40 to 50 mins.

98   *True Sponge Cake*

Preheat oven to 325°.
Select a 9″ tube pan and make sure that it is free of any grease.
Beat until frothy
  5 egg whites
Sprinkle with
  1 teaspoon cream of tartar
Continue beating until just stiff, but not dry.
Then gradually beat in
  ¼ cup fruit sugar
Set aside.
Beat until thick
  5 egg yolks
Gradually beat in
  5 tablespoons cold water
Then beat in
  ¾ cup fruit sugar
Blend or sift together
  ⅞ cup *Pre-Sifted* PURITY All-Purpose Flour
  ½ teaspoon salt
Sift or sprinkle the dry ingredients over the egg yolk mixture, a little at a time, combining lightly after each addition.
Fold in
  1 teaspoon vanilla
  1 teaspoon lemon extract
Carefully fold in the meringue.
Turn into pan. Cut through batter with a knife to eliminate air bubbles.
Bake in preheated 325° oven for 60 to 75 minutes.
As soon as the cake is baked, invert it and allow to hang suspended until cold. To remove from the pan, loosen with a knife and shake carefully from the pan.

99   *Hot Milk Sponge Cake*

Preheat oven to 350°.
Select an 8½″ or 9″ tube pan and make sure that it is free of any grease.
Beat until thick and lemon coloured
  3 eggs
Gradually beat in
  1¼ cups sugar
Then add
  1 teaspoon vanilla
Blend or sift together
  1½ cups *Pre-Sifted* PURITY All-Purpose Flour
  2¼ teaspoons baking powder
  ¼ teaspoon salt
Gradually sift or sprinkle the dry ingredients over the egg mixture and fold in carefully after each addition.
Then quickly fold in
  ¾ cup hot milk
(The milk should be at 120°—just a little warmer than *lukewarm*.)
Pour into the pan. Swirl a knife through the batter to remove air bubbles.
Bake in preheated 350° oven for about 50 minutes.
Invert the baked cake and allow it to hang suspended until cool. To remove from the pan, loosen with a knife or spatula and shake carefully from the pan.

100   *Angel Cake*

Preheat oven to 375°.
Select a 9″ tube pan and make sure that it is free of any grease.
Blend or sift together
  1 cup *Pre-Sifted* PURITY All-Purpose Flour
  ¼ cup fruit sugar
Set aside.
Beat until frothy
  1¼ cups egg whites
Sprinkle with
  ¼ teaspoon salt
  1¼ teaspoons cream of tartar
Continue beating until just stiff, but not dry.
Sift, 2 tablespoons at a time, over the egg whites
  1 cup fruit sugar
Fold in very carefully after each addition.

Then fold in
¾ teaspoon vanilla
¼ teaspoon almond extract

Sift or sprinkle the dry ingredients over the egg mixture, a little at a time. Fold in gently after each addition. Turn batter into the pan. Cut through batter with a knife to eliminate air bubbles.

Bake in preheated 375° oven for 45 to 50 minutes.

As soon as the cake is baked, invert it and allow to hang suspended until cold. To remove from the pan, loosen with a knife or spatula and shake carefully from the pan.

101 Coffee Sponge Cake

Preheat oven to 350°.

Select a 10″ tube pan and make sure it is free of any grease.

Beat until frothy
5 egg whites
Sprinkle with
½ teaspoon cream of tartar
Continue beating until soft peaks form.
Gradually beat in
⅓ cup fruit sugar
Beat until stiff, but not dry.
Beat until lemon coloured
5 egg yolks
Gradually beat in
1⅓ cups fruit sugar
Beat until thick.
Blend or sift together
1⅔ cups Pre-Sifted PURITY
All-Purpose Flour
2½ teaspoons baking powder
½ teaspoon salt
Stir dry ingredients into egg yolk mixture, alternately with
¾ cup cold strong coffee
Fold in
½ cup finely chopped pecans
Carefully fold batter into meringue.
Turn into pan. Cut through batter with a knife to eliminate air bubbles.
Bake in preheated 350° oven for 60 to 75 minutes.
As soon as the cake is baked, invert it and allow to hang suspended until cold. To remove from the pan, loosen with a knife or spatula and shake carefully from the pan.

102 Chiffon Cake

Preheat oven to 325°.

Select a 10″ tube pan and make sure that it is free of any grease.

Blend or sift together into a large mixing bowl
2 cups Pre-Sifted PURITY
All-Purpose Flour
1½ cups sugar
3 teaspoons baking powder
1 teaspoon salt
Make a well in centre of dry ingredients.
Add
½ cup vegetable oil
5 unbeaten egg yolks
¾ cup water
1 teaspoon vanilla
Beat with a wooden spoon until smooth.
Measure into a large mixing bowl
1 cup egg whites
Beat until frothy.
Sprinkle with
½ teaspoon cream of tartar
Continue beating until *very* stiff peaks form.
DO NOT UNDERBEAT.
Gradually *fold* batter into beaten egg whites. Turn batter into the tube pan. Cut through batter with a knife to eliminate air bubbles.
Bake in preheated 325° oven for 1 to 1¼ hours.
Invert cake immediately upon removal from the oven. Leave suspended until cold. Loosen with a knife or spatula and carefully shake cake from the pan.

VARIATIONS:

(a) Orange Chiffon Cake
Prepare as for Chiffon Cake, replacing the ¾ cup water with ½ cup orange juice plus ¼ cup water. Add 2 tablespoons finely grated orange rind to the batter.

(b) Lemon Chiffon Cake
Prepare as for Chiffon Cake, substituting 1 tablespoon finely grated lemon rind for the vanilla. Replace 1 tablespoon water with 1 tablespoon lemon juice.

(c) Spice Chiffon Cake
Prepare as for Chiffon Cake, adding 2 teaspoons cinnamon, 1 teaspoon ginger, ½ teaspoon nutmeg and ½ teaspoon cloves to the dry ingredients.

103 Cherry Chiffon Cake

Preheat oven to 325°.

Select a 10″ tube pan and make sure that it is free of any grease.

Blend or sift together into a large mixing bowl

**2 cups Pre-Sifted PURITY
All-Purpose Flour
1½ cups sugar
3 teaspoons baking powder
1 teaspoon salt**

Make a well in centre of dry ingredients.
Add

**½ cup vegetable oil
5 unbeaten egg yolks
¼ cup syrup from maraschino
cherries
½ cup water
2 teaspoons almond extract**

Beat with a wooden spoon until smooth.

Measure into a large mixing bowl

1 cup egg whites

Beat until frothy.

Sprinkle with

½ teaspoon cream of tartar

Continue beating until *very* stiff peaks form.
DO NOT UNDERBEAT.

Gradually *fold* batter into beaten egg whites.
Fold in

**⅔ cup finely chopped maraschino
cherries**

Turn batter into the tube pan. Cut through batter with a knife to eliminate air bubbles.

Bake in preheated 325° oven for 1 to 1¼ hours.

Invert cake immediately upon removal from the oven. Leave suspended until cold. Loosen with a knife or spatula and carefully shake cake from the pan.

104 Cocoa Chiffon Cake

Preheat oven to 325°.

Select a 10″ tube pan and make sure that it is free of any grease.

Blend or sift together in a large mixing bowl

**1¾ cups Pre-Sifted PURITY
All-Purpose Flour
1¾ cups sugar
⅓ cup cocoa
3 teaspoons baking powder
1 teaspoon salt**

Make a well in centre of dry ingredients.
Add

**½ cup vegetable oil
5 unbeaten egg yolks
1 cup water
1 teaspoon vanilla**

Beat with a wooden spoon until smooth.

Measure into a large mixing bowl

1 cup egg whites

Beat until frothy.

Sprinkle with

½ teaspoon cream of tartar

Continue beating until *very* stiff peaks form.
DO NOT UNDERBEAT.

Gradually *fold* batter into beaten egg whites.
Turn batter into the tube pan. Cut through batter with a knife to eliminate air bubbles.

Bake in preheated 325° oven for 1 to 1¼ hours.

Invert cake immediately upon removal from the oven. Leave suspended until cold. Loosen with a knife or spatula and carefully shake cake from the pan.

105 Banana Chiffon Cake

Preheat oven to 325°.

Select a 10″ tube pan and make sure that it is free of any grease.

Blend or sift together into a large mixing bowl

**2 cups Pre-Sifted PURITY
All-Purpose Flour
1½ cups sugar
3 teaspoons baking powder
1 teaspoon salt**

Make a well in centre of dry ingredients.
Add

**½ cup vegetable oil
5 unbeaten egg yolks
1 cup well mashed ripe bananas
1 teaspoon grated lemon rind
⅛ teaspoon nutmeg
¼ cup water
1 teaspoon vanilla**

Beat with a wooden spoon until smooth.

Measure into a large mixing bowl

1 cup egg whites

Beat until frothy.

Sprinkle with

½ teaspoon cream of tartar

Continue beating until *very* stiff peaks form.
DO NOT UNDERBEAT.

Gradually *fold* batter into beaten egg whites.
Turn batter into the tube pan. Cut through
batter with a knife to eliminate air bubbles.

Bake in preheated 325° oven for 1 to 1¼
hours.

Invert cake immediately upon removal from
the oven. Leave suspended until cold. Loosen
with a knife or spatula and carefully shake
cake from the pan.

106   Maple Walnut Chiffon Cake

Preheat oven to 325°.

Select a 10" tube pan and make sure that it is
free of any grease.

Blend or sift together into a large mixing bowl
**2 cups *Pre-Sifted* PURITY
All-Purpose Flour
1 cup granulated sugar
3 teaspoons baking powder
1 teaspoon salt**

Blend in
½ cup lightly-packed brown sugar

Make a well in centre of dry ingredients.

Add
**½ cup vegetable oil
5 unbeaten egg yolks
¾ cup water
1 teaspoon maple flavouring**

Beat with a wooden spoon until smooth.

Measure into a large mixing bowl
1 cup egg whites

Beat until frothy.

Sprinkle with
½ teaspoon cream of tartar

Continue beating until *very* stiff peaks form.
DO NOT UNDERBEAT.

Gradually *fold* batter into beaten egg whites.

Fold in
⅔ cup finely chopped walnuts

Turn batter into the tube pan. Cut through
batter with a knife to eliminate air bubbles.

Bake in preheated 325° oven for 1 to 1¼
hours.

Invert cake immediately upon removal from
the oven. Leave suspended until cold. Loosen
with a knife or spatula and carefully shake
cake from the pan.

---

*Pound cake improves if stored for a few days
before cutting.*

107   Pound Cake

Preheat oven to 325°.

Grease a 9" x 5" loaf pan and dust lightly
with flour.

Cream thoroughly
1 cup butter

Gradually beat in
1 cup fruit sugar

Beat until very light and fluffy.

One at a time, beat in
4 eggs

Beat for 2 minutes after each egg.

Blend in
1 teaspoon vanilla

Blend or sift together
**1½ cups *Pre-Sifted* PURITY
All-Purpose Flour
½ teaspoon cream of tartar
¼ teaspoon salt**

Gradually add the dry ingredients to the egg
mixture, folding in well. Then beat for 2
minutes (at low speed with electric mixer).

Turn into prepared pan.

Bake in preheated 325° oven for 60 to 70
minutes.

---

*Floured fruit is less likely to sink to the bottom.
Blend fruit and nuts with the measured dry
ingredients, or add about ¼ cup of the measured
flour and coat fruit thoroughly.*

108   Cherry Pound Cake

Preheat oven to 300°.

Grease a 10" x 5" loaf pan and dust lightly
with flour.

Cream
1 cup butter

Gradually blend in
1 cup fruit sugar

Beat until light and fluffy.

Then add, one at a time
3 eggs

Beat thoroughly after each addition.

Blend or sift together
**2 cups *Pre-Sifted* PURITY
All-Purpose Flour
½ teaspoon salt**

Add gradually to the creamed mixture,
blending thoroughly.

Fold in
1 cup red glacé cherries, halved
1 cup green glacé cherries, halved
2 teaspoons grated lemon rind
Pour into prepared pan.
Bake in preheated 300°oven for about 1 hour and 20 minutes.

Fruit cakes improve with age, so plan to bake them about 6 or 8 weeks before they will be required. Cut with a sawing motion, using a very sharp knife with a long blade.

109 Wedding Cake
(Rich Dark Fruit Cake)

This cake may be baked in any of the following combinations of pans:

Two 10″ tube pans; one 10″ tube pan plus two 8½″ x 4½″ loaf pans; one 8½″ square pan plus one 7″ square pan plus one 5″ pan for a tier cake. All pans must be at least 3″ deep.

Line pans with 2 or 3 thicknesses of heavy brown paper and grease well.
Combine
1 pound seedless raisins
1 pound sultana raisins
1 pound currants
1½ pounds seeded raisins
4 ounces green candied pineapple, chopped
8 ounces glacé cherries, halved
¾ pound dates, chopped
½ pound table figs, chopped
8 ounces candied citron, chopped
4 ounces candied lemon and orange peels, thinly shaved
1 cup blanched almonds, halved
1 cup shelled filberts, coarsely chopped
1 cup pecan halves
Cream until soft
1 pound butter
Gradually blend in
2 cups sugar
Cream until light and fluffy.
Beat in, one at a time
12 eggs
Beat until very light after each addition.
Add
½ cup fruit juice *or* red currant jelly
2 teaspoons vanilla

Blend or sift together
3½ cups *Pre-Sifted* PURITY All-Purpose Flour
½ teaspoon salt
2 teaspoons cinnamon
2 teaspoons nutmeg
½ teaspoon allspice
½ teaspoon ginger
½ teaspoon cloves
Add to the combined fruit and nuts. Mix very thoroughly to coat and separate all the fruit completely.
Turn the creamed mixture into the flour and fruit mixture and combine thoroughly. (Mix a large cake of this kind with the hands.)
Fill pans about ¾ full.
Bake in preheated 275° oven for 2½ to 3 hours, depending upon size of pans used.

Fruit cakes should be thoroughly cooled, wrapped tightly and stored in a closely covered crock or cookie tin.

110 Dark Fruit Cake

This cake may be baked in any of the following combinations of pans:

Three 10″ tube pans; three 9″ round or square pans; six 8½″ x 4½″ loaf pans. All pans must be at least 3″ deep.

Line pans with 2 or 3 thicknesses of heavy brown paper and grease well.
Combine and flour
2 pounds raisins
2 pounds currants
1½ pounds dates, chopped
2 cups glacé cherries, halved
1 cup candied pineapple, chopped
1 cup cut peel
2 cups chopped walnuts
1½ cups slivered blanched almonds
Cream
3 cups shortening
Blend in
2 teaspoons each of vanilla, lemon and almond extracts
Gradually add
5 cups lightly-packed brown sugar
Beat until light and fluffy.
Beat
10 egg yolks
until thick and lemon coloured.

Gradually add beaten yolks to the sugar mixture and beat thoroughly.

Blend or sift together

**8 cups *Pre-Sifted* PURITY
All-Purpose Flour
1 teaspoon baking soda
2 teaspoons salt
1 teaspoon cinnamon
1¼ teaspoons nutmeg
¾ teaspoon cloves**

Add dry ingredients to creamed mixture, alternately with

1 cup sour milk

Beat

10 egg whites

until stiff but not dry.

Fold beaten whites into the batter. Then add prepared fruit and nuts.

Fill each pan about ¾ full. Arrange glacé cherries and pecans or walnuts on the top, if desired.

Bake in preheated 325° oven for 2 to 3 hours, depending upon size of pans used. (Place a pan of water in the bottom of your oven to prevent drying out.)

Allow baked cakes to stand in pans for about ½ hour before removing.

NOTE: This recipe may be halved with the same excellent results.

111   Light Fruit Cake

This cake may be baked in any of the following combinations of pans:

Two 10″ tube pans; one 10″ tube pan plus a 10″ x 5″ loaf pan. All pans must be at least 3″ deep.

Line pans with 2 or 3 thicknesses of heavy brown paper and grease well.

Combine

**1 pound candied citron, slivered
1½ cups blanched almonds, sliced
1 pound red and green glacé
cherries, sliced
1 pound light sultana raisins**

Cream until soft

1 pound butter

Gradually blend in

2 cups fruit sugar

Cream until light and fluffy.

Beat until very light

8 eggs

Add to the butter and sugar mixture and combine well.

Add

**2 tablespoons grated lemon rind
2 tablespoons lemon juice *or* 1
teaspoon vanilla and 1 teaspoon
almond extract**

Blend or sift together

**4½ cups *Pre-Sifted* PURITY
All-Purpose Flour
2 teaspoons baking powder
1 teaspoon salt**

Thoroughly flour the combined fruit and nuts with part of the dry ingredients.

Mix very thoroughly to coat and separate all the fruit completely.

Gradually add remaining dry ingredients to the creamed mixture.

Combine very thoroughly.

Fold in the floured fruit and nuts.

Fill prepared pans about ¾ full.

Bake in preheated 325° oven for 1½ to 2 hours, depending upon size of pans used.

112   Balmoral Fruit Cake

Preheat oven to 325°.

Line a 10″ x 5″ loaf pan with heavy brown paper and grease it well.

Cream

¾ cup butter

Gradually blend in

1 cup fruit sugar

Cream until light and fluffy.

Beat thoroughly

3 eggs

Add to the creamed mixture and combine well.

Blend or sift together

**1½ cups *Pre-Sifted* PURITY
All-Purpose Flour
½ teaspoon baking powder
¼ teaspoon salt**

Combine and flour

**1 cup sultana raisins
3 tablespoons finely shaved candied
ginger
½ cup slivered blanched almonds**

Gradually add the dry ingredients to the creamed mixture.

Continue beating at low speed for 2 minutes after the last of the flour has been added.

Fold in the floured fruit and nuts.

Turn batter into prepared pan.

Bake in 325° oven for 65 to 70 minutes.

FILLINGS

113 Vanilla Cream Filling

Scald in top of double boiler
1 cup milk

Combine
**3 tablespoons *Pre-Sifted* PURITY
All-Purpose Flour
¼ cup sugar
⅛ teaspoon salt**

Gradually add some of the hot milk to the flour mixture, then return to double boiler top.

Cook over medium direct heat, stirring constantly, until mixture comes to a boil. Remove from heat.

Stir part of the hot mixture into
1 beaten egg

Return to double boiler top and cook over boiling water for 2 minutes, stirring constantly.

Remove from heat, cool slightly and then stir in
**1 tablespoon butter *or* margarine
½ teaspoon vanilla**

Cool, stirring occasionally.

Yield: Filling for an 8″ or 9″ layer cake, or for a jelly roll.

VARIATIONS:

(a) Coconut Cream Filling

Prepare as above, adding ½ cup desiccated coconut to the cooked filling.

(b) Almond Cream Filling

Prepare as for Vanilla Cream Filling, but replace the vanilla with ¼ teaspoon almond extract. Add ½ cup slivered blanched almonds to the cooked filling. For added flavour, toast the almonds.

(c) Banana Cream Filling

Prepare as for Vanilla Cream Filling, adding 1 banana, sliced, to the cooked filling just before using.

(d) Coffee Cream Filling

Prepare as for Vanilla Cream Filling, adding 2 teaspoons instant coffee powder to the scalded milk.

114 Lemon Filling

Combine in top of double boiler
**¾ cup sugar
3 tablespoons cornstarch
⅛ teaspoon salt**

Stir in
¾ cup boiling water

Cook over medium direct heat, stirring constantly, until mixture comes to a boil.

Place over boiling water. Cover and cook for 5 minutes, stirring occasionally.

Remove from heat and blend in
**1 tablespoon butter *or* margarine
1 tablespoon grated lemon rind
3 tablespoons lemon juice**

Cool, stirring occasionally.

Yield: Filling for an 8″ or 9″ layer cake.

NOTE: For a creamy lemon filling, beat one egg and add some of the hot mixture to it 2 minutes before end of cooking time. Add to remaining mixture, place over hot water and cook for 2 minutes, stirring constantly.

VARIATIONS:

(a) Orange Filling

Prepare as for Lemon Filling, substituting ¾ cup orange juice for the boiling water and 1 tablespoon grated orange rind for the lemon rind. Reduce the lemon juice to 2 tablespoons.

(b) Pineapple Filling

Prepare as for Lemon Filling, substituting ¾ cup unsweetened pineapple juice for the boiling water. Omit the lemon juice. Fold ½ cup well drained crushed pineapple into the cooked filling.

115 Marshmallow Filling

Prepare Seven-Minute Frosting (recipe No. 127). Just before removing from the heat, beat in 1 cup miniature marshmallows (or 10 regular marshmallows, quartered). Continue beating until the marshmallows melt. Use at once.

Yield: Filling for one Chocolate Roll or two 8″ or 9″ layer cakes.

116 Chocolate Cream Filling

Scald in top of double boiler
1 cup milk

Combine
3 tablespoons *Pre-Sifted* PURITY All-Purpose Flour
½ cup sugar
¼ cup cocoa
⅛ teaspoon salt

Gradually add some of the milk to the flour mixture and return to double boiler top.

Cook over medium direct heat, stirring constantly, until mixture comes to a boil. Remove from heat.

Stir part of the hot mixture into
1 beaten egg

Return to top of double boiler and cook over boiling water for 2 minutes, stirring constantly.

Remove from heat, cool slightly and stir in
1 tablespoon butter *or* margarine
½ teaspoon vanilla
Cool, stirring occasionally.
Yield: Filling for an 8″ or 9″ layer cake.

117 Lord Baltimore Filling

Prepare Boiled Frosting (recipe No. 126).
To about one-third of the frosting, add
½ cup maraschino cherries, halved
⅓ cup blanched almonds, chopped
Use this to fill an 8″ or 9″ layer cake. Ice the cake with the remaining frosting.

118 Lady Baltimore Filling

Prepare Boiled Frosting (recipe No. 126).
To about one-third of the frosting, add
⅓ cup raisins *or* chopped figs
½ cup chopped walnuts
Use this to fill an 8″ or 9″ layer cake. Ice the cake with the remaining frosting.

FROSTINGS

119 Butter Frosting

Cream
3 tablespoons soft butter *or* margarine

Beat in
½ teaspoon vanilla
Few grains salt

Blend in
2 cups sifted icing sugar
alternately with
2 to 2½ tablespoons warm cream *or* milk

Beat until smooth and of spreading consistency. Add more sifted icing sugar or milk, if necessary.

Yield: Frosts an 8″ or 9″ square cake or pan of squares, or about 1½ dozen medium-size cup cakes. Double the recipe to fill and frost an 8″ or 9″ layer cake.

NOTES: **1.** An egg yolk may be added for extra richness.

2. You may vary the frosting by using different flavouring extracts in place of the vanilla—maple, butterscotch, almond, coconut, strawberry, lemon, peppermint, etc.

VARIATIONS:

(a) Chocolate Butter Frosting

Prepare as for Butter Frosting, adding 1 square unsweetened chocolate, melted, to the creamed butter.   OR

Sift 3 tablespoons cocoa with the icing sugar and prepare as for Butter Frosting.

(b) Coffee Butter Frosting

Prepare as for Butter Frosting, omitting the vanilla. Dissolve ½ teaspoon instant coffee powder in 2 tablespoons boiling water and use it in place of the warm cream.

(c) Mocha Butter Frosting

Prepare as for Butter Frosting, adding 1 square unsweetened chocolate, melted, or 3 tablespoons cocoa, to the creamed butter. Substitute 2 to 2½ tablespoons hot coffee for the cream.

(d) Orange Butter Frosting

Prepare as for Butter Frosting, omitting the vanilla and substituting 2 to 2½ tablespoons orange juice for the cream. Finally, blend in 1 teaspoon finely grated orange rind.

120 Creamy Orange Frosting

Cream
> **2 tablespoons soft butter *or* margarine**

Add
> **½ cup sifted icing sugar**
> **Few grains salt**

Blend until smooth.

Add
> **1 egg yolk**
> **2 teaspoons finely grated orange rind**
> **1 tablespoon orange juice**

Beat well.

Then gradually beat in about
> **1½ cups sifted icing sugar**

Add enough icing sugar to make of spreading consistency. Beat until creamy.

Yield: Frosts an 8″ or 9″ square cake. Double the recipe to fill and frost an 8″ or 9″ layer cake.

NOTE: When doubling the recipe, you may use 2 egg yolks or 1 whole egg. If using a whole egg, it will be necessary to increase the amount of sifted icing sugar.

121 Creamy Lemon Frosting

Cream
> **2 tablespoons soft butter *or* margarine**

Add
> **½ cup sifted icing sugar**
> **Few grains salt**

Blend until smooth.

Add
> **1 egg yolk**
> **1 teaspoon finely grated lemon rind**
> **1½ teaspoons lemon juice**
> **1½ teaspoons milk**

Then gradually beat in
> **1½ cups sifted icing sugar**

Beat until of spreading consistency, adding a little more icing sugar or milk, if necessary.

Yield: Frosts an 8″ or 9″ square cake. Double the recipe to fill and frost an 8″ or 9″ layer cake.

NOTE: When doubling the recipe, you may use 2 egg yolks or 1 whole egg. If using a whole egg, it will be necessary to increase the amount of sifted icing sugar.

122 Café Royale Frosting

Melt over boiling water
> **2 squares unsweetened chocolate**
> **2 tablespoons butter *or* margarine**
> **2 teaspoons instant coffee powder**

Remove from heat and add
> **1 cup sifted icing sugar**
> **⅛ teaspoon salt**
> **1 egg**
> **¼ cup milk**
> **½ teaspoon rum flavouring**

Blend thoroughly.

Set in a pan of ice water and beat until stiff with an electric mixer or rotary beater. Add more sifted icing sugar, if necessary.

Yield: Frosts an 8″ or 9″ square cake. Double the recipe to fill and frost an 8″ or 9″ layer cake.

123 Chocolate Malt Frosting

Melt over hot water
> **3 squares semi-sweet chocolate**
> **2 tablespoons butter *or* margarine**

Remove from heat and beat in
> **2 tablespoons hot water**
> **1 egg yolk**
> **¼ cup instant chocolate malt powder**
> **Few grains salt**
> **½ teaspoon vanilla**

Gradually add about
> **1½ cups sifted icing sugar**

Beat until frosting is of spreading consistency.

Yield: Frosts an 8″ or 9″ square cake. Double the recipe to fill and frost an 8″ or 9″ layer cake.

NOTE: When doubling the recipe, you may use 2 egg yolks or 1 whole egg. If using a whole egg, it will be necessary to increase the amount of sifted icing sugar.

124 Whipped Chocolate Frosting

Melt
> **2 squares unsweetened chocolate**

Add
> **1 tablespoon butter *or* margarine**
> **1 cup sifted icing sugar**
> **⅛ teaspoon salt**
> **1 egg**
> **3 tablespoons milk**
> **½ teaspoon vanilla**

Combine well.

Set in a pan of ice water and beat until stiff with an electric mixer or rotary beater. Add more sifted icing sugar, if necessary.

Yield: Frosts an 8″ or 9″ square cake. Double the recipe to fill and frost an 8″ or 9″ layer cake.

125 Chocolate Fudge Frosting

Melt together

2 squares unsweetened chocolate
2 tablespoons butter *or* **margarine**

Add

1 cup sifted icing sugar
⅓ cup cream *or* **evaporated milk**
Few grains salt

Beat with a spoon until smooth. Place over low direct heat and stir until mixture bubbles well around the edges. Remove from heat.

Add

1 teaspoon vanilla

Then gradually add

1 cup sifted icing sugar

Beat until smooth after each addition.

Then set in a pan of ice water, stirring occasionally, until thick enough to spread.

Yield: Sufficient icing for an 8″ or 9″ square cake. Double the recipe to fill and frost an 8″ or 9″ layer cake.

126   Boiled Frosting
(*Mountain Cream Frosting*)

Combine in a saucepan

2 cups sugar
¼ teaspoon cream of tartar
⅔ cup water

Stir over low heat until sugar is dissolved.

Bring to a boil and cook, without stirring, until syrup reaches 245° or will spin a 6″ to 8″ thread. Remove from heat.

Beat to soft peaks

2 egg whites

As soon as the syrup stops bubbling, pour it *gradually* in a thin stream into the beaten whites. Beat with an electric mixer or rotary beater while adding the syrup and then continue beating until the frosting is of spreading consistency.

Then fold in

1 teaspoon vanilla

Yield: Fills and frosts an 8″ or 9″ layer cake.

VARIATIONS:

(*a*)   Chocolate Boiled Frosting

Prepare as for Boiled Frosting. Then fold in 2 squares unsweetened chocolate which have been melted and cooled.

(*b*)   Peppermint Boiled Frosting

Prepare as for Boiled Frosting, substituting 6 to 8 drops peppermint extract for the vanilla.

127   Seven-Minute Frosting

Combine in top of double boiler

¾ cup sugar
⅛ teaspoon cream of tartar
Few grains salt
3 tablespoons cold water
1 unbeaten egg white

Place over rapidly boiling water and beat constantly with an electric mixer or rotary beater until the frosting is stiff enough to stand in peaks. (This will take from 4 to 7 minutes.) Scrape sides and bottom of pan occasionally.

Remove from heat and fold in

½ teaspoon vanilla

Yield: Frosts an 8″ or 9″ square cake. Double the recipe to fill and frost an 8″ or 9″ layer cake. This will take a slightly longer beating time over rapidly boiling water.

VARIATIONS:

(*a*) Spiced Seven-Minute Frosting

Prepare as directed above, adding ¼ teaspoon cinnamon and ⅛ teaspoon ginger or ⅛ teaspoon nutmeg to the sugar.

(*b*) Peppermint Seven-Minute
Frosting

Prepare as for Seven-Minute Frosting, substituting 3 or 4 drops peppermint extract for the vanilla. Tint a pale green, if desired.

(*c*) Chocolate Seven-Minute Frosting

Prepare as for Seven-Minute Frosting. Then carefully *fold* in 1 square unsweetened chocolate which has been melted and cooled.

(*d*) Seafoam Seven-Minute Frosting

Prepare as for Seven-Minute Frosting, substituting 1 cup lightly-packed brown sugar for the granulated sugar. Omit the cream of tartar. Replace the vanilla with ½ teaspoon maple flavouring, if desired.

128   Broiled Frosting

Combine
- ¼ cup soft butter **or** margarine
- ½ cup lightly-packed brown sugar
- 3 tablespoons evaporated milk **or** cream
- ½ cup coconut **or** coarsely chopped nuts

Spread over top of warm 8″ or 9″ square cake. Placing 6″ from the heat, broil for 2 or 3 minutes or until the topping bubbles and browns.

VARIATION:

(a) Peanut Butter Broiled Frosting

Prepare as above, adding ¼ cup peanut butter and using 1 cup coarsely chopped peanuts for the nuts.

129   Praline Frosting

Combine
- ½ cup lightly-packed brown sugar
- 2 tablespoons *Pre-Sifted* PURITY All-Purpose Flour
- ¼ teaspoon salt

Add
- ¼ cup melted butter **or** margarine
- 1 tablespoon water
- ½ cup chopped walnuts **or** pecans

Blend thoroughly.

Spread over top of warm 8″ or 9″ square cake.

Place 6″ below broiler and broil for 2 to 3 minutes or until the topping bubbles and browns.

130   Fondant Frosting
(For Petits Fours)

Soften
- 1 teaspoon unflavoured gelatine

in
- 1 teaspoon cold water

Set aside.

Combine in top of double boiler
- ¼ cup sugar
- ¼ cup cold water
- 1 tablespoon corn syrup

Place over direct heat and bring to a full rolling boil, stirring to dissolve the sugar.

Remove from heat and stir in softened gelatine. Cool to 120° without stirring. (The bottom of the saucepan will feel warm.)

Stir in
- 3½ cups sifted icing sugar
- 1 unbeaten egg white
- 2 tablespoons shortening
- 1 teaspoon vanilla

Tint with food colouring, if desired.

Slowly pour the frosting over small pieces of cake placed on a rack. Return any "drippings" to the saucepan and heat over boiling water until again of pouring consistency.

Yield: Frosts about 2½ dozen petits fours.

131   Chocolate Glaze

Melt
- 1 square unsweetened chocolate
- 1 tablespoon butter **or** margarine

Add
- ¾ cup sifted icing sugar

Gradually blend in
- 2 tablespoons hot milk

Spread the warm glaze over éclairs, cream puffs, etc. Allow them to stand until the glaze becomes firm.

Yield: Sufficient glaze for 12 éclairs.

132   Whipped Cream

Using a rotary beater or electric mixer, beat chilled whipping cream (at least 30% butterfat) until it just moulds. For best results, use a small deep bowl.

To sweeten, allow about 3 tablespoons sugar for ½ pint of cream. Once the cream thickens, gradually beat in the sugar until the cream just holds its shape. Flavour to taste with a few drops vanilla or almond extract.

Yield: Cream doubles in volume when whipped, thus one-half pint provides about eight ¼ cup servings.

NOTES: 1. In hot weather, chill the bowl and beaters before whipping the chilled cream.

2. When a recipe calls for whipped cream, beaten stiff, measure the cream before whipping it.

VARIATION:

(a) Whipped Chocolate Cream

Beat ½ pint whipping cream until it just moulds, as above. Sift together ¼ cup cocoa and ¼ cup sugar. Gradually beat into the cream until it just holds its shape. Fold in ¼ teaspoon vanilla.

Cookies and Squares

DROP COOKIES / ROLLED COOKIES / REFRIGERATOR COOKIES
MOULDED COOKIES / NO-BAKE COOKIES / SQUARES AND BARS

THINGS TO REMEMBER WHEN MAKING COOKIES

Always grease the baking sheets with unsalted shortening.

If using only one rack when baking cookies, place it in the centre of the oven; if using two racks, divide the oven into thirds. To allow for proper circulation of heat, there should be at least 2″ of rack showing around the edges of each baking sheet. If using two racks, never place one sheet directly under the other.

If a recipe gives an approximate baking time, such as 12 to 15 minutes, check the cookies at the minimum time to avoid overbaking.

Always cool cookies on a rack.

Store crisp cookies in loosely covered containers; soft cookies in air-tight ones.

DROP COOKIES

Place drop cookies about 2″ apart on the greased baking sheets to allow for spreading.

133   Brown Sugar Cookies

Preheat oven to 350°.

Cream together
   ½ cup shortening
   1 cup lightly-packed brown sugar
Add
   2 beaten eggs
   ½ teaspoon vanilla
Beat until light and fluffy.

Blend or sift together
   1½ cups *Pre-Sifted* PURITY
      All-Purpose Flour
   1 teaspoon baking powder
   1 teaspoon baking soda
   ½ teaspoon salt
Add to creamed mixture alternately with
   ⅓ cup sour milk
Fold in
   ¾ cup raisins *or* chopped dates
   ½ cup chopped nuts

Drop from a teaspoon onto greased baking sheets. Bake in preheated 350° oven for about 12 minutes.

Yield: 4 dozen cookies.

134   Chocolate Chip Cookies

Preheat oven to 350°.

Cream thoroughly
   ½ cup shortening
   ½ cup granulated sugar
   ¼ cup lightly-packed brown sugar
Add
   1 beaten egg
   1 teaspoon vanilla
Beat thoroughly.

Blend or sift together and add to creamed mixture
   1 cup *Pre-Sifted* PURITY
      All-Purpose Flour
   ½ teaspoon baking soda
   ½ teaspoon salt
Combine well.

Fold in
   1 cup chocolate chips
      (6-ounce package)
   ½ cup chopped walnuts

Drop from a teaspoon onto greased baking sheets. Bake in preheated 350° oven for 10 to 12 minutes.

Yield: 3 dozen cookies.

135 Small Oatmeal Cakes

Preheat oven to 400°.

Cream thoroughly
> ½ cup shortening
> ¾ cup lightly-packed brown sugar

Beat in
> 1 egg
> 1 teaspoon vanilla

Blend or sift together
> 1 cup *Pre-Sifted* PURITY
> All-Purpose Flour
> ½ teaspoon baking soda
> ½ teaspoon salt

Add to creamed mixture.

Blend in
> 1 cup rolled oats
> ½ cup chopped walnuts
> ½ cup raisins

Add
> ¼ cup milk

Stir until mixture is well combined.

Drop from a teaspoon onto greased baking sheets. Bake in preheated 400° oven for 10 to 12 minutes.

Yield: 3 dozen cookies.

136 Hermits

Preheat oven to 350°.

Blend or sift together
> 1¾ cups *Pre-Sifted* PURITY
> All-Purpose Flour
> 1 teaspoon baking soda
> ½ teaspoon salt
> ½ teaspoon cinnamon
> ⅛ teaspoon allspice
> ⅛ teaspoon nutmeg

Add
> 1 cup raisins
> 1 cup chopped dates
> 1 cup coarsely chopped nuts

Blend with flour mixture to thoroughly coat the fruit.

Cream thoroughly
> ½ cup shortening
> 1 cup lightly-packed brown sugar

Beat until thick
> 2 eggs

Add them to the creamed mixture, a little at a time. Beat well after each addition.

Add
> ½ teaspoon vanilla

Add the flour mixture to the creamed mixture and blend until thoroughly combined.

Drop from a teaspoon onto greased baking sheets. Bake in preheated 350° oven for 10 to 12 minutes.

Yield: 5 dozen cookies.

137 Chocolate Drop Cookies

Preheat oven to 375°.

Cream together
> ½ cup shortening
> 1 cup sugar

Add
> 1 beaten egg
> 1 teaspoon vanilla

Beat well.

Blend in
> 2 squares unsweetened chocolate, melted
> ½ cup chopped walnuts

Blend or sift together
> 1½ cups *Pre-Sifted* PURITY
> All-Purpose Flour
> ½ teaspoon baking powder
> ½ teaspoon baking soda
> ½ teaspoon salt

Add to creamed mixture alternately with
> ⅓ cup sour milk

Drop from a teaspoon onto greased baking sheets. Bake in preheated 375° oven for 10 to 12 minutes.

Yield: 3 dozen cookies.

VARIATION:

(a) Fruit Drops

Prepare Chocolate Drop Cookie batter as above, replacing the vanilla with 1 teaspoon rum flavouring. Fold in ⅓ cup raisins and ⅓ cup chopped maraschino cherries. Bake as above.

138 Scrunchies

Preheat oven to 375°.

Combine
> 1 cup melted shortening *or* vegetable oil
> 1¼ cups lightly-packed brown sugar
> 2 tablespoons maple syrup
> 2 tablespoons milk
> 1 egg

Beat well.

Mix in
1 cup rolled oats
1 cup shredded coconut
½ cup chopped salted peanuts
½ cup chocolate chips

Chill for 10 minutes.

Blend or sift together
1¾ cups *Pre-Sifted* PURITY
All-Purpose Flour
2 teaspoons baking powder
¼ teaspoon baking soda
½ teaspoon salt

Add to chilled mixture and blend until well combined.

Drop from a teaspoon onto greased baking sheets. Bake in preheated 375° oven for 8 to 10 minutes.

Yield: 5 dozen cookies.

139   Molasses Drops

Preheat oven to 350°.

Cream together
¾ cup shortening
¾ cup lightly-packed brown sugar

Add
1 egg

Beat for 2 minutes.

Thoroughly blend in
¾ cup light molasses
¾ cup sour milk

Blend or sift together
3½ cups *Pre-Sifted* PURITY
All-Purpose Flour
1 teaspoon baking powder
1 teaspoon baking soda
1 teaspoon salt
2 teaspoons cinnamon
2 teaspoons ginger
½ teaspoon cloves

Add to the creamed mixture and combine well.

Drop from a teaspoon onto greased baking sheets. Bake in preheated 350° oven for 12 to 15 minutes.

Yield: 6 dozen cookies.

140   Glazed Molasses Cookies

Preheat oven to 350°.

Cream together
½ cup shortening
½ cup lightly-packed brown sugar

Add
1 egg
¼ cup light molasses

Beat well.

Blend or sift together and add to creamed mixture
1½ cups *Pre-Sifted* PURITY
All-Purpose Flour
½ teaspoon baking soda
½ teaspoon salt
½ teaspoon ginger
½ teaspoon cinnamon

Combine thoroughly.

Fold in
½ cup chopped walnuts
½ cup raisins

Drop from a teaspoon onto greased baking sheets. Bake in preheated 350° oven for about 12 minutes.

While the cookies are still slightly warm, glaze with a mixture of
1 tablespoon soft butter *or*
margarine
1 cup sifted icing sugar
Few grains salt
5 teaspoons cream *or* top milk
½ teaspoon vanilla

Yield: 3 dozen cookies.

141   Date and Nut Drops

Preheat oven to 350°.

Cream until light
1 cup shortening
1½ cups sugar

Beat in
3 beaten eggs

Add
2 cups chopped dates
1 cup chopped walnuts
1 teaspoon vanilla

Blend or sift together
2½ cups *Pre-Sifted* PURITY
All-Purpose Flour
1 teaspoon baking soda
½ teaspoon salt

Add to date mixture and combine thoroughly.

Drop batter from a teaspoon onto greased baking sheets. Bake in preheated 350° oven for 12 to 15 minutes.

Yield: 6 dozen cookies.

Purity Flour is vitamin-enriched for extra nutrition

142   Fruit Jumbles

Preheat oven to 375°.

Cream until light
- 1 cup shortening
- ¾ cup lightly-packed brown sugar

Stir in
- 1 egg yolk
- 1 teaspoon vanilla
- 2 tablespoons syrup from maraschino cherries

Blend or sift together and add to creamed mixture
- 1¾ cups *Pre-Sifted* PURITY All-Purpose Flour
- ¼ teaspoon salt

Mix well.

Add
- ½ cup chopped dates
- ½ cup raisins
- ½ cup shredded coconut
- ½ cup maraschino cherries, quartered
- 3 slices candied pineapple, chopped
- ⅔ cup chopped walnuts

Combine thoroughly.

Drop from a teaspoon onto greased baking sheets. Bake in preheated 375° oven for about 10 minutes.

Yield: 6 dozen cookies.

143   Coconut Crisps

Preheat oven to 350°

Cream until light
- 1 cup shortening
- 1½ cups sugar

Add
- 2 beaten eggs
- ½ teaspoon vanilla
- 1 cup desiccated coconut

Beat until well combined.

Blend or sift together
- 2¼ cups *Pre-Sifted* PURITY All-Purpose Flour
- 2 teaspoons baking powder
- ½ teaspoon salt

Add to first mixture and blend thoroughly.

Drop from a teaspoon onto greased baking sheets. Bake in preheated 350° oven for 10 to 12 minutes.

Yield: 4 dozen cookies.

144   Jumbo Raisin Cookies

Preheat oven to 400°.

Combine in a saucepan
- 2 cups raisins
- 1 cup boiling water

Bring to a boil and boil for 5 minutes. Cool.

Cream together
- 1 cup shortening
- 2 cups sugar

Add
- 3 eggs

Beat well.

Blend in
- Cooled raisin mixture
- 1 teaspoon vanilla

Blend or sift together
- 4 cups *Pre-Sifted* PURITY All-Purpose Flour
- 1 teaspoon baking powder
- 1 teaspoon baking soda
- 2 teaspoons salt
- 1½ teaspoons cinnamon
- ½ teaspoon nutmeg
- ¼ teaspoon allspice

Stir in
- 1 cup chopped nuts

Add to creamed mixture and combine thoroughly.

Drop from a teaspoon onto greased baking sheets. Bake in preheated 400° oven for 10 to 12 minutes.

Yield: 7 dozen cookies.

145   Apple 'n' Raisin Cookies

Preheat oven to 350°.

Peel and core apples and put through a food chopper to make
- ¾ cup ground apple

Grind
- 1 cup raisins

Blend together and set aside.

Cream together
- 1 cup shortening
- 2 cups lightly-packed brown sugar

Beat in
- 1 beaten egg
- 1 teaspoon vanilla

Blend or sift together
- 2½ cups *Pre-Sifted* PURITY All-Purpose Flour
- 2 teaspoons baking powder
- 1 teaspoon salt

Thimble Cookies: big favourite with small fry (Recipe No. 164)

Add to creamed mixture alternately with a mixture of

½ cup milk
¼ cup orange juice
1 tablespoon finely grated orange rind

Blend in

Apple and raisin mixture

Drop from a teaspoon onto greased baking sheets. Bake in preheated 350° oven for 12 to 15 minutes.

Yield: 5 dozen cookies.

146   Spice Gems

Preheat oven to 350°.

Cream together

½ cup shortening
1 cup lightly-packed brown sugar

Add

1 egg
½ cup applesauce

Beat well.

Blend or sift together and add to creamed mixture

1¾ cups *Pre-Sifted* PURITY
All-Purpose Flour
1 teaspoon baking soda
½ teaspoon salt
1 teaspoon cinnamon
1 teaspoon cloves
½ teaspoon nutmeg

Combine well.

Fold in

1 cup chopped walnuts
1 cup raisins

Drop from a teaspoon onto greased baking sheets. Bake in preheated 350° oven for 10 to 12 minutes.

While still warm, spread cookies with a mixture of

1 tablespoon soft butter *or*
margarine
1¼ cups sifted icing sugar
Few grains salt
2 tablespoons cream *or* top milk
½ teaspoon vanilla

Yield: 4 dozen cookies.

147   Sour Cream Cookies

Preheat oven to 375°.

Cream

⅓ cup butter *or* margarine

Blend in

⅔ cup commercial sour cream

Add

2 cups lightly-packed brown sugar
1 teaspoon vanilla
2 well-beaten eggs

Beat well.

Blend or sift together

3 cups *Pre-Sifted* PURITY
All-Purpose Flour
¾ teaspoon baking soda
½ teaspoon salt

Add

1 cup raisins *or* currants

Add flour mixture to the brown sugar mixture and combine thoroughly.

Drop from a teaspoon onto greased baking sheets. Bake in preheated 375° oven for 12 to 15 minutes.

Yield: 4 dozen cookies.

148   Coconut Kisses

Preheat oven to 325°.

Beat to soft peaks

3 egg whites

Gradually beat in

1½ cups sugar

Place bowl over hot water and stir mixture until a crust begins to form on bottom of the bowl. Remove from the heat.

Quickly stir in

2 cups desiccated coconut
½ teaspoon vanilla
¼ teaspoon salt

Drop from a teaspoon onto greased baking sheets. Bake in preheated 325° oven for 10 to 12 minutes.

Yield: 2½ dozen cookies.

149   Pineapple Nut Drops

Preheat oven to 375°.

Cream together

½ cup shortening
1 cup sugar

Add

1 beaten egg

Beat until light.

Stir in

1 cup crushed pineapple, well
drained
½ cup chopped nuts
1 tablespoon lemon juice

Blend or sift together and add to creamed mixture

**1¾ cups *Pre-Sifted* PURITY
All-Purpose Flour**
2 teaspoons baking powder
¼ teaspoon baking soda
½ teaspoon salt

Blend thoroughly.

Drop from a teaspoon onto greased baking sheets. Top each cookie with a walnut or pecan half. Bake in preheated 375° oven for 10 to 12 minutes.

Yield: 4 dozen cookies.

150   *Marmalade Chews*

Preheat oven to 350°.

Cream together

⅓ cup shortening
½ cup lightly-packed brown sugar
½ cup granulated sugar

Add

1 beaten egg
1 teaspoon vanilla

Beat well.

Blend or sift together

**1 cup *Pre-Sifted* PURITY
All-Purpose Flour**
½ teaspoon baking powder
½ teaspoon baking soda
½ teaspoon salt
½ teaspoon cinnamon

¼ teaspoon ginger
¼ teaspoon nutmeg

Add to creamed mixture and combine well.

Blend in

1 cup rolled oats
¼ cup orange marmalade
½ cup raisins

Drop from a teaspoon onto greased baking sheets. Bake in preheated 350° oven for 10 to 12 minutes.

Yield: 3 dozen cookies.

151   *Fruit Meringues*

Preheat oven to 275°.

Combine

1½ cups coarsely chopped dates
1 cup glacé cherries, halved
½ cup sifted icing sugar

Beat to soft peak stage

2 egg whites

Gradually beat in

½ cup sifted icing sugar

Beat until stiff.

Fold in

Date mixture
**1¾ cups coarsely chopped Brazil nuts
or walnuts**

Drop from a spoon onto well-greased baking sheets. Bake in preheated 275° oven for 12 to 15 minutes, or until a very light brown.

Yield: 4 dozen cookies.

ROLLED COOKIES

152   *Gingersnaps*

Preheat oven to 350°.

Cream thoroughly

1 cup shortening
1 cup sugar

Dissolve

1 teaspoon baking soda

in

1½ cups light molasses

Add to creamed mixture together with

2 tablespoons vinegar

Blend or sift together

**5 cups *Pre-Sifted* PURITY
All-Purpose Flour**

1 teaspoon salt
2 teaspoons ginger
1 teaspoon cloves
½ teaspoon cinnamon
½ teaspoon nutmeg

Gradually add to the creamed mixture and combine thoroughly.

Turn dough onto a lightly floured surface and roll to ⅛″ thickness. Cut out with floured cookie cutter. Place on greased baking sheets.

Bake in preheated 350° oven for 8 to 10 minutes.

Yield: About 10 dozen cookies.

———

To prevent sticking, use a pastry cloth and covered rolling pin when making rolled cookies.

153   Date Filled Cookies

DATE FILLING:

Combine in a saucepan
- **4 cups finely chopped dates**
- **1 cup water**
- **1 tablespoon granulated sugar**

Cook over medium heat until the dates are soft and the mixture is thickened and of spreading consistency; stir constantly. Remove from heat. Let cool while preparing Cookie Dough.

COOKIE DOUGH:

Preheat oven to 350°.

Blend or sift together
- **2 cups *Pre-Sifted* PURITY All-Purpose Flour**
- **1½ teaspoons baking soda**
- **1 teaspoon salt**

Add
- **2 cups lightly-packed brown sugar**
- **6 cups rolled oats**
- **1 cup melted shortening *or* vegetable oil**

Combine well.

Sprinkle with
- **About ⅞ cup cold water**

Add the water slowly, mixing with a fork to make a soft but not sticky dough.

Turn dough onto a lightly floured surface and roll very thin. Cut out with floured cookie cutter.

Place half the cookies on greased baking sheets. Spread each with about 1 teaspoon cooled Date Filling. Place remaining unbaked cookies on top. Bake in preheated 350° oven for 10 to 12 minutes.

OR

Place the cookies on greased baking sheets and bake in preheated 350° oven for 5 to 7 minutes. Cool the cookies and then sandwich together with cooled Date Filling.

Yield: About 6 dozen filled cookies.

NOTE: These cookies may be prepared without the date filling, if you wish.

———

Rolled cookie dough may be tightly covered and kept in the refrigerator for up to two weeks. Roll out and bake fresh cookies as desired.

154   Scotch Shortbread

Preheat oven to 300°.

Cream thoroughly
- **1 cup butter**
- **½ cup lightly-packed brown sugar**

Add
- **1 egg yolk**
- **1 teaspoon vanilla**

Beat until light and fluffy.

Blend or sift together
- **2 cups *Pre-Sifted* PURITY All-Purpose Flour**

Add to creamed mixture and combine well.

Turn dough onto a lightly floured surface.

Roll to ¼″ thickness. Cut into desired shapes with floured cutters.

Bake on ungreased baking sheets in preheated 300° oven for 18 to 20 minutes.

Yield: About 3 dozen shortbreads.

NOTE: The shortbread dough may be pressed into an ungreased 9″ square pan, if you prefer. Prick deeply with a fork.

Bake in preheated 300° oven for 30 to 35 minutes. Cut into fingers for serving.

155   Crisp Shortbread

Preheat oven to 300°.

Cream
- **1½ cups butter**
- **1 cup sifted icing sugar**

Add
- **½ teaspoon vanilla**

Beat thoroughly.

Blend or sift together
- **3 cups *Pre-Sifted* PURITY All-Purpose Flour**
- **¼ cup rice flour**

Gradually add to creamed mixture and combine well after each addition. Turn onto a lightly floured surface and roll to ¼″ thickness.

Cut into desired shapes with floured cutters.

Bake on ungreased baking sheets in preheated 300° oven for 18 to 20 minutes.

Yield: About 5 dozen shortbreads.

156 Sugar Cookies

Preheat oven to 375°.

Cream
- ½ cup shortening
- 1 cup sugar

Add
- 1 well-beaten egg
- 2 tablespoons milk or cream
- ½ teaspoon vanilla

Beat until light and fluffy.

Blend or sift together

- 1¾ cups Pre-Sifted PURITY All-Purpose Flour
- 2 teaspoons baking powder
- ½ teaspoon salt

Add to creamed mixture and combine well. Chill the dough.

Turn chilled dough onto a lightly floured surface. Roll to ⅛″ thickness. Cut out with floured cookie cutter.

Bake on greased baking sheets in preheated 375° oven for 6 to 8 minutes.

Yield: About 5 dozen cookies.

REFRIGERATOR COOKIES

157 Ginger Cookies

Cream thoroughly
- ½ cup shortening
- ½ cup sugar

Combine and add
- 1 beaten egg
- ¼ cup light molasses

Beat until light and fluffy.

Blend or sift together
- 1¾ cups Pre-Sifted PURITY All-Purpose Flour
- ½ teaspoon baking soda
- ½ teaspoon salt
- 2 teaspoons ginger

Gradually add to the creamed mixture, blending thoroughly.

Place the dough on pieces of waxed paper and shape into rolls which are about 2″ in diameter.

Wrap securely in waxed paper. Refrigerate overnight or until needed.

To bake, preheat oven to 400°. Slice off desired number of cookies, making each about ⅛″ thick. Place on greased baking sheets and bake in preheated oven for 5 to 7 minutes.

Wrap remaining cookie dough and return to refrigerator.

Yield: 6 dozen cookies.

To slice refrigerator cookies, use a sharp thin knife or serrated knife. Slicing may be easier if you dip the knife in hot water and then wipe dry.

158 Almond Cookies

Cream together
- 1 cup shortening
- 1 cup granulated sugar
- 1 cup lightly-packed brown sugar

Add
- 2 beaten eggs
- 1 teaspoon vanilla

Beat until light and fluffy.

Blend or sift together
- 2¾ cups Pre-Sifted PURITY All-Purpose Flour
- 1 teaspoon baking soda
- 1 teaspoon salt

Gradually add to the creamed mixture, blending thoroughly.

Stir in
- 1 cup finely chopped blanched almonds

Place the dough on pieces of waxed paper and shape into rolls which are about 2″ in diameter.

Wrap securely in waxed paper. Refrigerate overnight or until needed.

To bake, preheat oven to 400°. Slice off desired number of cookies, making each about ⅛″ thick. Place on greased baking sheets and bake in preheated oven for 5 to 7 minutes.

Wrap remaining cookie dough and return to refrigerator.

Yield: 10 dozen cookies.

VARIATION:

(a) Caraway Cookies

Substitute 1 tablespoon caraway seeds for the chopped almonds in above recipe.

159   Orange Slices

Cream thoroughly
>   1 cup shortening
>   1 cup sugar

Add
>   1 beaten egg
>   ⅓ cup orange juice
>   ½ teaspoon vanilla
>   2 tablespoons finely grated orange
>   rind

Beat well.

Blend or sift together
>   2¾ cups *Pre-Sifted* PURITY
>   All-Purpose Flour
>   1½ teaspoons baking powder
>   1 teaspoon salt

Add to creamed mixture and combine thoroughly.

Place dough on pieces of waxed paper and shape into rolls which are about 2″ in diameter.

Wrap securely in waxed paper. Refrigerate overnight or until needed.

To bake, preheat oven to 350°. Slice off desired number of cookies, making each about ⅛″ thick. Place on greased baking sheets and bake in preheated oven for 10 to 12 minutes.

Wrap remaining cookie dough and return to refrigerator.

Yield: 5 dozen cookies.

Refrigerator cookie dough will keep for 3 to 4 weeks if securely wrapped. If you prefer, freeze the securely wrapped rolls. The frozen dough will keep for 6 to 8 months.

160   Butterscotch Cookies

Cream thoroughly
>   ½ cup butter *or* margarine
>   2 cups lightly-packed brown sugar

Add
>   2 beaten eggs
>   ½ teaspoon vanilla

Beat until light and fluffy.

Blend or sift together
>   3 cups *Pre-Sifted* PURITY
>   All-Purpose Flour
>   1 teaspoon baking soda
>   ½ teaspoon cream of tartar
>   ¼ teaspoon salt

Gradually add to creamed mixture, blending thoroughly.

Then add
>   ½ cup chopped nuts
>   ½ cup maraschino cherries, quartered

Place the dough on pieces of waxed paper and shape into rolls which are about 2″ in diameter.

Wrap securely in waxed paper. Refrigerate overnight or until needed.

To bake, preheat oven to 375°. Slice off desired number of cookies, making each about ⅛″ thick. Place on greased baking sheets and bake in preheated oven for 5 to 7 minutes.

Wrap remaining cookie dough and return to the refrigerator.

Yield: 9 dozen cookies.

161   Chocolate Cookies

Cream together
>   ½ cup shortening
>   ½ cup lightly-packed brown sugar
>   ¼ cup granulated sugar

Add
>   1 beaten egg
>   1½ squares unsweetened chocolate,
>   melted
>   ½ teaspoon vanilla

Beat thoroughly.

Blend or sift together
>   1½ cups *Pre-Sifted* PURITY
>   All-Purpose Flour
>   ½ teaspoon baking powder
>   ½ teaspoon salt

Gradually add to the creamed mixture, blending thoroughly.

Place dough on pieces of waxed paper and shape into rolls which are about 2″ in diameter.

Wrap securely in waxed paper. Refrigerate overnight or until needed.

To bake, preheat oven to 375°. Slice off desired number of cookies, making each about ⅛″ thick. Place on greased baking sheets and bake in preheated oven for 5 to 6 minutes.

Wrap remaining cookie dough and return to refrigerator.

Yield: 6 dozen cookies.

NOTE: For variety, add ½ cup maraschino cherries, drained, or ½ cup chopped nuts. For Mint Chocolate Cookies, replace the vanilla with 3 or 4 drops peppermint extract.

162   Date Pinwheels

DATE FILLING:

Combine in a saucepan
- **2 cups chopped dates**
- **⅔ cup granulated sugar**
- **½ teaspoon salt**
- **1 cup water**

Cook over medium heat until mixture thickens to spreading consistency. Stir constantly.

Remove from heat and stir in
- **1 tablespoon lemon juice**
- **½ cup chopped walnuts**

Chill.

COOKIE DOUGH:

Cream thoroughly
- **1 cup shortening**
- **1 cup granulated sugar**
- **1 cup lightly-packed brown sugar**

Add
- **2 well-beaten eggs**
- **1 teaspoon vanilla**

Beat until light and fluffy.

Blend or sift together
- **2¾ cups *Pre-Sifted* PURITY All-Purpose Flour**
- **1 teaspoon baking soda**
- **1 teaspoon salt**
- **1 teaspoon cinnamon**

Add dry ingredients to the creamed mixture and combine thoroughly. Chill dough until firm.

Divide chilled dough into three balls. Roll each to an 8″ x 12″ rectangle. Spread with the date filling. Beginning at the narrow edge of each, roll up like jelly rolls. Wrap securely in waxed paper. Chill overnight or until needed.

To bake, preheat oven to 375°. Slice off desired number of cookies, making each about ¼″ thick. Place on greased baking sheets and bake in preheated oven for 10 to 12 minutes.

Wrap remaining cookie dough and return to refrigerator. Because of the date filling, all the cookies should be baked within a week or ten days unless the dough is frozen.

Yield: 7 dozen pinwheels.

MOULDED COOKIES

163   Almond Crisps

Preheat oven to 350°.

Cream together
- **½ cup butter *or* margarine**
- **½ cup shortening**
- **½ cup lightly-packed brown sugar**
- **½ cup granulated sugar**

Add
- **1 beaten egg**
- **1 teaspoon almond extract**

Beat well.

Blend or sift together
- **1¾ cups *Pre-Sifted* PURITY All-Purpose Flour**
- **2 teaspoons baking powder**
- **½ teaspoon baking soda**
- **½ teaspoon cream of tartar**
- **½ teaspoon salt**

Blend into creamed mixture until well combined.

Stir in
- **½ cup chopped blanched almonds**

Shape dough into balls which are about 1″ in diameter. Place on greased baking sheets and press down with a fork which has been dipped in warm water.

Bake in preheated 350° oven for about 10 minutes.

Yield: 4 dozen cookies.

164   Thimble Cookies

Preheat oven to 350°.

Cream together
- **½ cup butter *or* margarine**
- **¼ cup sugar**

Add
- **1 well-beaten egg yolk**
- **2 teaspoons lemon juice**

Beat well.

Add
- **1 cup *Pre-Sifted* PURITY All-Purpose Flour**

Combine until well blended.

Shape dough into balls which are about 1″ in diameter.

Dip balls in
- **1 slightly-beaten egg white**

Then roll in
About 1 cup finely chopped nuts

Place on greased baking sheets and make a fairly deep indentation in the centre of each cookie.

Bake in preheated 350° oven for 5 minutes and then quickly indent the centres a second time.

Bake for another 10 to 12 minutes.

Fill hot cookies with brightly coloured jelly or jam.

Yield: 2 dozen cookies.

165 Coffee Shortbread Fingers

Preheat oven to 300°.

Cream together
1 cup soft butter or margarine
¾ cup lightly-packed brown sugar

Blend in
1 teaspoon instant coffee powder

Gradually add
2 cups Pre-Sifted PURITY
All-Purpose Flour

Mix until well blended.

Chill the dough.

Roll chilled dough to ½" thickness on a lightly floured surface. Cut into 2" x ½" fingers.

Dip shortbread fingers in
1 slightly-beaten egg white

Roll in
About 1½ cups finely chopped nuts

Place on ungreased baking sheets. Bake in preheated 300° oven for 20 to 25 minutes.

Yield: 4 dozen fingers.

166 Peanut Butter Cookies

Preheat oven to 375°.

Cream together
½ cup shortening
½ cup peanut butter

Gradually beat in
½ cup granulated sugar
½ cup lightly-packed brown sugar

Add
1 egg
½ teaspoon vanilla

Beat well.

Blend or sift together
1¼ cups Pre-Sifted PURITY
All-Purpose Flour
1 teaspoon baking soda
½ teaspoon salt

Add to creamed mixture and combine thoroughly.

Shape dough into balls which are about 1" in diameter. Place on greased baking sheets and press down with a fork which has been dipped in warm water.

Bake in preheated 375° oven for 10 to 12 minutes.

Yield: 3 dozen cookies.

167 Fruit and Nut Cookies

Preheat oven to 350°.

Combine thoroughly
½ cup lightly-packed brown sugar
½ cup granulated sugar
½ cup melted shortening or
vegetable oil

Add
1 beaten egg
1 teaspoon vanilla

Beat well.

Blend in
½ cup mashed banana
½ cup coconut
½ cup chopped walnuts
½ cup raisins

Blend or sift together
1 cup Pre-Sifted PURITY
All-Purpose Flour
½ teaspoon baking soda
½ teaspoon salt

Add to first mixture along with
2 cups rolled oats

Blend until well combined.

Shape dough into balls which are about 1" in diameter. Place on greased baking sheets and press down with a fork which has been dipped in warm water.

Bake in preheated 350° oven for 12 to 14 minutes.

Yield: 4 dozen cookies.

NO-BAKE COOKIES

168   *Choco-Squares*

BASIC MIXTURE:

Melt in a saucepan over hot water
  ½ cup butter *or* margarine
  2 squares semi-sweet chocolate

Blend in
  ⅓ cup sugar
  1 teaspoon vanilla
  1 beaten egg
  1½ cups desiccated coconut
  1 cup rolled oats
  ½ cup chopped walnuts

Press this mixture into a buttered 9″ square pan.

ICING:

Spread with Butter Frosting (recipe No. 119).

Chill for a few minutes.

TOPPING:

Melt
  2 squares semi-sweet chocolate
  1 tablespoon butter *or* margarine

Spread over the icing. Cover and store in the refrigerator.

Cut into squares for serving.

VARIATION:

(a)   *Choco-Balls*

Prepare Basic Mixture as directed above, but form it into balls which are about 1″ in diameter. Roll the balls in chopped walnuts or desiccated coconut. Chill until needed.

Yield: 2½ dozen balls.

169   *Quick Drops*

Melt over hot water
  1 cup chocolate chips
  3 tablespoons butter *or* margarine

Blend in
  ¼ cup sifted icing sugar

Then add
  2 cups desiccated coconut

Drop from a teaspoon onto waxed paper.

Chill for 30 minutes. Store at room temperature.

Yield: 2½ dozen cookies.

170   *Christmas Fruit Balls*

Mix together
  30 marshmallows, quartered
  2 cups graham wafer crumbs
  ½ cup red maraschino cherries, halved
  ½ cup green maraschino cherries, halved
  1 (15-ounce) can sweetened condensed milk
  ½ cup chopped walnuts

Chill overnight.

Shape chilled mixture into balls which are about 1″ in diameter. Then roll in coconut.

Store in a covered container in the refrigerator.

Yield: 4 dozen balls.

171   *Apricot Balls*

Combine
  ¾ cup ground dried apricots
  2 cups desiccated coconut
  ¼ cup sifted icing sugar
  ½ cup sweetened condensed milk

Form into balls which are about 1″ in diameter.

Then roll in fine granulated sugar.

Store in a covered container.

Yield: 2 dozen balls.

172   *Saucepan Cookies*

Combine in a broad saucepan
  ½ cup butter *or* margarine
  ¾ cup sugar
  2 beaten eggs
  ½ teaspoon salt
  1 cup chopped dates
  ½ cup chopped walnuts

Cook over low heat for 10 minutes.

Remove from heat and add
  1 teaspoon vanilla

Cool for about 5 minutes and then fold in
  2 cups crisp rice cereal

Form into balls which are about 1″ in diameter.

Roll in
  About 1½ cups coconut

Yield: 3 dozen cookies.

173   Date Balls

Mix together
  16 marshmallows, quartered
  ½ cup finely chopped dates
  ½ cup chopped nuts
  3 tablespoons heavy cream
  1 tablespoon graham wafer crumbs
  ½ teaspoon vanilla

Shape into balls which are about 1″ in diameter.
Roll in
  About ¾ cup graham wafer crumbs

Store in a covered container. (The flavour will improve if the balls are stored for 24 hours before serving.)

Yield: 2 dozen balls.

SQUARES AND BARS

174   Fudge Brownies

Preheat oven to 325°.
Cream
  ½ cup shortening
Add
  1 cup sugar
Beat until light and fluffy.
Blend in
  2 beaten eggs
Then add
  **2 squares unsweetened chocolate,
    melted**
  ½ teaspoon vanilla
Blend or sift together
  **1 cup Pre-Sifted PURITY
    All-Purpose Flour**
  ¼ teaspoon salt
Add to creamed mixture and combine well.
Blend in
  ½ cup chopped walnuts or pecans
Spread batter in a greased 8″ square pan.
Bake in preheated 325° oven for 25 to 30 minutes.

175   Cake Brownies

Preheat oven to 350°.
Melt
  2 squares unsweetened chocolate
  ¼ cup shortening
Set aside.
Cream
  ¼ cup shortening
  1 cup sugar
Add
  2 beaten eggs
Beat well.
Add
  Chocolate mixture
  1 cup chopped nuts
  1 teaspoon vanilla

Blend or sift together
  **½ cup Pre-Sifted PURITY
    All-Purpose Flour**
  ½ teaspoon baking powder
  ½ teaspoon salt
Add to chocolate mixture and combine well.
Spread batter in a greased 8″ square pan.
Bake in preheated 350° oven for 30 to 35 minutes.
Frost with Chocolate Butter Frosting (recipe No. 119 (a).

176   Butterscotch Brownies

Preheat oven to 350°.
Melt
  ¼ cup butter or margarine
Add
  1 cup lightly-packed brown sugar
Blend thoroughly and cool to lukewarm.
Add
  1 egg
  1½ teaspoons vanilla
Beat well.
Blend or sift together
  **¾ cup Pre-Sifted PURITY
    All-Purpose Flour**
  1 teaspoon baking powder
  ¼ teaspoon salt
Add to creamed mixture and combine well.
Stir in
  ¼ cup chopped nuts
Spread in a greased 8″ square pan.
Bake in preheated 350° oven for about 20 minutes, or until a golden brown.
When cool, frost with Butter Frosting (recipe No. 119).

Many baked squares keep better when left in the pans in which they were baked. Be sure to keep them closely covered.

177　Chocolate Fingers

Preheat oven to 350°.

PASTRY:

Cream together
- ⅓ cup shortening
- ⅓ cup granulated sugar

Add
- 1 beaten egg

Beat well.

Blend or sift together
- ½ cup *Pre-Sifted* PURITY All-Purpose Flour
- ¼ teaspoon salt

Work into the creamed mixture until well combined.

Press into a greased 8″ square pan.

FILLING:

Melt over hot water
- ⅓ cup shortening
- 1½ squares unsweetened chocolate

Add
- ¾ cup granulated sugar
- ¾ teaspoon vanilla

Beat until light. Cool slightly.

Add
- 1 beaten egg

Blend or sift together
- ½ cup *Pre-Sifted* PURITY All-Purpose Flour
- ½ teaspoon baking powder
- ⅛ teaspoon salt

Add to chocolate mixture and combine well.

Fold in
- ⅓ cup raisins *or* chopped nuts

Spread over unbaked pastry.

Bake in preheated 350° oven for 30 to 35 minutes.

Cool.

TOPPING:

Combine
- ½ cup sifted icing sugar
- 1 tablespoon cocoa

Add
- 1 to 1½ tablespoons boiling water

(Use enough boiling water to make a thin icing.)

Add
- ¼ teaspoon vanilla

Beat until smooth.

Spread over cooled baked squares. Allow topping to set and then cut into fingers.

Refer to Freezing Section, Page No. 207, for information on the freezing of squares and bars.

178　Chinese Chews

Preheat oven to 350°.

Blend or sift together
- ¾ cup *Pre-Sifted* PURITY All-Purpose Flour
- 1 cup sugar
- 1 teaspoon baking powder
- ¼ teaspoon salt

Add
- 1 cup chopped dates
- ¾ cup chopped walnuts

Beat until light
- 2 eggs

Add to the flour mixture and combine well.

Spread batter in a greased 9″ square pan.

Bake in preheated 350° oven for about 30 minutes.

Cut into fingers while still warm, and then roll in fine granulated sugar.

179　Caramel Squares

Preheat oven to 350°.

Cream thoroughly
- ½ cup butter *or* margarine
- ½ cup lightly-packed brown sugar

Add
- 1 beaten egg yolk

Beat well.

Add
- 1¼ cups *Pre-Sifted* PURITY All-Purpose Flour

Combine thoroughly.

Spread this mixture over bottom of a greased 8″ square pan.

TOPPING:

Beat to stiff peaks
- 1 egg white

Then blend in
- 1 cup lightly-packed brown sugar
- 1 teaspoon vanilla
- ⅛ teaspoon salt
- 1 cup chopped nuts

Spread over batter in the pan.

Bake in preheated 350° oven for about 30 minutes.

180 Peanut Butterscotch Bars

Preheat oven to 350°.

Beat together
  1 whole egg
  1 egg white

Add
  ¼ cup milk
  1 teaspoon vanilla
  1½ cups lightly-packed brown sugar
  ½ cup peanut butter
  ¼ cup melted shortening or
     vegetable oil

Beat with a rotary beater.

Blend or sift together
  2 cups Pre-Sifted PURITY
     All-Purpose Flour
  2 teaspoons baking powder
  ½ teaspoon salt

Add to the first mixture and combine well.

Spread batter in 2 greased 9" square pans or one greased 10" x 15" pan.

Bake in preheated 350° oven for 18 to 20 minutes.

PEANUT BUTTER TOPPING:

Beat
  1 egg yolk

Blend in
  ¼ cup peanut butter
  2 tablespoons water
  ½ cup sifted icing sugar

Add
  ¾ cup chopped peanuts

Spread this topping over the baked squares while they are still slightly warm.

181 Date Squares
(Matrimonial Cake)

DATE FILLING:

Combine in a saucepan
  1 cup chopped dates
  1 tablespoon brown sugar
  ½ cup water

Bring to a boil and cook until dates are soft enough to be mashed with a fork (about 5 minutes). The mixture should be the consistency of jam.

Set aside to cool.

CRUMB MIXTURE:

Preheat oven to 325°.

Blend or sift together
  1 cup Pre-Sifted PURITY
     All-Purpose Flour
  ½ teaspoon baking soda
  ⅛ teaspoon salt

Cut in
  1 cup butter or margarine

Then blend in
  1 cup lightly-packed brown sugar
  2 cups rolled oats

Press half of this mixture over bottom of a greased 8" square pan. Cover evenly with cooled Date Filling. Then cover with remaining Crumb Mixture and pat until smooth.

Bake in preheated 325° oven for 35 to 40 minutes or until a light golden brown.

Cool before cutting into squares.

182 Dream Squares

Preheat oven to 350°.

Cream together
  ½ cup butter or margarine
  ½ cup lightly-packed brown sugar
  ½ teaspoon vanilla

Stir in
  1 cup Pre-Sifted PURITY
     All-Purpose Flour

Press into bottom of an ungreased 8-inch square cake pan. Bake in preheated 350° oven for 10 minutes.

Beat
  2 eggs

Blend in
  1 cup lightly-packed brown sugar

Stir in
  1 tablespoon Pre-Sifted PURITY
     All-Purpose Flour
  ½ teaspoon baking powder
     pinch of salt
  1 cup chopped walnuts
  ½ cup glacé cherries, quartered
  ½ cup desiccated coconut

Spread over the baked pastry.

Return to oven and bake for an additional 30 to 35 minutes, or until golden brown.

Cool and cut into bars.

Pastry and Pies

PASTRY

183   Purity Pastry

Yield: 1—9″ double crust pie, *or* 2—9″ shells, *or* 12 to 14 medium-sized tart shells, *or* 24 small tart shells.

Blend or sift together
   **2 cups *Pre-Sifted* PURITY
   All-Purpose Flour
   1 teaspoon salt**

Using a pastry blender or two knives, cut in
   ¾ cup shortening

Sprinkle with
   4 to 5 tablespoons cold water

Add the water one tablespoon at a time, mixing lightly with a fork until all the flour is dampened. Turn dough onto a piece of waxed paper and form into a ball. Chill if desired.

TO ROLL PASTRY:

Use a lightly floured surface, preferably a pastry cloth and a covered rolling pin. Divide pastry in two and form each half into a flattened ball. (If making a double crust pie, make one portion slightly larger and use it for the bottom crust.)

Roll lightly, from the centre to the edge each time, until the pastry is about 1″ larger than inverted pie plate. (When making tarts, roll to ⅛″ thickness.)

TO LINE A PIE PLATE:

Fold rolled pastry in half and transfer it to the pie plate. Unfold and ease loosely into place, being careful not to stretch the pastry. Trim off any extra pastry with scissors.

BAKED PIE SHELLS:

Flute edge of the pastry in your favourite way. Prick with a fork at 1″ intervals. Bake in a preheated 450° oven for 10 to 12 minutes or until golden brown. Cool before adding the cooked filling.

UNBAKED PIE SHELLS:

Prepare as above but do not prick the pastry. Add uncooked filling and bake as directed in the filling recipe.

DOUBLE CRUST PIES:

Add filling to the pastry lined pie plate and moisten the edge. Roll out top crust, fold over and make slits in the centre to allow for escape of the steam. Place top crust in position, unfold. Trim off excess pastry; seal the edge and flute.

Bake as directed in the filling recipe.

Avoid stretching the pastry, especially during rolling and when fitting pastry into a pie plate. Stretched pastry will shrink during baking.

184   Hot Water Pastry

Sprinkle
   1 teaspoon salt
over
   ⅔ cup shortening

Add
   ½ cup boiling water

Stir until shortening has melted and mixture is uniform. Cool to room temperature.

Blend or sift in
   **1¾ cups *Pre-Sifted* PURITY
   All-Purpose Flour
   ½ teaspoon baking powder**

Cut in flour with a pastry blender or two knives.

Chill thoroughly.

Roll out and use as for Purity Pastry (recipe No. 183).

Yield: 1—9″ double crust pie, *or* 2—9″ shells, *or* 12 to 14 medium-sized tart shells, *or* 24 small tart shells.

185 Refrigerator Pastry

Blend or sift together
**6 cups *Pre-Sifted* PURITY
All-Purpose Flour
1 tablespoon salt**
Using a pastry blender or two knives, cut in finely
1 pound shortening (2⅓ cups)
Sprinkle with
About 1 cup cold water
Add the water gradually, mixing lightly with a fork until all the flour is dampened.
Turn dough onto a large piece of waxed paper and form into a ball. Wrap securely.
Store in the refrigerator until needed.
To use, cut off portion required, roll out and use as Plain Pastry (recipe No. 183).
This pastry may be kept refrigerated for 3 to 4 weeks and used as needed. Keep it securely wrapped to prevent drying.
Yield: 3 double crust pies *or* 6 shells.

NOTE: A "dry mix" may be prepared by cutting the shortening into the flour and salt mixture in this recipe. This mix may be stored in a covered container on your kitchen shelf. Use 2½ cups of the mix and 4 to 5 tablespoons cold water for each 9″ double crust pie.

Pie tape, or a 1½″ strip of cloth or aluminum foil may be used to prevent the crust edge from becoming too brown. Dampen the tape or cloth before applying it to the pastry, and remove as soon as the pie is taken from the oven. Remove aluminum foil 15 minutes before end of the baking time.

186 Sweet Pastry

Preheat oven to 450°.
Blend or sift together
**2 cups *Pre-Sifted* PURITY
All-Purpose Flour
2 tablespoons sugar
½ teaspoon salt**
Cut in finely
**½ cup shortening
¼ cup butter**
Combine
**1 beaten egg
2 tablespoons cold water**
Sprinkle over flour mixture and toss lightly with a fork to make a soft dough. Turn onto a

lightly floured surface and knead gently 6 or 7 times.
Roll to ⅛″ thickness. Cut into 4″ rounds and line medium-sized muffin cups or tart pans with the pastry. (Or, place over inverted muffin cups or custard cups, pleating to make pastry fit smoothly.) Prick the pastry.
Bake in preheated 450° oven for 8 to 10 minutes. Cool.
Fill as desired.
Yield: 12 to 14 medium-sized tart shells.

187 Graham Cracker Crust

Place about 20 graham crackers in a plastic bag.
Roll to make
1¼ cups fine crumbs
Combine
**Graham cracker crumbs
¼ cup sugar**
Add
6 tablespoons melted butter
Mix thoroughly.
Reserve 2 tablespoons of this mixture to use for topping, if desired.
Press remaining crumb mixture into a well-greased 9″ pie plate, covering the bottom and sides with a firm, even layer of crumb. Chill.
Fill with a chiffon or cream type pie filling, sprinkling reserved crumb mixture over the top. Chill well before serving.
Yield: 1—9″ pie shell.

188 Puff Pastry

Wash **2 cups butter** in very cold water, squeezing lightly with the fingers until it is waxy and smooth. Double over and pat hard to remove the water. Reserve 2 tablespoons of this butter, and shape remainder into a flat oblong about ½″ thick. Chill.
Blend or sift together
**3 cups *Pre-Sifted* PURITY
All-Purpose Flour
1½ teaspoons salt**
Using a pastry blender or two knives, cut in
2 tablespoons reserved butter
Sprinkle with
1⅓ cups ice water
Add the water gradually, mixing lightly with a fork to form a soft dough.

Turn onto a lightly floured board and knead for 5 minutes. Then, cover and let stand for 10 minutes.

Roll pastry to ⅛" thickness, keeping it longer than it is wide, and the corners square.

Place chilled butter in centre of one side and fold other half of pastry over it. Seal edges to enclose as much air as possible.

Press until enclosed butter is within ½" of the edge. Fold ends over to make 3 layers. Chill thoroughly.

Roll pastry to ⅛" thickness, keeping it longer than it is wide. Be careful to prevent sticking.

Fold ends over to make 3 layers; fold again to make 6 layers. Chill thoroughly.

Repeat this rolling, folding and chilling three more times. After final rolling, chill until stiff (2 to 3 hours).

PATTY SHELLS:

Roll chilled pastry to ¼" thickness. Cut out with a round cutter. Using a smaller cutter, cut out centres from half the rounds.

Moisten edges of the complete rounds and place the rings on top. Press edges together. (The cut out centres may be baked and used as covers for the shells.)

Place on a baking sheet which has been covered with two layers of brown paper. Chill.

Bake in preheated 500° oven for 10 minutes, lower temperature to 375° and bake for another 10 to 15 minutes. (Turn during baking so shells will puff evenly.)

Yield: 12 to 16 large patty shells or 24 to 30 small patty shells.

NOTE: This pastry may also be used for cream rolls, horns, etc. Use the special forms which are available and follow manufacturer's directions for their use.

189   Danish Pastry

Wash ¾ cup butter in cold water, squeezing lightly with the fingers until it is waxy and smooth. Double over and pat hard to remove the water. Chill.

Sprinkle

   1 package active dry yeast

over

   ½ cup lukewarm water

in which has been dissolved

   1 teaspoon sugar

Let stand for 10 minutes. Stir with a fork.

Meanwhile, combine in a large bowl

   3 tablespoons sugar
   ¼ cup butter or margarine
   1 teaspoon salt
   ¾ cup scalded milk

Stir until butter melts. Cool to lukewarm.

Add

   Softened yeast
   1 well-beaten egg
   ¼ teaspoon vanilla
   ½ teaspoon crushed cardamon seeds
   or ¼ teaspoon mace
   1½ cups Pre-Sifted PURITY
   All-Purpose Flour

Beat well.

Then gradually add another

   1½ to 1¾ cups Pre-Sifted PURITY
   All-Purpose Flour

Stir to make a soft but not sticky dough.

Turn out onto a lightly floured surface. Roll to a square about ¼" thick. Place half of washed butter, in small bits, on the centre strip of the dough. Fold over one side of dough to cover butter. Place remaining butter on this layer, again in small pieces. Fold other side of dough over top. Press edges together.

Cover well and place in the refrigerator for 1 hour.

Roll to a square, about ¼" thick. Fold in such a way as to make a small square with 9 layers of dough. Chill for another hour.

Repeat this rolling, folding and chilling once more.

If you wish, the dough may be chilled overnight after the final rolling.

Then roll out the chilled dough and cut into desired shapes (next page). Place on baking sheets which have been covered with two layers of brown paper. Brush with melted butter or margarine. Let rise in a warm place for about 45 minutes, or until almost doubled in bulk.

Bake in preheated 375° oven for 18 to 20 minutes.

Glaze and decorate as desired (next page).

These are best when served while still slightly warm.

Yield: About 2½ dozen assorted pastries.

NOTE: The chilled dough may be cut into two or more pieces and each piece used to make a different shaped pastry.

TO SHAPE DANISH PASTRY:

1. Knots: Roll chilled pastry to ¼" thickness and cut into strips which are ½" wide and about 6" long. Tie each into a knot and place on a paper-covered baking sheet. Brush with melted butter or margarine. Let rise and bake as directed in recipe.

2. Braids: Roll chilled pastry to ¼" thickness and cut into long strips which are about ⅓" wide. Braid or twist these strips together in pairs. Cut each braid into 2" to 3" pieces. Place on a paper-covered baking sheet. Brush with melted butter or margarine. Allow to rise and then bake as directed in recipe.

3. Pinwheels: Roll chilled pastry to ⅛" thickness. Brush with melted butter or margarine. Sprinkle with a mixture of sugar and cinnamon. (Use ½ teaspoon cinnamon for each tablespoon of sugar.) Roll up like a jelly roll. Cut into ½" slices and place on a paper-covered baking sheet. Allow to rise and then bake as directed in recipe.

4. Filled Pastries: Roll chilled pastry to ⅛" thickness. Cut into 4" squares. Place about 1 tablespoon of desired filling in the centre of each. Bring two opposite corners together over the top, moisten and seal. Place on a paper-covered baking sheet. Brush with egg white. Allow to rise and then bake as directed in recipe.

Horns, cream shells, etc. may be made from Danish Pastry, if the special forms are available.

Suggested Fillings:

(a) Thick applesauce or jam may be used. If it is not thick enough, mix with a little cake crumb.

(b) Almond Filling: Combine thoroughly ¼ cup butter or margarine, ⅓ cup ground almonds and ½ cup sifted icing sugar. This makes filling for 10 to 12 pastries.

GLAZE FOR DANISH PASTRY:

Combine 1½ cups sifted icing sugar, few grains salt, 1 tablespoon soft butter or margarine and about 2 tablespoons milk. Blend until smooth. Add ½ teaspoon vanilla or ¼ teaspoon almond extract. Pour over warm Danish Pastries just before serving.

Sprinkle with chopped nuts, if desired.

Sufficient glaze for 2½ dozen pastries.

DOUBLE CRUST PIES

190   Apple Pie

Tart cooking apples which are firm and juicy make the best pies. You will need about 2 pounds for a 9" pie.

Preheat oven to 400°.

Prepare pastry, and line a 9" pie plate with the rolled pastry. Roll out the top crust; make slits in the centre.

Peel and core apples, cut into thin slices to make about

6 cups sliced apples

Combine

⅔ to 1 cup sugar (depending upon tartness of the apples)
½ teaspoon cinnamon or nutmeg
⅛ teaspoon salt

Place one-half of the apple slices in the pastry lined pie plate. Sprinkle with half the sugar mixture.

Add remaining apples, heaping them in the centre. Sprinkle rest of sugar mixture over the top.

Dot with

1 tablespoon butter or margarine

Moisten edge of pastry. Place top crust in position. Seal edge and flute.

Bake in preheated 400° oven for 40 to 50 minutes, or until the pastry is golden brown and the apples are tender.

NOTE: If apples are especially juicy, combine 1 tablespoon *Pre-Sifted* PURITY All-Purpose Flour with the sugar mixture. If apples are dry, sprinkle them with about 2 tablespoons water.

Fruit and mince pies may be covered and stored at room temperature. Freshen fruit pies for serving by heating in a 300° oven for about 15 minutes. Reheat mince pies in a 300° oven for about 20 minutes.

A favourite dessert at barbecue time, or any time, Cherry Pie (Recipe Nos. 195 and 196)

191 Fresh Berry Pie

Use strawberries, raspberries, blueberries, black-berries or loganberries. You will need about 4 cups of prepared berries for a 9" pie.

Preheat oven to 400°.

Prepare pastry, and line a 9" pie plate with the rolled pastry. Roll out top crust; make slits in the centre.

Prepare
  4 cups berries
Wash and drain.

Combine
  ¾ to 1 cup sugar (depending upon tartness of the berries)
  3 to 4 tablespoons *Pre-Sifted* **PURITY All-Purpose Flour**
  ⅛ teaspoon salt

Place one-half the berries in the pastry lined pie plate. Add half the sugar mixture. Add remaining berries and rest of sugar mixture.

Dot with
  1 tablespoon butter *or* **margarine**

Moisten edge of pastry. Place top crust in position. Seal edge and flute.

Bake in preheated 400° oven for 40 to 50 minutes or until pastry is golden brown.

VARIATION:

(a) Frozen Berry Pie

Frozen, unsweetened berries may be substituted for fresh berries. Partially thaw the berries and drain before using.

If you use sweetened frozen berries for a pie, reduce sugar to ¼ cup.

Baked or unbaked pie shells, fruit, mince and chiffon pies may all be frozen very successfully (see page 207.) Do not freeze custard pies or a pie which has a meringue on it.

192 Canned Fruit Pie Fillings

A wide variety of canned fruit pie fillings are available, mostly in the 20-ounce size. These are precooked and require no additional ingredients.

Prepare pastry and line a 9" pie plate with the rolled pastry. Roll out top crust; make slits in the centre.

Pour the canned pie filling into the pastry lined pie plate. Moisten edge of pastry. Place top crust in position. Seal and flute the edge.

Bake the pie as directed on the can. (This is usually in a preheated 425° oven for about 30 minutes.)

193 Rhubarb Pie

You will need about 4 cups of diced rhubarb for a 9" pie.

Preheat oven to 400°.

Prepare pastry, and line a 9" pie plate with the rolled pastry. Roll out top crust; make slits in the centre.

Peel rhubarb, if necessary. Cut into 1" pieces to make
  4 cups diced rhubarb

Combine
  1¼ to 1¾ cups sugar (depending upon tartness of the rhubarb)
  ⅓ cup *Pre-Sifted* **PURITY All-Purpose Flour**
  ⅛ teaspoon salt

Place one-half the rhubarb in the pastry lined pie plate, add about half the sugar mixture. Add remaining rhubarb and rest of the sugar mixture.

Dot with
  1 tablespoon butter *or* **margarine**

Moisten edge of pastry. Place top crust in position. Seal and flute the edge.

Bake in preheated 400° oven for 40 to 50 minutes or until the pastry is golden brown.

VARIATION:

(a) Frozen Rhubarb Pie

Unsweetened frozen rhubarb may be substituted for the fresh rhubarb. Partially thaw and drain before using.

Sweetened frozen rhubarb may also be used. Thaw and drain it, and reduce sugar to ⅓ cup.

194 Peach Pie

Select firm peaches for your pie. You will need about 1¾ pounds of peaches for a 9" pie.

Preheat oven to 400°.

Prepare pastry, and line a 9" pie plate with the rolled pastry. Roll out the top crust and cut slits in the centre.

Blanch the peaches in boiling water for 1 minute, place in cold water. Remove skins and stones. Slice to make about
  4 cups sliced peaches

Combine
⅔ to ¾ cup sugar
3 tablespoons *Pre-Sifted* PURITY
All-Purpose Flour
½ teaspoon cinnamon

Place one-half the peach slices in the pastry lined pie plate. Sprinkle with half the sugar mixture. Add remaining peaches and sugar.

Dot with
1 tablespoon butter *or* margarine

Moisten edge of pastry. Place top crust in position. Seal edge and flute.

Bake in preheated 400° oven for 40 to 50 minutes or until the pastry is golden brown.

VARIATION:

(a) *Fresh Apricot Pie*
Firm sliced apricots may be substituted for the peaches in the above recipe.

195 Fresh Cherry Pie

Choose sour red cherries for best results. You will need about 4 cups pitted cherries for a 9" pie.

Preheat oven to 400°.

Prepare pastry, and line a 9" pie plate with the rolled pastry. Roll out top crust and make slits in the centre, or cut top crust into strips to use for a lattice top.

Pit and wash sour cherries to make
4 cups cherries

Combine
1⅓ cups sugar
¼ cup *Pre-Sifted* PURITY
All-Purpose Flour
⅛ teaspoon salt
⅛ teaspoon almond extract
3 to 4 drops red food colouring

Spread one-half the cherries in the pastry lined pie plate, add half the sugar mixture.

Top with rest of cherries and sugar mixture.

Dot with
1 tablespoon butter *or* margarine

Moisten edge and place top crust in position, or arrange pastry strips on top, lattice style, moistening where necessary to seal.

Bake in preheated 400° oven for 40 to 50 minutes or until the pastry is golden brown and the cherries are tender.

196 Prize Winning Cherry Pie

Use two 15-ounce containers of pitted, red cherries, either canned or frozen. Thaw frozen cherries before using.

Preheat oven to 400°.

Drain
2 (15–ounce) containers of pitted, red cherries

Heat in a saucepan
¾ cup cherry juice

Meanwhile, blend together
⅓ cup *Pre-Sifted* PURITY
All-Purpose Flour
3 tablespoons cold cherry juice

Slowly add flour mixture to the heated cherry juice and cook over medium heat until thickened, stirring constantly.

Slowly add
¾ cup sugar

Cook for another 3 or 4 minutes. Remove from the heat.

Stir in
2 tablespoons lemon juice
1 tablespoon butter *or* margarine
⅛ teaspoon salt
2 to 3 drops red food colouring

Pour mixture over cherries and blend carefully but thoroughly. Allow to cool while making pastry.

Prepare pastry and line a 9" pie plate with the rolled pastry. Build up the edge as this makes a deep pie.

Roll out pastry for top crust. Cut into strips for lattice top.

Add cherry filling to the pastry lined pie plate.

Arrange pastry strips on top, lattice fashion.

Moisten and seal at edge and where strips cross.

Bake in preheated 400° oven for 15 minutes.

Reduce temperature to 350° and continue baking for another 25 to 30 minutes.

To make sure that the bottom crust is well done, place the rack about 4 or 5 inches from the bottom of the oven. This is particularly important in custard and fresh fruit pies.

197 Raisin Pie

Preheat oven to 400°.

Combine in a saucepan
> **1 cup lightly-packed brown sugar**
> **2 tablespoons** *Pre-Sifted* **PURITY All-Purpose Flour**
> **⅛ teaspoon salt**

Add
> **2 cups seedless raisins**
> **2 cups boiling water**

Bring to a boil. Simmer until raisins are plump and mixture starts to thicken (about 10 minutes). Stir constantly.

Remove from the heat and stir in
> **3 tablespoons lemon juice**
> **2 teaspoons finely grated lemon rind**

Cool while making the pastry.

Prepare pastry and line a 9″ pie plate with the rolled pastry. Roll out top crust and cut slits in the centre.

Pour cooled filling into pastry lined pie plate.

Moisten the edge. Place top crust in position. Seal and flute the edge.

Bake in preheated 400° oven for 35 to 45 minutes or until pastry is golden brown.

VARIATION:

(a) Raisin Nut Pie

Add ½ cup chopped walnuts to the cooked raisin mixture in above recipe.

198 Mince Pie

Preheat oven to 400°.

Prepare pastry and line a 9″ pie plate with the rolled pastry. Roll out top crust and make slits in the centre.

Use about
> **3 cups mincemeat (recipe No. 199)**

OR

Combine
> **1 (20-ounce) can mincemeat (2 cups)**

with
> **1 cup chopped apple,** *or* **applesauce** *or* **drained crushed pineapple**

Place mincemeat filling in the pastry lined pie plate. Moisten edge. Place top crust in position. Seal the edge and flute.

Bake in preheated 400° oven for about 30 minutes or until the pastry is golden brown. Serve hot.

To reheat: Place Mince Pie in a preheated 300° oven for about 20 minutes.

To protect the oven from spillovers when baking fruit pies, place a piece of foil on rack beneath pie. Do not lay foil on element or cover racks completely.

199 Mincemeat

Combine in a large kettle
> **3 cups ground suet**
> **1 sliced orange**
> **1 sliced lemon**
> **3 cups water**

Boil for 30 minutes and then strain out the sliced fruit.

Add to hot suet mixture
> **4 cups seedless raisins**
> **3 cups chopped cooked prunes**
> **8 cups chopped apples**
> **1½ cups cut citron** *or* **peel**
> **4 cups granulated sugar**
> **1½ cups lightly-packed brown sugar**
> **3 cups fruit juice (apple, pineapple** *or* **prune)**
> **¾ cup cider vinegar**
> **⅓ cup molasses**
> **2 teaspoons salt**
> **½ teaspoon pepper**
> **1 tablespoon nutmeg**
> **4 teaspoons cinnamon**
> **1½ teaspoons ground cloves**
> **1 teaspoon allspice**

Boil for 30 minutes, stirring very frequently to prevent sticking.

Pack in hot sterilized jars, seal tightly and store in a cool, dry place.

Yield: About 4 quarts.

Leftover mincemeat (from a partially used jar or can) can be used in tasty Mincemeat Tarts. Served hot, these are a popular Christmas treat.

For a lattice top pie, cut rolled pastry into strips which are about ⅓″ wide. Criss-cross the strips over the pie, trim and moisten at the edge to seal to bottom crust.

SINGLE CRUST PIES

200 Deep Dish Apple Pie

You will need about 3 pounds of tart, firm cooking apples for a 9″ square pie.

Preheat oven to 400°.

Prepare pastry and roll to a 10″ square and cut slits in the centre.

Peel and core apples; slice to make enough to just fill a 9″ square baking dish.

Sprinkle the apples with a mixture of
½ to ¾ cup granulated sugar (depending upon tartness of the apples)
¼ cup lightly-packed brown sugar
½ teaspoon cinnamon *or* nutmeg
¼ teaspoon salt

Dot with
2 tablespoons butter *or* margarine

Sprinkle with
1 teaspoon vanilla

Arrange pastry on top, folding edge under.

Flute along the edge.

Bake in preheated 400° oven for 30 to 40 minutes or until the apples are tender and the pastry is golden brown.

Cut into squares for serving. Top with ice cream or whipped cream.

Yield: 9 servings.

———————

To help prevent fruit pies from boiling over, a foil or glass cone may be set in the centre. This allows the steam to escape, but should be removed before serving, of course.

201 Upside Down Apple Pie

Preheat oven to 400°.

Line a 9″ pie plate with a circle of aluminum foil so there is a 1″ overhang at the edge.

Spread bottom and sides with
2 tablespoons soft butter *or* margarine

Arrange over the bottom
⅓ cup pecan halves

Sprinkle with
⅓ cup lightly-packed brown sugar

Combine
6 cups sliced, firm apples

with a mixture of
½ cup granulated sugar
2 tablespoons *Pre-Sifted* PURITY All-Purpose Flour
½ teaspoon cinnamon
¼ teaspoon nutmeg

Arrange in the prepared pie plate.

Prepare pastry and roll to a 10″ circle. Place over apple mixture. Fold under the edge and flute. Prick pastry to allow the steam to escape. Turn up edge of foil to prevent leaking.

Bake in preheated 400° oven for 35 to 40 minutes or until the apples are tender and the pastry is golden brown.

Invert on a serving plate. Remove pie plate and foil.

Serve warm, with ice cream or whipped cream if desired.

202 Rhubarb Cream Pie

Preheat oven to 425°.

Prepare pastry and line a 9″ pie plate with the rolled pastry. Flute the edge, but do not prick the pastry.

Fill with
3 cups finely-cut rhubarb

Combine
1 cup sugar
¼ cup *Pre-Sifted* PURITY All-Purpose Flour
¼ teaspoon salt

Blend in
¾ cup hot cream (18%)

Pour this mixture over the rhubarb.

Bake in preheated 425° oven for 12 minutes.

Reduce heat to 350° and bake for another 20 minutes, or until the rhubarb is tender and the pastry is nicely browned.

NOTE: Sweetened frozen rhubarb may be used for this pie. Partially thaw and drain the rhubarb. Reduce sugar to ¼ cup.

203 Peach Crumb Pie

Preheat oven to 450°.

Prepare pastry and line a 9″ pie plate with the rolled pastry. Flute the edge, but do not prick.

Combine
½ cup *Pre-Sifted* PURITY All-Purpose Flour
¼ cup granulated sugar
¼ cup lightly-packed brown sugar
½ teaspoon cinnamon

Cut in finely
¼ cup butter *or* margarine

Set aside one-half of this mixture.

To remaining half, add
½ cup chopped walnuts

Sprinkle nut mixture over bottom of pastry lined pie plate.

Drain
1 (28-ounce) can peach halves

Arrange the drained peaches, cut side down over the nut mixture. Sprinkle reserved crumb mixture over the top.

Bake in preheated 450° oven for 10 minutes. Lower temperature to 350° and bake for an additional 20 minutes.

Serve while warm.

204 Pear Streusel Pie

Preheat oven to 450°.

Prepare pastry and line a 9″ pie plate with the rolled pastry. Flute the edge, but do not prick.

Drain
1 (28-ounce) can pear halves

Slice lengthwise into thirds and arrange in the pastry lined pie plate.

Combine
⅓ cup *Pre-Sifted* PURITY All-Purpose Flour
⅓ cup lightly-packed brown sugar
1 teaspoon cinnamon
⅛ teaspoon nutmeg

Cut in finely
¼ cup butter *or* margarine

Sprinkle over the pears.

Bake in preheated 450° oven for 10 minutes. Lower temperature to 350° and bake for an additional 20 minutes.

Serve while warm.

205 Meringue for Pies

Preheat oven to 400°.

Beat to very soft peaks
2 egg whites
Few grains salt

Gradually beat in
4 tablespoons sugar

Beat until stiff. (Sugar should be completely dissolved.)

Beat in
¼ teaspoon vanilla *or* other flavouring

Pile meringue on warm pie filling. Spread to edge so that it joins the crust all the way around. (This prevents shrinking.) Swirl or peak for an attractive top.

Bake in preheated 400° oven for 7 to 8 minutes or until lightly browned.

Cool at room temperature, away from drafts.

VARIATION:

(a) Three Egg Meringue

Use 3 egg whites, few grains salt, 6 tablespoons sugar and ⅓ teaspoon flavouring. Prepare and bake as above.

If a meringue topped pie is difficult to cut, dip a sharp knife in water and shake off the excess. Repeat this between cuts.

206 Lemon Meringue Pie

Combine in top of double boiler
1 cup sugar
3 tablespoons *Pre-Sifted* PURITY All-Purpose Flour
3 tablespoons cornstarch
⅛ teaspoon salt

Stir in
1½ cups boiling water

Place over medium direct heat and bring to a boil, stirring constantly. Remove from the direct heat and place over boiling water. Cover and cook for an additional 5 to 7 minutes, stirring occasionally.

Pour some of this hot mixture into
2 beaten egg yolks

Return to double boiler top and cook over boiling water for another 2 minutes, stirring constantly.

Remove from the heat and blend in
1 tablespoon butter *or* margarine
¼ cup lemon juice
2 teaspoons finely-grated lemon rind

Cool slightly.

Pour into a baked 9″ pie shell.

Prepare Meringue (recipe No. 205), replacing vanilla with ½ teaspoon lemon juice. Spread over warm filling; swirl.

Bake in preheated 400° oven for 7 to 8 minutes or until meringue is lightly browned.

Let cool to room temperature, away from drafts.

Pudding and pie mixes may be used for quick cream pies. Do not bake a meringue on an instant type filling.

207 Vanilla Cream Pie

Scald

2 cups milk

Combine in top of double boiler

½ cup sugar
⅓ cup *Pre-Sifted* PURITY All-Purpose Flour
½ teaspoon salt

Slowly blend in

½ cup cold milk

Stir until smooth.

Add the hot milk.

Place over direct medium heat and bring to a boil, stirring constantly. Remove from the heat.

Stir part of the hot mixture into

2 beaten egg yolks

Return to double boiler top and cook over boiling water for 2 minutes, stirring constantly.

Remove from the heat and stir in

1 tablespoon butter *or* margarine
1 teaspoon vanilla

Cool slightly.

Pour filling into a baked 9″ pie shell.

Prepare Meringue (recipe No. 205). Swirl over warm filling.

Bake in preheated 400° oven for 7 to 8 minutes or until the meringue is a light brown.

Let cool to room temperature, away from drafts. Chill.

VARIATIONS:

(a) Banana Cream Pie

Prepare Vanilla Cream filling as directed. Cool to lukewarm. Pour half the filling into a baked 9″ pie shell. Cover with two layers of banana slices and then add rest of filling.

Top with meringue. Bake meringue as directed. Cool and then chill.

(b) Coconut Cream Pie

Prepare Vanilla Cream filling as directed, adding 1 cup coconut to the cooked filling. Sprinkle ½ cup coconut over the meringue and bake as directed. Cool and then chill.

(c) Peach Cream Pie

Prepare Vanilla Cream filling as directed. Cool slightly. Pour half the filling into a baked 9″ pie shell. Drain 1 (20-ounce) can peach slices. Arrange drained peaches over the filling and then cover with remaining filling. Top with meringue and bake as directed. Cool and then chill.

208 Chocolate Cream Pie

Scald

2 cups milk

Combine in top of double boiler

1 cup sugar
⅓ cup *Pre-Sifted* PURITY All-Purpose Flour
½ teaspoon salt

Slowly blend in

½ cup cold milk

Stir until smooth.

Add

Hot milk
2 squares unsweetened chocolate, cut up

Place over direct medium heat and bring to a boil, stirring constantly. Remove from the heat.

Stir part of the hot mixture into

2 beaten egg yolks

Return to top of double boiler. Cook over boiling water for 2 minutes, stirring constantly.

Remove from heat and stir in

1 tablespoon butter *or* margarine
1 teaspoon vanilla

Cool slightly.

Pour into baked 9″ pie shell.

Prepare Meringue (recipe No. 205). Swirl over warm filling.

Bake in preheated 400° oven for 7 to 8 minutes, or until a light brown.

Let cool to room temperature, away from drafts. Chill.

209   Butterscotch Cream Pie

Scald
    2 cups milk
Melt in top of a double boiler
    ¼ cup butter *or* margarine
Combine and add to melted butter
    1 cup lightly-packed brown sugar
    ⅓ cup *Pre-Sifted* PURITY
      All-Purpose Flour
    ½ teaspoon salt
Slowly blend in
    ½ cup cold milk
Stir until smooth.
Add the hot milk.
Place over direct medium heat and bring to a boil, stirring constantly. Remove from the heat.
Stir part of the hot mixture into
    2 beaten egg yolks
Return to top of double boiler. Cook over boiling water for 2 minutes, stirring constantly.
Remove from the heat and stir in
    1 teaspoon vanilla
Cool slightly.
Pour into a baked 9″ pie shell.
Prepare Meringue (recipe No. 205). Swirl over warm filling.
Bake in preheated 400° oven for 7 to 8 minutes, or until lightly browned.
Let cool to room temperature, away from drafts. Chill.

Cream and custard type pies must always be refrigerated if they are to be kept for more than an hour before serving. **This is necessary to prevent food poisoning.** *Keep any leftovers refrigerated as well, and serve them within 24 hours. Refrigerate chiffon pies to keep them firm and fresh for serving.*

210   Custard Pie

Preheat oven to 450°.
Prepare pastry and line a 9″ pie plate with the rolled pastry. Flute the edge, but do not prick.
Scald
    2 cups milk
Beat slightly with a fork
    3 eggs
Add
    ⅓ cup sugar
    ¼ teaspoon salt
Then slowly stir in the hot milk.

Add
    ½ teaspoon vanilla
Pour into pastry lined pie plate.
If desired, sprinkle with
    ¼ teaspoon grated nutmeg
Bake in preheated 450° oven for 10 minutes, then lower temperature to 325° and bake for another 25 minutes or until filling is just firm. (A metal skewer or knife will come out clean when inserted in the centre.)
Serve slightly warm or cold. Refrigerate if pie is to be kept more than an hour.

VARIATIONS:

(a)   Banana Custard Pie

Prepare Custard Pie filling as above. Line pastry with two layers of banana slices before adding the filling. Bake as for Custard Pie.

(b)   Custard Meringue Pie

Prepare and bake as for Custard Pie, substituting 2 eggs and 2 egg yolks for the 3 eggs called for in the recipe. Cool slightly.
Prepare Meringue (recipe No. 205) using the 2 egg whites. Pile on the baked pie. Return to a 400° oven and bake for 7 to 8 minutes or until the meringue is a light brown.

211   Pumpkin Pie

Preheat oven to 450°.
Prepare pastry and line a 9″ pie plate with the rolled pastry. Flute the edge but do not prick.
Blend together
    1 (15-ounce) can pumpkin (1½ cups)
    ⅔ cup lightly-packed brown sugar
    ¾ teaspoon cinnamon
    ½ teaspoon ginger
    ¼ teaspoon mace *or* nutmeg
    ½ teaspoon salt
Stir in
    2 well-beaten eggs
    ½ cup milk
    ⅔ cup evaporated milk
Blend until smoothly combined.
Pour into the unbaked pie shell.
Bake in preheated 450° oven for 10 minutes, then lower the temperature to 350° and bake for another 30 to 40 minutes, or until just firm in the centre. (A metal skewer or knife will come out clean when inserted.)
Serve slightly warm or cold. Refrigerate if the pie is to be kept more than an hour.

212   Lemon Chiffon Pie

Soften
   1 tablespoon gelatine
in
   ¼ cup cold water
Combine in top of double boiler
   ½ cup sugar
   ½ teaspoon salt
   2 teaspoons finely grated lemon rind
   ⅔ cup boiling water
Add
   Softened gelatine
   3 well-beaten egg yolks
Cook over boiling water until mixture coats
a metal spoon (8 to 10 minutes). Stir constantly.
Remove from heat.
Stir in
   ⅓ cup lemon juice
Pour into a bowl and chill the mixture until
it will mould slightly. Stir occasionally.
(This requires about 1 hour in the refrigerator
or about ½ hour if the bowl is set in a pan of
ice water.)
Beat to soft peaks
   3 egg whites
Gradually beat in
   ¼ cup sugar
Fold the meringue into cooled gelatine mixture. Pile into a baked 9″ pie shell.
Chill for 2 to 3 hours or until firm.

*If gelatine mixture for a chiffon filling becomes
too stiff, beat with rotary or electric mixer until
frothy, before adding the meringue mixture.*

213   Pumpkin Chiffon Pie

Soften
   1 tablespoon gelatine
in
   ¼ cup water
Combine in top of double boiler
   ½ cup lightly-packed brown sugar
   1 teaspoon cinnamon
   ½ teaspoon ginger
   ¼ teaspoon allspice
   ½ teaspoon salt
Add
   1 (15-ounce) can pumpkin (1½ cups)
   3 well-beaten egg yolks
   ½ cup milk
Beat until smooth.
Cook over boiling water until thick and
smooth (about 10 minutes). Stir constantly.
Remove from heat and blend in
   Softened gelatine
Pour into a bowl and chill until the mixture
will mould slightly. (This requires about 1
hour in the refrigerator or about ½ hour if the
bowl is set in a pan of ice water.) Stir occasionally.
Beat to soft peaks
   3 egg whites
Gradually beat in
   ¼ cup lightly-packed brown sugar
Fold meringue into chilled pumpkin mixture.
Pile into a baked 9″ pie shell.
Chill for 2 to 3 hours or until firm.
Serve cold, plain or topped with whipped
cream.

TARTS

214   Butter Tarts

Preheat oven to 375°.
Prepare pastry and roll to ⅛″ thickness. Cut
into 4″ rounds and line 12 medium-sized tart
pans or muffin cups. Do not prick.
Pour boiling water over
   ½ cup raisins
Let soak until edges of raisins begin to turn
white. Drain.
Cream
   ¼ cup butter *or* margarine

Add
   ½ cup lightly-packed brown sugar
Beat thoroughly.
Add
   ¼ teaspoon salt
   ½ cup corn syrup
   1 beaten egg
   ½ teaspoon vanilla
   Few drops lemon juice
Combine only until blended.
Fold in the drained raisins.

Spoon mixture into the unbaked tart shells, filling each about ⅔ full.

Bake in preheated 375° oven for 20 to 25 minutes.

Do not allow the filling to boil.

Yield: 12 medium-sized tarts.

215   Pineapple Tarts

Prepare pastry and roll to ⅛" thickness. Cut into 2½" rounds and line 24 small tart pans.

Prick bottom and sides of pastry with a fork. Bake in preheated 450° oven for 10 to 12 minutes. Cool.

Combine in top of double boiler

½ cup sugar
2 tablespoons *Pre-Sifted* **PURITY All-Purpose Flour**
¼ teaspoon salt

Slowly stir in

⅓ cup water

Place over direct medium heat and bring to a boil, stirring constantly.

Remove from the heat.

Slowly add some of the hot mixture to

2 beaten egg yolks

Return to double boiler top and cook over boiling water for 2 minutes, stirring constantly.

Remove from heat and add

⅔ cup crushed pineapple, undrained

Divide filling among the baked tart shells. Chill thoroughly. Serve plain or topped with whipped cream or meringue.

Yield: 24 small tarts.

FOR MERINGUE TOPPED TARTS:

Prepare Meringue (recipe No. 205).

Swirl over tops of the chilled tarts, using a cake decorator if desired.

Bake in preheated 400° oven for 5 minutes or until a light golden brown.

Cool to room temperature before serving.

216   Luscious Lemon Tarts

Preheat oven to 450°.

Prepare pastry and roll to ⅛" thickness. Cut into 4" rounds and line 12 to 14 medium-sized tart pans or muffin cups. Prick bottom and sides of pastry with a fork.

Bake in preheated 450° oven for 10 to 12 minutes.

Cool.

LEMON FILLING:

Combine in top of double boiler

3 beaten eggs
1 cup sugar
½ cup soft butter *or* **margarine**
3 tablespoons finely grated lemon rind

Cook over boiling water for 5 minutes, stirring constantly.

Add

6 tablespoons lemon juice

Continue to cook over boiling water until mixture is smoothly thickened (about 5 minutes). Stir constantly.

Chill thoroughly.

Fill baked tart shells with the chilled Lemon Filling. Keep refrigerated until serving time.

Yield: 12 to 14 medium-sized tarts.

217   Fruit Tarts

Prepare and bake 12 to 14 medium-sized tart shells, using the Sweet Pastry (recipe No. 186), or a plain pastry recipe.

Fill the baked tart shells with one of the following:

1. GLAZED TARTS:

Drain one 15- or 20-ounce container of frozen or canned strawberries, raspberries, cherries, peaches, or pineapple chunks. Measure the syrup and add enough water to it to make 1 cup.

Combine 2 tablespoons sugar and 1 tablespoon cornstarch in a saucepan. Blend in the fruit syrup mixture. Place over medium heat and boil for 5 minutes, stirring constantly.

Add a few drops of food colouring, if desired. Cool slightly.

Fold in the drained fruit and divide among 12 or 14 baked tart shells. Chill.

Serve plain or topped with sweetened whipped cream or vanilla ice cream. Garnish with chopped nuts, cinnamon or coconut, as desired.

2. QUICK TARTS:

Divide a 20-ounce can prepared pie filling among the baked tart shells. (Cherry, raspberry, peach and strawberry pie fillings are suggestions.) Top with whipped cream or ice cream.

Desserts

**BAKED DESSERTS / STEAMED DESSERTS / MILK AND CEREAL DESSERTS
FRUIT DESSERTS / ICE CREAM AND FROZEN DESSERTS / GELATINE DESSERTS**

BAKED DESSERTS

218 BASIC RECIPES   *Sweet Biscuit Doughs*

A. DROP:

Blend or sift together
- 1¼ cups *Pre-Sifted* PURITY All-Purpose Flour
- 3 tablespoons sugar
- 3 teaspoons baking powder
- ¼ teaspoon salt

Cut in finely
- ⅓ cup shortening

Add
- 1 beaten egg
- ½ cup milk

Stir with a fork to make a drop batter.

Use as directed in the following dessert recipes which call for a Sweet Drop Biscuit Dough.

B. ROLLED:

Blend or sift together
- 2 cups *Pre-Sifted* PURITY All-Purpose Flour
- 2 tablespoons sugar
- 3½ teaspoons baking powder
- ½ teaspoon salt

Cut in finely
- ⅓ cup shortening

Add
- ¾ cup plus 2 tablespoons milk

Stir with a fork to make a soft dough.
Turn onto a lightly floured surface and knead gently 8 to 10 times.

Use as directed in the following dessert recipes which call for a Sweet Rolled Biscuit Dough.

---

219   *Fresh Berry Cobbler*

Preheat oven to 375°.

Prepare and wash fresh berries to make
- 2½ cups

Add
- ½ cup sugar

Set aside.

Blend together in a saucepan
- 2 tablespoons *Pre-Sifted* PURITY All-Purpose Flour
- ¾ cup cold water *or* fruit juice

Cook over medium heat until mixture comes to a boil, stirring constantly.

Add berry mixture and cook over low heat until just tender.

Pour hot mixture into a 1½-quart casserole.

Dot with
- 1 tablespoon butter *or* margarine

Add spices, if desired.

Prepare Sweet Drop Biscuit Dough (recipe No. 218A).

Drop from a spoon onto berry mixture. Do not stir.

Bake in preheated 375° oven for 35 to 40 minutes.

Serve hot, with cream if desired.

Yield: 5 to 6 servings.

VARIATION:

(a)   *Rhubarb Cobbler*

Prepare as directed above, cutting rhubarb into ½" pieces. Add from ¾ cup to 1 cup sugar, depending upon tartness of the rhubarb.

220   *Canned Fruit Cobbler*

Preheat oven to 375°.

Drain
- 1 (20-ounce) can sweetened fruit

(Cherries, pineapple chunks, sliced peaches, blueberries and raspberries are suggestions.)

Place in a 1½-quart casserole.

Measure the fruit syrup and add sufficient cold water to make

1 cup

Blend together in a saucepan

2 tablespoons *Pre-Sifted* PURITY All-Purpose Flour
Fruit syrup mixture

Cook over medium heat until mixture comes to a boil, stirring constantly.

Pour thickened syrup over the fruit.

Dot with

1 tablespoon butter *or* margarine

Add spices, if desired.

Prepare Sweet Drop Biscuit Dough (recipe No. 218A). Drop from a spoon onto fruit mixture. Do not stir.

Bake in preheated 375° oven for 35 to 40 minutes.

Serve hot, with cream if desired.

Yield: 5 to 6 servings.

VARIATION:

(a)   Quick Fruit Cobbler

Empty 1 (20-ounce) can fruit pie filling into a 1½-quart casserole. (Cherry, raspberry, strawberry and blueberry pie fillings are suggestions.) Dot with 1 tablespoon butter or margarine. Top with Sweet Drop Biscuit Dough and bake as directed above.

221   Apple Pandowdy

Preheat oven to 375°.

Blend together in a saucepan

1 cup lightly-packed brown sugar
¼ cup *Pre-Sifted* PURITY All-Purpose Flour
¼ teaspoon cinnamon
¼ teaspoon salt

Stir in

1 cup water

Cook over medium heat until mixture comes to a boil and has thickened slightly (8 to 10 minutes).

Stir in

2 tablespoons butter *or* margarine
1 teaspoon vanilla
1 teaspoon lemon juice

Set aside.

Wash and peel tart apples, slice to make

4 cups

Arrange apple slices in a greased 9″ square pan which is at least 2″ deep.

Pour sauce over the apples.

Prepare Sweet Drop Biscuit Dough (recipe No. 218A) and drop from a spoon over the fruit mixture. Do not stir.

Bake in preheated 375° oven for 35 to 45 minutes.

Serve warm, plain or with whipped cream or ice cream.

Yield: 6 servings.

222   Apple Dumplings

Preheat oven to 450°.

Mix together

¾ cup lightly-packed brown sugar
¾ teaspoon cinnamon
¾ teaspoon nutmeg
¼ cup raisins

Set aside.

Prepare Sweet Rolled Biscuit Dough (recipe No. 218B). Roll to a 12″ x 18″ rectangle and cut into six 6″ squares. Place a peeled, cored apple in the centre of each pastry square.

Fill apples with the sugar mixture. Dot with butter or margarine.

Moisten edges of dough with milk. Bring dough up around each apple; seal the edges to within ½″ of the top. Turn back the four corners to expose tops of apples. Place in a greased baking pan.

Bake in preheated 450° oven for 10 minutes. Baste the top of each apple with about 1 teaspoon corn syrup. Then reduce oven temperature to 375° and continue baking for 30 to 35 minutes.

Serve hot, with Brown Sugar Sauce.

Yield: 6 dumplings.

NOTE: Fresh whole peaches or pears may be used in place of the apples.

"Minute Melba" is yours to serve in record time. For each serving, place a drained, canned peach half (cut side up) on a slice of plain cake or jelly roll. Place a small scoop of vanilla ice cream on the peach and top with heated, strained raspberry jam. Allow about ¼ cup of jam per serving.

223   Roly-Poly Pudding

Preheat oven to 400°.

This can be made with a variety of fresh or canned fruits. Apples, fresh or canned peaches, and fresh blueberries are suggestions.

Wash and prepare the fruit (apples and peaches should be chopped).

Combine
> **2 cups prepared fruit**
> **½ cup sugar**
> **½ teaspoon cinnamon**

Prepare Sweet Rolled Biscuit Dough (recipe No. 218B). Roll to a 9″ x 12″ rectangle.

Spread with fruit mixture to within ½″ of the edges. Roll up like a jelly roll, starting from the longer side. Dampen edges and seal.

Place in a greased baking dish and tuck the ends under.

Bake in preheated 400° oven for 10 minutes, then lower the temperature to 350° and bake for another 25 to 30 minutes.

Serve hot, with Lemon Sauce or Fruit Syrup Sauce.

Yield: 6 servings.

224   Fruit Shortcake

Preheat oven to 450°.

Prepare Sweet Rolled Biscuit Dough (recipe No. 218B), replacing 1 tablespoon of the milk with 1 beaten egg yolk.

Roll or pat the kneaded dough to a 6″ x 9″ rectangle. Cut into six 3″ biscuits. Place on an ungreased baking sheet.

Bake in preheated 450° oven for 10 to 12 minutes.

Split the hot biscuits, butter if desired.

Place sweetened fruit between layers and over the top. Serve with whipped cream.

NOTE: If you prefer a family size shortcake, divide kneaded dough in two. Pat or roll one half to fit an 8″ round layer cake pan. Brush with soft butter or margarine. Pat out rest of dough and place on top. Bake in preheated 450° oven for 15 to 18 minutes. Split; fill and top with sweetened fruit and serve with whipped cream.

Yield: 6 servings.

VARIATION:

(a)   Crunchy Pecan Shortcake

Prepare as directed for Fruit Shortcake, adding ½ cup coarsely chopped pecans to the dry ingredients before adding the liquids. Bake as directed above. Serve with sliced peaches and whipped cream.

225   Sunshine Cobbler

Preheat oven to 450°.

Combine
> **1½ cups fresh *or* frozen rhubarb (thawed)**
> **⅓ cup water**

Cook until tender.

Add a few drops red food colouring to make ruby red.

Add
> **1 cup crushed pineapple, undrained**
> **½ cup sugar**

Bring to a boil. Remove from heat and set aside.

Combine
> **½ can frozen orange juice concentrate (6-ounce size)**
> **2 teaspoons grated grapefruit rind**

Spread this over bottom of a 9″ square baking pan. Add the hot fruit mixture.

TOPPING:

Blend or sift together
> **1¼ cups *Pre-Sifted* PURITY All-Purpose Flour**
> **2½ teaspoons baking powder**
> **¼ teaspoon salt**

Add
> **3 tablespoons brown sugar**

Cut in
> **¼ cup butter *or* margarine**

Stir in
> **4 to 5 tablespoons commercial sour cream**

Stir with a fork to make a soft dough. Turn onto a lightly floured surface and knead gently 8 to 10 times. Pat or roll to an 8″ square. Cut into six pieces and place these on top of the fruit mixture.

Bake in preheated 450° oven for 15 to 18 minutes.

Serve warm with whipped cream flavoured to taste with brown sugar and allspice.

Yield: 6 servings.

226   Apple Crisp

Preheat oven to 350°.

Mix together

**1 cup *Pre-Sifted* PURITY
All-Purpose Flour
1 cup rolled oats
1 cup lightly-packed brown sugar
1 teaspoon cinnamon**

Cut in

½ cup butter *or* margarine

Set aside.

Wash, peel and slice apples to make

4 cups

Mix about ¼ of the crumb mixture with the apples and spread in a buttered 8″ x 12″ baking dish. Cover with remaining crumbs and pat down slightly.

Bake in preheated 350° oven for 35 to 40 minutes or until apples are tender.

Serve hot or cold, with cream.

Yield: 6 to 8 servings.

VARIATION:

(a)   Quick Apple Crisp

Prepare as directed above, replacing sliced apples with a 20-ounce can apple pie filling. Bake in preheated 350° oven for 25 to 30 minutes or until golden brown.

227   Apple Brown Betty

Preheat oven to 350°.

Mix together

**¾ cup lightly-packed brown sugar
¼ teaspoon salt
¼ teaspoon cinnamon
¼ teaspoon nutmeg**

Wash and peel apples, slice to make

4 cups

Prepare

2 cups fresh bread crumbs

Toss with

3 tablespoons melted butter *or* margarine

Butter a 1½-quart casserole.

Arrange alternate layers of apples, bread crumbs and sugar mixture.

Combine

**¼ cup water
1 tablespoon lemon juice**

Pour over top of the mixture.

Cover the casserole and bake in preheated 350° oven for 30 minutes. Remove cover and cook for another 10 to 15 minutes or until the apples are tender.

Serve hot, plain or with cream.

Yield: 4 to 6 servings.

228   Hot Water Gingerbread

Preheat oven to 350°.

Cream together

**⅓ cup shortening
½ cup lightly-packed brown sugar**

Add

1 egg

Beat until light.

Blend or sift together

**1½ cups *Pre-Sifted* PURITY
All-Purpose Flour
1 teaspoon baking soda
¼ teaspoon salt
1 teaspoon ginger
½ teaspoon cinnamon**

Combine

**½ cup light molasses
½ cup hot water**

Add dry ingredients to the creamed mixture, alternately with the molasses and hot water.

Blend until well combined. Pour batter into a greased 8″ square pan.

Bake in preheated 350° oven for 40 to 45 minutes.

Serve warm, with spiced whipped cream or Foamy Applesauce.

229   Sour Milk Gingerbread

Preheat oven to 350°.

Cream together until light and fluffy

**⅓ cup shortening
⅓ cup lightly-packed brown sugar**

Then beat in

**¾ cup light molasses
1 beaten egg**

Blend or sift together

**2 cups *Pre-Sifted* PURITY
All-Purpose Flour
¾ teaspoon baking soda
½ teaspoon salt
1½ teaspoons ginger**

Add to molasses mixture, alternately with

¾ cup sour milk

Pour into a greased 9″ square pan.

Bake in preheated 350° oven for about 45 minutes.

Serve warm, with whipped cream or Foamy Applesauce.

230 *Cottage Pudding*

Preheat oven to 350°.

Cream thoroughly
    ⅓ cup shortening
    1 cup sugar

Add
    1 egg
    1 teaspoon vanilla

Beat until light and fluffy.

Blend or sift together
    1½ cups *Pre-Sifted* PURITY
        All-Purpose Flour
    2 teaspoons baking powder
    ½ teaspoon salt

Add to creamed mixture alternately with
    1 cup milk

Beat well after each addition.

Pour batter into a greased 8″ or 9″ square cake pan.

Bake in preheated 350° oven for 35 to 45 minutes.

Serve warm, with a sauce.

Yield: About 9 servings.

231 *Dutch Apple Cake*

Preheat oven to 400°.

Prepare Cottage Pudding batter (recipe No. 230), adding ¼ teaspoon nutmeg to the dry ingredients. Pour batter into a greased 8″ or 9″ square cake pan.

Wash, pare and core
    3 medium-sized tart apples

Cut each in eighths, lengthwise.

Arrange apple slices over the batter, lightly pressing in the sharp edges.

Sprinkle with a mixture of
    ¼ cup lightly-packed brown sugar
    ½ teaspoon cinnamon

Bake in preheated 400° oven for 35 to 40 minutes.

Serve hot, with thick pouring cream, whipped cream or a sauce.

Yield: About 9 servings.

VARIATION:

(a)   *Dutch Peach Cake*

Prepare as above, using 1 (20-ounce) can drained peach slices in place of the apples.

232 *Upside Down Cake*

Preheat oven to 350°.

Melt in an 8″ square baking pan
    3 tablespoons butter *or* margarine

Sprinkle with
    ½ cup lightly-packed brown sugar

Cover with one of the following:

1. **Apple:** Slice 3 peeled apples over the sugar mixture.
2. **Peach:** Arrange 1 (20-ounce) can drained peach slices over the sugar mixture.
3. **Pineapple:** Place pineapple rings over the sugar mixture. Fill centres with cherries or nuts, if desired.
4. **Rhubarb:** Increase sugar to ¾ cup. Cover sugar mixture with 2 cups diced rhubarb.

Prepare batter for Cottage Pudding (recipe No. 230) and pour over the fruit.

Bake in preheated 350° oven for 40 to 50 minutes.

Invert at once on a serving plate.

Serve warm, with cream or a sauce, if desired.

Yield: About 9 servings.

233 *Lemon Sponge*

Preheat oven to 325°.

Cream together
    1 tablespoon butter *or* margarine
    ¾ cup sugar

Blend in
    3 tablespoons *Pre-Sifted* PURITY
        All-Purpose Flour
    ¼ teaspoon baking powder
    Few grains salt

Beat until thick
    2 egg yolks

Add
    2 teaspoons grated lemon rind
    ¼ cup lemon juice

Blend into the creamed mixture, then add
    1 cup scalded milk

Beat to soft peaks
    2 egg whites

Then beat in
    ¼ cup sugar

Fold egg yolk mixture into the whites. Pour into a 1½-quart casserole. Place casserole in a shallow pan of hot water.

Bake in preheated 325° oven for about 55 minutes.

Serve warm or cold.

Yield: 4 to 6 servings.

234   Saucy Mocha Pudding

Preheat oven to 350°.

Combine in top of double boiler
- ¼ cup cocoa
- ½ cup granulated sugar
- ½ cup lightly-packed brown sugar
- 3 tablespoons *Pre-Sifted* PURITY All-Purpose Flour

Gradually stir in
- 2 cups hot coffee

Keep hot over simmering water.

CAKE BATTER:

Cream together
- ⅓ cup shortening
- ⅔ cup granulated sugar

Add
- 1 egg
- ½ teaspoon vanilla

Beat until light and fluffy.

Blend or sift together
- 1 cup *Pre-Sifted* PURITY All-Purpose Flour
- 1½ teaspoons baking powder
- ¼ teaspoon salt

Add to creamed mixture, alternately with
- ⅓ cup milk

Combine well.

Turn batter into a greased 8″ square cake pan.

Pour hot coffee mixture over the batter. Do not stir.

Bake in preheated 350° oven for 45 to 50 minutes.

Serve warm.

Yield: About 6 servings.

235   Jelly Roll

Preheat oven to 400°.

Grease a 15 x 10 x 1-inch jelly roll pan and line with wax paper.

Whip until very thick and lemony
- 4 eggs

Beat in
- 1 teaspoon lemon juice
- 1 cup sugar

Meanwhile, scald together
- ¼ cup milk
- 1 tablespoon butter

Blend or sift together
- 1 cup *Pre-Sifted* PURITY All-Purpose Flour
- 1 teaspoon baking powder
- ¼ teaspoon salt

Sift dry ingredients over egg mixture alternately with hot milk, folding in gently after each addition. Turn into prepared pan.

Bake in preheated 400° oven for 10 to 12 minutes. Turn out immediately on towel sprinkled with icing sugar. Remove wax paper and roll, rolling towel up in cake. Cool. Unroll, fill with jam, jelly or filling and re-roll.

NOTE: Lemon Filling (recipe No. 114) or Cream Filling (recipe No. 113) may be used in this roll. Refrigerate until serving time. For variety, fold sliced strawberries into the cream filling.

236   Chocolate Roll

Preheat oven to 375°.

Beat until stiff but not dry
- 4 egg whites
- ½ teaspoon salt

Gradually beat in
- ½ cup sugar

Set aside.

Beat until thick
- 4 egg yolks

Gradually beat in
- ½ cup sugar

Then slowly stir in
- ¼ cup hot water
- 1 teaspoon vanilla

Carefully fold egg yolk mixture into the beaten whites.

Pineapple Upside-down Cake — listen for the 'Oohs' and 'Aahs' when you serve it (Recipe No. 232)

Blend or sift together
**½ cup *Pre-Sifted* PURITY
All-Purpose Flour
⅓ cup cocoa
1 teaspoon baking powder**

Gradually sift or sprinkle dry ingredients over the egg mixture and carefully fold in with a spatula.

Grease a 10″ x 15″ jelly roll pan and line bottom with waxed paper. Spread batter evenly in the pan.

Bake in preheated 375° oven for about 18 minutes.

Turn out at once onto a clean tea towel which has been dusted with icing sugar. Remove waxed paper and cut away any crisp edges. Starting from the narrow edge, roll up in the towel. Cool on a rack.

When cool, unroll and spread with ½ pint whipping cream which has been whipped and flavoured to taste, or spread with Marshmallow Filling (recipe No. 115). Roll up again.

NOTE: If whipped cream is used for filling, refrigerate until serving time and serve all of the roll the same day that it is made.

237   Almond Chiffon Roll

ALMOND FILLING:

Combine in top part of double boiler
**¼ cup sugar
¼ cup *Pre-Sifted* PURITY
All-Purpose Flour**

Gradually blend in
¾ cup milk

Cook over low direct heat, stirring constantly, until mixture comes to a boil and starts to thicken.

Add some of the hot mixture to
1 slightly-beaten egg yolk

Return to double boiler top and cook over boiling water for 2 minutes, stirring constantly. Remove from heat and cool.

Then gradually beat in
¼ cup soft butter *or* margarine
Add
**¼ cup slivered blanched almonds
1 teaspoon vanilla**

Chill thoroughly.

CHIFFON ROLL:

Preheat oven to 325°.

Beat until frothy
½ cup egg whites
Sprinkle with
¼ teaspoon cream of tartar

Continue to beat until stiff peaks are formed. Do not underbeat.

Blend or sift together
**1 cup *Pre-Sifted* PURITY
All-Purpose Flour
¾ cup sugar
1½ teaspoons baking powder
½ teaspoon salt**
Add
**¼ cup vegetable oil
2 egg yolks
2 teaspoons grated orange rind
¼ cup orange juice
2 tablespoons water
½ teaspoon vanilla**

Beat this mixture until smooth.

Gradually pour batter over the beaten egg whites, folding in gently after each addition.

Grease a 10″ x 15″ jelly roll pan and line bottom with waxed paper. Spread batter evenly in the pan.

Bake in preheated 325° oven for 20 to 25 minutes, or until cake springs back when lightly touched in the centre. Turn out at once on a clean tea towel which has been dusted with icing sugar. Remove waxed paper and trim off any crisp edges.

Spread with chilled Almond Filling. Roll up starting at the narrow side. Make a firm roll and wrap tightly in the tea towel. Chill before serving.

238   Boston Cream Pie

Preheat oven to 350°.

Beat until light and foamy
3 eggs
Gradually beat in
**¼ cup milk
1 cup sugar**
Continue beating until thick and light.

Blend or sift together
**1⅔ cups *Pre-Sifted* PURITY
All-Purpose Flour
2 teaspoons baking powder
½ teaspoon salt**

Gradually sift or sprinkle dry ingredients over the egg mixture, folding them in with a spatula.

Divide batter between 2 greased 8″ layer cake pans.

Bake in preheated 350° oven for 25 to 30 minutes.

Fill cooled layers with Cream Filling (recipe No. 113). Chill.

Serve, dusted with icing sugar or topped with whipped cream.

239 French Riviera Torte

Preheat oven to 350°.

Beat until stiff but not dry
5 egg whites

Set aside.

Beat until frothy
5 egg yolks

Gradually add
1 cup sugar

alternately with
¼ cup cold water

Continue beating until well blended.

Blend or sift together
1¼ cups *Pre-Sifted* PURITY All-Purpose Flour
1¼ teaspoons baking powder
¼ teaspoon salt

Add dry ingredients to the egg yolk mixture, one-quarter at a time. Blend after each addition.

Fold in
Stiffly-beaten whites
½ teaspoon vanilla

Divide batter among 4 well-greased 8″ round layer cake pans.

Bake in preheated 350° oven for 25 to 30 minutes.

Allow to cool for 10 minutes before removing from the pans. Cool thoroughly before filling and icing the Torte.

VANILLA CREAM FILLING:

Combine in a saucepan
½ cup sugar
⅓ cup *Pre-Sifted* PURITY All-Purpose Flour

Gradually add
1½ cups milk

Cook over medium heat until thickened, stirring constantly. Cool.

Cream
½ cup butter *or* margarine

Gradually beat in
Cooled milk mixture
½ teaspoon vanilla

Chill.

Place filling between layers of the Torte and allow to set before icing.

MOCHA ICING:

Cream
¼ cup butter *or* margarine

Add
2 tablespoons milk
¼ cup cold strong coffee
1 teaspoon vanilla
1 tablespoon cocoa

Blend well.

Gradually beat in about
4 cups sifted icing sugar

Beat until icing is of spreading consistency. Ice top and sides of the Torte.

Chill until serving time.

240 Cream Puffs

Preheat oven to 375°.

Combine in a saucepan
½ cup butter *or* margarine
1 cup boiling water

Bring to a boil.

Add all at once
1 cup *Pre-Sifted* PURITY All-Purpose Flour
¼ teaspoon salt

Beat vigorously until mixture leaves the sides of the pan. Remove from the heat and cool slightly.

Then add, one at a time
4 unbeaten eggs

Beat until smooth after adding each egg. Beat until glossy.

Drop batter from a spoon onto greased baking sheets, mounding each and swirling the top. Space at least 2″ apart.

Bake in preheated 375° oven for 30 to 40 minutes, or until light and dry.

Allow to cool slowly away from drafts.

Fill with flavoured whipped cream or a cream filling. Dust with icing sugar. Serve chilled.

Yield: 18 medium-sized cream puffs.

NOTE: For 8 to 10 large puffs, bake for 45 to 55 minutes. These may be split with a sharp knife, filled with ice cream and topped with sauce.

For small cream puffs (bouchées), bake for 25 to 30 minutes. (This recipe will make 3 to 4 dozen.) These may be served warm with a cream filling, or cold with a salad filling.

To Store: Place in a cookie tin and cover with a tea towel.

VARIATION:

(a) Éclairs

Prepare batter as for Cream Puffs. Shape on greased baking sheet into strips which are 4″ long and 1″ wide. Bake in preheated 375° oven for 45 to 50 minutes. Cool away from drafts.

Split and fill with Cream Filling (recipe No. 113) or ice cream. Top with Chocolate Glaze. Yield: 12 éclairs.

241 Dessert Meringues

Preheat oven to 250°.

Beat to soft peaks
   4 egg whites
   ¼ teaspoon cream of tartar
Gradually beat in
   1 cup fruit sugar
Beat until sugar dissolves and the meringue is stiff and glossy. Do not underbeat.
Fold in
   ½ teaspoon vanilla
Cover baking sheets with brown paper.

For each shell, drop about ⅓ cup meringue onto the brown paper. Using the back of a spoon, shape into shells. If you prefer, a pastry tube may be used for shaping the shells. Bake in preheated 250° oven for 1 hour. Turn off heat and leave meringues in the oven, door ajar, until cooled to room temperature.

Fill with ice cream and sweetened fruit.

Yield: 12 meringues.

NOTE: Food colouring may be added with the vanilla. To shape meringues for special occasions, such as St. Valentine's Day, draw appropriate outlines on the brown paper and shape the meringues to fit.

A single large meringue may be shaped on brown paper or in a lined 9″ pie plate. Fill and cut into wedges for serving.

To Store: Place in container and cover with tea towel.

_____

For a quick and attractive dessert, fill sherbets with cubes of varied-coloured jelly. Prepare 2 or 3 different jelly powders as directed and chill separately in 8″ square pans. Cut the jelly into ¾″ squares and lift out with a spatula.

242 Cheese Cake

Preheat oven to 350°.
Combine
   1½ cups graham cracker crumbs
   3 tablespoons sugar
   ¼ teaspoon cinnamon
Blend in
   ¼ cup melted butter *or* margarine
Press the crumb mixture firmly against the bottom and sides of a well-greased 9″ spring form pan, to the height of 1½″.
Chill the shell.
Beat thoroughly
   2 eggs
Then beat in
   ⅓ cup sugar
Add
   ½ teaspoon vanilla
   1 teaspoon grated lemon rind
   ½ teaspoon lemon juice
Gradually beat in
   ¾ pound softened cream cheese
Then beat in
   1½ cups commercial sour cream
Fold in
   2 tablespoons melted butter
Pour batter into prepared shell.
Bake in preheated 350° oven for 40 to 45 minutes.
Turn off the heat, open the oven door and leave cheese cake in the oven until cool.
Remove from pan. Chill for several hours before serving.

_____

For a flavour special, add drained mandarin orange sections and finely chopped preserved ginger to orange jelly powder.

STEAMED DESSERTS

243 Christmas Plum Pudding

Combine in a large bowl
- **4 cups seeded raisins**
- **2 cups seedless raisins**
- **1½ cups currants**
- **1 cup glacé cherries, halved**
- **1 cup candied peel, chopped**
- **½ cup chopped apple**
- **1 cup ground suet**
- **1 cup fine dry bread crumbs**
- **2 teaspoons grated lemon rind**

Flour the mixture and shake off the excess.

Beat until light
- **2 eggs**

Gradually beat in
- **½ cup sugar**

Blend in
- **½ cup light molasses**
- **½ cup milk**
- **½ teaspoon lemon extract**

Blend or sift together
- **1¼ cups *Pre-Sifted* PURITY All-Purpose Flour**
- **½ teaspoon baking soda**
- **1 teaspoon salt**
- **1½ teaspoons cinnamon**
- **½ teaspoon nutmeg**
- **¼ teaspoon mace**

Gradually combine the dry ingredients and egg mixture. Blend thoroughly.

Fold in the fruit mixture.

Divide batter between two 1-quart moulds which have been well-greased. Cover with aluminum foil and tie in place.

Steam for 2½ hours.

Cool thoroughly before storing. This pudding should be allowed to ripen for at least a month before serving. It will keep for months.

To reheat, steam for about 1 hour.

Serve hot, with Hard Sauce.

NOTE: This pudding may be steamed in four 20-ounce cans which have been well-greased. Reduce steaming time to about 1¾ hours.

For variety, try serving your festive steamed puddings with Lemon Sauce topped with Hard Sauce.

Small steamed puddings make attractive gifts. Cool thoroughly, wrap in saran and then in gay paper.

244 Carrot Pudding

Blend or sift together
- **¾ cup *Pre-Sifted* PURITY All-Purpose Flour**
- **½ teaspoon baking powder**
- **¾ teaspoon salt**
- **¾ teaspoon cinnamon**
- **¼ teaspoon allspice**

Stir in
- **¾ cup raisins**
- **¾ cup currants**

Combine well to coat the fruit. Set aside.

Cream together
- **⅓ cup butter *or* margarine**
- **⅓ cup lightly-packed brown sugar**

Dissolve
- **½ teaspoon baking soda**

in
- **1 well-beaten egg**

Gradually add to the creamed mixture.

Stir in
- **¾ cup grated raw carrot**
- **¾ cup grated raw potato**
- **¾ cup soft bread crumbs**

Add fruit mixture and combine thoroughly.

Turn batter into a well-greased 1-quart mould. Cover with aluminum foil and tie in place.

Steam for 2½ hours, then uncover and place in a preheated 350° oven for 10 minutes.

Recover and store in refrigerator.

To reheat, steam for about 1 hour.

Serve hot, with Lemon Sauce or Hard Sauce.

If you prefer individual steamed puddings, divide pudding batter among greased custard cups or small pudding moulds, filling each about ⅔ full. Cover each with aluminum foil and tie in place. Steam for about 1 hour. To reheat the individual puddings, steam for about 30 minutes.

245 Steamed Chocolate Pudding

Cream together
  ¼ cup shortening
  1 cup sugar
Add
  1 egg
Beat well.
Then add
  2 squares unsweetened chocolate, melted
Blend or sift together
  2¼ cups Pre-Sifted PURITY All-Purpose Flour
  4 teaspoons baking powder
  ½ teaspoon salt
Add to creamed mixture, alternately with
  1 cup milk
Mix well after each addition.

Turn batter into a greased 1-quart mould and steam for 2 hours.

Serve hot, with Marshmallow Sauce.

246 Steamed Fruit Pudding

Combine
  1 beaten egg
  ¼ cup lightly-packed brown sugar
  ½ cup corn syrup or light molasses
Beat well.
Then blend in
  ½ cup milk
Blend or sift together
  1½ cups Pre-Sifted PURITY All-Purpose Flour
  ½ teaspoon baking soda
  1 teaspoon salt
  ¾ teaspoon cinnamon
  ¼ teaspoon nutmeg
Add to liquid mixture and beat thoroughly.
Fold in
  ½ cup ground suet
  1 cup floured raisins, currants or chopped dates
Turn into a greased 1-quart mould. Cover with aluminum foil and tie in place.
Steam for 2½ hours. Cool thoroughly before storing.
To reheat, steam for about 1 hour.
Serve hot, with Lemon Sauce.

VARIATIONS:

(a) Ginger Pudding

Prepare as for Steamed Fruit Pudding, substituting 1½ teaspoons ground ginger for the spices. Use light molasses rather than the corn syrup. Steam in a 1-quart mould, as directed. Serve hot, with a sauce.

(b) Apple Pudding

Prepare as directed for Steamed Fruit Pudding, substituting whole wheat or graham flour for the Pre-Sifted PURITY All-Purpose Flour. Use corn syrup rather than molasses. Use only ½ cup floured dry fruit and add 1½ cups chopped apples. Steam in a 1-quart mould, as directed. Serve hot, with a sauce.

247 Crumb Pudding

Cream together
  ½ cup shortening
  ¾ cup lightly-packed brown sugar
Beat in
  1 egg
Add
  ¾ cup sour milk or buttermilk
Blend or sift together
  1 cup Pre-Sifted PURITY All-Purpose Flour
  ¾ teaspoon baking soda
  ½ teaspoon salt
  ¾ teaspoon cinnamon
Add to the liquid ingredients and beat thoroughly.
Fold in
  1½ cups fine dry bread crumbs
  1 cup chopped apples
  1 cup floured raisins, currants or chopped dates
Turn batter into a greased 1½-quart mould. Cover with aluminum foil and tie in place.
Steam for 2½ hours. Cool thoroughly before storing.
To reheat, steam for about 1¼ hours.
Serve hot, with Lemon Sauce.

VARIATION:

(a) Cranberry Pudding

Prepare as for Crumb Pudding, substituting 1 cup fresh cranberries, halved, and ¼ cup minced orange for the dried fruit. Steam, as directed above, and serve hot, with Fruit Syrup Sauce.

MILK AND CEREAL DESSERTS

248 Soft Custard

In top of double boiler, scald
2 cups milk

Meanwhile, beat slightly
3 eggs or 6 yolks

Add
¼ cup sugar
¼ teaspoon salt

Gradually stir in a little of the scalded milk.

Return to double boiler top and cook over simmering water, stirring constantly, until the custard coats a metal spoon.

Remove from heat, strain, and stir in
½ teaspoon vanilla

Chill.

Yield: 4 to 6 servings.

NOTE: If custard should curdle with over-cooking, pour it quickly into a cold bowl and beat with an egg beater. This should restore the smoothness, but it will be less thick.

This may be used as a rich Custard Sauce for desserts.

249 Trifle Pudding

A light, plain cake or sponge cake may be used.

Cut one-half of an 8″ or 9″ cake into ½″ slices. Spread sliced cake with raspberry jam.

Sprinkle generously with fruit juice or sherry.

Allow to stand for 3 hours.

Prepare Soft Custard (recipe No. 248).

In large serving bowl, arrange alternate layers of cake slices and custard.

Chill thoroughly.

Serve with sweetened whipped cream, and garnish with toasted almonds.

Yield: 5 to 6 servings.

250 Floating Island

Scald in top of double boiler
1 cup milk

Meanwhile, beat slightly
3 egg yolks

Add
2 tablespoons sugar
⅛ teaspoon salt

Gradually stir in a little of the hot milk.

Return to double boiler top and cook over simmering water, stirring constantly, until the custard coats a metal spoon.

Remove from heat, strain and stir in
¼ teaspoon vanilla

Pour custard into serving dish. Chill.

Beat until frothy
3 egg whites

Gradually add
6 tablespoons sugar

Beat until stiff peaks form.

Drop meringue by large spoonfuls onto a pan of hot water. Brown in a 400° oven, 3 to 5 minutes. Carefully lift from water and place on custard.

Garnish with fresh strawberries, if desired.

Yield: 4 to 6 servings.

Baked custard made with homogenized milk requires longer baking time, but is firmer than that made with non-homogenized milk.

251 Baked Custard

Preheat oven to 350°.

Scald
2 cups milk

Beat slightly
3 eggs or 6 yolks

Add
¼ cup sugar
¼ teaspoon salt
½ teaspoon vanilla

Gradually pour the hot milk over the egg mixture, stirring constantly.

Stir until sugar is thoroughly dissolved.

Pour into buttered individual custard cups, set in a pan of hot water.

Sprinkle each with a dash of nutmeg, if desired.

Bake in preheated 350° oven for 30 minutes, or until just firm in centre.

To test baked custard for doneness, insert a knife or metal skewer in centre. If it comes out clean, the custard is baked. Do not overcook.

Yield: 5 to 6 servings.

252   Lemon Fluff

Scald in double boiler top
  1½ cups milk
Combine
  ¾ cup sugar
  6 tablespoons *Pre-Sifted* **PURITY All-Purpose Flour**
  ¼ teaspoon salt
Add
  ½ cup cold milk
Stir to make a smooth paste.
Gradually stir into the hot milk.
Cook over direct heat, stirring constantly, until mixture begins to boil.
Add a little of the hot mixture to
  2 slightly-beaten egg yolks
Return to double boiler and cook over boiling water for 2 minutes. Stirring constantly.
Cool slightly and add
  ½ teaspoon vanilla
  ⅓ cup lemon juice
  1 teaspoon grated lemon rind
Fold in
  2 stiffly-beaten egg whites
Chill before serving.
Yield: 6 to 8 servings.

253 Blanc Mange Pudding

Scald
  1½ cups milk
Combine
  ⅓ cup *Pre-Sifted* **PURITY All-Purpose Flour**
  ¼ cup sugar
  ¼ teaspoon salt
Add
  ½ cup cold milk
Stir to make a smooth paste.
Gradually stir into the hot milk.
Cook over direct heat, stirring constantly, until mixture begins to boil.
Cool slightly and add
  1 teaspoon vanilla
Chill thoroughly and serve with fresh or preserved fruit.
Yield: 4 servings.

VARIATION:

(a)   Butterscotch Blanc Mange
Prepare as for Blanc Mange Pudding, substituting brown sugar for granulated and 1½ teaspoons butterscotch flavouring for vanilla.

––––––––––

To colour coconut: Add food colouring to 1 teaspoon water and toss the coconut until evenly coloured.

254   Chocolate Soufflé

Preheat oven to 350°.
Melt in double boiler top
  3 tablespoons butter or margarine
Blend in
  3 tablespoons *Pre-Sifted* **PURITY All-Purpose Flour**
  ⅛ teaspoon salt
Gradually add
  1 cup milk
Cook, stirring constantly, until smoothly thickened.
Beat until creamy
  3 egg yolks
Gradually beat in
  6 tablespoons sugar
Add a little of the hot mixture to the yolks.
Return to double boiler top and cook over hot water for 2 minutes, stirring constantly.
Remove from heat and add
  1 teaspoon vanilla
  1 ounce unsweetened chocolate, melted
Cool.
Carefully fold in
  3 stiffly-beaten egg whites
Turn into buttered 1½-quart soufflé dish, set in a shallow pan of hot water. Bake in preheated 350° oven for 45 to 50 minutes or until firm.
Serve at once with whipped cream.
Yield: 6 servings.

255   Tapioca Cream

Combine in saucepan
  3 tablespoons minute tapioca
  2 tablespoons sugar
  1 beaten egg yolk
  2 cups milk
  ⅛ teaspoon salt
Cook over moderate heat, stirring constantly, until mixture comes to a full boil.
Remove from heat.

Beat until stiff
1 egg white
Gradually beat in
2 tablespoons sugar
½ teaspoon vanilla
Gradually fold tapioca mixture into meringue.
Serve warm or chilled, with cream.
Yield: 4 to 5 servings.
NOTE: Quick-cooking sago may be used in place of tapioca in this recipe.

VARIATION:

(a)   Chocolate Tapioca

Add 2½ tablespoons instant chocolate drink powder to milk in above recipe.

256   Creamy Rice Pudding

Combine in top of double boiler
1½ cups cooked rice
1 cup milk
2 slightly-beaten eggs
⅓ cup sugar
Cook over simmering water, stirring constantly, until mixture coats a metal spoon.
Remove from heat.
Add
1 tablespoon butter *or* margarine
1 teaspoon vanilla
⅓ cup raisins, currants *or* chopped dates
Pour into serving bowl and allow to stand, without stirring, for 30 minutes.
Serve warm or chilled, with cream.
Yield: 5 to 6 servings.

257   Old-Fashioned Rice Pudding

Preheat oven to 325°.
Combine in a buttered 1½-quart casserole
½ cup uncooked regular rice
3 cups milk
¼ cup sugar
½ teaspoon salt
1 tablespoon butter *or* margarine
1 teaspoon vanilla
Few grains nutmeg
Stir until sugar is dissolved.
Bake in preheated 325° oven for 1 hour, stirring every 20 minutes.

At the end of the hour, add
½ cup raisins
Bake for another 15 minutes.
Serve warm with cream.
Yield: 5 to 6 servings.

258   Baked Rice Custard

Preheat oven to 350°.
Beat until light
3 egg yolks
Gradually stir in
2 cups hot milk
Add
¼ cup sugar
1 teaspoon vanilla
¼ teaspoon salt
Stir until sugar is dissolved.
Add
⅔ cup cooked rice
Pour into a buttered 1-quart baking dish.
Place in a shallow pan of hot water.
Bake in preheated 350° oven for 60 minutes or until just firm.
Beat until stiff
3 egg whites
Gradually beat in
6 tablespoons sugar
Pile meringue on rice custard and brown in a 400° oven for 7 to 8 minutes.
Serve warm, with cream or fresh fruit.
Yield: 6 servings.

259   Hawaiian Rice

Combine in a bowl
1½ cups cooked rice
1 cup miniature *or* quartered marshmallows
¾ cup well-drained crushed pineapple
Chill 2 to 3 hours.
Beat until stiff
½ pint whipping cream
Fold in
3 tablespoons sugar
Fold sweetened whipped cream lightly into rice mixture. Garnish with red maraschino cherries, almonds or toasted coconut.
Yield: 6 servings.

FRUIT DESSERTS

260 Stewed Fresh Fruits
(Apples, cherries, pears, peaches, plums, rhubarb, etc.)

Wash fruit and remove stems, hulls, leaves, and any spoiled portions. Remove cores or stones from larger fruit, pare, and cut into ½″ slices. Place in a saucepan and add water to about 1″ below the top of the fruit. Simmer until fruit is tender. Add sugar to taste and cook 2 minutes longer. Cool.

For added flavour, a few drops of lemon juice or a dash of nutmeg, cinnamon or ground cloves may be added with the sugar.

261 Stewed Dried Fruits
(Prunes, apricots, peaches)

Rinse fruit. Cover with hot water and simmer until tender (approximately 30 to 40 minutes). Add sugar to taste and cook 2 minutes longer. Cool.

NOTE: Certain dried fruits are packed with extra moisture (see label) and should be cooked for a shorter length of time.

Cooking time may be reduced, also, by covering the fruit with boiling water and allowing it to soak for 1 hour. Cook in the same water. For added flavour, a slice of lemon, a piece of ginger or a few cloves may be added.

262 Fruit Whip
(Banana, peach, apple, apricot, prune)

Purée or mash sweetened drained fruit to make
> **1 cup**

(Canned baby fruits may be used.)
Add
> **1 tablespoon lemon juice**

Beat until frothy
> **2 egg whites**

Beat in
> **¼ teaspoon cream of tartar**
> **¼ cup sugar**

Fold meringue into fruit pulp.
Serve with Custard Sauce.
Yield: 4 servings.

VARIATION:

(a) Baked Fruit Whip
Prepare Fruit Whip as in above recipe. Turn into a buttered 1-quart casserole and bake in preheated 325° oven for 30 to 35 minutes. Serve immediately with Custard Sauce.

263 Apple Compote

Boil together for 5 minutes in a broad saucepan
> **1 cup sugar**
> **2 cups water**
> **1 slice lemon or**
> **1 piece stick cinnamon**

Remove lemon or cinnamon.
Pare and core
> **4 large apples**

Slice thickly, quarter, or section the apples.

Stew a few pieces of apple at a time in the syrup. Carefully turn fruit to cook both sides.

Lift from syrup when tender.

When apples are cooked, boil syrup for about 5 minutes, or until slightly thickened. Pour over fruit and serve hot or chilled.

If desired, the apples may be left whole and the centres filled with jelly to serve.

Yield: 4 servings.

NOTE: Peaches, pears and oranges may be prepared by the above method.

VARIATION:

(a) Rosy Apple Compote
Dissolve ¼ cup red cinnamon candies in the syrup in the above recipe.

264 Strained Applesauce

Use tart, well flavoured apples which break up readily on cooking. Wash, remove stems and blossom ends. Cut in quarters. Place in saucepan, and add water to about 1″ below the top of the fruit. Simmer until the fruit is tender. Press fruit through a purée or coarse sieve. Add sugar to taste and a dash of salt. Cook 3 minutes longer, stirring frequently.

Spiced fruit is a welcome change for dessert. Drain a suitable size can of peaches or pears and simmer the juice for 10 minutes with a piece of stick cinnamon and a few whole cloves. Strain, pour over fruit and refrigerate until cold.

265   Baked Apples

Preheat oven to 375°.

For baking, select large tart apples. Wash and remove cores. Slash skin around top or pare a ½″ band of skin from the top of each apple. Arrange in a baking dish and fill the centre of each with approximately 1 tablespoon of granulated or brown sugar, or maple syrup. Top with a small piece of butter or margarine. Add water to a depth of about ½″.

Bake in preheated 375° oven until tender (30 to 60 minutes, depending on variety of apple). Serve hot or chilled, with cream.

VARIATION:

(a)   Baked Stuffed Apples

The cavity in the centre of the apple may be filled with one of the following: mincemeat, raisins, cranberry sauce, chopped dates or prunes with nuts. Bake as above.

266   Caramel Apples

Pare, core and halve
   6 apples

Arrange in large flat pan or skillet.

Sprinkle with
   ¾ cup lightly-packed brown sugar
   2 tablespoons melted butter or
      margarine
   ⅓ cup raisins
Add
   ⅓ cup water

Cook over low heat until the apples are tender. Turn apples to cook both sides.

Baste frequently with the caramel syrup.

Serve warm with cream.

Yield: 6 servings.

267   Baked Bananas

Preheat oven to 350°.

Remove the skins from slightly under-ripe bananas. Cut in halves lengthwise or leave whole. Place bananas in a buttered baking dish. Sprinkle with lemon juice, brown sugar and melted butter, allowing about 1 teaspoon of each for a banana. Bake in preheated 350° oven for about 20 minutes or until tender.

268   Fried Bananas

Remove the skins from slightly under-ripe bananas. Cut in halves lengthwise. Fry in shortening in a moderately hot pan, turning to brown both sides. Cook until tender, approximately 3 to 5 minutes on each side. Serve as dessert with Lemon Sauce or as a meat accompaniment.

NOTE: Sliced cored apples or sliced canned pineapple may be prepared by the above method.

269   Broiled Grapefruit

Cut grapefruit in half and remove seeds. Cut around each section, then remove membrane at the core with scissors. Sprinkle each half with brown sugar and dot with butter or margarine. Broil until lightly browned. Serve immediately, garnished with a maraschino cherry. If desired, a tablespoon of sherry may be added to each half just before serving.

Don't overlook the delightful eating of whole fresh or frozen strawberries served on a mound of commercial sour cream. Sprinkle the berries with fruit sugar.

270   Winter Fruit Cup

Drain and save syrup from
   1 (11-ounce) can mandarin oranges
   1 (15-ounce) can grapefruit sections
   1 (15-ounce) can pineapple (crushed
      or tid bits)
Combine drained fruits and add
   2 bananas, sliced
Chill.

About 30 minutes before serving, pour combined fruit juices into ice cube tray.

Freeze until mushy. Mixture freezes quickly and should not be hard.

To serve, spoon fruits into 6 sherbet glasses and top with partially frozen juices. Garnish with maraschino cherries.

Serve immediately.

Yield: 6 servings.

For a new touch in fruit cups, combine the usual fruits, drained, and top with a sauce made by heating 1 cup raspberry jam with 1 teaspoon lemon juice. Strain and pour over fruit, allowing about ¼ cup sauce per serving.

ICE CREAM AND FROZEN DESSERTS

So Easy To Buy: Delicious ice cream is available prepackaged in pint, half-gallon and gallon containers. The larger the carton, the more economical the buy, but of course you must have proper facilities for storage.

So Easy To Keep: A freezer (in combination with a refrigerator, or separate) is best suited for ice cream storage. Store unopened containers in the coldest section—against the freezing coils or shelves. Allow to stand at room temperature for a few minutes for easier serving.

Reseal opened containers tightly to prevent loss of flavour and accumulation of ice crystals. Ice cream desserts should be wrapped carefully to protect flavour, and stored in the coldest part of the freezer.

Ice cream may be stored for two or three days in a conventional refrigerator. It will stay firmer if removed from the carton and stored in ice cube trays. Cover tightly with waxed paper or foil. If necessary, turn down the temperature control for a few hours. If the temperature is lowered for a longer period, it may freeze foods in the refrigerator section.

So Easy To Use: What could be easier than serving ice cream in such a wide variety of flavours. Once in a while, however, for a family treat or special occasion, you may want to "dress up" ice cream a little.

---

271   Ice Cream

Snow Balls: Scoop out ice cream balls, then roll in fine cake crumbs, chocolate shot, finely chopped nuts, toasted coconut, or finely crushed peanut brittle. Store in freezer until serving time.

Parfaits: In parfait or sherbet glasses, alternate layers of ice cream with sauce and sherbet. Top with whipped cream. For a delightful dessert, try a combination of coffee ice cream, orange sherbet and marshmallow sauce; or vanilla ice cream, drained crushed pineapple and frozen orange juice concentrate, thawed.

Ripple: Turn softened pint of vanilla ice cream into ice cube tray, lined, if desired, with graham cracker crumb pie shell mixture. Swirl in one of the following:

    1 cup strawberries *or* raspberries, fresh or frozen (thawed)

    ⅔ cup thawed frozen orange *or* grape juice concentrate

    1 cup broken ginger snaps *or* macaroons

    ¼ cup chopped candied pineapple mixed with ¼ cup chopped maraschino cherries and ¼ cup blanched slivered almonds

272   French Ice Cream
(For Dasher Type Freezer)

Scald can and dasher. Assemble the freezer. Pack with ice and salt mixture. (Six parts ice to one part salt is the usual proportion.)

Scald in top of double boiler

    2½ cups milk

Beat slightly

    2 eggs

Add

    1 cup sugar
    ¼ teaspoon salt

Mix a little of the hot milk with the egg mixture and then return to double boiler top.

Cook over simmering water, stirring constantly, until custard coats a metal spoon. Remove from heat, strain and cool.

Add

    4 cups 18% cream
    1 tablespoon vanilla

Pour mixture into cold freezer can, filling no more than ¾ full. Cover securely and let stand until thoroughly chilled.

Then turn slowly until the ice cream is firm. Add additional ice and salt mixture to the tub as required.

When frozen, drain water from the tub, remove dasher and crank. Scrape ice cream from sides of can. Replace the cover and seal, being careful that no brine gets into the ice cream.

Pack the freezer with a mixture of eight parts ice to one part of salt. Keep in a cool place until ready to serve.

Yield: About 2½ quarts.

VARIATIONS:

(a) Strawberry Ice Cream

Prepare custard as for French Ice Cream. When cool, add 3 cups 18% cream and 1 quart strawberries, mashed with ¼ cup sugar.

(b) Chocolate Ice Cream

Prepare as for French Ice Cream, adding 2 ounces unsweetened chocolate to the milk. Scald until the chocolate has melted; beat until smooth. Increase sugar to 1⅓ cups.

273 Vanilla Ice Cream

Combine in top of double boiler
20 marshmallows
1 cup whole milk *or* 10% cream

Place over simmering water and stir until marshmallows are melted. Cool, stirring occasionally, until partially set.

Fold in
1 cup whipping cream, beaten stiff
1 teaspoon vanilla
Few grains salt

Pour into refrigerator tray or a 9″ x 5″ loaf pan. Place in freezer, and stir every 15 minutes for 1 hour, then continue freezing until very firm.

Yield: 6 servings.

274 Orange Sherbet

Soften
1 tablespoon gelatine
in
¼ cup water
Combine in saucepan
1¾ cups orange juice
½ cup water
1 cup sugar
¼ teaspoon salt

Bring to a boil, stirring to dissolve sugar. Remove from heat.
Stir in softened gelatine until dissolved.
Add
¼ cup lemon juice

Pour into refrigerator tray or a 9″ x 5″ loaf pan.

Place in freezer, stirring every 15 minutes for 1 hour, then continue freezing until very firm.

Yield: 6 servings.

275 Baked Alaska

Beat until frothy
4 egg whites
Gradually beat in
½ cup fruit sugar
¼ teaspoon cream of tartar
½ teaspoon vanilla

Cover a board with aluminum foil. Cut a 1″ thick piece of sponge or plain cake 1″ larger than an ice cream brick. Place on the board.

Place a pint brick of ice cream on the cake.

Quickly cover cake and ice cream completely with meringue. Place in freezer until needed, or bake at once.

When ready to serve, place in a preheated 475° oven, 3 to 5 minutes, to brown meringue lightly and quickly.

Serve immediately.

Yield: 6 servings.

NOTE: If you prefer, an 8″ square cake which is about 1″ thick may be used for a Baked Alaska. Slice the brick of ice cream in four, lengthwise. Place on the cake and finish as above.

276 Gingerbread Baked Alaska

Beat to soft peak stage
4 egg whites
Beat in
⅓ cup lightly-packed brown sugar

Cover a board with aluminum foil. Place an 8″ or 9″ square gingerbread on the board. The gingerbread should not be more than 1½″ thick.

Slice two pint bricks of vanilla ice cream, lengthwise, into two pieces. Place on the gingerbread so there is at least ½″ of cake showing around the edges.

Quickly cover the ice cream and cake with meringue, being careful to leave no spot uncovered.

Sprinkle top with
¼ cup slivered blanched almonds

Place in the freezer until needed, or bake at once.

To bake, place in preheated 475° oven for 3 to 5 minutes to lightly brown the meringue.
Serve at once.

Yield: 9 servings.

GELATINE DESSERTS

Gelatine desserts are easy to prepare and there is a wide variety, from simple to elaborate. There are two types of gelatine:

Unflavoured Gelatine: This must be soaked (or hydrated) in cold water before dissolving, and is available in 1-ounce envelopes which measure 1 tablespoon each. Flavouring and sugar must be added.

Flavoured Gelatine Powder: This is available in a wide range of flavours and need only be dissolved in hot water. For variety, fruit juice, canned fruit syrup, or ginger ale may be used in place of all or part of the liquid in preparing gelatine powders. When fruit is to be added, fold it into the slightly thickened gelatine mixture. Do *not* use fresh pineapple because it prevents gelatine of either type from setting.

JELLY MOULDS:

Metal moulds will chill more quickly than china or glass.

To unmould a jelly, dip a paring knife in hot water and run it around the top edge of the mould. Then quickly dip the mould to the top in lukewarm water. (If the water is too hot, it will melt the jelly.) Shake the mould slightly to loosen. Cover with a plate and turn plate and mould over together. Lift off the mould.

There is a trick to centering a large gelatine mould on the plate. Slightly moisten the top of the jelly in the mould, and also the serving plate. Unmould as above and slide to centre.

---

277 Apricot Jelly

Dissolve
1 (3-ounce) package lemon jelly powder
in
1 cup boiling water
Add
1 cup apricot nectar
1 tablespoon lemon juice
Pour into serving dishes and chill until firm.
Yield: 4 servings.

278 Lemon Snow

Soften
1 tablespoon gelatine
in
¼ cup cold water
Combine
1 cup boiling water
1 teaspoon grated lemon rind
¾ cup sugar
¼ teaspoon salt
Add softened gelatine and stir until dissolved.
Add
¼ cup lemon juice
Chill until partially set.
Beat gelatine mixture until frothy, and fold in
2 stiffly-beaten egg whites

Pour into moulds or sherbet glasses and chill until firm. If desired, unmould before serving. Serve with Custard Sauce.
Yield: 4 servings.

VARIATION:

(a) Banana Snow

Add two mashed bananas to partially set gelatine in above recipe.

279 Peach Chiffon

Drain syrup from
1 (20-ounce) can peaches
Mash or purée peaches (approximately 1½ cups)
Soften
1 tablespoon gelatine
in
¼ cup syrup from peaches
Scald in top of double boiler
1 cup milk
Add
¼ cup sugar
¼ teaspoon salt
Mix a little of the hot mixture with
2 beaten egg yolks
Return to double boiler top and cook over

simmering water, stirring constantly, until mixture coats a metal spoon.

Remove from heat and add softened gelatine. Stir until gelatine is dissolved.

Chill until partially set.

Fold in
1 tablespoon lemon juice
Mashed or puréed peaches
2 stiffly-beaten egg whites

Spoon into serving dishes and chill until set.

Serve with cream or Custard Sauce.

Yield: 8 servings.

280   Spanish Cream

Soften
1 tablespoon gelatine
in
½ cup milk
Heat in double boiler top
1½ cups milk
Add hot milk to
2 beaten egg yolks
Return to double boiler top and add
⅓ cup sugar
¼ teaspoon salt
Cook over simmering water, stirring constantly, until mixture coats a metal spoon.

Remove from heat and add softened gelatine. Stir until gelatine is dissolved.

Cool and add
½ teaspoon vanilla
Chill until partially set.

Fold in
2 stiffly-beaten egg whites
Pour into serving dishes and chill until set.

Serve with fresh fruit garnish or whipped cream.

Yield: 8 servings.

VARIATIONS:

(a)   Chocolate Spanish Cream

Prepare as above, melting 1 ounce unsweetened chocolate in the hot milk. (Blend evenly by beating with rotary beater.)

(b)   Coffee Spanish Cream

Prepare as for Spanish Cream, adding 2½ tablespoons instant coffee powder to the hot milk.

281   Coffee Mallow

Combine in double boiler top
½ pound marshmallows (5 cups miniature or quartered)
1 cup hot coffee
⅛ teaspoon salt
Heat over boiling water until marshmallows are melted, stirring frequently.

Chill. When partially set, beat until frothy.

Fold in
½ pint whipping cream, beaten stiff
1 teaspoon vanilla
Spoon into sherbet dishes and garnish with toasted slivered almonds.

Chill thoroughly.

Yield: 8 servings.

282   Bavarian Cream

Soften
1 tablespoon gelatine
in
¼ cup cold water
Add
1¼ cups hot milk
⅓ cup sugar
¼ teaspoon salt
Stir until gelatine and sugar are dissolved.

Cool and add
1 teaspoon vanilla
Chill until partially set. Beat until frothy.

Fold in
½ pint whipping cream, beaten stiff
Spoon into serving dishes and chill until firm.

Yield: 8 servings.

VARIATIONS:

(a)   Chocolate Bavarian Cream

Prepare as for Bavarian Cream, melting 1 ounce unsweetened chocolate in the hot milk. (Blend evenly by beating with rotary beater.)

(b)   Coffee Bavarian Cream

Prepare as for Bavarian Cream, adding 2½ tablespoons instant coffee powder to the hot milk.

(c)   Orange Bavarian Cream

Prepare as for Bavarian Cream, replacing the hot milk with 1 cup hot orange juice and ¼ cup lemon juice. After the whipped cream has been added, fold in 1 (11-ounce) can mandarin orange sections which have been well drained.

283　　Mocha Soufflé

Soften
>**1 tablespoon gelatine**

in
>**¼ cup cold water**

Combine
>**2 tablespoons instant coffee powder**
>**⅓ cup sugar**
>**⅛ teaspoon salt**
>**1 cup boiling water**

Add softened gelatine and stir until gelatine is melted.

Chill until partially set.

Beat until light
>**2 egg yolks**

Beat egg yolks into coffee mixture until foamy.

Beat until stiff
>**2 egg whites**

Gradually beat in
>**⅓ cup sugar**

Beat until stiff
>**½ pint whipping cream**

Add
>**½ teaspoon vanilla**

Fold meringue and whipped cream into coffee mixture.

Spoon into sherbet glasses and chill thoroughly.

Garnish with whipped cream and finely chopped cashew nuts.

Yield: 10 to 12 servings.

284　　Cheese Cake

Combine
>**½ cup graham cracker crumbs**
>**   (8 single wafers)**
>**2 tablespoons melted butter *or* margarine**
>**2 tablespoons brown sugar**
>**⅛ teaspoon cinnamon**
>**Few grains salt**

Butter an 8″ or 9″ spring form ring pan. Press crumb mixture into bottom of pan.

In double boiler top, combine
>**2 tablespoons gelatine**
>**⅔ cup granulated sugar**
>**⅛ teaspoon salt**

Beat slightly
>**2 egg yolks**

with
>**½ cup milk**

Add to gelatine mixture and blend well.

Cook over simmering water, stirring constantly, until mixture coats a metal spoon.

Remove from heat and stir in
>**1 teaspoon grated orange rind**

Cool, stirring frequently.

Meanwhile, press through ricer or coarse sieve
>**3 cups creamed cottage cheese**

Combine gelatine mixture with cottage cheese, beating until smooth.

Add
>**⅓ cup orange juice**

Cool until mixture begins to set.

Beat until stiff, but not dry
>**2 egg whites**

Fold cottage cheese mixture into egg whites with
>**½ pint whipping cream, beaten stiff**

When evenly blended, turn into crumb lined pan and chill until firm.

Unmould, crumb side up, and garnish with orange sections.

Yield: 10 to 12 servings.

285　　Ban-Orange Chiffon

Soften
>**2 tablespoons gelatine**

in
>**½ cup cold water**

Heat together
>**1½ cups orange juice**
>**½ cup sugar**

Add softened gelatine to hot orange juice and stir until dissolved. Chill until partially set, then beat until frothy.

Mix
>**½ cup instant skim milk powder**

with
>**½ cup ice water**

Beat until soft peaks form (3 to 4 minutes).

Add
>**2 tablespoons lemon juice**

Continue beating until stiff peaks form (3 to 4 minutes longer).

Beat into orange mixture, just until evenly combined.

Fold in
>**1 cup sliced bananas**
>**1 teaspoon grated orange rind**

Spoon into sherbet glasses and chill.

Yield: 8 servings.

Sweet Sauces

286 Butterscotch Sauce

Combine in a saucepan
1¼ cups lightly-packed brown sugar
¾ cup white corn syrup
¼ cup butter

Bring to a boil over medium heat, stirring constantly. Cook, without stirring, until mixture reaches 238° on candy thermometer (soft ball stage). Remove from heat and let cool to lukewarm.

Blend in
½ cup cream
1 teaspoon vanilla

Serve at room temperature on ice cream or ice cream desserts.

To store, refrigerate in covered jar.

Thin with cream, if desired.

Yield: 2 cups.

VARIATIONS:

(a) Holiday Sauce

To 1 cup Butterscotch Sauce, add 2 tablespoons finely chopped maraschino cherries and 1 tablespoon each of chopped peel, chopped raisins and chopped almonds, and 1 tablespoon brandy, if desired.

(b) Coffee Sauce

Dissolve 1 tablespoon instant coffee powder in 1 tablespoon boiling water and blend into 1 cup Butterscotch Sauce.

(c) Pineapple Butterscotch Sauce

Fold ¼ cup well drained crushed pineapple into 1 cup Butterscotch Sauce.

287 Brown Sugar Sauce

Melt in a saucepan
2 tablespoons butter
Add
2 tablespoons *Pre-Sifted* PURITY All-Purpose Flour
¼ teaspoon salt
Stir until smooth.

Add
½ cup lightly-packed brown sugar

Blend thoroughly and cook over medium direct heat, stirring constantly, until mixture bubbles and is lightly browned (about 5 minutes).

Remove from heat.

Blend in
1 cup boiling water

Stir until well combined.

Return to heat and bring to a boil, stirring constantly, until smoothly thickened.

Add
1 teaspoon vanilla

Serve hot on steamed or baked puddings.

Yield: 1¼ cups.

VARIATIONS:

(a) Raisin Brown Sugar Sauce

Add ⅓ cup raisins and ¼ teaspoon grated lemon rind to the Brown Sugar Sauce.

(b) Spiced Brown Sugar Sauce

Add ¼ teaspoon cinnamon and ⅛ teaspoon nutmeg to the Brown Sugar Sauce.

288 Chocolate Pudding Sauce

Combine in a saucepan
⅓ cup cocoa
1 cup sugar
3 tablespoons *Pre-Sifted* PURITY All-Purpose Flour

Gradually stir in
2 cups boiling water

Cook over medium direct heat, stirring constantly, until smoothly thickened.

Remove from heat and blend in
2 tablespoons butter *or* margarine
1 teaspoon vanilla

Serve hot on steamed or baked puddings, or warm banana cake squares.

Yield: 2½ cups.

289 Deluxe Chocolate Sauce

Combine in a saucepan
1 cup lightly-packed brown sugar
1 cup white corn syrup
½ cup boiling water
Bring to a boil, stirring constantly. Reduce heat and cook 2 minutes longer.
Meanwhile, melt in top of double boiler
4 squares unsweetened chocolate
Remove from heat.
Add hot syrup gradually, stirring constantly. Blend in
¼ teaspoon salt
1 teaspoon vanilla
The mixture should be very smooth and glossy. If the chocolate appears to be flaky, beat mixture briskly with rotary beater.
Serve at room temperature on ice cream or ice cream desserts.
To store, refrigerate in covered jar.
Thin with hot water, if desired.
Heat over hot water for hot fudge sauce.
Yield: 2¼ cups.

290 Marshmallow Sauce

Combine in a saucepan
½ cup sugar
⅓ cup hot water
Heat until sugar is dissolved.
Reduce heat and add
¼ pound (20 to 22) large marshmallows, cut in pieces
Stir until melted.
Pour gradually into
1 beaten egg white
Beat until mixture thickens.
Serve at room temperature on ice cream or ice cream desserts. Serve warm on hot gingerbread, baked chocolate pudding, etc.
To store, refrigerate in covered jar.
Thin with hot water, if desired.
Yield: 2¾ cups.

VARIATIONS:

(a) Mint Marshmallow Sauce

Add ¼ teaspoon peppermint extract to Marshmallow Sauce. Tint mixture a pale green with food colouring. Especially nice on chocolate ice cream.

(b) Fruit Marshmallow Sauce

To 1½ cups Marshmallow Sauce, add ¼ cup chopped maraschino cherries, 2 tablespoons each of chopped candied pineapple and raisins. Tint mixture a pale pink with food colouring.

291 Quick Vanilla Sauce

Combine in a saucepan
1 cup lightly-packed brown sugar
3 tablespoons *Pre-Sifted* PURITY All-Purpose Flour
¼ teaspoon salt
Gradually stir in
2 cups boiling water
Bring to a boil over medium direct heat. Cook until smoothly thickened, stirring constantly.
Remove from heat and stir in
2 tablespoons butter *or* margarine
1½ teaspoons vanilla
Serve with baked or steamed puddings, or with apple dumplings.
Yield: 2 cups.

292 Custard Sauce

Heat in top of double boiler
2 cups milk
Combine in a bowl
2 well-beaten eggs
¼ cup sugar
2 tablespoons *Pre-Sifted* PURITY All-Purpose Flour
¼ teaspoon salt
Gradually stir a little of the hot milk into the egg mixture.
Return mixture to milk in double boiler, stirring briskly to combine.
Cook over boiling water, stirring constantly, until mixture is thickened (about 10 minutes).
Remove from heat and set in a pan of cold water. Stir frequently.
Add
1 teaspoon vanilla *or* almond flavouring
Serve well chilled with steamed puddings, pineapple upside down cake, fruit or gelatine desserts.
Beat with rotary beater for extra smoothness when cold.
Thin with cream, if desired.
Yield: 2 cups.
For a rich Custard Sauce, see recipe No. 248.

293 Lemon Sauce

Combine in a saucepan
½ cup sugar
3 tablespoons *Pre-Sifted* PURITY All-Purpose Flour
1 teaspoon grated lemon rind
¼ teaspoon salt
Gradually add
1¼ cups boiling water
Cook, stirring constantly, over medium direct heat until sauce is thickened (5 to 7 minutes).
Blend in
3 tablespoons lemon juice
2 tablespoons butter *or* margarine
Serve hot on steamed or baked puddings.
Yield: 1½ cups.

VARIATION:

(a) Orange Sauce

Prepare as for Lemon Sauce, substituting 1 teaspoon grated orange rind for the lemon rind, and 3 tablespoons orange juice and 1 tablespoon lemon juice for the 3 tablespoons lemon juice.

294 Fruit Syrup Sauce

Measure into a saucepan
1 cup syrup from canned fruit
Bring to a boil.
Combine
¼ cup sugar
3 tablespoons *Pre-Sifted* PURITY All-Purpose Flour
¼ teaspoon salt
Stir in
¼ cup cold water
Gradually add
Boiling syrup
Return to saucepan. Cook, stirring constantly, over medium direct heat until sauce is thickened (5 to 7 minutes).
Blend in
2 tablespoons butter *or* margarine
1 tablespoon lemon juice
Serve hot on Roly-Poly Pudding or squares of gold cake.
Yield: 1¼ cups.
NOTE: If necessary, water may be added to the syrup to make up the required volume.

295 Hard Sauce

Cream
⅓ cup soft butter
Gradually add
1 cup sifted icing sugar *or* lightly-packed brown sugar
Beat until creamy.
Gradually beat in
1 teaspoon vanilla *or* 1 tablespoon brandy, sherry *or* rum
Place in serving dish and chill thoroughly.
If desired, use a pastry tube to make individual rosettes. Serve well chilled on hot steamed or baked puddings.
Yield: 1 cup.

VARIATION:

(a) Fluffy Hard Sauce

Fold ¼ cup whipping cream, beaten stiff, into the Hard Sauce before chilling.

296 Egg-Nog Sauce

To
1 well-beaten egg
Add
1½ cups sifted icing sugar
Blend thoroughly.
Gradually add
⅓ cup melted butter
Blend in
1 teaspoon rum flavouring
⅛ teaspoon nutmeg
Fold in
1 cup whipping cream, beaten stiff
Do not overmix. Chill thoroughly.
Serve on steamed or baked puddings.
Especially delicious with rich fruit puddings and warm chocolate cake squares.
Yield: 3 cups.

297 Foamy Applesauce

Combine in a bowl
1 (15-ounce) can sweetened applesauce
¼ teaspoon cinnamon
Fold in
2 stiffly-beaten egg whites
¼ cup whipping cream, beaten stiff
Serve on hot gingerbread or spice cake squares.
Yield: 2⅔ cups.

Beverages

298 Milk Shake

Combine with rotary beater, electric mixer or blender

1 cup milk
1 scoop vanilla ice cream

Yield: 1 serving.

VARIATIONS:

(a) Chocolate Milk Shake

Add 1½ tablespoons instant chocolate drink powder to above recipe.

(b) Strawberry Milk Shake

Add 1 tablespoon instant strawberry drink powder to above recipe.

(c) Coffee Milk Shake

Add 2 teaspoons instant coffee powder to above recipe.

Your cocoa and chocolate beverages will be creamier if made with homogenized milk. They will also have a heavier body with less cocoa settling out than those made with non-homogenized milk.

299 Banana Milk Shake

Mash

1 medium-sized fully ripe banana

Beat with

1 cup milk
2 teaspoons lemon juice
1 tablespoon sugar

Serve immediately with ice.

Yield: 2 servings.

NOTE: With an electric blender, combine all ingredients and blend until smooth and light.

Add taste and eye appeal to tall "coolers" by making ice cubes of tea, fruit juice, ginger ale or coloured water.

300 Mocha Bounce

Combine

2 cups milk
1 teaspoon instant coffee powder
2 tablespoons instant chocolate drink powder

Pour flavoured milk over a scoop of vanilla ice cream in each of two tall glasses. Serve immediately.

Yield: 2 servings.

NOTE: With an electric blender, combine milk, instant coffee, chocolate powder and 2 scoops ice cream. Blend until ice cream is just melted. Serve immediately.

Garnish cool drinks with fruit kabobs made by arranging maraschino cherries, orange sections and lemon slices on toothpicks.

301 Cocoa Syrup

Combine in a saucepan

½ cup cocoa
1¼ cups sugar
½ teaspoon salt
1 cup water

Place over moderate heat and boil for three minutes, stirring constantly. Remove from heat, cool slightly, and add

1 teaspoon vanilla

Pour into a scalded pint sealer, cover and store in refrigerator. Use as a sauce for ice cream or use 1 to 2 tablespoons in a glass of milk.

Yield: 1 pint.

302 Chocolate Float

For each serving, combine in a tall glass

2 tablespoons Cocoa Syrup (recipe No. 301)
1 cup milk

Add a scoop of vanilla ice cream and serve.

303 Hot Chocolate

Scald in double boiler
4 cups milk
Melt in a small saucepan
2 squares unsweetened chocolate
Add
¼ cup sugar
¼ teaspoon salt
Blend in
1 cup boiling water
Stir briskly until smooth, bring to a boil and boil for 5 minutes.
Pour into scalded milk and stir to combine evenly.
Serve in cups garnished with a marshmallow, or whipped cream sprinkled with nutmeg.
Yield: 6 servings.

_____

Chill summer drinks with ice cubes frozen with a maraschino cherry, sprig of mint or one-quarter lemon slice in centre.

304 Lemon Syrup

Combine
3 cups sugar
2 cups water
Boil together for 5 minutes.
Add
1 cup lemon juice
2 tablespoons grated lemon rind
Pour into scalded quart sealer, cover and store in refrigerator.
To serve, fill glass about ¼ full with syrup; add ice and cold water. Stir and garnish with lemon slice and maraschino cherry.
Yield: 1 quart syrup.

305 Egg-Nog

Beat together in a small bowl or electric blender
1 egg
1½ tablespoons sugar
1 cup milk
¼ teaspoon vanilla
Strain into a tall glass and serve.
                    OR
Separate
1 egg
Beat the white until stiff, then beat in
1½ tablespoons sugar

Then beat the yolk with
1 cup milk
¼ teaspoon vanilla
Stir the yolk mixture into the egg white but do not blend completely. Pour into a tall glass and serve.
Yield: 1 serving.
NOTE: For flavour variety, instant chocolate or strawberry drink powder may be added to taste.

306 Orange-Nog

For each serving, beat with rotary beater, electric mixer or blender
1 egg
Gradually add
1 cup orange juice
Serve immediately, with a scoop of vanilla ice cream, if desired.
NOTE: Equally good with apricot nectar or prune juice.

_____

After skating, youngsters will welcome mugs of Mulled Apple Juice. Heat a 48-ounce can of apple juice in double boiler with 6 to 8 whole cloves and a 4" or 5" piece of stick cinnamon. Remove spices after 30 minutes. Serve moderately hot, but not scalding. This makes eight 6-ounce servings.

307 Pineapple Sparkle

Combine equal quantities of pineapple juice and ginger ale. Serve with ice, garnished with thin lemon slices and maraschino cherries.
NOTE: Grape juice, orange juice or grapefruit juice may be used in place of the pineapple juice.

308 Sparkling Tea Punch

Combine in a pitcher
2 cups cold strong tea
2 tablespoons lime juice
3 tablespoons sugar
Stir to dissolve sugar.
Just before serving add
2 cups ginger ale
Serve with ice, garnished with a slice of lemon or lime.
Yield: About 4 servings.

309 Orange Punch

Combine
  ½ cup sugar
  3 cups water
Boil together for 5 minutes.
Add
  1 cup orange juice
  ¼ cup lemon juice
Chill.
Just before serving add
  4 cups ginger ale
  Crushed *or* cubed ice
Serve from a punch bowl or in glasses.
Yield: About 2 quarts.

310 Christmas Egg-Nog

Separate
  6 eggs
Beat egg whites until stiff but not dry.
Then gradually beat in
  ½ cup sugar
Beat egg yolks with
  ¼ cup sugar
  2½ cups milk
Fold egg yolk mixture into egg whites.
When blended, add
  2½ cups whipping cream
  Rum flavouring to taste
Chill.
Pour into a large punch bowl and lightly sprinkle with grated nutmeg.
Yield: About 15 (4-ounce) servings.

311 Christmas Cranberry Cocktail

Defrost
  1 (6-ounce) can frozen limeade
Combine with
  3 (6-ounce) cans water
  2 cups bottled cranberry juice
Chill.
Just before serving, add
  2 cups ginger ale
Serve with ice.
Yield: About 12 (4-ounce) servings.

312 Tea

For the best flavour, tea must be of good quality and be properly made.
For quality, you must depend on the brand name.

To make good tea:
1. Use fresh water from the cold water tap—bring to a boil.
2. Scald the tea-pot.
3. Allow one teaspoon tea per person and "one for the pot"; or one tea bag for every two cups of tea.
4. Pour freshly boiling water over tea.
5. Allow it to brew for 5 minutes. Then strain or remove tea bag and serve.

313 Iced Tea

Prepare tea as usual, making it twice the usual strength. Allow tea to brew for 5 minutes, strain or remove tea bags. Cool slightly to avoid cloudiness. Pour into tall glasses filled with ice.
Garnish with lemon or mint.

314 Coffee

Coffee may be purchased in various grinds to suit any type of coffee-maker.
  Coarse—for old-fashioned coffee-pot or large quantity open pot.
  Medium—for percolator.
  Fine—for drip or vacuum-type coffee-makers.
Unless coffee is "vacuum-packed", it is best freshly ground when purchased.
Once coffee is ground, the flavour begins to deteriorate. Purchase weekly in the required amount. Storing coffee in the refrigerator will help to retain the fresh flavour.
Follow manufacturer's directions for your particular coffee-maker, allowing approximately 2 to 3 level tablespoons for each 8-ounce cup water.
Best results are obtained when a coffee-maker is filled to capacity.

315 Iced Coffee

Instant: For each serving, dissolve 1 tablespoon instant coffee powder in a small amount of hot water in a tall glass. Fill glasses with ice cubes and add water or milk. Stir before serving.
Regular: Prepare coffee as usual, making it twice the usual strength.
Pour over crushed ice in tall glasses.

Appetizers

COCKTAILS

THINGS TO REMEMBER ABOUT FRUIT JUICE COCKTAILS

Fruit juice cocktails are at their best when well chilled, so refrigerate until serving time and serve in chilled glasses.

Garnish fruit juice cocktails with a sprig of fresh mint; lemon, lime or orange twists; tiny scoops of sherbet; or very thin slices of lemon or lime.

Brighten your cocktails by adding a few drops of food colouring.

---

316   Tomato Juice Cocktail

Combine

1 (20-ounce) can tomato juice
1 teaspoon Worcestershire sauce
¼ teaspoon salt
Few grains celery salt
Few grains pepper
Few drops lemon juice

Chill.

Yield: 5 (4-ounce) servings.

317   Golden Glow Cocktail

Combine

1 (6-ounce) can frozen lemonade concentrate
2¼ cups cold water
2 (13-ounce) cans apricot nectar

Blend juices thoroughly.

Chill before serving.

Yield: 12 (4-ounce) servings.

318   Tangarine Sparkle

Combine equal parts chilled tangarine juice and gingerale. Serve chilled in glasses.

319   Citrus Mint Cocktail

Serve chilled citrus fruit juices in tall glasses. Garnish with a sprig of fresh mint.

320   Mix and Match Cocktails

There are many pleasing fruit juice combinations.

Here are a few suggestions:

(a)   Apricot and Grapefruit Cocktail

Combine 2 parts apricot nectar and 1 part grapefruit juice. Chill.

(b)   Cranberry and Lemonade Cocktail

Combine 2 parts bottled cranberry juice and 1 part lemonade.   The flavours will blend during chilling, so prepare at least an hour before serving.

(c)   Grape and Limeade Cocktail

Combine 1 part grape juice and 3 parts limeade. Chill.

(d)   Sparkling Fruit Cocktails

Reconstitute frozen fruit juice concentrates with chilled ginger ale. Serve at once.

OR

Combine equal parts chilled canned fruit juice and chilled ginger ale. (Apple, grapefruit, cranberry and pineapple juices are suggestions.) Serve at once.

There are a variety of canned and frozen fruit drinks on the market. Keep some on hand to brighten family meals and for spur-of-the-moment entertaining.

THINGS TO REMEMBER ABOUT FRUIT COCKTAILS

Fresh, frozen or canned fruits may be combined in many ways for delightful fruit cocktails. When using several fruits, combine them an hour or so before serving so the flavours will mingle. Have the fruits well chilled and serve them whole or in "bite-size" pieces (not too small). Partially thaw frozen fruits—there should still be a few ice crystals present.

The syrup from canned and frozen fruits may be frozen to a mush (this takes about 20 minutes) and spooned over the chilled fruit just before serving.

Garnish your fruit cocktails with cherries, whole strawberries or raspberries, a tiny scoop of sherbet, or a sprig of fresh mint. The fruit syrup may be tinted with food colouring.

321 Fruit Cups

There are many possible combinations for these, especially when fresh fruits are available. Here are two suggestions for year round use:

(a) Fruit Medley

Drain and measure
> 1 cup pears, cut in bite-size pieces
> 1 cup pineapple chunks
> 1 cup apricots, sliced
> ½ cup maraschino cherries, halved

Combine with
> 1 banana, sliced

Cover and chill to blend flavours.

Combine
> ¾ cup orange juice
> ¾ cup pineapple syrup drained from fruit

Freeze to a mush (about 20 minutes). Spoon over fruit mixture in chilled sherbet glasses. Serve at once.

Yield: 6 to 8 servings.

(b) Minted Fruit Cocktail

Drain and measure
> 2 cups minted pineapple chunks
> 1½ cups peaches, cut in bite-size pieces

Combine with
> 1 cup halved and seeded red grapes
> 1 large red apple, cut in thin wedges

Cover and chill to blend flavours.

To serve, arrange fruit in chilled sherbets and spoon chilled orange juice over it.

Yield: 6 to 8 servings.

322 Honeydew Melon Deluxe

Sprinkle chilled honeydew melon wedges with ground nutmeg. Drape clusters of red grapes over each wedge.

323 Ambrosia

Combine
> 2 oranges, sectioned
> 1 large grapefruit, sectioned
> 1 cup crushed pineapple, undrained
> ½ cup desiccated coconut
> ½ cup whole strawberries

Cover and chill to blend flavours.

Serve in chilled sherbets. Sprinkle with coconut and garnish with a sprig of mint.

Yield: 6 to 8 servings.

324 Hawaiian Cocktail

Arrange equal parts mandarin orange sections and pineapple chunks in chilled sherbets. Spoon pineapple juice over the fruit. Sprinkle with fruit sugar.

Chill before serving.

325 Melon Ball Cocktail

Combine equal parts cantaloupe, honeydew melon and watermelon balls. Place in chilled sherbets and spoon grapefruit juice or ginger ale over the mixture.

Chill thoroughly. Garnish with a sprig of mint, a cherry or fresh strawberry.

326 Apple and Grapefruit Cocktail

Alternate chilled grapefruit sections and un-peeled red apple wedges in chilled sherbets. Spoon a mixture of equal parts orange juice and grapefruit juice over the fruit. Sprinkle with fruit sugar, if desired.

Chill before serving.

For an easy cocktail, add 1 tablespoon honey to each grapefruit half. Chill 1 hour. Add 1 tablespoon sherry, if desired, before serving.

FINGER FOODS

HORS D'OEUVRES:

These dainty finger foods may be simple or exotic, hot or cold. Serve hot hors d'oeuvres from a chafing dish or entrée dish. If you like, spear cold hors d'oeuvres with cocktail picks or toothpicks and arrange them in a holder, a red apple or cheese, or in a grapefruit or pineapple.

Ideas are endless for these tasty morsels of food. We have included but a few suggestions which you may enjoy trying.

Hot Hors d'Oeuvres

327 Pigs in Blankets

TO PREPARE THE SAUSAGES:

The sausages must be completely cooked before they are wrapped in dough. If tiny cocktail sausages are not available, you can make your own by twisting regular sausages into two or three sections. Cook these and then cut. Regular sausages may also be cooked as usual and then cut into two or three pieces. If using bottled or canned cocktail sausages, prepare as directed.

TO PREPARE THE DOUGH:

Preheat oven to 450°.

Prepare one-half the Basic Tea Biscuit dough (recipe No. 42). Divide dough in two and roll each piece to an 8" square. Cut into 2" squares and spread with prepared mustard.

Place a cooked sausage piece on each square of dough. Roll up diagonally and seal. Place on baking sheets.

Bake in preheated 450° oven about 10 minutes or until golden.

Serve hot.

Yield: 32 tiny rolls.

328 Hot Kebabs

Various foods, in bite-size pieces may be placed on toothpicks and broiled to make tasty Hot Kebabs. Here are some suggested combinations:

1. Arrange on each toothpick: A maraschino cherry; pineapple chunk; cube of ham, luncheon meat or wiener; and another maraschino cherry.

2. Cook sausage and cut into bite-size pieces. Roll cubes of unpeeled red apple in brown sugar. Arrange these on toothpicks, a piece of sausage between two apple cubes.

3. Place on each toothpick: A mandarin orange section, a cube of ham and a pineapple chunk.

Place the kebabs about 5" below the broiler. Broil until golden brown (3 to 5 minutes), turning frequently.

For added flavour, the kebabs may be basted with melted butter or a sauce during the broiling.

PINEAPPLE SAUCE:

Combine

   ⅓ cup melted butter *or* margarine
   ¼ cup pineapple juice
   2 tablespoons brown sugar
   1 tablespoon lemon juice
   ⅛ teaspoon cloves

This will baste about 20 kebabs.

329 Cheese Dreams

Remove crusts from bread and cut into 2" squares or into fingers. Sprinkle with shredded Cheddar cheese. Top each with a piece of side bacon and arrange on a baking sheet. Place about 5" below the broiler and broil until bacon begins to crisp and the cheese has melted (3 to 5 minutes). Serve hot.

330 Bouchées

Prepare tiny Bouchée cases as directed in recipe No. 240. Fill with a hot cream filling—shrimp, lobster, chicken or ham. Garnish and serve hot.

If preferred, the Bouchées may be filled with a tasty salad filling and served cold.

331 Nibblers

Preheat oven to 400°.

Spread potato chips and assorted small crackers on a baking sheet. Sprinkle generously with grated Parmesan cheese. Bake in preheated 400° oven for 2 to 3 minutes or until golden brown. Serve hot.

332   Tasty Rolls

Split finger rolls or tiny hamburger buns and spread with soft butter or margarine. Toast lightly under the broiler.

Cover toasted buns with thin slices of turkey, ham or luncheon meat. Season with salt and pepper.

Top with a slice of cranberry jelly and a cheese slice. Place about 5″ below the broiler. Broil until the cheese melts (about 3 minutes). Serve hot.

333   Pineapple and Sausage Nibblers

Brown and cook
½ pound sausages
Cut each sausage into thirds.
Heat syrup from
1 (20-ounce) can pineapple chunks
Arrange pineapple chunks and sausage pieces on toothpicks. Place in hot syrup.
Keep warm over candle warmer or prepare and serve from a chafing dish.
Yield: 2 dozen nibblers.

Cold Hors d'Oeuvres

334   Meat Teasers

1. Spread thin slices of cooked meat (ham, salami, tongue, bologna) with a flavourful cheese spread. Roll up tightly and chill. Cut into bite-size pieces and secure with toothpicks.

2. Wrap pineapple chunks in ham slices. Fasten with toothpicks.

3. Shape thin slices of cooked meat into small cones and fasten with toothpicks. Fill with rosettes of tasty cheese.

4. Sandwich four or five slices of cooked meat together with cheese—sliced or a spread. Cut into wedges and serve on toothpicks.

5. Dip thin apple wedges in lemon juice and wrap in thin slices of salami. Secure with toothpicks.

6. Split wieners in two, lengthwise. Fill with cheese and cut into bite-size pieces. Spear with toothpicks.

335   Cheese Log

Cream thoroughly
½ pound soft process cheese
3 tablespoons mayonnaise
Add
2 tablespoons finely chopped onion
2 tablespoons finely chopped green pepper
3 stuffed olives, chopped
⅓ cup finely crushed salted soda crackers
Combine ingredients thoroughly and form into a long roll. Wrap in waxed paper and chill until firm (about 3 hours).
Serve with assorted, crisp crackers.

336   Seafood Teasers

1. Lobster, shrimp, smoked salmon, oysters and sardines all make tasty bite-size morsels to serve with cocktails.

2. Top cucumber slices with a piece of smoked salmon or a dab of seafood paste.

337   Cheese Balls

Soften cream or process cheese and season to taste with mustard, horseradish, etc. Shape into small balls and roll in finely chopped parsley, chives or nuts, or in crushed potato chips. Refrigerate until firm.

338   Cold Kebabs

It's fun to try two or three different foods together on a toothpick. Cubes of cooked meat go well with pineapple chunks, maraschino cherries, olives, pickles, cheese cubes, sautéed mushroom caps, etc. Cooked shrimp or lobster pieces may be combined with mandarin orange sections, cherries or pineapple chunks.

339   Sardine Hors D'Oeuvres

Drain
2 (3¼ ounce) cans sardines
Dip sardines in
¾ cup PURITY Corn Meal
Then dip in a mixture of
1 beaten egg
1 tablespoon milk
Dip again in corn meal.
Fry in hot butter until golden (3 to 5 minutes).
Serve hot or cold.

Canapés

340 Canapé Bases

To avoid waste, use unsliced bread for canapé bases. Remove crusts and then slice the bread lengthwise into ¼" thick slices. Cut into rounds, stars, triangles, oblongs, crescents, etc. Toast, on one side only, until golden brown, using a hot frying pan with butter or margarine. Cover and set aside until about ½ hour before serving time.

Then, spread the untoasted side with mayonnaise or soft cheese and garnish attractively, or top with one of the spreads suggested in the following recipes and then garnish.

Other bases may be used for canapés—small crisp crackers, melba toast, crisp thin pastry cut in various shapes, tiny yeast rolls, thick slices of cucumber or pickle.

Prepare canapés only ½ hour before serving as they wilt and become very uninteresting if allowed to stand.

341 Shrimp and Cucumber Canapés

Spread 2" canapé bases with soft cream cheese. Place a thin slice of cucumber on each prepared round. Top with a cooked shrimp and garnish.

342 Shrimp Canapés

Combine thoroughly
   1 (4½-ounce) can shrimps, minced
   3 tablespoons mayonnaise
   1 tablespoon minced green pepper
   1 teaspoon lemon juice
   Few drops tabasco sauce

Spread the canapé bases with mayonnaise and top with the shrimp mixture.

Garnish with a piece of cucumber pickle.

Yield: 2 dozen (1½") canapés.

343 Sardine Fingers

Spread canapé fingers with cream cheese which has been seasoned with Worcestershire sauce. Top each with a drained sardine. Garnish with parsley, olive slices or strips of pimiento.

344 Chicken-Almond Canapés

Combine
   ¾ cup minced cooked chicken
   ¼ cup chopped blanched almonds
   1½ tablespoons mayonnaise
   ⅛ teaspoon celery salt
   Few grains salt and pepper

Blend thoroughly.

Spread canapé bases with mayonnaise and top with chicken-almond mixture. Garnish.

Yield: 2 dozen (1½") canapés.

345 Ham Pick-Ups

Combine
   1 (2¼-ounce) can devilled ham
   1 teaspoon horseradish

Spread canapé bases with the devilled ham mixture.

Top with a small mound of commercial sour cream.

Press a piece of pickle, pimiento or an olive slice into the sour cream.

Yield: 2½ dozen (1½") canapés.

346 Egg and Olive Canapés

Combine thoroughly
   2 hard-cooked eggs, finely chopped
   2 tablespoons mayonnaise
   1 teaspoon chopped parsley
   6 stuffed olives, finely chopped
   Few grains paprika and onion salt

Spread the mixture on canapé bases.

Garnish with thin slices of stuffed olive, pickle or a sprig of parsley.

Yield: 2 dozen (1½") canapés.

347 Green Onion Canapés

Combine
   1 cup commercial sour cream
   3 tablespoons finely chopped green onion
   ¼ teaspoon salt

Cover and chill to blend flavours.

Spread the mixture on canapé bases. Garnish.

Yield: 2 dozen (1½") canapés.

SPREADS AND DIPS

For casual entertaining, prepare one or two spreads and dips and surround them with a variety of crisp crackers, potato chips, unusual breads. Everyone will enjoy helping themselves, especially the teenagers. Many of the recipes for spreads may also be used for canapés—just spread them on canapé bases, crackers, etc., and garnish.

348   Ham Spread

Combine
  ⅔ cup minced cooked ham
  ¼ cup chopped stuffed olives
  1 tablespoon chopped parsley
  3 tablespoons mayonnaise
  1 teaspoon Worcestershire sauce
  ¼ teaspoon prepared mustard
Blend thoroughly.
Cover and chill to blend flavours.
Yield: 1 cup

349   Shrimp Spread

Combine thoroughly
  ¼ cup mayonnaise
  3 tablespoons sweet pickle relish
  2 tablespoons catsup
  1 tablespoon finely chopped celery
  2 teaspoons grated onion
  1 teaspoon horseradish
  2 teaspoons lemon juice
Fold in
  1 (4½-ounce) can shrimp, flaked
Cover and chill to blend flavours.
Yield: 1¼ cups.

350   Nippy Spread

Beat until creamy
  1 (4-ounce) package soft cream cheese
  1 tablespoon mayonnaise
  1 tablespoon cream
Add
  2 tablespoons sweet pickle relish
  1 tablespoon finely chopped onion
  1 teaspoon horseradish
  Few drops tabasco sauce
  Few grains garlic salt
Blend thoroughly.
Cover and chill to blend flavours.
Yield: ¾ cup.

_____

For a quick dip, add mayonnaise or cream to softened pimiento or pineapple cream cheese, etc.

351   Piquant Dip

Beat until creamy
  1 cup commercial sour cream
  1 (4-ounce) package soft cream cheese
Blend in
  1 hard-cooked egg, finely chopped
  ¼ cup finely chopped green peppers
  1 tablespoon catsup
  1½ teaspoons horseradish
  1 teaspoon Worcestershire sauce
  ½ teaspoon salt
  ½ teaspoon dry mustard
  ½ small clove of garlic, finely chopped
Cover and chill to blend flavours.
Yield: 1¾ cups.

352   Party Dip

Beat until creamy
  1 (8-ounce) package soft cream cheese
  3 tablespoons mayonnaise
Add
  3 tablespoons chili sauce
  2 tablespoons finely grated onion
  ¼ teaspoon salt
  ¼ teaspoon prepared mustard
  Few grains pepper
Blend until smooth.
Cover and chill to blend flavours.
Yield: 1½ cups.

353   Cucumber Dip

Beat until creamy
  1 (8-ounce) package soft cream cheese
  3 tablespoons mayonnaise
  1 tablespoon milk
Add
  ¼ cup grated, unpeeled cucumber
  ¼ teaspoon Worcestershire sauce
  Few grains garlic salt
Blend thoroughly.
Cover and chill to blend flavours.
Yield: 1¼ cups.

Soups

THINGS TO REMEMBER ABOUT SOUPS

"Season to taste" is mentioned in all recipes and this is the place to add salt and seasonings to suit your requirements. Seasoning salt, soy sauce, poultry seasoning, powdered herbs and curry powder are among the many seasonings which will add that special touch. Monosodium glutamate is a flavour intensifier and can be used in soups with excellent results—just follow the directions given with the product.

Most soups, like stews, improve in flavour the second day of using. When reheating, thin with vegetable liquids, soup stock, milk or water depending upon the type of soup.

To remove fat from hot soup stock, skim with a metal spoon. Then roll up paper towelling tightly and use end to blot up fat from surface. Snip off end of paper as it becomes saturated.

A pressure cooker is recommended where long cooking periods are necessary. Follow manufacturer's directions for the steps called for in the recipes.

---

354   Beef Soup Stock

Purchase
    2 pounds soup bones
    2 pounds lean stewing beef
If bones are meaty, reduce the amount of lean beef purchased. Cut meat and fat from bones.

Dice the meat, including that cut from the bones, and brown in beef drippings in pressure cooker.

Add
    Soup bones
    6 cups cold water
    2 teaspoons salt
    ½ teaspoon peppercorns
    ½ bay leaf
    ¼ teaspoon thyme
    ¼ teaspoon marjoram
    2 cloves
    1 cup sliced onions
    1 cup cut celery leaves and stalks
    1 large sliced carrot
Bring cooker to 15 pounds pressure and process 30 minutes.

Cool cooker, remove bones and discard. Remove meat and save it to add to soup, etc. Strain broth through fine sieve or cheesecloth in a colander. Cool quickly and refrigerate.

Remove chilled fat from surface and store stock in covered container in refrigerator. Use as needed in soup or sauce recipes.

Yield: 6 cups.

Long Cooking Method: Proceed as directed in recipe *except* substitute 12 cups cold water for 6 cups water and cook in a deep heavy kettle with cover. Let simmer 3 hours.

VARIATION:

(a)   Beef and Rice Soup

To 2 cups Beef Soup Stock, add 1 cup water, 1 cup diced beef (cooked with the soup bones) and ½ cup cooked rice. Let simmer 10 minutes, season to taste and serve.

Yield: 4 cups.

355 Vegetable Medley Soup

Melt in a large saucepan
    2 tablespoons butter *or* margarine
Add
    ½ cup green beans, cut in 1″ pieces
    ½ cup diced celery
    ½ cup sliced carrots
    ½ cup diced turnip
    ½ cup finely chopped onions
Toss vegetables in butter and cook for about 5 minutes.
Add
    1½ cups canned tomatoes
    2 cups Beef Soup Stock
    1 cup water
Bring to a boil, cover and simmer 20 minutes or until vegetables are tender. Season to taste.

Yield: 6 cups.

356   Onion Soup au Gratin

Melt in a heavy saucepan

3 tablespoons butter *or* margarine

Add

3 cups thinly sliced onions

Fry onions until a deep golden brown.

Add

2½ cups Beef Soup Stock
1½ cups water

Stir well. Bring to a boil, cover and simmer 20 minutes.

Add

1 teaspoon Worcestershire sauce

Season to taste.

Meanwhile butter 4 slices French bread and sprinkle with grated Parmesan cheese. Toast under broiler.

Ladle hot soup into dishes and float the toast on top.

Yield: 4 cups.

NOTE: If desired, use 2 cans consommé and 1 soup can of water in place of Beef Soup Stock and water.

357   Chicken Broth

Wash and disjoint

4 to 4½ pound fowl

Place in pressure cooker and add

2 teaspoons salt
¼ teaspoon pepper
¼ teaspoon poultry seasoning
1 cup celery leaves and stalks, cut-up
1 medium onion, sliced
1 large carrot, sliced
5 cups cold water

Bring cooker to 15 pounds pressure and process 30 minutes. Cool quickly and remove chicken and bones from broth. Save chicken meat to add to soups, etc. Discard bones.

Strain soup through fine sieve or cheesecloth in a colander.

Cool quickly and refrigerate.

Remove chilled fat from surface and store broth in covered container in refrigerator.

Use as needed in soups or sauces.

Yield: 6 cups.

Long Cooking Method: Use a large heavy kettle with cover and increase water to 8 cups. Cook until chicken is tender, 2 to 3 hours. Add water from time to time as needed. When chicken meat is tender, remove from bones. Return bones and skin to broth and cook 30 minutes longer.

VARIATION:

(a)   Jellied Chicken Bouillon

To 4 cups hot Chicken Broth add 1 envelope gelatine softened in ¼ cup water. Stir until dissolved. Season to taste.

Cool and refrigerate until set.

To serve, break up with a fork and fill chilled consommé cups. Garnish with lemon wedges and parsley or commercial sour cream and chopped chives.

Yield: 4 servings.

358   Turkey Soup

Break apart carcass of leftover turkey or chicken and place in large kettle along with skin and trimmings.

Add

6 cups cold water
1 cup celery leaves
2 sprigs parsley
1 large onion, sliced
1 large carrot, sliced
2 teaspoons salt
3 peppercorns
1 bay leaf
1 teaspoon poultry seasoning

Bring to a boil. Cover and simmer 3 hours.

Remove bones. Strain broth through fine sieve or cheesecloth in a colander. Cool quickly and refrigerate. Remove chilled fat if necessary.

Measure and make up volume to 6 cups with water or vegetable stock.

Add

1 (12-ounce) package frozen mixed vegetables
⅓ cup packaged precooked rice
Any diced leftover poultry

Bring to a boil. Cover and simmer 15 minutes. Season to taste.

Yield: 6 cups.

NOTES: **1.** For large turkey carcass, allow 8 or more cups water.

2. Pressure cook if desired, using 4 to 6 cups water depending upon size of bird. Process at 15 pounds pressure for 20 minutes. Proceed as directed in recipe.

359 Old Fashioned Split Pea Soup

Pick over and wash

2 cups (1 pound) dried yellow *or* green split peas

Soak overnight in

12 cups cold water

Do not drain.

Add

1 ham bone (trim off fat)
1 cup finely chopped onions
1 cup finely diced celery

Bring slowly to boiling point. Cover and simmer 3 hours or until peas are tender.

Remove ham bone. Cut off any meat, finely dice and return to soup. Skim off fat.

Combine

3 tablespoons soft butter *or* margarine
3 tablespoons *Pre-Sifted* PURITY All-Purpose Flour

Blend in about

1 cup soup

Stir this mixture into soup and bring to a boil, stirring constantly. Season to taste — the amount of salt will vary with saltiness of the ham.

Serve garnished with slices of small ring bologna.

Yield: 10 to 11 cups.

NOTE: Do not pressure cook, since split peas tend to clog the vent pipe.

360 Scotch Broth

Purchase **3 pounds neck, shank or stewing lamb.**

Cut meat from bones and trim off *all fat possible* and discard.

Cut meat into ¾″ pieces.

Loosely tie bones in cheesecloth.

Place meat and bones in pressure cooker.

Add

6 cups cold water
1½ teaspoons salt
⅛ teaspoon pepper
½ bay leaf, crushed
½ cup chopped onions
¼ cup whole barley

Bring pressure to 15 pounds and process 20 minutes. Cool cooker quickly. Skim off fat, if necessary.

Remove bones and add

½ cup diced turnip
½ cup diced carrots
½ cup sliced celery
½ cup diced potatoes
½ cup chopped onions

Bring pressure to 15 pounds and process 5 minutes. Cool cooker quickly. Skim off fat.

Combine

3 tablespoons soft butter *or* margarine
3 tablespoons *Pre-Sifted* PURITY All-Purpose Flour

Blend in about

1 cup soup

Stir this mixture into soup in cooker and bring to a boil, stirring constantly. Season to taste.

Serve piping hot garnished with chopped parsley.

Yield: 8 cups.

361 Potato Soup Country Style

Cut 4 peeled medium potatoes, lengthwise, into quarters. Then slice thinly and measure

4 cups

Place in a large saucepan and add

1 cup thinly sliced onions
1 teaspoon celery salt
½ teaspoon salt
¼ teaspoon pepper
2 cups boiling water

Bring to a boil. Cover and simmer 30 minutes or until vegetables are tender.

Add

2 cups milk
¼ cup chopped parsley

Cover and simmer 10 minutes longer. Season to taste.

Sprinkle each serving with 1 tablespoon shredded old Cheddar cheese.

Yield: 6 cups.

362 Corn Chowder

Fry until crisp in a deep heavy saucepan

4 slices side bacon, cut in small pieces

Remove bacon bits and drain on paper towelling.

Pour off fat. Measure 2 tablespoons and return to saucepan.

Add

½ cup finely chopped onions

Cook until transparent but not brown.

Add

2 cups diced raw potatoes
1 cup boiling water

Bring to a boil. Reduce heat, cover and cook 8 to 10 minutes or until tender.

Add

3 cups warm milk
1 (14-ounce) can whole kernel corn
or 1½ cups cooked corn
Crisp bacon bits
1 teaspoon salt
¼ teaspoon pepper

Heat just to boiling. Season to taste.

Serve garnished with paprika.

Yield: 6 cups.

363 Delicious Fish Chowder

Melt in a large heavy saucepan

2 tablespoons butter or margarine

Add

¾ cup thinly sliced onions
½ cup diced celery

Cook, stirring frequently, until transparent.

Add

2 cups diced raw potatoes
½ cup sliced carrots
1½ teaspoons salt
⅛ teaspoon pepper
2 cups boiling water

Bring to a boil. Cover and simmer until vegetables are tender—about 15 minutes.

Add

1 pound uncooked fish fillets, cut in bite-size pieces (haddock, sole or halibut)

Cover and simmer 10 minutes longer.

Add

2 cups milk

Heat but do not allow to boil. Season to taste.

Serve garnished with chopped parsley.

Yield: 6 cups.

364 Clam Chowder

Fry in a large heavy saucepan

4 slices side bacon, finely diced

Drain the crisp bacon on absorbent paper. Set aside until needed.

Pour off fat. Measure 2 tablespoons and return to saucepan.

Add

½ cup very finely chopped onions

Cook until transparent.

Add

2 cups diced raw potatoes
1 cup boiling water

Bring to a boil, then reduce heat. Cover and cook 10 minutes or until potatoes are just tender.

Add

2 (10-ounce) cans clams or
1 pint fresh clams and liquor
2½ cups milk
1 teaspoon salt
½ teaspoon celery salt
⅛ teaspoon pepper
Crisp bacon bits

Stir well to combine and heat until just boiling. Season to taste.

Serve garnished with paprika.

Yield: 8½ cups.

NOTE: If a thicker chowder is desired, mix to a paste

3 tablespoons Pre-Sifted PURITY All-Purpose Flour
¼ cup milk

Combine with about 1 cup of the chowder broth and then stir back into the chowder. Stir gently until thickened. Season to taste.

365 Lydia's Oyster Stew

Heat in double boiler

4 cups milk
2 tablespoons butter or margarine
1 teaspoon salt
½ teaspoon celery salt
⅛ teaspoon pepper

Keep mixture hot over simmering water.

Heat to simmering

1 pint oysters and liquor

until the oysters are plump and the edges curl (3 to 4 minutes).

Add to hot seasoned milk in double boiler.

Combine and let stand 10 minutes for flavours to blend.

Serve steaming hot with oyster crackers.

Sprinkle with paprika.

Yield: 6 cups.

Main Dishes

THINGS TO REMEMBER ABOUT MAIN DISHES

Most of the recipes in this section can be prepared ahead of time, refrigerated and then cooked. Allow longer baking time for a refrigerated casserole. To prevent breakage, avoid placing icy cold glass or china casseroles in the oven.

How to cook Pasta (noodles, spaghetti, macaroni, etc.): Drop pasta into a large amount of boiling salted water. Cook, uncovered, keeping the water boiling briskly. Stir occasionally. Never overcook pasta. If it is firm all the way through but not hard in the centre, it is just right. Rinse with cold water. Noodles do not increase in size when cooked; spaghetti increases about one and one-half times its original size; macaroni swells to double its original size when cooked.

How to cook Rice: Quick-cooking varieties of rice should be cooked according to package directions.

Regular rice should be cooked in a large amount of boiling salted water, uncovered. Keep water boiling briskly. Do not stir. Cook until tender, about 25 minutes. Rinse with cold water.

When cooked, regular rice has swelled to three times its original size.

Toppings for casseroles are many and varied. Choose from one of the following:
Biscuit topping (drop, rolled or pinwheel—plain, savoury or cheese).
Pastry — plain or latticed.
Buttered sliced bread, cut into small cubes.
Triangular cheese slices on toast.
Dried bread crumbs mixed with commercially grated cheese.
Corn bread.

---

366 Devilled Chicken Wings

Heat in a large frying pan
   3 tablespoons vegetable oil or shortening
Add
   ⅓ cup sliced onions
   2 pounds chicken wings (approximately 15 to 18 wings)
Cook over moderate heat until browned (about 10 minutes).
Then add
   1 (28-ounce) can tomatoes
   ⅔ cup packaged precooked rice
   ⅓ cup water
   1 teaspoon salt
   ½ teaspoon dried parsley flakes
   ¼ teaspoon chili powder
Stir to moisten rice and combine ingredients.
Cover pan and simmer slowly for 25 to 30 minutes. Stir occasionally, adding water if necessary.
Yield: 6 servings.

367 Chicken Tetrazzini

Preheat oven to 375°.
Melt in a frying pan
   2 tablespoons butter or margarine
Add
   ¼ pound fresh mushrooms, sliced
Cook until tender.
Meanwhile, melt in a saucepan
   3 tablespoons butter or margarine
Blend in
   ¼ cup Pre-Sifted PURITY All-Purpose Flour
   ½ teaspoon salt
   ⅛ teaspoon paprika
   Few grains pepper

Slowly stir in
  2 cups milk
Cook until smoothly thickened, stirring constantly.
Then add
  2 tablespoons diced pimiento
Place in a buttered 1½-quart casserole
  1 cup cooked spaghetti
Add
  1 cup diced cooked chicken
  Cooked mushrooms
Top with the cream sauce and sprinkle with
  ⅓ cup grated Parmesan cheese
Bake in preheated 375° oven for 25 to 30 minutes, until cheese is bubbly and browned.
Yield: 4 servings.

368   Chicken Pie Pronto

Preheat oven to 450°.
Heat in a frying pan
  2 tablespoons vegetable oil *or* shortening
Add
  ½ cup sliced onions
Cook until tender but not browned.
Blend together
  1 (10-ounce) can cream of mushroom soup
  ½ cup milk
  ⅛ teaspoon marjoram
Add to the cooked onions and heat to the simmering point.
Arrange in an 8″ baking dish or deep pie plate
  1 cup diced cooked chicken
  1 cup canned whole potatoes *or* cubed leftover potatoes
Pour the hot mushroom sauce over top.
Prepare one-half recipe for Savoury Biscuits (recipe No. 42 (f) and roll to a 9″ circle. Place over chicken mixture, flute edge and prick top.
Bake in preheated 450° oven for 15 minutes.
Yield: 4 servings.

369   Chicken Supreme

Preheat oven to 350°.
Melt in top of double boiler over direct heat
  5 tablespoons butter *or* margarine
Blend in
  6 tablespoons *Pre-Sifted* PURITY All-Purpose Flour

  1 teaspoon salt
  Few grains pepper
  ⅛ teaspoon monosodium glutamate
Slowly stir in
  1 cup chicken stock *or* bouillon (1 cup water with 1 chicken bouillon cube)
  2 cups cream (18%)
Stir until smoothly thickened.
Add a little of the hot sauce to
  2 slightly-beaten egg yolks
Blend, then return to double boiler top and cook over boiling water for 2 minutes, stirring constantly.
Remove from heat and stir in
  1 tablespoon lemon juice
  2 tablespoons sherry, if desired
Butter a 2-quart casserole. Arrange in layers
  3 cups cooked diced chicken
  1 cup cooked sliced mushrooms
  1 cup drained sliced water chestnuts
  Cream sauce
End with a layer of sauce.
Top with
  ¼ cup slivered blanched almonds
Bake in preheated 350° oven for 30 to 40 minutes, until bubbly.
Yield: 6 to 8 servings.

370   Chicken à la King

Melt in a frying pan
  2 tablespoons butter *or* margarine
Add
  ⅓ cup diced green peppers
  ¼ pound fresh mushrooms, sliced
Cook slowly until tender, but not browned.
Melt in a saucepan
  2 tablespoons butter *or* margarine
Blend in
  ¼ cup *Pre-Sifted* PURITY All-Purpose Flour
  ½ teaspoon salt
  Few grains pepper
Slowly stir in
  1 cup milk
  1 cup chicken stock *or* bouillon (1 cup water with 1 chicken bouillon cube)
  ⅛ teaspoon ground nutmeg
Stir until smoothly thickened.

Add
**Cooked green peppers and
mushrooms
3 cups cooked diced chicken
2 tablespoons diced pimiento**

Serve on hot buttered biscuits, toast or in patty shells.

Yield: 6 servings.

VARIATION:

(a) *Eggs à la King*

Prepare as above, substituting 6 sliced hard-cooked eggs for the chicken.

371 Jambalaya

Preheat oven to 350°.

Cook in a frying pan over moderate heat
**4 slices side bacon, cut in 1" pieces
½ cup chopped onions
½ cup diced green peppers**

Combine in a buttered 1½-quart casserole
**3 cups hot water
3 chicken bouillon cubes
½ cup catsup
2 tablespoons brown sugar
1⅓ cups packaged precooked rice
½ teaspoon salt**

Stir to blend well.

Add cooked bacon, onions and green peppers.

Then add
**3 (4¼-ounce) cans drained shrimp
or 2 cups diced cooked ham**

Cover casserole and bake in preheated 350° oven for 25 minutes. Stir 2 or 3 times during baking.

Yield: 6 to 8 servings.

If the recipe calls for a "covered" casserole or skillet, a piece of aluminum foil can be used.

372 Creole Shrimp

Melt in a frying pan
3 tablespoons butter *or* margarine
Add
**½ cup chopped onions
½ cup diced green peppers
½ cup diced celery**

Cook slowly until tender, but not browned.

Blend in
**3 tablespoons *Pre-Sifted* PURITY
All-Purpose Flour**

**½ teaspoon Worcestershire sauce
½ teaspoon salt
½ teaspoon monosodium glutamate
⅛ teaspoon marjoram
Few drops tabasco sauce**

Slowly stir in
**1 (7½-ounce) can tomato sauce
2 cups water**

Stir until smoothly thickened. Simmer gently, uncovered, for 30 minutes. Stir occasionally.

Stir in
2 cups cooked shrimp

Cook just until shrimps are heated.

Serve on hot buttered biscuits or cooked rice.

Yield: 6 servings.

373 Rice and Crab Meat Bake

Preheat oven to 350°.

Cook
½ pound fresh mushrooms, sliced
in
2 tablespoons butter *or* margarine

When mushrooms are tender, add
**1 (7-ounce) can crab meat, drained
and flaked
1½ cups cooked rice
1 cup shredded Cheddar cheese
½ cup milk
3 tablespoons catsup
½ teaspoon Worcestershire sauce
½ teaspoon salt
⅛ teaspoon pepper**

Turn mixture into a buttered 1½-quart casserole.

Top with
**¼ cup catsup
½ cup shredded Cheddar cheese**

Bake in preheated 350° oven for 25 to 30 minutes.

Yield: 4 to 5 servings.

374 Salmon Casserole

Preheat oven to 325°.

Heat in top of double boiler over simmering water
**1 (10-ounce) can cream of mushroom
soup
½ cup milk**

When smoothly blended and hot, add
1 cup cubed process cheese

Continue heating until cheese is melted, stirring frequently.

Combine in a buttered 1½-quart casserole
> **2 cups cooked noodles**
> **1 (7¾-ounce) can salmon, flaked**

Add the cheese sauce.

Around the edge, arrange a border of
> **½ cup Chinese noodles**

Bake in preheated 325° oven for 20 minutes.

Yield: 6 servings.

375   Salmon Delight

Preheat oven to 450°.

Melt in a saucepan
> **⅓ cup butter or margarine**

Add
> **½ cup finely chopped onions**

Cook until tender.

Blend in
> **⅓ cup Pre-Sifted PURITY**
> **All-Purpose Flour**
> **½ teaspoon salt**
> **Few grains pepper**

Slowly stir in
> **1½ cups milk**

Cook until smoothly thickened.

Stir in
> **¼ cup shredded Cheddar cheese**
> **1 (7¾-ounce) can salmon, flaked**
> **1 cup canned tomatoes**
> **Few drops Worcestershire sauce**

Pour into a buttered 2-quart casserole.

Prepare Drop Biscuits (recipe No. 43), adding ¼ cup shredded Cheddar cheese to the dry ingredients. Drop by large spoonfuls around edge of the casserole.

Bake in preheated 450° oven for about 20 minutes.

Yield: 6 servings.

376   Shellfish Special

Preheat oven to 350°.

Heat about 1½″ of water in a broad saucepan.

Add
> **1 teaspoon salt**
> **1 teaspoon lemon juice**
> **1 pound scallops (defrosted, if frozen)**

Poach for 10 minutes.

Melt in a saucepan
> **½ cup butter or margarine**

Blend in
> **½ cup Pre-Sifted PURITY**
> **All-Purpose Flour**
> **1 teaspoon salt**
> **½ teaspoon monosodium glutamate**
> **¼ teaspoon pepper**
> **¼ teaspoon dry mustard**

Gradually stir in
> **2¼ cups milk**

Cook, stirring constantly, until thickened.

Remove from heat, and add
> **1½ cups shredded Cheddar cheese**
> **1 tablespoon lemon juice**

Blend well.

Butter a 2-quart casserole. Arrange in layers
> **3 cups cooked rice**
> **Poached scallops**
> **1 (14-ounce) package frozen shrimp, cooked**
> **1 (10-ounce) can sliced mushrooms, drained**
> **Cheese sauce**

End with a layer of sauce.

Sprinkle with
> **3 slices bread, buttered and cubed**

Bake in preheated 350° oven for 30 minutes or until browned and bubbly.

Yield: 8 servings.

377   Speedy Shrimp Newburg

Combine in top of double boiler
> **1 (10-ounce) can frozen cream of shrimp soup**
> **½ cup milk**
> **¼ cup cubed process cheese**

Heat over simmering water, stirring until blended.

Add
> **1 cup cooked shrimp**
> **1 cup cooked peas**
> **½ teaspoon salt**

Heat to serving temperature.

Serve over hot cooked rice.

Yield: 4 servings.

Remember the threesome: flavour, colour, texture. They are important in all your meal planning and food preparation, and particularly so in casserole and skillet dishes. Keep pieces of onion, celery, green pepper, etc. large enough to be recognized.

378   Tuna Casserole

Preheat oven to 425°.

Combine

1 (7-ounce) can tuna
2 tablespoons chopped onion
1 tablespoon chopped green pepper
or celery
¾ cup cooked peas, drained
1 (10-ounce) can cream of celery soup
⅓ cup milk
Few grains pepper

Pour into a 1-quart casserole or into individual ramekins. Prepare one-half recipe for Basic Tea Biscuits (recipe No. 42), adding ⅛ teaspoon each of sage, thyme and savoury to the dry ingredients. Roll to about ½″ thickness. Cut dough into interesting shapes.

Place on tuna mixture.

Bake in preheated 425° oven for 20 to 25 minutes.

Yield: 4 to 5 servings.

379 Individual Tuna Pizzas

PIZZA DOUGH:

Sprinkle

1 package active dry yeast*

over

½ cup lukewarm water

in which has been dissolved

1 teaspoon sugar

Let stand in a warm place for 10 minutes.

Then stir briskly with a fork.

Meanwhile, scald

¼ cup milk
2 tablespoons shortening
1 tablespoon sugar

Cool to lukewarm.

Add softened yeast and stir well.

Then add

2 cups *Pre-Sifted* PURITY
All-Purpose Flour

Combine well.

Knead for 3 minutes on a lightly floured board.

Place in a greased bowl and grease dough slightly. Cover and set in a warm place until doubled in bulk (about 45 minutes). Keep at a temperature of about 80°.

Punch down and rest the dough for 10 minutes.

Roll to a 9″ x 12″ rectangle. Cut into twelve 3″ circles. Place on a greased baking sheet. Spread with the Tuna Mixture.

TUNA MIXTURE:

Heat in a frying pan

2 tablespoons vegetable oil *or*
shortening

Add

½ cup chopped cooked mushrooms
⅓ cup chopped onions

Fry only until tender.

Combine

1 (7-ounce) can tuna, flaked
1 (10-ounce) can tomato soup
¼ teaspoon garlic powder
¼ teaspoon chili powder
⅛ teaspoon pepper

Add mushroom mixture and combine evenly.

When this mixture has been spread on rounds of dough, sprinkle with grated cheese.

Set pizzas in a warm place (80°) to rise again for 45 minutes.

Bake in preheated 425° oven for 12 to 15 minutes.

Yield: 12 small pizzas.

380   Sausage Pizza

Prepare the Pizza Dough as for Individual Tuna Pizzas (recipe No. 379).

Roll the rested dough to fit a 14″ pizza pan and ease it into the pan. Fill with the Sausage Filling.

SAUSAGE FILLING:

Combine in a frying pan

½ pound sausage meat
⅓ cup chopped onions

Cook until meat shows no pink colour and onions are tender.

Add

1 (10-ounce) can sliced mushrooms,
drained
1 (6-ounce) can tomato paste
¼ teaspoon salt
⅛ teaspoon pepper
¼ teaspoon garlic powder
¼ teaspoon chili powder
¼ teaspoon oregano
½ cup water

Blend well and spread on the pizza dough.

Set in a warm place (80°) and allow to rise for 45 minutes.

*To use fresh yeast see "Note" page 6.

Then bake in preheated 450° oven for 15 minutes.

Place 3 slices Mozzarella cheese (about 4 ounces) on top of filling 5 minutes before removing from the oven.

Yield: 8 to 10 servings.

381   Martha's Casserole

Preheat oven to 350°.

Cook until tender in boiling salted water
  8 ounces noodles

Meanwhile, heat in large heavy frying pan
  **3 tablespoons vegetable oil *or*
    shortening**

Add
  **1 cup sliced onions
  ½ cup diced green peppers
  1 pound minced beef
  ½ pound minced pork**

Cook slowly until tender and lightly browned.

Add
  **1 (10-ounce) can mushroom pieces,
    undrained
  1 (10-ounce) can tomato soup
  1 (4-ounce) package cream cheese
  1 tablespoon Worcestershire sauce
  ½ teaspoon salt
  ¼ teaspoon pepper**

Blend over low heat for 10 minutes.

Arrange cooked noodles in buttered 2-quart casserole. Cover with meat mixture.

Combine
  **1 cup corn flakes
  ½ cup slivered blanched almonds**

Sprinkle over the top.

Bake in preheated 350° oven for 30 minutes.

Yield: 8 to 10 servings.

382   Mafalda Supreme

Preheat oven to 350°.

Combine in a large frying pan
  **¾ pound minced beef
  ¼ cup chopped onions
  ¼ teaspoon basil
  ¼ teaspoon oregano
  ¼ teaspoon black pepper
  ⅛ teaspoon rosemary
  1 clove of garlic, crushed
  1 teaspoon salt
  1½ cups canned tomatoes
  1 (6-ounce) can tomato paste
  ¼ cup water**

Cover and simmer gently for 45 minutes. Stir occasionally.

Meanwhile, cook until tender in boiling salted water
  8 ounces thin noodles

CHEESE SAUCE:

Melt in top of double boiler over direct heat
  2 tablespoons butter *or* margarine

Blend in
  **1½ tablespoons *Pre-Sifted* PURITY
    All-Purpose Flour**

Slowly stir in
  1 cup milk

Stir until smoothly thickened.

Add
  **2 tablespoons finely chopped onion
  ½ cup shredded Mozzarella cheese
  ¼ cup shredded Parmesan cheese**

When cheese has melted and sauce is smooth, add a little to
  1 slightly-beaten egg yolk

Blend well and return to double boiler, stirring briskly. Cook over boiling water 2 minutes longer. Remove from heat.

Butter a 2-quart casserole.

Arrange meat and tomato mixture in layers with the cooked noodles, cheese sauce and ½ cup cottage cheese. Top with a layer of cheese sauce.

Bake in preheated 350° oven for about 30 minutes.

Yield: 6 to 8 servings.

383   Spaghetti with Italian Sauce

Brush large frying pan with
  **1 tablespoon melted shortening *or*
    vegetable oil**

Add
  **1 pound minced beef
  ½ cup diced celery
  ½ cup sliced onions
  ½ cup diced green peppers
  1 (28-ounce) can tomatoes
  1 (15-ounce) can spaghetti sauce
  1 (10-ounce) can mushroom pieces,
    drained
  1 teaspoon salt
  ¼ teaspoon oregano
  ⅛ teaspoon pepper
  1 clove of garlic, crushed**

Combine and simmer gently for 30 minutes. Meanwhile, cook until tender in boiling salted water

16 ounces spaghetti

Drain.

Pour sauce over the spaghetti and sprinkle with commercially grated Parmesan cheese.

Yield: 8 servings.

384   French Meat Roll

Preheat oven to 425°.

Mix thoroughly

¾ pound minced beef
½ cup diced celery
¼ cup diced green peppers
¼ cup chopped onions
1 tablespoon Worcestershire sauce
¼ cup catsup
2 unbeaten eggs
¼ cup rolled oats
1 teaspoon salt

Prepare Basic Tea Biscuit dough (recipe No. 42), adding 1 teaspoon dry mustard and 1 teaspoon dried parsley flakes to the dry ingredients.   Roll to a 10″ x 12″ rectangle. Spread meat filling to within ½″ of the edges. Roll up like a jelly roll, starting from the long side. Moisten edge and seal.

Place on greased baking sheet, tuck ends under.

Bake in preheated 425° oven for 30 to 35 minutes.

Serve plain or with tomato or mushroom sauce.

Yield: 6 servings.

385   Chili Con Carne

Heat in a large heavy frying pan

1 tablespoon vegetable oil or shortening

Add and cook together over moderate heat

1 pound minced beef
½ cup sliced onions
½ cup diced green peppers

When meat is lightly browned, add

1 (15-ounce) can red kidney beans
1 (10-ounce) can tomato soup
2 teaspoons chili powder
1 teaspoon salt
¼ teaspoon oregano
⅔ cup water

Blend, cover and simmer gently for 20 minutes.

Yield: 4 to 6 servings.

386   Baked Ham Rolls

Preheat oven to 350 .

Combine in top of double boiler

½ pound process cheese, cubed
½ cup milk

Heat and stir until smooth.

Spread with prepared mustard

4 thin slices cooked ham

Peel

4 slightly under-ripe bananas

Roll each banana in a slice of ham.

Arrange ham rolls in a buttered casserole. Pour cheese sauce over top.

Bake in preheated 350° oven for about 20 minutes.

Yield: 4 servings.

VARIATION:

(a)   Pineapple Ham Rolls

Prepare as directed above, omitting the bananas and filling the rolls with a combination of:

⅔ cup cooked rice
⅔ cup well-drained crushed pineapple
½ teaspoon curry powder

387   Spanish Rice

Melt in a frying pan

¼ cup butter or margarine

Add

⅓ cup chopped onions
⅓ cup chopped green peppers
¼ cup diced celery
½ pound fresh mushrooms, sliced

Cook slowly until tender, but not browned.

Add

1 (20-ounce) can tomatoes
1 teaspoon salt
⅛ teaspoon pepper

Simmer gently, uncovered, for 10 minutes.

Stir in

2 cups cooked rice

Cover and simmer gently for another 10 minutes.

More tomatoes or tomato juice may be added, if desired.

Yield: 6 servings.

Cheese and Eggs

THINGS TO REMEMBER ABOUT CHEESE

There is a wide assortment of Canadian and imported cheeses in our food stores: hard and soft, sharp and mild, natural and process. Do serve new flavours and include different varieties in your cooking.

Cheese should be stored in the refrigerator, tightly wrapped in waxed paper or saran. Small portions of firm cheeses, such as Cheddar and Swiss, may be kept in this way for 2 to 3 weeks. For larger portions, such as the rounds of cheese, seal the cut edge with cheesecloth dipped in melted paraffin and keep the wrapped cheese covered with a cloth dampened with water to which a little vinegar has been added. The soft cheeses such as Roquefort, Blue and Camembert should be kept well covered and used within a few days. Purchase cream cheese and cottage cheese as needed as they do not improve with age.

Cheese should be melted and cooked at low temperatures to prevent toughness and stringiness. Either natural Cheddar or process cheese may be used in main dishes. Process cheese melts more uniformly than the Cheddar and gives a milder flavour.

---

388   Cheese Puff

Preheat oven to 325°.

Remove crusts from
  12 slices day-old white bread

Arrange 6 slices in bottom of 12" x 8" x 2" casserole or baking dish.

Place **6 slices Canadian process cheese (6 ounces)** on top of the bread. Arrange remaining bread slices over the cheese.

Combine
  4 slightly-beaten eggs
  2½ cups milk
  1 teaspoon salt
  Few grains pepper
  ⅛ teaspoon dry mustard

Pour egg mixture over bread and cheese and allow to stand for 1 hour.

Bake in preheated 325° oven for about 1 hour, until puffed and browned.

Yield: 6 servings.

VARIATION:

(a)   Tomato-Cheese Puff

Prepare recipe for Cheese Puff, replacing the 2½ cups milk with 1 (8-ounce) can tomato sauce and 1½ cups milk. Combine and bake as above.

389   Cheese Soufflé

Preheat oven to 300°.

Melt in a saucepan
  3 tablespoons butter or margarine

Blend in
  3 tablespoons *Pre-Sifted* PURITY All-Purpose Flour
  ½ teaspoon salt
  ⅛ teaspoon dry mustard
  Few grains pepper

Gradually stir in
  1 cup milk

Cook, stirring constantly, until thickened.

Add
  1 cup shredded Cheddar cheese

Stir until cheese is melted. Remove from heat.

Beat until light
  3 egg yolks

Stir hot cheese mixture into yolks, blending thoroughly. Cool.

Beat until stiff, but not dry
  3 egg whites

Carefully fold cheese mixture into egg whites.

Turn into an ungreased 1½-quart casserole.

Bake in preheated 300° oven for about 60

minutes, until firm, dry and lightly browned.
Yield: 4 to 5 servings.

NOTES: **1.** Run the tip of a teaspoon around the unbaked soufflé about an inch in from the edge of the casserole, making a slight depression. This forms a high centre or "top hat" on the soufflé as it bakes.

2. A soufflé will stand for 10 to 15 minutes after baking with very little shrinkage. Keep it in the oven, with the heat off.

3. For a soft crust, place casserole in a shallow pan of hot water. If a crisp, firmer crust is preferred, bake without water.

VARIATIONS:

(a)   Chicken or Fish Soufflé

Prepare Cheese Soufflé as directed above, adding 1 cup diced cooked chicken or 1 cup flaked cooked fish to the mixture *before* folding it into the beaten egg whites. Bake as directed above.

(b)   Ham-Cheese Soufflé

Prepare Cheese Soufflé as directed above, adding ½ cup minced cooked ham to the mixture *before* folding it into the beaten egg whites. Bake as directed above.

390   Mushroom Cheese Soufflé

Preheat oven to 300°.

Heat
   **1 (10-ounce) can condensed cream
      of mushroom soup**

Add
   1 cup shredded Cheddar cheese

Stir over low heat until cheese is melted.

Gradually stir into
   6 slightly-beaten egg yolks

Cool.

Beat until stiff, but not dry
   6 egg whites

Carefully fold mushroom mixture into egg whites. Turn into an ungreased 2-quart casserole.

Bake in preheated 300° oven for 1 to 1¼ hours, until firm, dry and lightly browned.
Yield: 6 servings.

391   Macaroni and Cheese

Preheat oven to 375°.

Cook **1 cup macaroni** until tender in boiling salted water.

Drain.

Meanwhile, melt in a saucepan
   ¼ cup butter *or* margarine

Add
   1 tablespoon chopped onion

Cook slowly until tender but not browned.

Blend in
   **¼ cup *Pre-Sifted* PURITY
      All-Purpose Flour**
   ½ teaspoon salt
   ¼ teaspoon dry mustard
   Few grains pepper

Gradually stir in
   2 cups milk

Cook over medium heat, stirring constantly, until thickened.

Add
   1 cup shredded Cheddar cheese

Stir until cheese is melted.

Add cooked macaroni and blend well.

Pour into a buttered 1½- or 2-quart casserole.

Sprinkle with
   ⅔ cup buttered bread crumbs

Bake in preheated 375° oven for 30 minutes or until bubbly and browned.
Yield: 4 to 6 servings.

Slice or cube process cheese before adding it to other foods. Harder Cheddar cheese should be shredded, ¼ pound makes 1 cup shredded cheese, lightly-packed.

392   Rice and Cheese

Combine in top of double boiler
   2 slightly-beaten eggs
   3 cups cooked rice
   1 cup shredded Cheddar cheese
   1½ cups milk
   ¼ teaspoon salt
   ¼ teaspoon Worcestershire sauce
   Few grains cayenne

Cook over simmering water until mixture is thickened slightly and cheese is melted. Let stand in a warm place for 10 minutes. Do not cook further. Serve on toast with a crisp salad.
Yield: 6 servings.

393   Welsh Rabbit

Melt over simmering water in top of double boiler

1 tablespoon butter *or* margarine

Add

½ pound process cheese, sliced or cubed
½ teaspoon dry mustard
¼ teaspoon salt
Few grains cayenne

As cheese begins to melt, gradually stir in

½ cup milk

Continue stirring until sauce is smooth and well blended.

Gradually add cheese sauce to

1 slightly-beaten egg

Stir briskly until evenly combined.

Serve immediately, on toast.

Yield: 4 to 6 servings.

Cheese is best when served at room temperature. Remove it from the refrigerator at least an hour before serving (except for cottage cheese).

394   Pink Poodle (*Tomato Rabbit*)

Melt in top of double boiler

3 tablespoons butter *or* margarine

Blend in

¼ cup *Pre-Sifted* PURITY All-Purpose Flour
1 tablespoon finely grated onion
½ teaspoon salt
¼ teaspoon dry mustard
¼ teaspoon Worcestershire sauce
Few grains cayenne

Gradually stir in

¾ cup milk

Cook over direct medium heat until smoothly thickened, stirring constantly.

Remove from heat and gradually stir in

¾ cup tomato juice

Place over hot (not boiling) water and add

1½ cups shredded Cheddar cheese

Stir constantly until cheese is melted.

Serve on toast, with a tossed salad.

Yield: 4 to 6 servings.

THINGS TO REMEMBER ABOUT EGGS

Eggs purchased from refrigerated display cases will generally have retained better quality than those displayed on open counters.

At home, eggs should be stored in the refrigerator, away from strong-smelling foods.

Eggs beat up to a larger volume when at room temperature. The whites will not beat up to full volume or stiffness if *any* yolk or bit of fat gets into the bowl. If eggs are to be beaten separately, beat the whites first and then the yolks, using the same beater.

Store leftover whites in a tightly covered jar in the refrigerator. They will keep about 10 days. Cover leftover yolks with water or milk and use within 2 or 3 days.

Eggs toughen at high temperatures, so no matter what method is used for cooking them, the temperature should be low.

---

395   Soft-Cooked Eggs

Cover eggs with water at least 1″ above the eggs. Quickly bring water to a boil and then remove from the heat. Cover pan, and let stand for 3 to 5 minutes, depending on individual taste.

When cooking more than 4 eggs, do not remove pan from heat but keep water below simmering point. Allow eggs to cook for 4 to 6 minutes.

When hard-cooking eggs for later use, add a few drops of vegetable colouring to the cooking water. The cooked eggs are then easily distinguished from the uncooked ones in your refrigerator.

396   Hard-Cooked Eggs

Cover eggs with water at least 1″ above the eggs. Quickly bring water to a boil and then lower heat and keep water below the simmering point. Allow eggs to cook for about 15 minutes.

If the hard-cooked eggs are to be used for salads, etc. cool at once under cold running water. This prevents the formation of a dark ring around the yolk.

There is no difference between white and brown eggs. They are alike in flavour, yolk colour and nutritive value.

397   Poached Eggs

Butter frying pan. Add water to a depth of 1½" to 2". Add salt and bring to boiling point. Lower heat to keep water just below simmering. Break eggs carefully, one at a time, into a saucer, and slip gently into water. Cook until eggs are set, 3 to 5 minutes. Remove eggs from pan with slotted pancake lifter, drain and serve.

NOTE: For luncheon, serve poached eggs on cooked spinach or corned beef hash with Hollandaise Sauce or Cheese Sauce.

VARIATION:

(a)   Eggs Benedict

Top toasted English muffin halves with slices of hot ham, poached egg and Hollandaise Sauce.

398   Fried Eggs

For every 2 eggs, place about 1 tablespoon fat in a frying pan. Place pan over heat until just hot enough to make a drop of water sizzle. Lower heat. Break eggs into pan. Cook gently for 3 to 5 minutes or until of desired firmness, spooning hot fat over eggs. Remove with pancake lifter, tilting against side of pan to drain well. Season before serving.

If frying bacon with eggs, cook bacon first in ungreased frying pan. When done, drain on absorbent paper towel. Pour off all but fat required for eggs, lower heat and proceed as above.

399   Scrambled Eggs

For each egg, add 1 tablespoon milk, few grains of salt and pepper. Beat just until blended. Melt butter or margarine to cover bottom of frying pan. Cook egg mixture over moderate heat until creamy, stirring lightly. Serve immediately.

NOTE: If desired, chopped ham, cooked mushrooms or asparagus may be added.

Egg yolks may be hard-cooked separately. Drop gently into simmering water and cook for 8 to 10 minutes. Use in salads, sandwiches, casseroles, etc.

400   Shirred Eggs

Preheat oven to 350°.

Butter individual baking dishes, custard cups or a large casserole, depending upon number of eggs to be served. Break eggs and slip, one at a time, into dish. Season with salt and pepper and top with a little butter, cream, fine bread crumbs, or shredded cheese. Bake in preheated 350° oven for 12 to 18 minutes, depending upon firmness desired.

401   Creamy Eggs

For each egg, add 2 tablespoons milk, few grains of salt and pepper. Beat until just blended.

Melt about 1 tablespoon butter or margarine in double boiler top. Add egg mixture and cook over simmering water. As eggs cook, draw away from sides and bottom of the pan with a spoon. Continue until eggs are set but still moist. Do not overcook.

Serve at once.

402   French Toast

Beat together until blended
   2 eggs
   1 tablespoon sugar
   ¼ teaspoon salt
   Few grains pepper
   ½ cup milk

Place in broad, shallow dish.

Dip into egg mixture
   6 slices bread

Drain bread slightly and brown in butter in moderately hot frying pan. Turn to brown second side, adding more butter if necessary.

Serve with maple syrup and bacon.

VARIATION:

(a)   French-Toasted Sandwiches

Prepare cheese, chopped fish, chicken, meat, or egg salad sandwiches as usual. Dip in the egg mixture above, and cook as for French Toast.

403   French Omelet

For each egg, add 1 tablespoon water, milk or tomato juice, few grains of salt and pepper. Beat just until blended. Pour egg mixture into moderately hot, heavy frying pan containing

2 to 3 tablespoons melted butter or margarine. As egg cooks at edge, lift and allow uncooked portion to flow to the bottom. Do not stir. Shake pan to keep omelet sliding freely. When eggs are set but still moist (about 3 minutes), increase heat to brown bottom quickly. Fold in half and serve immediately.

404   Spanish Omelet

SPANISH SAUCE:

Heat in a frying pan
>   **2 tablespoons vegetable oil**

Add
>   **3 tablespoons chopped onions**
>   **3 tablespoons chopped celery**
>   **3 tablespoons chopped green peppers**

Fry until tender.

Blend in
>   **1 tablespoon *Pre-Sifted* PURITY All-Purpose Flour**

Gradually add
>   **1 cup canned tomatoes**

Stir until thickened.

Add
>   **¼ teaspoon chili powder**
>   **¼ teaspoon salt**
>   **¼ teaspoon monosodium glutamate**

Simmer slowly for 5 minutes, stirring occasionally.

Keep hot while preparing omelet.

OMELET:

Beat together until blended
>   **4 eggs**
>   **¼ cup milk**
>   **½ teaspoon salt**
>   **Few grains pepper**

Pour egg mixture into moderately hot buttered frying pan. As egg cooks at edge, lift and allow uncooked portion to flow to the bottom.

Do not stir. Shake pan to keep omelet sliding freely. When eggs are set but still moist (about 3 minutes), increase heat to brown bottom quickly. Place Spanish Sauce on one half of omelet and fold over.

Serve at once.

Yield: 3 servings.

Hard-cooked eggs are easily and quickly prepared for sandwich fillings by pressing through a potato ricer.

405   Omelet Shortcake

Preheat oven to 350°.

Measure 2 tablespoons butter or margarine into each of two 8″ round layer cake pans. Place pans in 350° oven.

Separate
>   **4 eggs**

Beat whites until stiff but not dry.

Beat yolks with
>   **¼ cup milk**
>   **½ teaspoon salt**
>   **Few grains pepper**

Fold yolk mixture into beaten whites.

Divide omelet mixture between the two heated pans. Bake in preheated 350° oven for 15 minutes or until knife inserted in centre comes out clean.

Meanwhile prepare Cheese Sauce (recipe 498 (a).

To serve, invert one layer onto serving dish, pour cheese sauce over it. Cover with second layer. Pour more cheese sauce over this layer.

Cut or tear into wedges and serve additional sauce at the table.

Yield: 6 servings.

NOTE: This Shortcake is delicious filled with creamed chicken or fish.

406   Fluffy Omelet

Preheat oven to 350°.

Separate eggs. Beat whites until stiff but not dry. Beat yolks until thick, add 1 tablespoon milk or water for each egg and few grains of salt and pepper. Fold yolk mixture carefully into whites. Pour into moderately hot greased frying pan containing 2 or 3 tablespoons melted butter or margarine. Cook over low heat until omelet is puffy, and brown on under side (about 5 minutes). Place in a preheated 350° oven for 10 to 15 minutes, or until a knife inserted in the centre comes out clean.

To serve, fold in half, or tear into wedges with two forks, and serve browned side up.

NOTE: Grated cheese, chopped ham or chicken, cooked mushrooms or bacon may be added to the French or Fluffy Omelet mixtures before cooking. Omelets may be filled with tart jelly, grated cheese, mushroom or cheese sauce, creamed fish or chicken, etc.

Poultry

Poultry includes all domestic fowl such as chicken, turkey, duck, goose and guinea hen.

HOW TO BUY POULTRY:

Fresh poultry is available in two forms:

1. *Eviscerated* (also called oven-ready and ready-to-cook) refers to poultry which has been drawn and is ready for use.

2. *Dressed* refers to poultry from which only the blood and feathers have been removed. While this type will cost less per pound, remember that it includes head, feet and entrails which you must remove.

Frozen poultry is eviscerated. Thaw frozen poultry before cooking, except for stewing.

Do not refreeze poultry once it has thawed. *Do not thaw frozen stuffed poultry before cooking. Follow directions on the label.*

Amount To Buy: For roasting, allow ½ to ¾ pound eviscerated poultry per serving. For broiling or frying, allow ¾ to 1 pound. Plan for extra servings and some leftovers too.

HOW TO PREPARE POULTRY FOR COOKING:

If necessary, singe the bird with a candle or gas flame. Remove any large pin feathers. Pull out any large leg tendons by using a heavy metal skewer.

TO EVISCERATE:

Using a sharp knife, make a 3″ or 4″ cut in the skin from the tail piece up towards the keel or breast bone. Insert the hand, pressing it well up against the breast bone and ribs. Loosen and then draw out the entrails. Be careful not to break the gall bladder (small yellow-green pocket in the liver).

Loosen the skin at the neck and remove the crop and windpipe.

Cut the oil sac from the tail.

Be sure the lungs are removed from the upper back and the kidneys from the lower back.

Hold the bird under cold running water and wash thoroughly inside and out and then pat dry with a cloth.

Stuff and cook immediately or cover loosely and store in refrigerator. Cook within 24 hours.

TIPS ON POULTRY STUFFING:

Crumbs may be prepared a day ahead, but do not combine with other stuffing ingredients. Because of the danger of food poisoning, do not stuff poultry until you are ready to cook it. Extra stuffing may be baked in a casserole or open pan. Cover with sliced bacon. Bake for 1 hour in oven with poultry.

HOW TO MAKE GRAVY:

After roasting, remove poultry to heated platter. Keep warm in oven with heat off.

Pour fat and drippings from pan. For each cup of gravy, measure 1 to 2 tablespoons drippings back into pan. Blend in 2 tablespoons *Pre-Sifted* PURITY All-Purpose Flour. Slowly add 1 cup liquid (water, milk, chicken broth or cooking water from giblets). Stir constantly until gravy boils and is smoothly thickened. Season to taste with salt and pepper. For a more flavourful gravy, add a dash of mustard, monosodium glutamate, onion or garlic salt, or Worcestershire sauce.

Allow approximately ¼ cup gravy per serving (remember to allow enough for leftovers).

Giblet Gravy: Add chopped cooked giblets to the gravy and heat thoroughly.

To Cook Giblets: Rinse giblets thoroughly, discarding any yellowish parts of the liver. Place gizzard, heart and neck in a saucepan, cover with salted water and simmer gently for about one hour or until tender. Add liver during the last half hour of cooking time. Then chop giblets finely and add to gravy. Turkey giblets, being larger, will require about 1½ to 2 hours cooking.

TIPS ON BUYING:

Broiler-Fryers: small tender birds of 1½ to 3½ pounds ready-to-cook weight, available whole or cut up.

Roasters: tender birds weighing over 3½ pounds, usually purchased whole but may be cut up.

Capons: exceptionally tender birds weighing 4 to 8 pounds, having a large proportion of white meat.

Fowl (or stewing chickens): mature less tender birds, but flavourful for fricassée if simmered slowly.

Chicken

407   *Roast Chicken*

Preheat oven to 325°.

Rinse eviscerated roasting chicken or capon. Remove any bits of lung, veins, etc. and cut off oil sac on tail. Pat dry.

Prepare stuffing (see below) allowing about 1 cup per pound. Stuff loosely into both neck and body cavities. Pull neck skin to the back, over the stuffing, and skewer securely. Fold wings across the back with tips touching. Truss body opening with skewers and lace with string, or sew with a heavy thread. Tie legs together closely, winding string around tail.

Place bird, breast side up, on a rack in a shallow pan in preheated 325° oven. If desired, bird may be covered loosely with foil or with cheesecloth dipped in melted butter or vegetable oil. To brown the chicken, it may be necessary to remove covering ½ hour before roasting time is up. Roast bird, without water, until drumstick twists easily and meat thermometer reads 190°. The thermometer should be inserted in middle of the thick muscle inside the thigh and should not rest on bone.

Time tables estimate the approximate cooking time to help you plan the meal, but a thermometer is the most accurate guide. It is wise to start the chicken about ½ hour ahead of schedule. This will avoid delay should the roasting take longer than expected. In addition, carving is easier if the bird has been allowed to "rest" for 15 to 20 minutes.

(a) *Bread and Celery Stuffing*

Combine
> **5 cups soft bread crumbs**
> **1 cup finely diced celery**
> **¼ cup melted butter or margarine**
> **1 teaspoon salt**
> **⅛ teaspoon pepper**
> **1 teaspoon dried parsley flakes**
> **1 teaspoon marjoram**
> **½ teaspoon poultry seasoning**
> **⅓ cup chopped onions**

Yield: Stuffing for a 6 to 8 pound bird

(b)   *Sausage Stuffing*

Brown in a frying pan
> **½ pound sausage meat**

Pour off accumulated fat.

Add sausage meat to
> **6 cups soft bread crumbs**
> **1 teaspoon salt**
> **1 teaspoon dried parsley flakes**
> **1 teaspoon poultry seasoning**
> **3 tablespoons melted butter or margarine**
> **¼ cup chopped onions**
> **¼ cup diced celery**

Yield: Stuffing for a 6 to 8 pound bird.

> **Never partially roast poultry one day and complete it the next. Arrange to roast the bird completely at one time and so avoid the possibility of spoilage.**

ROASTING TIMES FOR CHICKEN (325°)	
Eviscerated Weight	**Approximate Total Cooking Time (Stuffed Bird)**
1½ to 2½ pounds	1¼ to 2 hours
2½ to 3½ pounds	2 to 3 hours
3½ to 4¾ pounds	3 to 3½ hours
4¾ to 6 pounds	3½ to 4 hours

408 Broiled Chicken

Use 1½ to 2½ pound broiler-fryers, split in half lengthwise, or small chicken pieces.

Brush generously with melted butter *or* margarine.

Sprinkle with salt, pepper and paprika.

Place chicken, skin side down, in greased broiler pan (without the broiler rack). This allows the chicken to keep moist in the pan juices. Set pan in oven so that chicken pieces are 6″ to 8″ below the broiler. Turn chicken and brush with melted butter or oil every 15 minutes. Broiling time will vary with the size of chicken. Allow approximately 50 to 60 minutes, or until leg twists easily and meatiest parts are tender.

409 Fried Chicken

Cut a 2 to 2½ pound broiler-fryer chicken into serving pieces.

Combine in a paper bag
**⅓ cup *Pre-Sifted* PURITY
All-Purpose Flour
1 teaspoon salt
1 teaspoon paprika
⅛ teaspoon pepper**

Add chicken pieces a few at a time and shake to cover completely. Heat vegetable oil or shortening in a large heavy frying pan, using enough to cover bottom of pan to a depth of about ¼″. Brown chicken pieces, 2 or 3 at a time, turning with tongs to brown all sides. Reduce heat, cover pan, and cook slowly for 50 to 60 minutes or until chicken is tender. Add hot water, if necessary. Uncover pan during last few minutes cooking to crisp the coating.

Yield: 4 to 6 servings.

NOTES: **1.** Fried Chicken may be prepared in the oven (recipe No. 411) or coated with batter and Deep Fat Fried (recipe No. 482).

2. Fried chicken pieces add a special treat when included in lunch boxes or picnic meals. Keep well chilled until serving time.

In recipes calling for chicken broth, you may use chicken bouillon cubes dissolved in water according to package directions.

410 Simmered Chicken

Use simmered chicken in pie, salad, à la king and other recepies calling for cooked chicken.

TO SIMMER CHICKEN:

Place a 4 to 5 pound fowl, whole or cut up, in a large kettle or Dutch oven.

Add
**3 cups water
2 teaspoons salt
1 teaspoon monosodium glutamate
Few celery leaves
1 medium onion, sliced**

Cover tightly and bring to a boil. Skim if necessary. Reduce heat and simmer until meat is tender (2 to 3 hours).

TO PREPARE IN PRESSURE COOKER:

Follow directions for simmering chicken but reduce water to 1½ cups.

Cook chicken in pressure cooker at 15 pounds pressure for 35 minutes, or as manufacturer recommends.

NOTE: When chicken is cooked by either method, chill chicken and broth separately to hasten cooling. Remove chicken from bones and use in any recipe calling for cooked chicken.

Turkey leftovers can be used in any recipe calling for cooked chicken.

411 Oven-Crisp Chicken

Preheat oven to 350°.

Cut a 2½ pound broiler-fryer chicken into serving pieces or use 6 leg or breast pieces.

Dredge chicken pieces in
**½ cup *Pre-Sifted* PURITY
All-Purpose Flour**

Dip in
½ cup evaporated milk

Finally coat with mixture of
**1 cup fine dry bread crumbs
1 teaspoon salt
Few grains pepper**

Lay chicken pieces, skin side up, in greased roast pan. Bake in preheated 350° oven, uncovered, for 1 hour or until chicken is tender. Do not add water or turn the chicken pieces. For easier clean-up, line roast pan with foil.

Serve with cranberry sauce.

Yield: 6 servings.

412 Chicken Fricassée

Cut a 4½ to 5 pound fowl into serving pieces.

Combine in a paper bag
**½ cup *Pre-Sifted* PURITY
All-Purpose Flour
1 teaspoon salt
2 teaspoons paprika
⅛ teaspoon pepper**

Add chicken pieces a few at a time and shake to cover completely.

Heat in a large frying pan
¼ cup shortening *or* vegetable oil

Add chicken and brown.

Then add
**1 cup water
¼ cup chopped celery leaves
⅓ cup chopped onions**

Cover and cook over low heat (or in 325° oven) for 2½ to 3 hours, or until meatiest pieces are tender. Add water if necessary during cooking. Season gravy to taste and thicken if desired. (Use 1 tablespoon flour to 2 tablespoons water and blend together until smooth before adding to the gravy.)

Yield: 6 servings.

NOTES: **1.** Chicken may be cooked in pressure cooker at 15 pounds pressure for 35 minutes.

2. If desired, the completed Chicken Fricassée may be placed in a buttered casserole and covered with pastry. Slit to allow steam to escape. Bake at 450° for 20 minutes or until pastry is golden.

413 Barbecued Chicken

This may be done on a charcoal or oven rotisserie.

Sprinkle body cavities of 2 broiler-fryer chickens with salt and monosodium glutamate.

Truss chickens and secure on spit. Brush generously with melted butter or margarine. Cook on revolving spit at medium heat. Baste occasionally with additional butter, French dressing or sauce. Allow 1 to 1½ hours or until leg twists easily and meatiest parts are tender.

Yield: About 6 servings.

NOTE: Barbecue sauces with sugar and tomato burn easily, so use for basting only during the last ½ hour of cooking.

414 Mom's Chicken Stew with Dumplings

Cut a 4½ to 5 pound fowl into serving pieces.

Place in pressure cooker with
**3 cups water
2 teaspoons salt
1 teaspoon monosodium glutamate
1 medium onion, sliced
Few celery leaves**

Cook at 15 pounds pressure for 35 minutes.

OR

Simmer chicken and other ingredients in covered pan or Dutch oven for 2½ to 3 hours, or until tender.

Remove chicken pieces from broth and discard celery leaves.

Add water, if necessary, to give about 3 cups of gravy.

Blend together
**3 tablespoons *Pre-Sifted* PURITY
All-Purpose Flour
6 tablespoons water**

Add flour mixture to hot broth until gravy is the consistency of thin cream sauce. Season to taste. Return chicken pieces to gravy and heat until simmering. Meanwhile, prepare Dumplings (recipe below).

Serve as soon as the dumplings are cooked.

Yield: 6 to 8 servings.

NOTE: Chicken wings may be used in place of fowl. Allow 1½ hours simmering or 20 minutes in pressure cooker.

(a) Dumplings

Blend or sift together
**1 cup *Pre-Sifted* PURITY
All-Purpose Flour
2 teaspoons baking powder
½ teaspoon salt**

Using two knives or a pastry blender, cut in
3 tablespoons shortening

Stir in
**½ cup milk
1 teaspoon dried parsley flakes
¼ cup grated raw carrots**

Blend just until flour is moistened.

Drop by large spoonfuls on simmering stew.

Cover pan tightly and cook for 15 minutes. Do not lift cover during cooking.

Yield: 6 dumplings.

415   Chicken Pie

Preheat oven to 450°.

Melt in a saucepan over moderate heat
   ½ cup butter *or* margarine

Blend in
   ½ cup *Pre-Sifted* PURITY
      All-Purpose Flour
   1 teaspoon salt
   ⅛ teaspoon pepper
   1 tablespoon dried minced onion

Gradually stir in
   3 cups chicken broth

Cook, stirring constantly, until smoothly thickened.

Meanwhile cook
   ½ pound mushrooms, sliced
in
   3 tablespoons butter *or* margarine

Add cooked mushrooms to sauce with
   3 cups cooked diced chicken
   1 cup cooked lima beans
   1 cup cooked carrots

Combine evenly and turn into 2½- or 3-quart casserole. Cover with pastry. Slash pastry to allow steam to escape.

Bake in preheated 450° oven about 20 minutes or until pastry is golden and chicken mixture bubbly.

Yield: 6 to 8 servings.

416   Barbecued Supper Surprises

Prepare barbecue fire and allow white ash to form over red coals. For each serving, proceed as follows:

Place on a piece of greased heavy aluminum foil
   1 serving piece broiler-fryer chicken, skin side down

Place on top
   1 small potato, sliced
   1 slice onion
   1 small carrot, sliced
   1 large mushroom, sliced
   Few grains salt and pepper
   2 teaspoons butter *or* margarine

Close foil package with a double fold on top and tuck ends in to keep juices from leaking out.

Place on rack over hot coals, chicken side down, and barbecue for 40 minutes. Turn package with tongs and cook 20 minutes longer. Open one package to see if chicken and vegetables are tender. If not, continue cooking until tender.

Chicken will brown if fire is quite hot to start. Serve in the foil.

NOTE: A spoonful of barbecue sauce or moistened dried onion soup mix makes a delicious addition.

Turkey

417   Roast Turkey

Preheat oven to 325°.

Rinse eviscerated turkey and remove any bits of lungs, veins, etc. Cut off oil sac on tail. Pat dry.

Prepare stuffing (next page), allowing about 1 cup per pound. Stuff loosely into both neck and body cavities. Pull neck skin to the back, over the stuffing, and skewer securely. Fold wings across the back, with tips touching. Truss body opening with skewers and lace with string or sew with a heavy thread. Tie legs together closely, winding string around tail.

Place bird, breast side up, on a rack in a shallow pan in preheated 325° oven.

Cover with double thickness of cheesecloth dipped in melted butter or vegetable oil or brush with fat and cover loosely with foil. Baste with fat during roasting. Remove covering to brown turkey during last hour, if necessary.

Roast the turkey, without water, until drumstick twists easily and meat thermometer, inserted in middle of the thick muscle inside the thigh, reads 190°. Be sure the thermometer does not rest on bone.

Time tables estimate the approximate cooking time to help you plan the meal, but a thermometer is the most accurate guide. It is wise to start the turkey about one hour ahead of schedule. This will avoid delay should the roasting take longer than expected. In addition, carving is easier if the bird has been allowed to "rest" for 20 to 30 minutes before serving.

ROASTING TIMES FOR TURKEY (325°)	
Eviscerated Weight	Approximate Total Cooking Time (Stuffed Bird)
6 to 8 pounds	3¾ to 4 hours
8 to 10 pounds	4 to 4½ hours
10 to 12 pounds	4½ to 5 hours
12 to 14 pounds	5 to 5¼ hours
14 to 16 pounds	5¼ to 6 hours
16 to 18 pounds	6 to 6½ hours
18 to 20 pounds	6½ to 7½ hours
20 to 24 pounds	7½ to 9 hours

(a)   Chestnut Stuffing

Combine

5 cups soft bread crumbs
1 teaspoon salt
¼ teaspoon pepper
1 teaspoon sage
1 teaspoon dried parsley flakes
1 teaspoon monosodium glutamate
**1 (10-ounce) can water chestnuts,
    drained and sliced**
¼ cup melted butter or margarine
⅓ cup finely chopped onions

Yield: Stuffing for a 6 to 8 pound bird.

NOTES: **1.** For a crisp delicious skin, spread a mixture of equal parts *Pre-Sifted* PURITY All-Purpose Flour and butter over entire surface of turkey. Cover with foil and roast as above. For a 12 pound turkey, you will need about ¼ cup each of flour and butter.

2. If your turkey is very large and fills your oven almost completely, allow extra cooking time. A filled oven means poor circulation of heat and so requires a longer cooking time.

418   Half Turkey

TO ROAST:

Tie leg to tail and skewer wing flat against the body. If desired, dressing may be placed on foil on the rack and the turkey, skin side up, laid over it.

Roast the turkey, skin side up, on a rack in a shallow pan. Cover with foil or cheesecloth which has been dipped in melted butter or vegetable oil, as for whole turkey. Roast at 325° without water. For 5 to 8 pounds, allow 3½ to 4 hours; for 8 to 12 pounds, allow 4 to 4½ hours. Drumstick will move easily when turkey is done. Meat thermometer inserted into inside of thigh should read 190°.

TO BROIL:

Skewer wing flat against the body. Brush generously with melted butter or vegetable oil. Sprinkle lightly with salt and paprika.

Place in greased broiler pan, skin side down, not on the rack, so that turkey can cook in its own juices.

Broil 8″ to 10″ below heat, brushing occasionally with fat. Turn turkey after 15 minutes, brush skin with fat and continue cooking, turning and basting every 15 minutes. Broil until leg twists easily and meat is tender with no pink tinge. Allow about 1½ to 2 hours, depending on size. For added flavour, turkey may be brushed with French dressing or barbecue sauce during last half hour.

STORAGE OF LEFTOVERS

Remove stuffing from body and neck cavities, cover and refrigerate leftover poultry promptly. Place stuffing in bowl, cover and refrigerate. To serve stuffing, place amount desired in foil, wrap and heat in 350° oven for about half an hour.

Fish

THINGS TO REMEMBER ABOUT FISH

TO KEEP FISH:

Fresh fish should be washed in cold water and dried. Wrap securely in waxed paper, store in refrigerator. Use within a day or two.

Frozen fish should be kept in freezer in original package until ready to use. Depending upon recipe, frozen fish may be cooked frozen or thawed.

Smoked fish should be handled the same as fresh. Smoking retards spoilage in addition to adding a distinctive flavour, but does not preserve fish.

Salted dried fish will keep without refrigeration.

TO COOK FISH:

Cook fish quickly at a high temperature to retain the flavour and juiciness. Fish should be cooked just until the flesh is opaque and flakes readily. An approximate guide is to allow 10 minutes cooking time per inch of thickness. (Double this time for frozen fish.) If fish is covered with a sauce, allow 15 to 20 minutes per inch thickness. Always test for flakiness with a fork to be sure the fish is cooked.

> **Do not overcook fish as it will become tasteless and dry.**
>
> **Serve fish as soon as it is cooked, because the flavour and texture deteriorate rapidly on standing.**

TO CLEAN FRESH FISH:

For those of you who have a fisherman in the family.

To Scale: Holding the tail firmly and using the dull edge of a knife held at a 45° angle, loosen the scales from tail to head. This is best done under running water so the scales do not scatter.

To Clean: Using a thin sharp knife, or kitchen shears, slit skin from vent to gills. Remove viscera. Wash in running water and brush to clean thoroughly. Remove the fins by cutting the flesh along both sides of the fins, and then pull each fin sharply towards head to remove root bones. Remove the head and tail. Dry thoroughly.

TO USE CANNED FISH:

Tuna: Pour off oil and place in a sieve. Pour boiling water over the tuna.

Salmon: Bones may be mashed with a fork and retained with the juices for extra flavour and nutrition.

Shrimps: Drain and rinse with cold water. Remove black vein, if necessary.

Lobster, Crab: Drain.

Clams, Oysters: Most recipes call for use of liquor. Strain to remove sand and small pieces of shell.

419   Baked Fish Fillets or Steaks

Preheat oven to 450°.

Arrange fish fillets or steaks in a greased baking dish. Brush with vegetable oil or melted shortening, season with salt and pepper.

Bake in preheated 450° oven, allowing 10 minutes baking time per inch thickness. Allow 20 minutes per inch if frozen.

Turning is not necessary. Do not add water.

NOTE: Whole fish may be baked in the same way, but if stuffing is desired see recipe No. 425.

420   Broiled Fish

Small fish may be broiled whole. Medium-sized fish are split in half lengthwise. Steaks and fillets are also excellent for broiling.

Season fish and arrange on well greased broiler rack. Brush with vegetable oil or melted shortening. Place 2″ to 4″ below the preheated broiler, depending on thickness. (Place thicker pieces farther from the heat.) Allow 10 minutes broiling time per inch thickness. Turn fish at half time, season and baste the other side.

NOTES: **1.** Thin cuts of fish (½″ or less) may be broiled without turning.
2. If broiling unthawed frozen fish, place it about 6″ below the broiler and allow 18 to 20 minutes per inch thickness.

421   Pan Fried Fish

Fillets, steaks or small whole fish are suitable for frying.

Cut fish into serving-size pieces. Coat with seasoned flour; dip in salted milk or beaten egg; and then roll in fine dry bread crumbs, cracker crumbs, or cornmeal, etc.

Heat vegetable oil or shortening in frying pan, using enough to cover bottom of pan to a depth of about ⅛″.

Fry fish quickly on each side, turning once during the frying. Allow about 10 minutes per inch thickness.

NOTE: For deep fat frying of fish see recipe No. 483.

> *When buying fish, allow ⅓ pound of steak or fillets, or ½ pound whole fish, per person.*

422   Poaching Fish

If possible, poach fish in pan from which it can be served. This avoids the problem of the fillets breaking when they are moved from pan to platter.

(a)   Milk Poaching

Smoked fish is traditionally cooked by poaching in milk. However, if fish is heavily smoked, the milk may curdle. To prevent this, poach in water for most of the allotted cooking time, then drain off the water and replace it with warm milk. Finish cooking.

FINNAN HADDIE:

Place fish in a broad, flat pan and cover with water. Simmer gently for 5 to 8 minutes. Drain off water and barely cover with warm milk; dot with butter. Continue to cook slowly, until fish flakes easily, allowing a total cooking time of about 10 minutes per inch thickness.

After the fish is cooked, the milk may be thickened by stirring in a mixture of flour and water and cooking until smooth. Serve garnished with chopped parsley.

NOTE: Fish may also be poached in a preheated 450° oven.

(b)   Poaching in Court Bouillon

Court Bouillon is a stock in which fish is poached and is especially suited for large pieces of fish such as salmon and whitefish. It is used to enhance the flavour of the fish and, incidentally, reduces cooking odours. Enough should be used to cover the fish. The seasonings may be varied or extended according to taste and availability.

COURT BOUILLON:

To
   5 cups boiling water
add
   1 tablespoon salt
   1 large stalk celery with leaves
   1 medium-size onion, sliced
   1 tablespoon chopped parsley
   1 bay leaf
   ¼ teaspoon thyme
   Few peppercorns
   ¼ cup lemon juice *or* wine vinegar
Cover and simmer for 10 minutes.

Yield: About 1 quart.

To Use: Loosely tie fish in cheesecloth and lower into hot Court Bouillon. Bring to a boil and then reduce heat. Cover and simmer for 10 minutes per inch thickness (measured at the thickest part).

Fish should flake easily with a fork when tested near the back bone. Remove fish, handling carefully to avoid breakage. Remove skin and lift out the back bone, thus removing nearly all the bones at once.

Serve hot with Cream Sauce, or cold with lemon wedges and Cucumber Sauce.

423 Steamed Fish

Arrange serving-size pieces of fish on plate or aluminum foil. Season with salt and pepper. Cover with foil.

Place over rapidly boiling water, cover and steam approximately 15 minutes per inch thickness (30 minutes if frozen).

Serve with a Caper Sauce, or use in salads, casseroles, etc.

424 Spencer Baked Fish

Preheat oven to 450°.

Cut into serving-size pieces
    2 pounds fish fillets or steaks
Combine
    ½ cup evaporated milk
    1 teaspoon salt
Soak fish for 3 to 5 minutes in salted milk.
Drain and roll in
    ½ cup fine dry bread crumbs or cracker crumbs

Arrange fish in greased baking dish.
Sprinkle with
    2 tablespoons melted butter or margarine
Bake in preheated 450° oven for 10 minutes per inch thickness. If fish is frozen allow 20 minutes per inch thickness. Serve with Tomato or Cheese Sauce.

Yield: 6 servings.

VARIATION:

(a) Crunchy Fish

Prepare as above, sprinkling 2 tablespoons lemon juice over fillets or steaks with the melted butter. Top with ¼ cup blanched sliced almonds. Bake as above.

425 Baked Stuffed Fish

Preheat oven to 450°.

Wash and dry a dressed whole fish which weighs about 4 pounds.

Sprinkle inside lightly with salt.

Stuff fish loosely with dressing (see below), allowing about ¾ cup for each pound of dressed fish. Fasten opening with small skewers or toothpicks and lace with string, or sew opening with coarse thread.

Place fish on well greased foil in baking pan and brush with vegetable oil or melted shortening. Measure the stuffed fish at the thickest part. Bake in preheated 450° oven, allowing 10 minutes cooking time for each inch of stuffed thickness.

Serve immediately with lemon wedges or Lemon Butter.

Yield: About 8 servings.

DRESSINGS:

(a) Savoury Bread Dressing

Melt in a frying pan
    3 tablespoons butter or margarine
Add
    ⅓ cup chopped onions
    ⅓ cup diced celery
Cook until tender.
Toss with
    3 cups soft bread crumbs
    1 teaspoon salt
    ⅛ teaspoon pepper
    ½ teaspoon thyme
    ½ teaspoon marjoram
    1½ teaspoons dried parsley flakes
Yield: Sufficient to stuff a 4-pound dressed fish.

(b) Lemon Rice Dressing

Melt in a frying pan
    ⅓ cup butter or margarine
Add
    1 cup finely diced celery
    ⅓ cup chopped onions
Cook until tender.
Toss lightly with
    3 cups cooked rice
    1 tablespoon grated lemon rind
    ½ teaspoon salt
    ¼ teaspoon thyme
    ¼ cup lemon juice
Yield: Sufficient to stuff a 4-pound dressed fish.

426 Kippered Herring
(Kippers)

TO BAKE:

Preheat oven to 450°.

Wrap kippered herring individually in greased aluminum foil, sealing tightly.

Bake in preheated oven for 10 minutes.

TO POACH:

Cover kippered herring with Court Bouillon (recipe No. 422 (b) or water. Simmer for 10 minutes. Drain and serve with butter.

427 Winnipeg Gold-Eye

Preheat oven to 400°.

Allowing one gold-eye per person, arrange in a greased baking dish. Brush generously with melted butter or margarine. Bake in pre-heated oven for 15 minutes, basting occasionally with butter.

Gold-eye is usually prepared and served with head and tail attached.

428 Fillet Rolls

Preheat oven to 475°.

Melt in a frying pan

    3 tablespoons butter or margarine

Add

    ¼ cup diced celery
    2 tablespoons chopped onion

Cook slowly until tender.

Combine with

    1 cup soft bread crumbs
    ½ teaspoon salt
    ½ teaspoon dried parsley flakes
    ¼ teaspoon thyme
    Few grains pepper

Spread out

    1 pound sole fillets (about 4 fillets)

Cover each with the bread dressing. Roll up loosely, jelly roll fashion.

Wrap each fillet roll with

    1 slice side bacon

Fasten with metal skewers or toothpicks.

Place in a greased baking dish. Bake in pre-heated 475° oven for 20 to 25 minutes.

Serve with Cucumber Sauce.

Yield: 4 servings.

429 Baked Salmon Steaks

Preheat oven to 450°.

Dredge

    4 salmon steaks (about 2 pounds)

in mixture of

    ½ cup Pre-Sifted PURITY All-Purpose Flour
    ½ teaspoon salt

Arrange steaks in greased baking dish. Avoid overlapping.

Melt in a frying pan

    3 tablespoons butter or margarine

Add

    2 tablespoons chopped onion
    2 tablespoons diced celery

Cook until tender.

Combine with

    1½ cups soft bread crumbs
    ½ teaspoon salt
    ¼ teaspoon marjoram
    Few grains freshly ground black pepper

Spread the dressing over the salmon steaks.

Bake in preheated 450° oven for 20 to 25 minutes, or until fish flakes easily at the bone.

Serve with Hollandaise Sauce.

Yield: 4 servings.

430 Salmon Puffs

Preheat oven to 375°.

Remove skin from

    1 (15-ounce) can salmon

Mash bones and flake salmon with juices.

Add

    2 well-beaten eggs
    ½ cup fine dry bread crumbs
    1 teaspoon dried parsley flakes
    1 teaspoon instant minced onion
    ¼ teaspoon salt
    Few grains pepper
    1 tablespoon lemon juice

Combine well and pack lightly into 6 well buttered custard cups or small casseroles.

Place custard cups in a pan of hot water.

Bake in preheated 375° oven for 30 minutes.

Serve with Tomato Sauce.

Yield: 6 servings.

NOTE: This may be baked in a greased 7½" x 3½" loaf pan for about 50 minutes.

431 Salmon Roll

Preheat oven to 425°.

Remove skin from

1 (15-ounce) can salmon

Mash bones and flake salmon with juices.

Mix with

¼ cup chopped onions
2 tablespoons chopped green pepper or celery
2 tablespoons catsup
½ teaspoon dry mustard
1 beaten egg
Few grains salt and pepper

Prepare dough for Basic Tea Biscuits (recipe No. 42). Roll to a 10″ x 12″ rectangle. Spread salmon mixture to within ½″ of the edges. Roll up like a jelly roll, starting from the longer side. Moisten edge and seal.

Place on greased baking sheet and tuck ends under.

Bake in preheated 425° oven for 25 to 30 minutes.

Serve plain or with Cheese Sauce.

Yield: 6 servings.

Most fish can be cooked by any method, so remember that you can substitute one fish for another in these recipes.

432 Salmon Pot Pie

Preheat oven to 450°.

Cut into 1″ pieces

5 slices side bacon

Fry until crisp and then drain on absorbent paper.

Measure into a saucepan

¼ cup bacon drippings (add shortening if necessary)

Blend in

⅓ cup *Pre-Sifted* PURITY All-Purpose Flour
½ teaspoon salt
Few grains pepper
1 teaspoon instant minced onion
½ teaspoon dried parsley flakes
⅛ teaspoon savoury

Gradually add, stirring constantly

2 cups milk

Stir and cook until smoothly thickened.

Drain and remove skin and bones from

1 (15-ounce) can salmon

Break into bite-size pieces.

Combine

Cream sauce
Crisp bacon pieces
Salmon
1½ cups cooked mixed vegetables

Turn into buttered 1½-quart casserole.

Prepare half the recipe for Basic Tea Biscuits (recipe No. 42).

Cut dough into six 1½″ to 2″ rounds and arrange around edge of casserole on fish mixture.

Bake in preheated 450° oven for 18 to 20 minutes.

Yield: 6 servings.

Cooking times in recipes are for fresh fish, unless otherwise specified.

433 Tuna Fondue

Preheat oven to 350°.

Remove crusts from day old bread and cut into cubes to make

3 cups

Melt in a frying pan

3 tablespoons butter *or* margarine

Add the bread cubes and brown lightly.

Place in a buttered 1½-quart casserole.

Top with

2 (7-ounce) cans tuna, drained and flaked
1 cup shredded Cheddar cheese

Beat together

3 eggs
½ teaspoon salt
½ teaspoon dry mustard
Few drops tabasco sauce
½ teaspoon instant minced onion

Add

1½ cups scalded milk

Pour egg mixture over the fish.

Place casserole in pan of hot water in preheated 350° oven. Bake for 50 to 60 minutes, or until just firm in centre.

Serve with Creole Sauce or Chili Sauce.

Yield: 6 servings.

NOTE: This is very good with shrimps in place of tuna. Chop shrimps coarsely.

Frozen fillets may be prepared quickly for frying or baking by cutting a 1-pound block into sections, rather than waiting for the fillets to thaw enough to separate.

434   Haddock Creole

Preheat oven to 450°.

Melt in a frying pan
3 tablespoons butter or margarine

Add
¼ cup chopped onions
¼ cup diced green peppers

Cook slowly until tender.

Blend in
1 tablespoon *Pre-Sifted* PURITY
All-Purpose Flour

Add
1 (7½-ounce) can tomato sauce

Stir until blended.

Arrange in a greased baking dish, without overlapping
1 pound haddock fillets

Pour tomato sauce over the fillets. Bake in covered baking dish in preheated 450° oven for 20 minutes, or until fish flakes readily with a fork.

Yield: 3 servings.

435   Halibut Oriental

Dip
4 halibut steaks (about 2 pounds)
in a mixture of
½ cup milk
1 teaspoon salt

Drain slightly, then dip in
½ cup *Pre-Sifted* PURITY
All-Purpose Flour

Pan fry the steaks in ⅛″ vegetable oil or melted shortening (hot but not smoking).

Fry quickly on one side, turn and brown the other side. Complete cooking time will be about 10 minutes per inch thickness.

Meanwhile, combine in small saucepan
2 tablespoons brown sugar
3 tablespoons *Pre-Sifted* PURITY
All-Purpose Flour
¼ teaspoon salt
Few grains garlic powder
2 tablespoons vinegar

Slowly stir in
1 cup syrup from 15-ounce can crushed pineapple (add water if necessary)

Cook, stirring constantly, until smoothly thickened.

Remove from heat and add
½ cup drained crushed pineapple
¼ cup sliced gherkin pickles
½ teaspoon soy sauce

Serve sauce over the fish.

Yield: 4 servings.

436 Hawaiian Sole Casserole

Preheat oven to 350°.

Place in a buttered 1½-quart casserole
½ cup drained, crushed pineapple

Combine
2 cups cooked flaked sole
¼ cup cream or evaporated milk
½ teaspoon salt
⅛ teaspoon pepper

Place fish mixture on top of pineapple.

Combine
1 cup mashed potatoes
1 well-beaten egg
2 tablespoons milk

Spread potato mixture on top of the fish.

Top with
¼ cup commercially grated Cheddar cheese
Few grains paprika

Bake in preheated 350° oven for 30 minutes.

Yield: 4 to 6 servings.

437   Cod Fish Cakes

Combine
1½ cups cooked flaked salt cod
1½ cups mashed potatoes

Add
3 tablespoons finely grated onion
1 teaspoon dried parsley flakes
⅛ teaspoon pepper
1 beaten egg

Blend well and form into 6 flattened balls or cakes. Roll in finely crushed corn flakes.

Fry in about 3 tablespoons vegetable oil or melted shortening over moderate heat. Allow 4 to 5 minutes frying on each side, or until nicely browned and heated through.

Serve with chutney or chili sauce.

Yield: 6 fish cakes.

NOTE: To freshen boneless salt fish, soak overnight in cold water to cover. Drain. Add fresh water and slowly bring to a simmer. Drain and repeat if fish is still too salty. To cook, simmer until fish flakes easily.

THINGS TO REMEMBER ABOUT SHELLFISH

Lobsters may be purchased alive, cooked and frozen, or canned. The shell of live lobsters varies from dark green to blue, and turns bright red when cooked.

Crabs are available cooked—fresh, frozen, or canned. Live crabs are sold only in areas close to fishing centres.

Oysters from the Atlantic coast are sold in the shell or shucked. The shells should be tightly closed. Pacific (or Japanese) oysters from the west coast of Canada are larger and always sold shucked. They may be fresh, frozen, canned or smoked.

Clams are sold alive in the shell, or shucked in fresh, frozen or canned forms. Like the oyster, the shell of a live clam should be tightly closed.

Scallops are always sold shucked, either fresh or frozen. Thaw frozen scallops before using.

Shrimps are available fresh, frozen and canned. Most frozen and some canned shrimps have the dark vein removed. If not, it should be lifted out with the point of a knife.

438　Boiled Lobster

Thrust the live lobsters, head first, into boiling salted water. Cover, simmer 15 to 20 minutes depending on size.

To Serve Hot: Remove from boiling water, place lobster on its back and split lengthwise with sharp knife or scissors. Remove dark vein and small sac behind the head. Crack large claws.

Serve piping hot with melted butter and lemon wedges.

To Serve Cold: Cool cooked lobster quickly in cold running water. Chill thoroughly in refrigerator, then prepare for serving as above. Serve with vinegar or Tartar Sauce.

For salads and main dishes, remove meat from claws, legs and tail and break into bite-size pieces. Be sure to remove the flat thin pieces of cartilage in the claw meat of both cooked and canned lobster.

439　Lobster Newburg

Break into bite-size pieces
> **2 (5-ounce) cans lobster**

Melt in a frying pan
> **2 tablespoons butter *or* margarine**

Add
> **½ pound mushrooms, sliced**

Cook until tender.

Melt in top of double boiler, over direct heat
> **2 tablespoons butter *or* margarine**

Blend in
> **3 tablespoons *Pre-Sifted* PURITY All-Purpose Flour**
> **½ teaspoon salt**
> **¼ teaspoon paprika**
> **¼ teaspoon dry mustard**

Gradually add, stirring constantly
> **1½ cups milk**

Stir and cook until smoothly thickened.

Add
> **⅓ cup shredded Cheddar cheese**

Add a little of the hot sauce to
> **2 slightly-beaten egg yolks**

Return to double boiler and cook, over boiling water, stirring constantly for 2 minutes.

Add the lobster meat and cooked mushrooms.

Heat thoroughly, stirring frequently.

If desired, add
> **3 tablespoons sherry**

Serve immediately over hot cooked rice.

Yield: 5 to 6 servings.

440　Baked Scallops

Preheat oven to 450°.

Dredge
> **1 pound scallops**

in mixture of
> **½ cup *Pre-Sifted* PURITY All-Purpose Flour**
> **½ teaspoon salt**
> **Few grains pepper**

Divide scallops among four buttered scallop shells or individual baking dishes. Place on a baking sheet for easier handling.

To each, add
> **1 tablespoon cream**
> **1 teaspoon fine dry bread crumbs**
> **1 teaspoon butter *or* margarine**

Bake scallops in preheated 450° oven for 20 minutes, or until cooked.

Serve with Tartar Sauce or lemon wedges.

Yield: 4 servings.

441   Shrimp Curry

Melt in a saucepan
   ⅓ cup butter or margarine
Add, cooking until tender
   ½ cup finely chopped onions
Blend in
   **⅓ cup Pre-Sifted Purity
   All-Purpose Flour
   2½ teaspoons curry powder
   1 teaspoon salt
   ¼ teaspoon ground ginger**
Gradually add, stirring constantly
   **2 cups cream or evaporated milk
   1 cup chicken broth or bouillon**
Stir and cook until smoothly thickened.
Add
   **4 cups cooked shrimps
   (two 14-ounce packages frozen
   shrimps)
   1 teaspoon lemon juice**
Heat thoroughly, stirring frequently.
Serve on hot cooked rice with side dishes of chutney, pineapple chunks, salted peanuts, fresh shredded coconut, crisp bacon bits, sliced avocado or fried bananas.
Yield: 8 servings.
NOTE: This is a moderately flavoured curry. If a hotter flavour is desired, increase curry accordingly.

442   Crab Deluxe

Melt in top of double boiler, over direct heat
   3 tablespoons butter or margarine
Add
   ½ pound mushrooms, sliced
Cook until tender.
Then place over boiling water.
Blend in
   **¼ cup Pre-Sifted PURITY
   All-Purpose Flour**
Slowly stir in
   **1 cup chicken broth or bouillon
   1 cup cream**
Cook, stirring constantly, until sauce is smoothly thickened.
Add
   **½ cup shredded Cheddar cheese
   ½ teaspoon salt
   Few grains paprika and pepper
   1 (6-ounce) can crab meat, drained**
Heat thoroughly.

If desired, just before serving add
   3 tablespoons sherry
Serve on hot buttered tea biscuits or patty shells.
Yield: 6 servings.

443 Oysters on the Half-Shell

Wash oyster shells thoroughly. Insert blunt knife near the hinge, and with a twisting motion, pry the shells apart. Separate the shells by cutting the connecting muscle, and loosen the oyster. Try to retain as much juice as possible. Discard one of each pair of shells. Serve the oyster on the other.

Allow approximately six oysters per serving.

Arrange on crushed ice, with a small dish of Cocktail Sauce in the centre. Garnish with lemon wedges.

444   Seafood Cocktail

SAUCE:

Combine
   **1 cup catsup
   2 tablespoons finely chopped onion
   2 tablespoons lemon juice
   1 tablespoon horseradish
   1 tablespoon Worcestershire sauce
   ½ teaspoon celery salt
   ½ teaspoon dried parsley flakes**
Chill thoroughly.
Yield: Sauce for 6 to 8 servings.

SEAFOOD:

For each serving, allow about ⅓ cup cooked shrimp, crab meat, lobster, or a mixture of these.

Serving Suggestions:

1. Line chilled sherbets with shredded lettuce. Add about 3 tablespoons Cocktail Sauce and arrange the chilled seafood on top.

2. Dip chilled seafood in Cocktail Sauce and serve in scooped out small tomatoes.

3. Cover small glass plates with shredded lettuce. Place about 3 tablespoons Cocktail Sauce in the centre and arrange the chilled seafood around it.

Serve at once.

Meats

THINGS TO REMEMBER ABOUT MEAT

BUY WISELY:

Amount to Buy: The number of servings in a pound of meat depends on the amount of bone, fat and gristle; the size of servings; added ingredients or extenders; and the shrinkage during cooking. Generally, boneless meat will give three to four servings per pound, bone-in meat two to three servings per pound.

Recognize Quality and Cuts: Particularly in beef, it is wise to look for creamy white fat of moderate thickness. The lean should be firm, smooth and moist with good marbling of fat (this means flecks of fat evenly distributed through the lean).

Take time to learn the various cuts and how they are best prepared. The cost of meat varies with the demand and less popular cuts can mean a real saving.

HOW TO STORE MEAT:

Remove butcher's wrapping, wipe meat with a clean damp cloth and cover loosely with waxed paper. Store in the refrigerator and use within a day or two—minced beef should be used within one day. Meats may be wrapped securely in freezer wrap and frozen. Thaw before cooking. Cured meats may be kept in store wrappings for up to a week. Cooked meats should be cooled quickly, then tightly wrapped and refrigerated.

To Cook Meats

A low temperature gives better flavour and less shrinkage.

HOW TO PANBROIL

Panbroiling is recommended for dry heat cooking of tender cuts of meat on top of the range. It is sometimes called pan frying.

Slash fat edge of meat to prevent curling. Place meat in a hot, heavy frying pan which has been lightly greased. Cook over moderate heat, turning frequently. Pour off fat as it accumulates. Season meat after browning, adding salt, pepper and monosodium glutamate.

HOW TO BROIL

Broiling is a dry heat method of cooking tender cuts of meat.

Follow instructions for your range concerning preheating broiler and door position (opened or closed). Do not broil veal, or pork except sausages.

Slash fat edge of meat to prevent curling. Meat should be no less than ½″ thick for best results. Place meat on cold broiler rack 4″ to 5″ below heat. Increase distance for thicker cuts. If meat should spit or smoke, it is too close to the heat. Broil meat on one side, season and turn with tongs and broil other side. Test by cutting meat close to bone.

Barbecuing is actually broiling—upside down. Adjust distance from coals according to intensity of heat.

HOW TO ROAST:

Roasting is used to cook large tender cuts by dry heat.

Roast meats in an open, shallow pan at 325°. Do not add water; do not cover the pan; and do not sear the meat. If used, insert a meat thermometer into the meatiest part so that the tip does not touch fat or bone. Roast meat to required internal temperature or to desired degree of doneness. Season when roast is half done. Allow a roast to stand for 10 minutes to make carving easier.

Time Table for Roasting Meat

Preheat oven to 325°

Cut	Minutes Per Pound	Final Internal Temperature
BEEF *Cook rare to medium for tenderness*		
Standing Rib		
rare	18–20	140°
medium	22–24	160°
Rolled Rib		
rare	28–30	140°
medium	32–34	160°
Round or Rump (red brand)		
rare	20–22	140°
medium	25–30	160°
VEAL *Should be well done, but do not overcook*		
Leg, Loin, Shoulder, Rump	40	180°
Rolled Front	50	180°
LAMB *Never serve rare*		
Leg, Loin	30–35	180°
Shoulder (bone-in)	30–35	180°
Rolled Front	45	180°
PORK *Must be well done*		
Fresh		
Loin, Leg, Butt	40–45	185°
Smoked		
Ham—whole	15–18	160°
half	22	160°
Picnic Shoulder	30	170°
Cottage Roll	35	170°
Midget Loin	40	170°

NOTE: Ready-to-serve hams require no further cooking. They may be served cold or heated by baking in a 325° oven to an internal temperature of 130°. This will require 10 minutes per pound for whole hams and 15 minutes per pound for half hams.

445   *Gravy*

Remove roast from pan and keep in a warm place.

Measure.................................¼ **cup pan drippings**

Blend in................................¼ **cup** *Pre-Sifted* **PURITY All-Purpose Flour**
1 teaspoon salt

Gradually stir in..........................**2 cups water, cream** *or* **vegetable stock**

Stir briskly until gravy boils and is smoothly thickened.

Season to taste.

Yield: 2 cups.

HOW TO POT ROAST

Pot roasting is moist heat cookery for large, less tender cuts.

Rub meat with seasoned flour. Brown meat well on both sides in hot fat in a heavy skillet or Dutch oven. Season well. Add a small amount of liquid (to the depth of about 1″). Cover pan tightly and cook slowly on top of range or in 325° oven until tender. Allow 30 to 35 minutes per pound for bone-in roasts and 40 to 45 minutes per pound for boneless or rolled roasts. Add more liquid as required. Vegetables may be added during the last half hour of cooking. Thicken flavourful pan juices with flour and water mixture to make gravy.

HOW TO BRAISE

Braising is a moist heat method of cooking the smaller, less tender cuts.

Flour meat and brown in hot fat in heavy frying pan. Add liquid, cover pan and cook slowly until tender on top of the range or in a 325° oven. Add water to prevent drying out during cooking.

HOW TO STEW

Less tender meat is made tender and flavourful by long, slow cooking in moist heat.

Trim off any excess fat and yellow gristle. Cut meat into 1″ cubes. Meat may be browned in fat, depending on type of stew. Half cover the meat with liquid. Cook slowly until tender in a tightly covered kettle. Simmer, do not boil. Add vegetables and seasonings about 30 minutes before meat is done. Thicken gravy with flour and water mixture.

Stew is quickly made in a pressure cooker—just follow manufacturer's directions.

Beef

446 Hamburger Stroganoff

Melt in large frying pan
   3 tablespoons butter *or* margarine

Add
   ½ cup chopped onions
   ½ pound mushrooms, sliced

Cook slowly until tender.

Add
   1 pound minced beef
   2 tablespoons *Pre-Sifted* PURITY
     All-Purpose Flour
   ½ teaspoon salt
   ½ teaspoon monosodium glutamate
   ¼ teaspoon pepper
   ⅛ teaspoon garlic powder
   ½ teaspoon Worcestershire sauce

Cook over moderate heat for 5 minutes or until meat has lost its pink colour.

Blend in
   1 (10-ounce) can cream of chicken
     soup

Simmer uncovered for 10 minutes.

Remove from heat and stir in
   ½ pint commercial sour cream

Garnish with chopped chives and serve immediately.

Yield: 4 to 6 servings.

447 Italian Beef with Noodles

Heat in frying pan
   1 tablespoon shortening

Add and brown lightly
   1 pound minced beef
   ½ cup chopped onions
   ⅓ cup sliced green peppers

Reduce heat and add
   2 cups canned tomatoes, drained
   1 (14-ounce) can kernel corn,
     drained
   1 (10-ounce) can tomato soup
   1 teaspoon salt
   ¼ teaspoon oregano
   ¼ teaspoon garlic powder
   Few grains cayenne

Stir to combine and then simmer very slowly for 20 minutes.

Just before serving, stir in
   ¾ cup shredded Cheddar cheese

Heat until cheese is just melted.

Serve with hot buttered noodles.

Yield: 6 servings.

NOTE: This is an excellent way to use left-over roast. Mince and use in place of fresh beef.

448   Family Meat Loaf

Preheat oven to 350°.
Combine
  1½ pounds minced beef
  1 beaten egg
  1 cup rolled oats
  1 cup milk
  1½ teaspoons instant minced onion
  ½ teaspoon dried parsley flakes
  1½ teaspobns salt
  ⅛ teaspoon pepper
  ¼ teaspoon monosodium glutamate
  1 teaspoon Worcestershire sauce

Blend thoroughly. Pack lightly into a 9″ x 5″ loaf pan.
Make three diagonal indentations across the top and fill with
  3 tablespoons catsup

Bake in preheated 350° oven for 1¼ to 1½ hours.
Yield: 6 to 8 servings.

VARIATIONS:

(a)   Frosted Meat Loaf

Prepare 2 cups instant mashed potatoes according to package directions. Season well. Spread over top and sides of hot baked meat loaf and brown in hot oven.

(b)   Cheddar Meat Loaf

Prepare Family Meat Loaf mixture as directed and spread half in a loaf pan. Cover with 1 cup shredded Cheddar cheese. Then add remaining meat mixture. Bake as directed. Leave baked meat loaf in pan for about 10 minutes before removing.

449   Sour Cream Meat Pie

Preheat oven to 375°.
Prepare dough for Parsley Tea Biscuits (recipe No. 42 (d).
Roll into a 12″ square. Line an 8″ square pan with the dough.
Melt in a frying pan
  2 tablespoons butter or margarine
Add
  ½ cup thinly sliced onions
Cook until tender.
Add
  1 pound minced beef
Cook until brown.

Stir in
  1 teaspoon salt
  ½ teaspoon pepper
  2 tablespoons fine dry bread crumbs
Remove from heat.
Blend together
  1 cup commercial sour cream
  1 well-beaten egg
  1 tablespoon catsup
  1 tablespoon Worcestershire sauce
  2 tablespoons finely chopped green pepper
  1 teaspoon dry mustard
  Few drops tabasco sauce
Combine
  ½ cup of this sour cream mixture
  1 tablespoon catsup
Set aside for topping.
Combine the meat and remaining sour cream mixture. Pour into the biscuit lined pan. Top with the reserved sour cream mixture.
Bake in preheated 375° oven about 30 minutes.
Yield: 9 servings.

450   Cheddar Burgers

Combine and blend thoroughly
  1½ pounds minced beef
  ⅔ cup evaporated milk
  ½ cup fine dry bread or cracker crumbs
  1 egg
  ¼ cup chopped onions
  1 teaspoon salt
  ⅛ teaspoon pepper
  1 teaspoon prepared mustard
  ½ teaspoon monosodium glutamate
  1 cup shredded Cheddar cheese
Form into 8 to 12 patties.
Cook in a greased heavy frying pan over moderate heat for 20 to 30 minutes. Turn occasionally during cooking.
Yield: 6 to 8 servings.

Beef is the only meat which can be purchased by grade. In most centres, there are three grades available to the homemaker:
  Red Brand—top quality, premium price
  Blue Brand—good quality, excellent eating
  Top Commercial (standard)—good eating, economical
Lower grades are usually not sold to the consumer.

451 Swiss Steak

Combine
> ½ cup *Pre-Sifted* PURITY
> All-Purpose Flour
> 1 teaspoon salt

Using a mallet or the edge of a plate, pound the flour into both sides of
> 2 pounds round steak

Cut steak into 6 or 8 pieces.

Heat in large frying pan
> 3 tablespoons shortening

Brown meat on both sides.

Reduce heat and add
> 1 (10-ounce) can consommé
> ½ cup water
> ¼ cup catsup
> 1 teaspoon prepared mustard
> 1 medium onion, sliced

Tightly cover pan and simmer slowly for 1½ hours or until meat is tender. Add water to keep meat moist, if necessary. About 20 minutes before cooking time is up, add
> ½ pound mushrooms, sliced

Yield: 6 to 8 servings.

452 Shish Kebabs

Cut into 1½″ to 2″ cubes
> 2 pounds sirloin steak

Marinate, overnight if desired, in Basic Marinade (recipe No. 476).

Thread meat cubes on 10″ or 12″ metal skewers with
> 6 small tomatoes, whole *or* halved
> 12 whole canned onions *or* potatoes
> 12 mushroom caps
> 6 (1-inch) squares green *or* red pepper

Arrange the meat and vegetables alternately. Other foods may be used, such as bacon, chicken livers, sausages, lamb, zucchini, cucumber, small pre-cooked carrots, etc.

Broil kebabs in oven or over barbecue coals. Brush frequently with salad oil, butter, French dressing or barbecue sauce and turn to cook evenly on all sides. Total cooking time will be about 10 to 15 minutes, depending on variety and size of meat and vegetables.

When arranging foods on skewer, place those requiring more cooking (such as raw vegetables) near point of skewer so they will be closer to the centre of heat.

If you choose foods that vary greatly in cooking times, place only one variety on each skewer. Plan cooking so that all are done at one time. In this way, the selection of foods is much wider and you can be sure each will be completely cooked. Serve each person one or two pieces from each skewer.

Yield: 6 servings.

453 Pot Roast with Vegetables

Rub
> 3 to 3½ pound pot roast (round, chuck *or* rump)

with mixture of
> ¼ cup *Pre-Sifted* PURITY
> All-Purpose Flour
> 1 teaspoon salt
> ¼ teaspoon pepper
> ½ teaspoon monosodium glutamate

Heat in heavy pan or Dutch oven
> 3 tablespoons shortening

Brown roast on all sides in hot fat.

Lower heat and slip a rack under the meat.

Add
> 1 (28-ounce) can tomatoes
> 2 onions, quartered

Cover tightly and simmer until tender, adding water during cooking if necessary. Allow 30 to 35 minutes per pound for bone-in roasts, 40 to 45 minutes per pound for rolled roasts.

Add
> 1½ teaspoons salt
> 6 medium carrots, quartered lengthwise
> 4 medium potatoes, quartered

Cover and cook 30 minutes longer.

Remove meat to hot serving platter and arrange vegetables around it. Season gravy to taste. Thicken with flour and water mixture. Serve gravy with pot roast and vegetables.

Yield: 6 to 8 servings.

To Thicken with a Flour and Water Mixture

To thicken stews, pot roast gravies, etc., estimate the amount of liquid left at the end of the cooking time. For each cup, combine 2 tablespoons *Pre-Sifted* PURITY All-Purpose Flour and ¼ cup water. Stir into the simmering liquid and bring to a full boil, stirring briskly.

---

454 Savoury Beef Stew

Cut into 1″ pieces
1 pound stewing beef
Dredge with
**¼ cup *Pre-Sifted* PURITY
All-Purpose Flour**
Heat in heavy pan, Dutch oven or pressure cooker
3 tablespoons shortening
Add floured meat pieces and brown well.
Add
**½ cup chopped onions
1 cup tomato juice
1 teaspoon salt
⅛ teaspoon pepper
½ teaspoon monosodium glutamate
¼ teaspoon garlic powder**
Stir to blend evenly. Cover pan and simmer very slowly for 2½ hours, stirring occasionally and adding water if necessary, *or* cook in pressure cooker at 15 pounds pressure for 15 minutes.
Add
**1 cup diced potatoes
1 cup sliced carrots
1 cup sliced celery
½ teaspoon salt
½ teaspoon Worcestershire sauce
1 teaspoon dried parsley flakes
1 cup water (more or less,
as necessary)**

Continue simmering, covered, for 30 minutes *or* in pressure cooker at 15 pounds pressure for 3 minutes.

Thicken gravy with flour and water mixture.

If desired, serve with Dumplings.

Yield: 6 servings.

(a) Dumplings

Blend or sift together
**1 cup *Pre-Sifted* PURITY
All-Purpose Flour
2 teaspoons baking powder
½ teaspoon salt**
Using two knives or a pastry blender, cut in
3 tablespoons shortening
Stir in
½ cup milk

Blend just until flour is moistened.

Drop by large spoonfuls on simmering stew. Cover pan tightly and cook for 15 minutes. Do not lift cover during cooking.

Yield: 6 dumplings.

The brown "CANADA APPROVED" stamp on wholesale cuts of meat is your guarantee that the meat has met Federal Government standards for health, cleanliness and wholesomeness. Shop for meat only where all meat sold has been properly inspected to ensure your family's good health.

Veal

455 Veal Pot Roast

Rub Seasoned Flour (recipe No. 477) into
**4 pound veal pot roast (rolled front,
shoulder, etc.)**
Heat in heavy kettle or Dutch oven
3 tablespoons shortening
Brown meat well on all sides.
Reduce heat and add
**¾ cup water
2 tablespoons vinegar
1 onion, sliced
½ teaspoon Worcestershire sauce**
Cover and simmer slowly until tender, about 45 minutes per pound.

Add water during cooking, if necessary. Vegetables may be added during last ½ hour of cooking.

Yield: 6 to 8 servings.

456 Stuffed Veal Rolls

Place **2 pounds veal cutlet,** thinly sliced, between sheets of waxed paper and pound to ⅛″ thickness. Use a meat cleaver or heavy frying pan to do this.

Cut meat slices into 6 rectangular serving pieces.

Combine in a small frying pan
**⅓ pound sausage meat
¼ cup finely chopped onions**
Cook until pink colour of meat disappears.
Add
**½ teaspoon salt
Few grains pepper
¼ teaspoon mixed herbs
½ cup fine dry bread crumbs**
Spread sausage mixture on veal slices. Roll up from narrow side and tie or skewer.

Brown veal rolls on all sides in
¼ cup shortening
Reduce heat and add
**1 (10-ounce) can cream of
mushroom soup
⅓ cup milk
2 tablespoons sherry, if desired**
Cover and cook over low heat for 30 minutes.
Stir and turn meat rolls occasionally.
Yield: 6 servings.

457   *Veal Paprika*

Cut into 6 or 8 serving pieces
2 pounds veal cutlet
Dredge in
½ cup Seasoned Flour (recipe No. 477)
Heat in large frying pan
3 tablespoons shortening
Brown meat pieces well on both sides.
Reduce heat and add
1 (10-ounce) can consommé
Tightly cover pan and cook 40 to 50 minutes
or until meat is tender. Add water if necessary
during cooking.
Blend together
**2 teaspoons paprika
½ pint commercial sour cream**
Remove pan from heat and blend sour cream
into consommé pan gravy. Stir until just
blended. Serve immediately.
Yield: 6 to 8 servings.

-----

*A generous sprinkle of paprika will add a
note of colour to broiled or roasted meats.*

458   *Veal Parmigiana*

Combine
**1 beaten egg
1 tablespoon water
1 teaspoon salt
¼ teaspoon pepper**
Blend together
**1 cup fine dry bread crumbs
3 tablespoons grated Parmesan
cheese**
Dip
4 veal chops
in egg mixture, then in crumb mixture.
Heat in a heavy frying pan
6 tablespoons shortening
Brown coated chops in the shortening over
moderate heat.

When chops are browned on both sides, pour
off excess fat. Lower heat and pour around
(not over) the meat
1 (7½-ounce) can tomato sauce
Top each chop with
1 slice Mozzarella cheese
Cover pan and cook slowly for 35 to 40
minutes or until meat is tender. If necessary, a
little water may be added to the tomato sauce
during cooking.
Yield: 4 servings.

459   *Stuffed Roast Veal*

Have butcher remove bone from
4 to 5 pound veal leg *or* rump
Preheat oven to 325°.
Fill pocket with Fruit Stuffing (recipe below).
Skewer together or tie with string.
Roast in shallow pan, uncovered, in preheated
325° oven. Allow 40 minutes per pound, or
until meat thermometer registers 180°. Meat
thermometer should be inserted into meat, not
stuffing.
Yield: 8 to 10 servings.

(a)   *Fruit Stuffing*
Combine
**2 cups soft bread crumbs
¼ cup chopped onions
1 teaspoon salt
½ cup chopped cooked prunes *or*
apricots, *or* diced celery
½ teaspoon dried parsley flakes
¼ teaspoon marjoram
2½ tablespoons melted butter *or*
margarine**
Use as stuffing in filleted veal roast.
NOTE: The amount of stuffing required will
vary but the above should be
adequate for the average size pocket.

-----

*Barbecuing is a favourite summer pastime.
Steaks, chops, chicken (pieces or whole), spareribs and roasts, are all popular. Be sure that
coals are burning with a white ash for maximum
heat. Meat may be marinated for added flavour
and less tender cuts treated by sprinkling with
commercial tenderizer. (Follow manufacturer's
directions.) To prevent drying out, baste with
butter, barbecue sauce, French dressing, etc.
during cooking. Sauces with tomato or sugar
burn readily, and so should be used only during
the last few minutes of cooking.*

460 Veal Jellies

Place in deep kettle
  1 veal knuckle (bone cracked)
  2 pounds stewing veal
  3 carrots
  1 onion
  1 tablespoon salt
  4 cloves
  ½ bay leaf
  Few celery leaves
  Sprig of parsley

Cover with water and bring to a boil. Skim. Reduce heat, cover, and simmer slowly 1½ to 2 hours or until meat is tender. Remove cover during last ½ hour to allow broth to boil down. When done, remove meat from broth.

Strain broth and chill quickly.

Meanwhile remove fat and gristle from meat and cut meat into ½″ cubes.

Combine meat with
  ¾ cup finely sliced celery

Place half of meat in 12 individual moulds and put a slice of hard cooked egg on each.

Add remaining meat.

Remove fat from surface of cooled broth. Heat and season to taste. There should be 1 to 1½ cups broth. If more, boil down, uncovered, to required volume.

Cool slightly and pour over meat. Chill thoroughly.

Yield: 12 moulds.

Lamb

461 Foil-Baked Lamb Chops

Preheat oven to 400°.

Heat in a frying pan
  2 tablespoons shortening
Add and brown well
  8 loin lamb chops, 1″ thick
Remove chops.

Add to fat
  ⅓ cup chopped onions
  2 tablespoons chopped green pepper
  ½ cup fresh or canned whole mushrooms
Cook gently for 5 minutes.

Have ready 4 sheets heavy aluminum foil about 15″ square. Place two browned chops in the centre of each square and top with onion and mushroom mixture.

On each portion, arrange
  2 tiny peeled onions
  1 or 2 small peeled potatoes
  1 small peeled tomato, cut in half
Sprinkle with salt, pepper and paprika.

Fold foil over top and seal securely. Place packages in shallow baking pan. Cook in preheated 400° oven for 1 hour.

Yield: 4 servings.

_____

The tough, thin, paper-like covering on lamb roasts (called the fell) is tasteless and makes carving difficult. It should be removed before roasting. Mutton (from mature sheep) is sold in limited quantities. It is made tender by cooking with moist heat (braising, pot roasting, stewing).

462 Mixed Grill

For each serving allow
  2 slices side bacon
  1 loin or rib lamb chop, 1″ thick
  2 pork sausages
  1 tomato slice, 1½″ thick

Broil the bacon first, remove and keep warm.

Pour off fat and arrange the lamb chops and sausages on broiler rack. Allow 15 minutes broiling time (7 to 8 minutes per side). Add tomato slices to broiler rack 10 minutes before chops are done. Do not turn.

If preferred, the sausages may be panbroiled.

463 Lamb Curry

Cut into 1½″ pieces
  2 pounds boned lamb shoulder
Dredge pieces lightly with
  ⅓ cup Pre-Sifted PURITY All-Purpose Flour
Melt in a heavy kettle
  ¼ cup butter or margarine
Add meat and brown thoroughly.

Then add
  ¾ cup finely chopped onions
  ¼ cup finely diced celery
  2 to 3 teaspoons curry powder
  1 teaspoon salt
  ⅛ teaspoon thyme
Combine and cook gently for 3 minutes.

Now add
  1 (10-ounce) can consommé
  2 cups boiling water

Cover and let simmer for 1 to 1½ hours or until meat is tender.

Add

    1 cup peeled, diced apple
    ½ cup raisins
    2 tablespoons chutney

Let simmer 10 minutes. Season to taste.

Blend together
    ¼ cup *Pre-Sifted* PURITY All-Purpose Flour
    ½ cup cream

Stir into sauce and cook gently until thickened.

Serve with hot, fluffy rice and side dishes of salted almonds, crisp bacon bits, pineapple chunks and chutney.

Yield: 6 servings.

464   *Irish Stew*

Remove excess fat, skin and gristle from
    2 pounds boned lamb shoulder

Cut meat into 2″ pieces.

Place in a heavy kettle and add
    1½ teaspoons salt
    ⅛ teaspoon pepper
    1 bay leaf
    ¼ cup chopped onions
    3 cups boiling water

Cover tightly and cook gently for 1 to 1½ hours or until meat is almost tender. Remove any excess fat from surface of broth.

Add
    1¼ cups carrots, cut in 1″ pieces
    1¼ cups turnip, cut in 1″ cubes
    3 medium onions, quartered
    4 to 5 medium potatoes, quartered

Cover and cook 30 minutes longer until vegetables are done and meat is very tender.

Remove vegetables and meat from broth and keep warm. Skim off any excess fat.

Blend together
    3 tablespoons *Pre-Sifted* PURITY All-Purpose Flour
    ¼ cup water

Stir into simmering broth and cook, stirring constantly, until thickened.

Add
    2 teaspoons Worcestershire sauce
    1 tablespoon snipped parsley

Season to taste.

Return meat and vegetables to gravy and reheat.

Serve with Dumplings (recipe No. 454 (a), if desired.

Yield: 4 to 6 servings.

465   *Shepherd's Pie*

Preheat oven to 375°.

Combine
    3 cups minced cooked lamb *or* beef
    1 tablespoon instant minced onion
    1 teaspoon Worcestershire sauce
    ⅔ to ¾ cup gravy
    Salt and pepper

Prepare
    3 cups seasoned mashed potatoes

Butter a shallow casserole and spread about one-third of the potatoes around the sides. Add meat mixture. Top with remaining mashed potatoes — either spread over the top or as a border around rim of the dish.

Bake in preheated 375° oven for 25 to 30 minutes or until the mixture is bubbling and the potatoes lightly browned.

Serve with tomato sauce, if desired.

Yield: 4 servings.

Pork

466   **Baked Pork Chops**

Preheat oven to 350°.

Dredge
    6 pork chops
in
    ½ cup Seasoned Flour (Recipe No. 477)

Heat in frying pan
    2 tablespoons shortening

Brown chops on both sides in hot fat.

Arrange in shallow baking dish.

Top each chop with
    1 lemon slice

Combine
    ⅔ cup catsup
    ⅔ cup water
    3 tablespoons brown sugar

Pour catsup mixture around the chops.

Cover and bake in preheated 350° oven for 30 minutes. Uncover and bake a further 20 to 30 minutes. Add water, if necessary.

Yield: 6 servings.

467 Baked Stuffed Tenderloin

Preheat oven to 325°.

Prepare **4 pork tenderloins** (about 3 pounds) by cutting each lengthwise, not quite through. Open each flat.

Prepare stuffing by combining

    2 cups dry bread cubes
    3 tablespoons chopped onions
    1 teaspoon salt
    ¾ cup well drained pineapple tidbits
    2 tablespoons melted butter *or* margarine

Spread stuffing on two of the tenderloins and top with the other two.

Tie each pair with string, and top with

    1 slice side bacon

Place on a rack in roast pan. Do not add water. Do not cover.

Roast in preheated 325° oven for 1½ hours.

Remove strings before serving. Nice with applesauce.

Yield: 6 to 8 servings.

468 Stuffed Pork Loin Roast

Have butcher bone **2 pork loins** weighing 1½ to 2 pounds each when boned.

Preheat oven to 325°.

Spread Apple Stuffing (recipe below) between the two pieces of meat (fat side out) and tie securely together.

Rub surfaces with Seasoned Flour (recipe No. 477). Place on rack in open roast pan in preheated 325° oven. Roast for 45 minutes per pound or until a thermometer inserted in meat reads 185°.

Serve with spiced applesauce.

Yield: 6 to 8 servings.

(a) Apple Stuffing

Fry slowly

    2 tablespoons butter *or* margarine
    2 tablespoons chopped onion
    2 tablespoons diced celery

When onion is transparent and celery tender, add

    2 cups soft bread crumbs
    1 large apple, coarsely shredded
    1 tablespoon chopped parsley
    ½ teaspoon thyme
    1 teaspoon salt
    Few grains pepper

469 Barbecued Spareribs

Preheat oven to 350°.

Arrange in a shallow roasting pan

    3 pounds pork spareribs (back)

Sprinkle with salt and pepper.

Roast uncovered in preheated 350° oven for 1¼ hours.

Meanwhile combine

    ⅓ cup finely chopped onions
    ⅓ cup finely chopped green peppers
    ½ cup chili sauce
    ½ cup canned crushed pineapple, undrained
    1 (7½-ounce) can tomato sauce
    ¼ cup lemon juice
    ¼ cup brown sugar
    ½ teaspoon dry mustard

Mix well and allow to stand to blend flavours.

Pour off any accumulated fat after 1¼ hours of baking. Pour sauce over ribs and bake 45 minutes longer. Baste frequently.

Yield: 4 to 6 servings.

470 Stuffed Spareribs

Purchase two sets of matching pork spareribs (back), weighing about 1½ pounds each.

Preheat oven to 350°.

Place half the ribs, meaty side down, on rack in shallow pan. Cover with stuffing (recipe below) and top with remaining ribs, meaty side up.

Sprinkle with salt, pepper and thyme.

Add ½ cup water to pan. Roast in preheated 350° oven for 1¾ to 2 hours. Add a little water during cooking if meat is drying out.

Do not cover pan.

To serve, cut between ribs.

Yield: 4 servings.

(a) Sparerib Stuffing

Heat in frying pan

    3 tablespoons butter *or* margarine

Add and brown lightly

    ⅓ cup chopped onions
    ½ cup diced celery

Then add

    1 cup coarsely shredded apple
    2 tablespoons chopped parsley
    1 teaspoon salt
    3 cups soft bread crumbs

Combine evenly.

Roast Beef and Yorkshire Pudding to satisfy your whole family (Page 151, 152 and Recipe No. 75 (a)

471   Pineapple Ham Loaf

Preheat oven to 350°.

Combine

3 cups minced cooked ham
1 cup fine dry bread crumbs
2 beaten eggs
¾ cup milk
2 teaspoons instant minced onion
½ teaspoon salt
½ teaspoon monosodium glutamate
1 teaspoon prepared mustard
1 teaspoon dried parsley flakes
1 teaspoon Worcestershire sauce

Blend well.

Place in a 9″ x 5″ loaf pan

⅓ cup lightly-packed brown sugar
½ cup drained crushed pineapple
½ teaspoon dry mustard

Stir lightly with a fork to blend and spread evenly in pan.

Cover with meat loaf mixture, packing down firmly.

Bake in preheated 350° oven for one hour.

Allow to stand in pan for about 5 minutes. Invert onto plate and serve in slices.

Yield: 6 servings.

472   Perfect Ham Glaze

Bake ham according to directions on wrapper or see Roasting Time Table page 152.

When ham is baked, cut or peel off skin. Using a sharp knife, score fat by cutting about ¼″ deep in 1 to 1½″ diamonds.

Increase oven temperature to 500°.

Brush fat surface with

½ cup corn syrup or honey

Combine

1 cup lightly-packed brown sugar
2 tablespoons *Pre-Sifted* PURITY All-Purpose Flour
1 tablespoon dry mustard

with enough **vinegar** to make a thick paste.

Spread over surface of ham.

If desired, fasten maraschino cherries and pineapple slices to the ham with toothpicks.

Place in preheated 500° oven for 10 to 15 minutes to brown glaze.

Baste frequently with syrup and sugar mixture that drips into pan.

Remove from oven and continue to baste with syrup for 10 minutes.

Glaze should be firm enough at the end of this time to hold cherries and pineapple without the toothpicks.

Yield: Glaze for whole ham (12-15 pounds).

NOTE: This glaze may be used on half hams, cottage rolls, etc. Reduce quantities depending on size.

473   Ham Steaks

Panbroil: Brown ham steaks quickly in a lightly greased pan. Reduce heat and cook slowly, turning occasionally. Allow 12 to 15 minutes for ½″ steaks, 18 to 20 minutes for 1″ steaks.

Broil: Place steaks on cold broiler rack and broil 3″ below heat. Allow times as for panbroiling. Brush with barbecue sauce or herb butter after turning.

Bake: Place steaks in shallow baking pan and sprinkle with brown sugar or honey, and mustard. Bake in preheated 325° oven, allowing 25 to 30 minutes for ½″ steaks, 50 to 55 minutes for 1″ steaks. If desired, ½ cup apple, pineapple or orange juice may be added during last half of baking time.

474   Sausages

Sausages are prepared from pork or pork and beef, with cereal and seasonings added. They are sold fresh, smoked or cooked.

When fresh, sausages are pink in colour. They should be purchased as fresh as possible, refrigerated and used promptly. Cooked sausages should be uniformly grey inside and show no tinge of pink.

Link sausages are sold with casing or skinless. To cook, place sausages in cold, lightly greased frying pan over moderate heat. Cook slowly for 20 to 30 minutes, turning frequently. Do not prick. Drain well before serving.

Farmer style sausage (large sausage, in casing). Place in a heavy frying pan with ½″ water. Cook slowly for 35 to 40 minutes. When water has evaporated, turn sausage occasionally to brown evenly.

Sausage meat may be formed into patties. Brown in lightly greased frying pan and cook slowly over moderate heat for about 20 minutes. Turn frequently.

Any kind of sausage may be baked or broiled. Sausages should be partially cooked before adding to casserole or skillet dishes.

475 Variety Meats

Liver: Remove outer skin and cut away tubes if necessary. Soak beef and pork liver in milk for 2 hours in refrigerator for a milder flavour. Calf and baby liver are considered the choicest. Allow ¼ pound per serving.

To panbroil—flour liver slices and cook over moderate heat in a small amount of fat for 2 to 3 minutes on each side. Cook until pink colour in centre just disappears. Do not overcook or liver will be very tough. Season.

To broil—calf and baby beef liver may be cooked in this way. Brush generously with fat and place 3″ below heat. Broil 4 to 5 minutes on each side. Season.

Kidney: These vary in flavour and tenderness. Before cooking kidney, remove the membrane, fat and tubes. Cut kidney in half lengthwise for panbroiling or broiling. Allow ⅓ pound per serving.

To panbroil—brown kidney in a small amount of fat and cook 3 to 5 minutes, turning frequently. For kidney halves, allow 7 to 9 minutes cooking time. Do not overcook. Season.

To broil—brush generously with fat and place 3″ below heat.

Broil 4 to 7 minutes on each side. Season.

To braise—beef and pork kidneys are generally cooked in this way. Soak in salted water for 1 hour in refrigerator. Flour and brown in a small amount of fat. Add liquid to about ¼″ depth, cover and cook slowly 35 to 40 minutes.

Heart: All types of heart require long slow cooking at a low temperature. A beef heart that has passed government inspection will be cut in two. Heart is generally stuffed and baked. Allow approximately ½ pound per person; 2 cups stuffing for 6 servings.

Wash thoroughly, wipe dry and cut away coarse tubes and excess fat. Trim out heart cavity and fill with well-seasoned bread stuffing. Fasten with skewers and string, if necessary. Place bacon strips on top. Bake in preheated 325° oven, basting frequently, for following times:

Beef   2½ to 3 hours; Pork 2 to 2½ hours; Lamb   1 to 1¼ hours; Veal 1½ to 2 hours.

Tongue: Tongue requires long, slow cooking in moist heat. Beef, veal and pork tongues are sold fresh. Beef is also sold pickled (which adds greatly to the flavour). Allow ½ pound per serving. Wash tongue thoroughly and

cover with water. Simmer in a covered saucepan. Allow time as follows:

Fresh beef. . .60 minutes per pound
Pickled beef. .50 minutes per pound
Lamb, Pork, Veal . . . . .2 hours

Tongue should be cooked until tender.

Remove skin, excess fat, glands and bones while still hot.

476 Basic Marinade

Meats and vegetables are marinated or soaked for added flavour. Less tender cuts of meat are also made more tender by marinating overnight. For salads, marinate cooked, chilled vegetables for about an hour.

For barbecued meats, marinate for several hours, then brush meat with marinade during barbecuing.

Combine in a jar

⅔ cup vegetable oil
⅓ cup tarragon *or* wine vinegar
1 teaspoon salt
½ teaspoon dry mustard
1 teaspoon sugar
Dash tabasco sauce

Cover jar and store in refrigerator. Shake well before using. The marinade may be re-used.

Yield: 1 cup.

477 Seasoned Flour

For convenience, prepare seasoned flour to use for dredging meat and poultry.
Combine

2 cups *Pre-Sifted* PURITY
  All-Purpose Flour
2 tablespoons salt
1 tablespoon celery salt
1 tablespoon pepper
2 tablespoons dry mustard
4 tablespoons paprika
2 tablespoons garlic powder
3 tablespoons monosodium
  glutamate
1 teaspoon ginger
½ teaspoon thyme
½ teaspoon sweet basil
½ teaspoon oregano

Sift together to blend evenly. Store in a tightly covered jar.

For a crumb coating, combine 1½ tablespoons of the basic Seasoned Flour with 1 cup fine dry bread crumbs.

Deep Fat Frying

THINGS TO REMEMBER ABOUT DEEP FAT FRYING

Vegetable oils (such as peanut oil, corn oil or cottonseed oil) or hydrogenated vegetable shortenings are best suited for deep fat frying. Properly cooked by this method, food is flavourful, attractive and digestible.

To be sure that the flavour is sealed in and that the heat, not the oil, penetrates the food evenly, a thermometer or thermostatically controlled fryer should be used.

It is wise to test the accuracy of any cooking thermometer by checking its reading in boiling water. Adjust for any variation from 212°.

Add the oil or shortening to about one-third the depth of the pan. Be sure the fat is preheated to the recommended temperature before the food is added. Cook a few pieces of food at a time, using tongs for handling. Do not crowd or overload the fryer.

As the pieces of food are browned and cooked, remove them carefully with tongs and drain on absorbent paper towels.

Keep fried foods warm in a 300° oven. They may also be reheated by placing them in a 300° oven for 15 to 20 minutes.

After cooking, cool the fat, strain through cheese cloth into original container and store. Carefully handled, it may be used over and over again. Do not allow the temperature to rise any higher than recommended for the particular food you are cooking. Overheating will cause the fat to smoke and develop off flavours. Such fat cannot be used again and must be discarded.

---

478 Croquettes

Melt over moderate heat
    2 tablespoons butter *or* margarine
Add
    2 tablespoons chopped onion
Cook until onion is tender.
Blend in
    ¼ cup *Pre-Sifted* PURITY All-Purpose Flour
    ½ teaspoon salt
    Few grains pepper
Gradually add, stirring constantly
    1 cup milk
Cook until mixture begins to boil and is smoothly thickened. Stir constantly.
Remove from heat and add
    2 cups cooked chopped chicken, turkey, meat *or* grated cheese
    1 teaspoon finely chopped parsley *or* ½ teaspoon dried parsley flakes

Cool mixture for easier handling.

Form into croquettes, allowing about 1 large spoonful for each.

Roll in
    Fine, dry bread crumbs
Dip breaded croquettes in
    1 slightly-beaten egg
Drain off excess egg and roll again in bread crumbs.

Chill until ready to fry.

Fry in preheated deep fat at 375° for 3 to 5 minutes.

Drain on absorbent paper.

Yield: 6 croquettes.

Chill breaded foods for a few minutes before frying in deep fat. This will allow the coating to set so the crumbs will not come off during frying.

479   Banana Fritters

Cut peeled bananas in 2″ pieces.

Dust lightly and evenly with *Pre-Sifted* PURITY All-Purpose Flour

Prepare batter by combining

  2 eggs
  ½ cup milk
  ½ cup *Pre-Sifted* PURITY
    All-Purpose Flour
  1 tablespoon sugar
  1½ teaspoons baking powder
  ¼ teaspoon salt

Beat with rotary beater until batter is smooth.

Dip floured banana pieces in batter to coat entire surface.   Drain off excess.

Fry in preheated deep fat at 375° for 3 to 4 minutes. Turn frequently to brown evenly.

Drain on absorbent paper.

Serve hot with meat, or as dessert with lemon sauce.

Yield: Sufficient batter for about 6 bananas.

NOTE: This batter recipe may be used for coating apple slices or sections, pineapple slices or apricot halves. Prepare and deep fry as above.

480   Mammy's Corn Fritters

Blend or sift together

  1¾ cups *Pre-Sifted* PURITY
    All-Purpose Flour
  3 teaspoons baking powder
  1 teaspoon salt
  Few grains cayenne

Beat until light
  2 eggs

Add

  1 tablespoon melted butter *or*
    margarine

Add egg mixture to the dry ingredients and beat with a fork until smooth.

Stir in

  1½ cups cream style corn

Drop by spoonfuls into preheated deep fat at 375°. Fry for 4 to 5 minutes, or until evenly browned.

Serve hot with maple syrup and crisp side bacon.

Yield: 15 to 18 fritters.

481   Batter for Deep Frying

Blend or sift together
  1 cup *Pre-Sifted* PURITY
    All-Purpose Flour
  1 teaspoon baking powder
  1 teaspoon salt

Combine
  2 beaten eggs
  ⅔ cup milk
  1 tablespoon vegetable oil *or*
    melted butter

Gradually add to dry ingredients, stirring until well blended.

Use this batter for coating chicken, fish, etc. as directed in the following recipes.

482   Fried Chicken

Prepare Batter for Deep Frying (recipe No. 481).

Dust

  6 to 8 chicken pieces (fryers *or*
    broilers)

with *Pre-Sifted* PURITY All-Purpose Flour.

Dip floured chicken pieces in batter, drain off excess. Place carefully in preheated deep fat at 350°. Turn frequently to brown evenly.

Cook 20 to 30 minutes, depending on size of chicken pieces. Drain on absorbent paper.

Yield: 6 to 8 servings.

NOTE: Meatier chicken pieces may be steamed or simmered until tender, cooled quickly and then dipped in batter as above. Fry in preheated deep fat at 375° for 5 to 7 minutes.

483   Fish in Batter

Prepare Batter for Deep Frying (recipe No. 481).

Cut 1½ to 2 pounds fish fillets into pieces which are about 2″ square. (Haddock, halibut, cod and sole fillets are especially good. If using frozen fish, thaw completely.) Dry the fish thoroughly and then dust with *Pre-Sifted* PURITY All-Purpose Flour.

Dip floured fish in batter, drain off excess.

Fry in preheated deep fat at 375° for 5 to 7 minutes, turning frequently for even browning.

Drain on absorbent paper.

Yield: 6 to 8 servings.

484 Deep Fried Scallops

Beat together in a shallow bowl
1 egg
1 tablespoon water

Place ¼ cup *Pre-Sifted* PURITY All-Purpose Flour on one plate; 1 cup fine dry bread crumbs on a second plate.

Drain
1 pound scallops

Dip scallops in flour, then in egg mixture and finally in the crumbs. Be sure that each one is completely coated. Allow to stand for about 20 minutes so the crumbs will dry and not come off during frying.

Fry in preheated deep fat at 375° for 3 to 4 minutes. Turn frequently for even browning.

Drain on absorbent paper.

Yield: 3 to 4 servings.

NOTE: Fish fillets may be prepared in the same way. Deep fry at 375° for 5 to 7 minutes.

485 French Fried Potatoes

One Step Method (4 servings or less): Allow 1 medium or 1 large potato for each serving. Peel and cut into ⅜″ slices, then into lengthwise strips which are ⅜″ wide. Wash in cold water and dry thoroughly.

Just cover the bottom of the fryer basket with potatoes, and lower slowly into deep fat preheated to 380°. If fat bubbles violently due to moisture of the potatoes, remove basket for a second. Fry, shaking occasionally until potatoes are crisp and brown — about 7 to 10 minutes. Drain on absorbent paper, salt to taste just before serving.

Two Step Method (5 or more servings): Prepare potatoes as above then fry in preheated deep fat at 370° as directed until potatoes are tender but not brown — about 5 minutes.

Drain on a baking sheet or tray covered with absorbent paper. When cold, cover loosely with waxed paper. The first frying can be done several hours in advance or whenever convenient. Just before serving, refry potatoes in preheated deep fat at 390° until crisp and brown—about 2 to 3 minutes. A large quantity of potatoes may be fried at a time on second frying. Drain, salt to taste and serve at once.

486 Cheese Bites

Beat until stiff
2 egg whites

Fold in
1 cup shredded Cheddar cheese
¼ cup fine dry bread crumbs
½ teaspoon Worcestershire sauce

Combine evenly and form into small balls (approximately 1 tablespoon in each). Fry in preheated deep fat at 350° for 2 to 3 minutes.

Serve hot with tomato juice or fruit salad.

Yield: 12 to 15 small balls.

487 Doughnuts

Beat thoroughly
2 egg yolks

Beat in
1 cup sugar
3 tablespoons soft shortening

Stir in
¾ cup sour milk

Blend or sift together
3 cups *Pre-Sifted* PURITY All-Purpose Flour
2 teaspoons baking powder
1 teaspoon baking soda
1 teaspoon salt
½ teaspoon cinnamon
¼ teaspoon nutmeg
¼ teaspoon mace

Add to egg yolk mixture, stir to make a soft dough.

Then fold in
2 stiffly-beaten egg whites

Cover and chill for 1 hour.

Turn chilled dough onto a lightly floured surface and roll to ⅓″ thickness. Cut out with a floured 2½″ doughnut cutter.

Fry in preheated deep fat at 370° for about 1 minute on each side.

Drain on absorbent paper.

Sugar, if desired.

Yield: About 2 dozen doughnuts.

To sugar doughnuts: Combine ½ cup sugar and ½ teaspoon cinnamon or ¼ teaspoon nutmeg in a paper bag. Add the drained doughnuts, 2 or 3 at a time, and shake to coat.

Vegetables

THINGS TO REMEMBER ABOUT COOKING VEGETABLES

To get your money's worth in nutrition and flavour, cook vegetables with care and season subtly to enhance their natural goodness.

Store fresh vegetables in a cool dry place or refrigerator after purchasing and use within two or three days.

Pare vegetables thinly when necessary and avoid soaking. The exception is for vegetables such as broccoli and cauliflower where there might be insects. Soak these in salted water for ½ hour.

Cook only enough vegetables for one meal. Do not start in cold water. Cook only until tender crisp.

COOKING METHODS

Boiling: Cook vegetables in a deep, heavy saucepan which has a tight fitting lid, using as little water as possible. Add vegetables and salt to boiling water, cover and bring to the boil quickly, reducing heat enough to just keep vegetables boiling. Cook until just tender. Drain, season to taste and serve immediately.

Pressure Cooking: This method provides an ideal way of cooking vegetables to help retain colour, flavour and nutritive value. Follow manufacturer's directions carefully.

Steaming: This is another excellent method of cooking vegetables. Allow 10-20 minutes more cooking time than for boiling vegetables (see Chart pages 170-172).

Oven Steaming: Do this when cooking an oven meal. Cook prepared vegetables in a tightly covered casserole with a small amount of salted water. Allow three times as long as for boiling vegetables.

Braising: This is another way to steam vegetables. Allow 2 tablespoons each of butter and water to every 4 cups of shredded or thinly sliced vegetables.

Baking: Place prepared vegetables in oven on rack, baking sheet or casserole. Bake along with an oven meal, adjusting cooking time with temperature required for the main dish.

Frying: This gives special flavour and crispness to raw or cooked vegetables. Use a heavy frying pan and small amount of shortening. For French fried vegetables see section on Deep Fat Frying.

Canned Vegetables: Drain liquid from vegetables into saucepan. Boil to reduce liquid to half. Add vegetables, heat gently and season to taste.

Frozen Vegetables: For commercially frozen vegetables, carefully follow the directions on the package. See page 205 for cooking home frozen vegetables.

---

488 — *Baked Potatoes*

Preheat oven to 425°.

Choose medium or large potatoes of uniform size. Scrub thoroughly and remove any blemishes. Rub each with salad oil or soft butter and arrange on a baking sheet or oven rack.

Bake in preheated 425° oven for 55 minutes or until tender.

To serve: Make two diagonal cross cuts about 1½" long. Holding the potato in a clean towel, press upward from the bottom to force open the slits. Fluff up the potato with a fork. Serve immediately with butter, salt and pepper.

If desired, top with one of the following: Commercial sour cream, snipped chives, process cheese spread, Lemon Butter Sauce.

NOTE: Potatoes may be baked at varying oven temperatures along with any oven meal. For instance, if baked in a 375° oven, medium potatoes will require about 75 minutes.

489 Stuffed Baked Potatoes

For 6 servings, bake **7 medium - sized potatoes.**

When tender, cut a slice from the top of each potato and scoop out potato leaving skin intact.

Mash well and beat in
> **¼ cup hot milk**
> **1 tablespoon melted butter *or* margarine**
> **½ teaspoon salt**

Season to taste. Refill 6 shells, mounding the tops of each. Brush with melted butter or margarine and dust with paprika. Brown lightly under broiler for about 10 minutes before serving, or reheat in 400° oven for 15 minutes.

The potato filling may be varied by adding 2 or more tablespoons of chopped parsley, chives or onion; ⅓ to ½ cup shredded old cheese, diced cooked ham, corned beef or crumbled crisp bacon.

Yield: 6 servings.

490 Pan Roast Potatoes

Method 1: Choose small potatoes of uniform size, allowing 2 to 3 per serving. Pare, wash and place around the meat in roasting pan about 1¼ hours before roast is done. Add salt and paprika. If potatoes are medium or large, cut in halves or quarters. Bake 60 to 70 minutes or until tender, turning occasionally and basting with pan drippings. If potatoes are not brown enough, place under broiler (after roast has been removed), turning potatoes to brown evenly.

Method 2: Parboil potatoes 10 minutes in boiling, salted water to cover. Drain well. Arrange in drippings around the roast and bake 40 to 50 minutes or until tender. Turn potatoes and baste as in Method 1. Potatoes are fluffier when roasted by this method.

491 Duchess Potatoes

Preheat oven to 450°.

Prepare, then boil **6 medium potatoes** until just tender. Mash.

Have ready
> **¼ cup hot milk**
> **3 tablespoons butter *or* margarine**
> **1 teaspoon salt**
> **⅛ teaspoon pepper**

Add gradually to hot, mashed potatoes and beat thoroughly.

Blend in
> **3 beaten egg yolks**

Continue to beat until mixture is smooth and fluffy.

Arrange in 12 mounds on buttered baking sheet. If desired, use pastry bag and star tube to make 12 rosettes.

Bake in preheated 450° oven for 15 minutes or brush with melted butter and brown under broiler.

Yield: 6 servings.

492 Scalloped Potatoes

Preheat oven to 375°.

Peel 4 or 5 medium potatoes, thinly slice and measure
> **4 cups**

Combine
> **2 tablespoons *Pre-Sifted* PURITY All-Purpose Flour**
> **1½ teaspoons salt**
> **⅛ teaspoon pepper**

Have ready
> **½ cup chopped onions**
> **2 tablespoons butter *or* margarine**
> **1½ cups hot milk**

Arrange alternate layers of potatoes, onions and seasoned flour in a greased 2-quart casserole. Dot with butter.

Pour hot milk over top and sprinkle with paprika.

Bake, covered, in preheated 375° oven for 45 minutes. Uncover and bake 15 minutes longer or until potatoes are tender and top lightly browned.

Yield: 4 servings.

NOTE: If desired, arrange 2 cups diced, cooked ham between potato layers.

493 Baked Pepper Squash

Preheat oven to 400°.

Prepare 2 pepper squash (see Chart page 172).

Brush cut edges with melted butter or margarine. Arrange in a greased baking pan, cut side down. Bake in preheated 400° oven for 45 minutes.

Turn squash cut side up and brush with melted butter. Sprinkle each half with 1 tablespoon brown sugar and a little salt.

Bake 15 minutes longer or until squash is tender and sugar melted.

Yield: 4 servings.

494 Stuffed Baked Tomatoes

Preheat oven to 400°.

Wash **4 large firm tomatoes.** Cut slice off top of each and scoop out pulp with spoon or grapefruit knife, leaving shells ¼" thick.

Invert tomatoes to drain.

Combine
- **1 cup hot cooked rice**
- **3 tablespoons chopped tomato pulp**
- **1 tablespoon finely diced green pepper**
- **1 tablespoon chopped onion**
- **1 tablespoon chopped parsley**
- **½ teaspoon salt**
- **1 teaspoon Worcestershire sauce**
- **2 tablespoons melted butter *or* margarine**

Fill tomato shells and place in shallow baking pan.

Bake in preheated 400° oven about 20 to 25 minutes.

Yield: 4 servings.

NOTE: If smaller tomatoes are used, bake in muffin cups and reduce baking time to 15 minutes.

Sweet potatoes are yellow and mealy while yams are orange and moist. They may be used interchangeably.

495 Glazed Carrots

Prepare **1 pound fresh carrots,** cut in half lengthwise and crosswise. If small, leave whole. Cook until just tender (see Chart page 171). Drain.

Melt in a frying pan
- **2 tablespoons butter *or* margarine**

Stir in
- **⅓ cup sugar**
- **1 tablespoon water**

Heat until sugar is dissolved.

Add carrots and cook over medium heat, turning frequently, until carrots are glazed—about 10 to 15 minutes. Do not cook glaze too long or it will caramelize and become hard.

Yield: 4 to 6 servings.

VARIATION:

(a) Glazed Onions

Prepare 1½ pounds small, white cooking onions and cook until just tender (see Chart page 171). Glaze as directed in above recipe.

496 Wax Beans Lyonnaise

Prepare **1 pound fresh wax beans** and cut into 1" pieces. Cook until just tender (see Chart page 170). Drain.

Melt
- **¼ cup butter *or* margarine**

Add
- **¼ cup finely chopped onions**

Cook, stirring frequently, for 5 minutes.

Add to the cooked beans
- **Butter and onions**
- **1 tablespoon snipped parsley**
- **½ teaspoon salt**
- **Few grains pepper**
- **Few grains nutmeg**

Combine gently. Cover and let simmer over low heat for 10 minutes. Shake the saucepan occasionally to prevent scorching. Season to taste.

Yield: 4 to 6 servings.

497 Harvard Beets

Drain
- **2 (20-ounce) cans sliced beets**

Reserve
- **⅔ cup beet liquid**

Combine in top of double boiler
- **⅓ cup sugar**
- **½ teaspoon salt**
- **2 tablespoons *Pre-Sifted* PURITY All-Purpose Flour**

Mix together
- **Reserved beet liquid**
- **⅓ cup vinegar**

Stir gradually into dry ingredients. Place over medium heat and cook, stirring constantly, until smoothly thickened.

Add
- **Drained sliced beets**
- **¼ teaspoon instant minced onion**

Set over boiling water for 15 minutes or until beets are hot.

Stir in
- **1 tablespoon butter *or* margarine**

Yield: 6 to 8 servings.

NOTE: If desired, use cooked fresh beets in place of canned. Substitute ⅔ cup water for the beet liquid and use 4 cups sliced, cooked fresh beets.

VEGETABLE CHART

Use about 1 inch boiling salted water for mild flavoured vegetables. Use more water for potatoes, strong flavoured vegetables and those which require long cooking times. Cooking times given in the chart are approximate.

Vegetable	Amount to Purchase For 4	Preparation	Boiling Time (Minutes)	Suggestions
Asparagus	2 pounds	Cut off tough ends. Remove scales. Wash. *Lay in 9" or 10" skillet. Add 1" boiling, salted water. Cook covered.* Whole Cut in 1" pieces	15-20 10-15	Drizzle with melted butter. *Sauces:*—Hollandaise, Cheese, Mushroom, Egg.
Beans Green and Wax	1 pound	Wash. Snip off ends and remove strings if any. Whole Cut in 1" straight or diagonal slices French cut in thin lengthwise strips	20-30 10-20 10-20	Sprinkle with slivered toasted almonds, diced pimiento, or grated Parmesan cheese. *Sauces:*—Cream, Mustard, Mushroom
Beets	2 pounds	Cut off tops, leaving 1" stem and root. Scrub well. *Use boiling, salted water to cover.* Small, whole Large, whole	30-60 1-2 hours	Slip off skins under cold water. Leave whole, slice or dice. Reheat with seasonings and butter. Serve with vinegar or lemon juice.
Broccoli	2 pounds	Cut off large leaves and tough ends. Slit stems lengthwise to flowerets if larger than ½". *Lay in 9" or 10" skillet. Add 1" boiling, salted water. Cook covered.*	10-15	Serve with melted butter, lemon wedges or grated Parmesan cheese. *Sauces:*—Hollandaise, Cheese, Mustard.
Brussels Sprouts	1 pound	Remove wilted leaves. Cut off stem end. Wash thoroughly. Whole	10-25	Serve with lemon juice, snipped parsley, chives or fresh chopped dill. *Sauce:*—Lemon Butter.
Cabbage Green and Savoy Wedges Shredded	 1¼ pounds 1 pound	Remove wilted leaves. Wash. Cut in wedges. Leave enough core to hold shape. Cut in quarters. Shred with very sharp knife or coarse grater.	 8-12 5-10	*Sauces:*—Cream, Egg, Mustard, Cheese.

Vegetable	Amount to Purchase For 4	Preparation	Boiling Time (Minutes)	Suggestions
Carrots	1 pound	Scrub, scrape or thinly pare. Small whole Halved or quartered Thin strips or slices	 20-30 15-20 10-15	Sprinkle with snipped parsley, mint or chives. *Sauces:*—Cream, Parsley, Lemon Butter.
Cauliflower	1 medium head	Remove outer leaves. Cut off any blemishes. Wash thoroughly. Cut out centre core. Whole Break into flowerets	 20-30 8-15	Top with buttered crumbs and grated cheese. Broil. Sprinkle with snipped chives or parsley. *Sauces:*—Cheese, Hollandaise.
Celery	Allow ⅔ cup diced or sliced raw per serving.	Remove leaves, trim roots. Scrub. Dice or slice diagonally in ½″ or 1″ pieces	 15-20	Brown in butter and cook until tender in consommé or bouillon. *Sauces:*—Cream, Parsley, Hollandaise
Corn on the Cob	8 ears	Remove husks, silk and any blemishes just before cooking. *Cook in boiling, salted water to cover.*	5-8	Wrap in foil and roast or barbecue. Cut fresh corn off cob. Simmer 10 minutes with butter and milk.
Onions Yellow Small White Spanish *or* Bermuda	1½ pounds	Cut slices from stem and root ends. Peel and remove loose layers under cold running water. Whole (2″ or larger) Whole For slices, cut ¼″-½″ thick. Cut into slices.	 30-35 20-25 10	Serve whole—boiled, baked, or glazed. *Sauces:*—Cream, Cheese. Serve raw or deep fat fried.
Parsnips	1½ pounds	Wash, pare, cut into halves or quarters. Remove woody cores. Halved or quartered Sliced or diced	 20-30 8-15	Mash, pan fry, or cream. Cook with carrots and mash.
Peas	2 pounds	Shell and wash just before cooking. Add 1 teaspoon sugar to water.	8-20	Combine with tiny cooked onions, new potatoes, or pan fried mushrooms. *Sauces:*—Cream, Mushroom.

Purity Flour is vitamin-enriched for extra nutrition

Vegetable	Amount to Purchase For 4	Preparation	Boiling Time (Minutes)	Suggestions
Potatoes Sweet *or* Yams White	2 pounds 2 pounds (1 medium potato = ⅓ pound)	Scrub well. Remove blemishes. Do not pare. Scrub well, remove blemishes and eyes. Cook in skins, scrape or thinly pare. Whole Cut in halves or quarters	30-35 35-40 20-25	Boil, bake, mash or candy. Boil, mash, bake, cream, pan fry, scallop, or deep fat fry.
Spinach and Greens	2 pounds	Discard ends, tough stalks and yellow leaves. Wash in warm water 3-4 times, lifting greens out of water. *If greens are young, cook without adding water. Otherwise use ½" boiling, salted water.* Spinach Beet Tops Swiss Chard	 6-10 5-15 3-10	Cut cooked greens before serving. Sprinkle with chopped hard cooked egg, chopped beets, lemon juice or vinegar. *Sauces:*—French Dressing, Cream, Egg.
Summer Squash Yellow Crookneck	2 pounds	Scrub well. Cut slices from stem and blossom ends. Do not pare (unless old). Do not remove seeds. Cut into thin slices. *Cook in ½" boiling, salted water.*	 15-20	Boil, mash, or use in casseroles *Sauces:*—Tomato, Cheese.
Winter Squash Pepper Hubbard Butternut	2 whole 2½ to 3 pounds	Scrub well. Cut in half lengthwise. Remove seeds and stringy portions. Scrub well, cut into pieces. Remove seeds and stringy portions.	 25-30 25-30	Bake. (See recipe 493) Mash or bake.
Tomatoes	2 pounds	Wash, pare thinly or scald and slip off skins. *Quarter and cook without water.*	 5-15	Stew, bake, broil or serve in casseroles.
Turnip Yellow *or* Rutabaga White	2 pounds 2 pounds	Scrub well. Cut into ½" slices and pare. Cut into cubes or strips Scrub well. Cut into ½" slices and pare. Cut into cubes or strips	 20-30 15-20	Cook with potatoes and onions for flavour and texture. Sprinkle with chopped parsley.

Savoury Sauces

498 BASIC RECIPE *Cream Sauce*
(Medium Sauce)

Melt in a saucepan over low heat
2 tablespoons butter *or* margarine
Blend in
**2 tablespoons *Pre-Sifted* PURITY
All-Purpose Flour**
½ teaspoon salt
Few grains pepper
Few grains paprika
Stir until smooth. Remove from heat.
Gradually blend in
1 cup milk

Return to direct medium heat and stir
constantly until smoothly thickened. Season
to taste.
Use with vegetables, chicken, seafood or in
casserole dishes. To keep hot, cover and place
over simmering water.
Yield: 1 cup.
NOTE: For a thin Cream Sauce, decrease
butter and flour to 1 tablespoon each.
For a thick Cream Sauce, increase the
butter and flour to ¼ cup each.

(a) Cheese Sauce

Add ½ cup shredded old Cheddar cheese or ¾
cup diced process cheese and 1 teaspoon
Worcestershire sauce to the Cream Sauce.

(b) Curry Sauce

Add 2 tablespoons finely minced onion and ½
to 1 teaspoon curry powder to melted butter
in Cream Sauce recipe. Cook stirring constantly
for 2 to 3 minutes then proceed as directed.
Use with seafood, rice or hard-cooked eggs.

(c) Mustard Sauce

Blend 1 tablespoon prepared mustard and ½
teaspoon onion powder into the Cream Sauce.
Nice with green or wax beans.

(d) Egg Sauce

Increase milk in Cream Sauce recipe to 1¼
cups and add 2 chopped or sliced hard-cooked
eggs and 1 teaspoon Worcestershire sauce.
Serve with poached fresh or smoked fish,
croquettes or toast.

(e) Parsley Sauce

Add ¼ cup finely chopped parsley and ½
teaspoon celery salt to Cream Sauce. Nice
with new boiled potatoes, fish or croquettes.

(f) Shrimp Sauce

Add 1 teaspoon Worcestershire sauce, ¼ teaspoon paprika and ½ cup diced cooked
shrimps to Cream Sauce. Cooked crabmeat,
lobster or oysters may also be used. Serve with
poached or broiled fish.

---

499 *Mornay Sauce*

Melt in top of double boiler
3 tablespoons butter
Blend in
**3 tablespoons *Pre-Sifted* PURITY
All-Purpose Flour**
Remove from heat.
Gradually stir in
1 cup well-flavoured chicken broth
½ cup cream
½ teaspoon instant minced onion

Cook over direct medium heat stirring
constantly until smoothly thickened.
Place over hot water and add
**2 to 3 tablespoons grated Parmesan
cheese**
Season to taste. Serve with chicken, seafood,
asparagus, broccoli or cauliflower.
Yield: About 1⅔ cups.
NOTE: If chicken broth is not available, use 2
chicken bouillon cubes dissolved in 1
cup boiling water.

500 Brown Sauce

Melt in a medium-sized heavy frying pan
2 tablespoons butter
Heat until frothy and light brown.
Blend in
2 tablespoons Pre-Sifted PURITY All-Purpose Flour
Cook over medium heat stirring constantly until a rich brown.
Remove from heat.
Gradually stir in
1 cup beef stock, canned consommé or beef bouillon
½ teaspoon instant minced onion
Cook over medium heat stirring constantly until thickened and smooth.
Season to taste.
Yield: 1 cup.

VARIATIONS:

(a) Piquant Sauce

Combine 2 tablespoons vinegar, 1 teaspoon sugar and 1 tablespoon each of minced onion and green pepper. Simmer together for 5 minutes. Add to Brown Sauce along with 2 tablespoons chopped sweet gherkins. Use with hot tongue, ham or game.

(b) Mushroom Sauce

Slowly cook ½ cup sliced fresh mushrooms in the butter before adding and browning the flour. Complete as for Brown Sauce, then add 1 teaspoon Worcestershire sauce and a dash of nutmeg. Nice with lamb or veal chops, or hamburgers.

501 Hollandaise Sauce

Melt in top of double boiler over hot (not boiling) water
½ cup butter
Blend in, stirring constantly
4 well-beaten egg yolks
Gradually stir in
¾ cup boiling water
Cook over hot water, stirring constantly, until mixture begins to thicken. It will be the consistency of soft custard.
Remove from heat.
Beat in
2 tablespoons lemon juice
¼ teaspoon salt

Cover and place over hot water until ready to serve.
Should the mixture curdle, beat rapidly with rotary beater until smooth and creamy.
Serve with fish dishes, asparagus, cauliflower or broccoli.
Yield: About 2 cups.

502 Tomato Sauce

Melt in a saucepan
2 tablespoons butter or margarine
Add
2 tablespoons chopped green pepper
2 tablespoons chopped onion
Cook, stirring constantly, for 5 minutes.
Blend in
2 tablespoons Pre-Sifted PURITY All-Purpose Flour
Add
1 cup tomato juice
1 teaspoon salt
1 teaspoon sugar
1 teaspoon Worcestershire sauce
1 tablespoon catsup
Cook, stirring constantly, until thickened.
Stir in
1 tablespoon chopped parsley
Season to taste. If a smooth sauce is desired, strain to remove green pepper and onion, and omit the parsley. Serve with deep fried fish, meats or vegetables.
Yield: 1¼ cups.

503 Barbecue Sauce

Combine in a saucepan
1 beef bouillon cube dissolved in
1 cup boiling water
½ cup catsup
2 tablespoons Worcestershire sauce
1 teaspoon dry mustard
1 teaspoon instant minced onion
1 teaspoon salt
1 tablespoon sugar
⅛ teaspoon cayenne
2 tablespoons butter or salad oil
1 slice lemon
Bring to a boil and simmer 10 minutes, uncovered. Remove lemon slice. Leave overnight before using to allow flavours to blend.
Use to brush on spareribs, chicken or other meats while barbecuing or broiling.
Yield: About 1¼ cups.

504 Raisin Sauce

Melt in a saucepan
2 tablespoons butter *or* margarine
Blend in
**2 tablespoons *Pre-Sifted* PURITY
All-Purpose Flour**
Gradually add
1 cup consommé
Stir constantly until smoothly thickened.
Add
½ teaspoon grated lemon rind
1 teaspoon sugar
1 teaspoon Worcestershire sauce
1 teaspoon lemon juice
⅓ cup raisins
Combine and heat thoroughly. Serve with
baked ham, ham steaks or tongue.
Yield: About 1⅓ cups.

505 Lemon Butter

Cream well
¼ cup soft butter
Blend in
½ teaspoon salt
⅛ teaspoon pepper
1 tablespoon lemon juice
1 tablespoon finely chopped parsley
Spread on broiled fish, steaks or chicken just
before serving.
Yield: About ⅓ cup (4 to 5 servings).

VARIATIONS:

(a) Herb Butter

To soft Lemon Butter add 1 tablespoon
snipped chives and 1 teaspoon snipped fresh
dill.

(b) Hot Lemon Butter

Melt butter and add remaining ingredients.
Pour over vegetables, steaks, chops or fish.

506 Mint Sauce

Combine and bring to a boil
¼ cup cider vinegar
¼ cup water
2 tablespoons sugar
¼ teaspoon salt
Pour over
**¼ cup finely chopped fresh mint
leaves**
Let stand 30 minutes. Serve with lamb.
Yield: ¾ cup.

507 Tartar Sauce

Combine
1 cup mayonnaise
1 tablespoon chopped stuffed olives
1 tablespoon chopped capers
1 tablespoon chopped gherkins
1 tablespoon chopped parsley
1 teaspoon grated onion
Blend thoroughly.
Serve chilled with fried or broiled fish, shellfish
or as a dressing with cold salmon.
Yield: 1¼ cups.

508 Cucumber Sauce

Peel, cut in quarters and remove seedy portion
from a small cucumber.
Finely chop the firm portion and measure
⅔ cup
Drain well.
Combine
Chopped cucumber
½ cup commercial sour cream
1 teaspoon onion salt
⅛ teaspoon paprika
Blend thoroughly and serve well chilled.
Very nice with seafood or cold meats.
Yield: 1⅓ cups.

509 Cumberland Sauce

Combine in a saucepan
1 cup red currant jelly
1 tablespoon lemon juice
1 tablespoon orange juice
1 tablespoon vinegar
1 tablespoon grated orange rind
1 teaspoon prepared mustard
½ teaspoon ginger
½ teaspoon paprika
Heat sufficiently to melt the jelly and blend
with the other ingredients.
Chill and serve with duck, chicken or lamb.
Yield: 1¼ cups.

510 Creamy Horseradish Sauce

Beat until stiff
½ cup whipping cream
Fold in
½ teaspoon salt
¼ cup horseradish
Serve chilled with steaks, roast beef or ham.
Yield: 1 cup.

Salads and Salad Dressings

THINGS TO REMEMBER ABOUT SALADS

Salads fit into many places in the daily menu, from appetizer to dessert course. Delightful miniature salads can be served as a first course to whet the appetite; tossed and side salads usually accompany the entrée; salads of the more robust variety are headliners at luncheons and patio suppers. Fruit gelatine moulds and frozen salads are excellent for late evening refreshment as well as dessert. A salad does not have to be intricate—garden lettuce dressed with oil, vinegar and seasonings is just as much a salad as one requiring many more ingredients.

Attractive salad bowls, servers and platters greatly enhance your efforts as a salad maker and give shape and form to salads. These need not be expensive or exotic but colourful and suited to your needs. A good wooden salad bowl for daily use is an excellent investment.

SALAD GREENS:

Head and leaf lettuce are the most popular salad greens. Purchase a variety of green salad vegetables according to the season—curly endive, escarole, romaine, Bibb lettuce, spinach, chard and watercress. They should be fresh, young and crisp.

Care of Salad Greens:

Remove any woody stems or bruised portions and wash under cold running water. Shake off excess water, dry and store loosely packed in covered container or plastic bag in refrigerator. Do this as soon as possible after purchasing. Keep salad greens chilled at all times. Watercress and pepper (garden) cress are quite fragile and should be used soon after purchasing.

Spinach:

Wash thoroughly in several changes of cold water, lifting the vegetable out of the water each time. Dry thoroughly. Use only tender young leaves for salads. Usually served in tossed salads.

Lettuce:

For Cups: Cut out the core, then loosen leaves by holding head, cored side up, under cold running water. Slip off leaves, shake dry in a towel or in a mesh salad basket. Use as needed to hold salad mixtures.

To Shred: Cut head lettuce in half then shred quite finely with a very sharp knife. Often used as a base or bed for arranged salads.

To Tear: Break or tear chilled washed greens into bite-size pieces. Use in tossed salads.

For Wedges: Cut chilled washed head lettuce into quarters or sixths. Use in head lettuce salads. You can also slice head lettuce into four or six slices and use as you would the wedges.

Leaf Lettuce (also endive, romaine and escarole): Separate leaf by leaf and wash very thoroughly. Break off woody stems and bruised portions. Dry well in towel or salad basket. Use for platter garnishes, sandwiches, tossed salads, etc.

511   Tossed Green Salad

Wash, dry and chill lettuce or a selection of salad greens (head lettuce, endive and watercress is a nice combination).

Sprinkle a small amount of salt in a wooden salad bowl and rub a cut clove of garlic over the bowl.

Tear cold dry greens into bite-size pieces and measure 8 cups. Place in prepared salad bowl.

Toss with **¼ cup salad oil** until the leaves glisten.

Mix together in a small bowl
¼ teaspoon dry mustard
½ teaspoon salt
¼ teaspoon freshly ground pepper
Gradually stir in
2 tablespoons vinegar *or* lemon juice
Set aside.

If adding extra ingredients for colour and texture (see below), prepare them now and place on top of salad greens. Pour the mustard-vinegar mixture over all and toss thoroughly.

Serve at once.

Yield: 6 to 8 servings.

NOTE: If desired, use prepared French dressing. Omit salad oil and mustard-vinegar mixture. Assemble all desired ingredients in salad bowl, add French dressing allowing 1 tablespoon per serving. Toss thoroughly and serve at once.

FOR COLOUR AND TEXTURE

Add one or more of these ingredients (about ¼ to ½ cup) to the basic Tossed Green Salad recipe: cauliflowerets, celery, parsley, chives, radishes, cucumbers, tomatoes, green onions, pineapple tidbits, avocado, hard-cooked eggs, bacon bits, olives, Parmesan or blue cheese, garlic croutons.

FOR A CHANGE OF FLAVOUR

Add a small amount of one or more of these flavour extras to the dressing and combine well: chili sauce, horseradish, Worcestershire sauce, anchovy paste, curry powder, onion or celery salt, fresh or diced herbs, dill, sesame or celery seeds.

---

512   Chef's Salad

Prepare one of the following:

(a) HAM AND CHICKEN:

Cut into thin strips
1¼ cups cooked chicken
1¼ cups cooked ham
¼ pound Swiss cheese

Peel and cut into wedges
2 tomatoes

Score and then slice
1 small unpeeled cucumber

Prepare
8 radish roses

(b) SALAMI AND CHEESE:

Cut into thin strips
¼ pound salami
¼ pound bologna
¼ pound Cheddar *or* process cheese

Prepare
1 cup tiny raw cauliflowerets

(c) CORNED BEEF AND EGGS:

Cut into thin strips
1 (12-ounce) can corned beef, chilled
¼ pound Swiss *or* process cheese

Slice
3 hard-cooked eggs

Thinly slice
1 medium-sized onion

(*Tongue or canned luncheon meat can be used instead of the corned beef.*)

Cover and refrigerate until needed.

Prepare Tossed Green Salad (recipe No. 511) as directed. Dress with either oil, vinegar and seasonings or a French dressing. Omit additional ingredients. Add about two-thirds of your prepared meat mixture and toss gently. Arrange remaining meat mixture and other ingredients in alternate groups, spoke-fashion, on top of the salad. Garnish with watercress and serve with extra dressing. If preferred, arrange in individual salad bowls.

Yield: 6 luncheon servings or 12 buffet servings.

To make a radish rose, cut radish in six or eight sections or petals to within ¼ inch of the bottom. To open, place in cold water for about an hour.

513 Tossed Vegetable Salad

Combine in a salad bowl
   4 cups torn chilled salad greens
   3 cups vegetables (choose one or more from those given below)
   ¼ cup French dressing *or* equal parts of mayonnaise and French dressing
Toss gently.
Yield: 4 servings.

VEGETABLES:

Raw: Broccoli or cauliflower, red cabbage, carrots, cucumber, green or white onions, parsnips, radishes, tomatoes.

Cooked: Fresh, frozen or canned vegetables— asparagus, green beans, carrots, mixed vegetables, baby lima beans, green peas.

FOR A CHANGE OF FLAVOUR
Add a small amount of one or two of these: bacon bits, anchovy fillets, chopped hard-cooked eggs, Swiss or blue cheese, pineapple tidbits, sliced ripe or green olives.

---

514 Coleslaw

Combine in a bowl
   4 cups shredded cabbage
   ½ cup diced celery
   ⅓ cup finely diced green peppers
   ⅓ cup coarsely grated carrots
   ¼ cup sliced radishes
Toss with
   ½ cup Coleslaw Dressing
Place in lettuce lined salad bowl and garnish as desired.
Yield: 4 to 6 servings.

VARIATIONS:

(a) Tomato Coleslaw
Prepare as for Coleslaw, omitting the carrots and radishes. Add 1 cup peeled diced tomatoes and ¼ cup sliced green onions.

(b) Olive and Onion Coleslaw
To 4 cups shredded cabbage, add ¾ teaspoon celery seeds, ½ cup sliced stuffed olives, ¼ cup chopped ripe olives and ½ cup thinly sliced sweet onions. Toss with ½ cup Coleslaw Dressing.

(c) Apple Coleslaw
To 4 cups shredded cabbage and ½ cup diced celery, add 1 cup diced unpeeled red apples, ½ cup raisins and ¼ cup chopped walnuts. Toss with ½ cup Coleslaw Dressing.

(d) Pineapple Coleslaw
To 4 cups shredded cabbage and ½ cup diced celery, add ½ cup well-drained pineapple tidbits and ½ cup halved and seeded red grapes. Toss with ½ cup Coleslaw Dressing.

(e) Orange and Peanut Coleslaw
To 4 cups shredded cabbage and ½ cup diced celery, add 1 cup well-drained fresh orange sections or mandarin orange sections, and ½ cup chopped peanuts. Toss with ½ cup Coleslaw Dressing.

(f) Cabbage Bowl
This is a buffet specialty, quite easy to do and very effective.

Slice off one-third of the top of a large firm head of cabbage; save trimmings. Turn cabbage over and carefully cut out centre of core end; scoop out cabbage leaving ½" shell intact. Wrap in damp towel and refrigerate. Shred cabbage trimmings and prepare any of the Coleslaw variations given above.

To serve, place cabbage "bowl" on bed of lettuce on a large plate. Fill with Coleslaw and surround with garnishes which complement the filling. Devilled egg halves, rosebud beets, pickled crab apples, peach halves, tomato wedges are suggestions.
Yield: 6 to 8 servings.

515 Stuffed Tomato Salads

TO PREPARE:

1. Cut peeled tomatoes, poinsettia-fashion, into sections. To do this, peel firm ripe tomatoes and remove hard core at each stem end. Turn tomato over and cut into 5 sections almost to stem end. Then carefully spread apart the petals. Chill until ready to serve. Stuff with one of the suggested fillings.

OR

2. Peel firm ripe tomatoes, cut ¼" slice from each stem end and scoop out pulp with a spoon, leaving the shells. Chill until ready to serve. Stuff with one of the suggested fillings.

TO FILL:

The following recipes will yield sufficient filling to stuff 4 to 6 tomatoes depending upon size of the tomatoes:

(a) Chicken Salad: Prepare one-half Chicken Salad recipe No. 517. The chicken and celery should be finely diced for stuffing tomatoes.

(b) Tuna Salad: Combine 1 cup flaked tuna, ½ cup finely diced celery, 1 tablespoon chopped sweet pickles and ¼ cup mayonnaise or salad dressing.

(c) Cottage Cheese Salad: Combine 2 cups cottage cheese with 1 teaspoon horseradish, 1 tablespoon chopped chives, 2 tablespoons chopped ripe or stuffed olives and 2 tablespoons mayonnaise.

516 Devilled Egg Salad

Hard cook 6 eggs. Cool and peel the eggs.

Cut in half lengthwise, remove yolks and press them through a sieve or potato ricer.

Add to egg yolks

> ¼ to ⅓ cup mayonnaise or salad
> dressing (depending on size of
> eggs)
> ½ teaspoon prepared mustard
> ½ teaspoon onion juice or
> onion powder
> ½ teaspoon salt
> Few grains pepper

Blend to a creamy consistency.

Refill egg whites. (Use a pastry tube, or stuff the eggs and then score with a fork.)

Dust lightly with paprika and garnish with a tiny piece of parsley.

Serve as a salad on salad greens; as hors d'oeuvres; as a garnish for chicken, meat, fish or vegetable salads; or with cold meat platter.

Yield: 12 halves.

FOR ADDED FLAVOUR

Vary the egg filling by adding one or two of the following:

Fish or anchovy paste, devilled ham, crumbled crisp bacon, liver sausage, finely cut chicken or ham, cut up shrimp or crab meat, curry powder, tabasco sauce or pickle relish. Adjust mayonnaise if necessary.

---

517 Chicken Salad

Combine in a mixing bowl

> **4 cups cooked diced chicken**
> **1 cup diced *or* sliced celery**
> **1 cup diced green peppers**
> **1 teaspoon grated onion**

Mix together in a small bowl

> **⅔ cup mayonnaise *or* salad dressing**
> **1 tablespoon vinegar *or* lemon juice**
> **1 teaspoon salt**

Gradually stir in

> **¼ cup cold chicken broth *or* cream**

Pour dressing over chicken mixture. Combine thoroughly and refrigerate until needed.

Serve on salad greens and garnish with asparagus tips, peach halves filled with cranberry jelly, watercress or parsley.

Yield: 6 (1-cup) servings.

NOTE: Green pepper can be replaced wholly or in part with celery or other ingredients, if desired.

VARIATIONS:

(a) Southern Chicken Salad

Prepare as for Chicken Salad, omitting the green peppers and adding ½ cup halved and seeded red grapes and ½ cup canned drained pineapple tidbits. Serve in a lettuce lined bowl and garnish with an additional ½ cup grapes and pineapple, and ⅓ cup toasted sliced almonds.

(b) Crunchy Chicken Salad

Prepare as for Chicken Salad, omitting the green peppers. Increase the celery to 1½ cups and add ¼ cup coarsely chopped pecans and ¼ cup sliced stuffed olives.

518 Carrot and Raisin Salad

Combine in a mixing bowl

> **2 cups shredded carrots**
> **½ cup diced celery**
> **½ cup raisins**
> **⅓ cup mayonnaise *or* salad dressing**
> **1 tablespoon vinegar**

Toss lightly with two forks and turn into lettuce lined serving bowl. This is an excellent lunch box salad.

Yield: 4 to 6 servings.

519 Dutch Potato Salad

Cook until just tender
6 medium potatoes

Measure 6 cups sliced potatoes and place in a heatproof serving dish. Keep warm until needed.

Cook in a frying pan until crisp
6 slices side bacon

Remove bacon, drain on absorbent paper and crumble finely. Add to the potatoes.

Pour off bacon fat, measure ¼ cup (add shortening if necessary) and return it to frying pan. Add
¼ cup finely chopped onions

Cook until transparent. Add
¼ cup vinegar
¼ cup water
1 tablespoon sugar
1 teaspoon salt
½ teaspoon celery seeds
Few grains pepper

Bring to a boil, remove from heat and pour over potatoes and bacon. Add
1 tablespoon chopped parsley

Combine gently. Serve warm.
Yield: 6 servings.

> **WARNING: Keep potato salad well chilled until serving time. Serious food poisoning can result if potato salad is allowed to stand in a warm place for any length of time.**

520 Potato Salad

Combine in a mixing bowl
4 cups diced cold cooked potatoes
1½ cups sliced or diced celery
2 tablespoons finely chopped onion
2 tablespoons snipped parsley

Mix together
¾ cup mayonnaise or salad dressing
1 tablespoon vinegar
1 teaspoon prepared mustard
2 teaspoons salt
Few grains freshly ground pepper

Pour over potatoes and toss lightly with 2 forks until well blended.
Chill at least 1 hour before serving.
Yield: 6 servings.

NOTES: **1.** Since the mealiness of potatoes will vary, add more mayonnaise or salad dressing if needed to make a moist salad.

2. For better flavour, carefully combine one-half the dressing mixture with the potatoes while they are still warm. Refrigerate until 1 hour before serving. Then add vegetables and remaining dressing. Toss and refrigerate until needed.

3. For moulded potato salad, pack salad in oiled ring mould, loaf pan or individual custard cups. Chill 1 hour.

521 Seafood Salad

Combine in a mixing bowl
2 cups cooked or canned shrimps
1 cup sliced celery
¼ cup sliced stuffed olives
¼ cup diced green peppers

Mix together in a small bowl
½ cup mayonnaise or salad dressing
1 tablespoon lemon juice
½ teaspoon onion salt
Few grains pepper

Pour over shrimp mixture, toss gently and chill until needed. Serve in lettuce cups or in centre of Tomato Aspic Ring (recipe No. 526 (b).

Garnish with wedges of hard-cooked egg and watercress.
Yield: 4 (1-cup) servings.

VARIATIONS:

(a) Lobster or Crab Meat Salad

Prepare as for Seafood Salad, substituting 2 cups cooked or canned lobster, or crab meat (in chunks) for the shrimp.

(b) Tuna Salad

Prepare as for Seafood Salad, substituting 2 cups flaked solid pack tuna for the shrimp. Omit the stuffed olives if desired and add 2 tablespoons chopped sweet pickles and ¼ cup chopped nuts.

(c) Salmon Salad

Prepare as for Seafood Salad, substituting 2 cups canned salmon (in chunks) for the shrimp. Omit the stuffed olives and substitute 2 coarsely chopped hard-cooked eggs.

522   Waldorf Salad

Dice enough unpeeled red apples to measure
   3 cups
Toss with
   3 tablespoons lemon juice
   1 teaspoon sugar
      or
   ¼ cup orange juice
Add
   1 cup thinly sliced celery
   ½ cup dark seedless raisins
   ½ cup coarsely chopped walnuts
   ½ to ⅔ cup mayonnaise
Toss and chill.
Serve in lettuce lined shallow salad bowl or on individual plates in lettuce cups.
Garnish with unpeeled apple wedges and parsley.
For a more spectacular salad, place in a mound on lettuce covered serving plate. Press 6 unpeeled apple wedges into the mound to form "ribs", garnish top with additional mayonnaise. Alternate clusters of grapes and orange slices around the mound and scatter with walnut halves.
Yield: 6 servings.

NOTE: If apple skins are tough or poorly coloured, peel the apples.

VARIATION:

(a)   Pear Waldorf Salad
Substitute 3 cups diced peeled fresh pears for the apples. Omit the raisins.

523   Fruit and Nut Cottage Cheese Salad

Combine in a mixing bowl
   2 cups cottage cheese
   ¼ cup mayonnaise *or* salad dressing
   1 teaspoon lemon juice
Add
   1½ cups diced canned pineapple *or* diced unpeeled red apples
   ½ cup raisins
   ½ cup chopped nuts
Mix lightly with two forks.
Pile into lettuce cups. If using pineapple, garnish each serving with a maraschino cherry and parsley. If using apple, garnish with an unpeeled apple wedge dipped in lemon juice.
Yield: 4 (1-cup) servings.

MOULDED SALADS

THINGS TO REMEMBER ABOUT MOULDED SALADS

Size of Moulds: The salad mixture should come to the top of the mould for best results as it will be easier to unmould and be more perfectly shaped. To determine the size of the mould, measure the amount of water it will hold.

Preparation of Moulds: Moulds may be coated lightly with salad oil, rinsed with cold water or not treated at all. If heavy meat or vegetable mixtures are used in fancy moulds, it is advisable to use salad oil.

To Unmould: See Gelatine Desserts page 106. If unmoulding a heavy mixture in a fancy mould, loosen edge of jelly with a hot knife and invert on serving plate. Wring out a tea towel in hot water (wear rubber gloves) and cover mould with the towel. Do this two or three times leaving the towel on the mould for a short period until the mould slips out easily. This is helpful for tube pans, ring moulds and some very ornate moulds.

Gelatine: See Gelatine Desserts page 106.

Setting Gelatine Salads: If the salad requires partial setting before adding other ingredients, you can hasten the procedure by placing the gelatine mixture in a pan of ice cubes. Stir occasionally to chill evenly. When mixture is cool but has not begun to jell, place in refrigerator (in pan of ice cubes) to further lessen the setting time.

For even distribution of the added ingredients, chill gelatine until it is the consistency of unbeaten egg whites or liquid honey. For layered salads, allow the first layer to set until *almost* firm before adding the second layer which should be slightly thickened.

Chilling Time: Allow 5 to 6 hours for medium-sized moulds, 12 hours or overnight for large moulds. Individual moulds set quickly and are excellent if time is short.

524 Cranberry Relish Mould

Put through food chopper
**4 cups washed cranberries
(1 pound)
1 unpeeled orange**
Add
1½ cups sugar
Set aside.
Soften
1 envelope gelatine
in
¼ cup cold water
Combine
**2 (3-ounce) packages lemon jelly
powder
Softened gelatine
3 cups boiling water**
Stir until completely dissolved. Chill until slightly thickened.
Fold in cranberry-orange mixture.
Pour into a 7- or 8-cup mould, a 10″ ring mould or star shaped mould.
If serving-size slices or squares are desired, use loaf or square pans.
Chill until firm, preferably overnight.
Yield: 15 to 20 servings.

525 Jellied Apple and Celery Salad

Soften
2 envelopes gelatine
in
½ cup apple juice
Heat to boiling
3 cups apple juice
Remove from heat and add
**Softened gelatine
¼ cup sugar
½ teaspoon salt
2 tablespoons vinegar**
Stir until completely dissolved.
Chill until slightly thickened.
Then fold in
**1½ cups finely diced unpeeled red
apples
¾ cup finely diced celery**
Pour into a 6-cup mould or 8 to 10 individual moulds. Chill until firm.
This is nice with cold roast pork or chicken.
Yield: 8 to 10 servings.

526 Tomato Aspic

Combine in a mixing bowl
**2 envelopes gelatine
⅔ cup tomato juice**
Let stand to soften gelatine.
Combine in a saucepan
**3 cups tomato juice
1 tablespoon dried onion flakes
1 tablespoon dried celery flakes
2 tablespoons sugar
1 teaspoon salt
1 teaspoon Worcestershire sauce
2 slices lemon**
Bring to a boil and let simmer 10 minutes.
Strain hot mixture into softened gelatine and stir thoroughly to dissolve gelatine.
Pour into a 6-cup mould or 6 to 8 individual moulds. Chill until firm. Unmould and garnish as desired.
Yield: 6 to 8 servings.

VARIATIONS:

(a) Vegetable-Tomato Aspic

Prepare Tomato Aspic and chill until slightly thickened. Fold in 1½ cups chopped raw or cooked mixed vegetables. Pour into individual moulds.

(b) Tomato Aspic Ring

Prepare Tomato Aspic. Pour into a 6-cup ring mould. Fill centre of unmoulded ring with crisp salad greens, cottage cheese or any of the fillings suggested for Stuffed Tomato Salads (recipe No. 515).

527 Seafoam Mould

Dissolve
**1 (3-ounce) package lime jelly
powder**
in
1 cup boiling water
Add
**1 cup grated unpeeled cucumber
1 tablespoon grated onion
2 tablespoons vinegar
½ teaspoon celery salt
Few grains pepper**
Pour into a 3-cup mould or pan.
Chill until firm.
Unmould on lettuce-lined plate, garnish with radish roses. Nice with chicken, ham or seafood.

528   Jellied Perfection Salad

Soften
    2 envelopes gelatine
in
    1 cup cold water
Add
    1½ cups boiling water

Stir until dissolved. Heat if necessary.
Add
    ⅓ cup sugar
    1 teaspoon salt
    ¼ cup vinegar
    ¼ cup lemon juice
    3 to 4 drops yellow food colouring

Chill until slightly thickened.

Then fold in
    1½ cups shredded cabbage
    ¾ cup diced celery
    ¾ cup grated carrots
    ¼ cup chopped green peppers
    2 tablespoons chopped pimiento

Pour into a 6-cup mould or an 8″ square pan.

Chill until firm.

Yield: 8 to 12 servings.

VARIATIONS:

(a)   Seafood Perfection Salad

Prepare as above, omitting the cabbage and carrots. Add 1½ cups tuna, salmon, lobster or shrimps and ¾ cup peeled diced cucumber.

(b)   Pineapple-Ham Perfection Salad

Prepare as for Jellied Perfection Salad, omitting the celery and carrots and reducing the vinegar to 2 tablespoons and the cabbage to 1 cup. Add 1 cup canned drained crushed pineapple and 1 cup diced cooked ham.

529   Frozen Fruit Salad

In a large mixing bowl, cream
    1 (8-ounce) package cream cheese
Add
    1 teaspoon grated lemon rind
    1 tablespoon lemon juice
    2 tablespoons sifted icing sugar
    ⅔ cup mayonnaise
    4 or 5 drops red food colouring

Blend thoroughly until mixture is smooth.

Drain and measure
    1 cup pineapple tidbits
    1 cup mandarin orange sections or diced canned apricots
    ½ cup sliced maraschino cherries

Add to cream cheese mixture and combine gently.

Fold in
    1 cup whipping cream, beaten stiff
    2 cups miniature marshmallows

Pour into an 8″ or 9″ square pan or a loaf pan.

Cover with foil or saran. Freeze until firm.

Cut in slices or squares and place on individual plates. Garnish with apricot halves, fresh strawberries and sprigs of mint.

Serve with party sandwiches or small rolls.

Yield: 8 to 12 servings.

530   Sparkling Fruit Mould

Soften
    2 envelopes gelatine
in
    ½ cup lemon juice

Place over hot water and stir until dissolved.

Combine in a bowl
    ½ cup sugar
    ½ teaspoon salt
    1 cup fruit syrup (drained from canned fruits)
    2 cups ginger ale

Stir in dissolved gelatine and blend well.

Refrigerate, stirring occasionally until slightly thickened.

Then fold in
    1 cup halved and seeded red grapes
    ¾ cup drained diced pineapple
    ¾ cup drained mandarin orange sections

Pour into a 6- to 8-cup mould or 8 to 10 individual moulds. Chill until firm.

Unmould and garnish with fruit and sprigs of mint. If a ring mould is used, fill centre of unmoulded jelly with cottage cheese. Serve with Fluffy Lemon Dressing.

Yield: 8 to 10 servings.

NOTE: Other fruits, in any desired combination, may be used in above mould.

SALAD DRESSINGS

THINGS TO REMEMBER ABOUT SALAD DRESSINGS

There are just a few basic salad dressings but many, many variations. Whether you make your own or use commercially prepared dressings, you can team up your salads with complementary dressings.

Mayonnaise: This is a rich mixture of oil, vinegar and egg yolks which is the choice dressing for meat, seafood, poultry and cooked vegetable salads. If modified with whipped cream and fruit juice it is most enjoyable with moulded and fruit salads.

French Dressing: This is the easiest dressing to make and historically the oldest. It is a simple combination of oil, vinegar and seasonings. Since it is a temporary emulsion, it has to be shaken before serving. It is the classic dressing for salad greens. However, it has many variations which complement fruit, cooked vegetable, poultry and seafood salads.

Cooked Salad Dressing: Sometimes referred to as "boiled" dressing, this is basically a cream sauce mixture of eggs, water, oil and vinegar. It is not as rich as mayonnaise but is very flavourful and sharp and it is especially good with potato salad, coleslaw and some fruit salad mixtures. Many commercial salad dressings are mixtures of cooked and mayonnaise dressings.

---

531 BASIC RECIPE *Mayonnaise*

Combine in a small deep bowl
  1 teaspoon dry mustard
  1 teaspoon salt
  1 teaspoon sugar
  Few grains cayenne
Using electric mixer or blender at medium speed, beat in
  2 egg yolks
Beat in, drop by drop
  ¼ cup salad oil
(During this first addition of oil, if too much is added at a time, the mixture may curdle.)
Beat in
  1 tablespoon vinegar

Now beat in, in a slow stream
  ¾ cup salad oil
As the mixture thickens, alternate
  1 tablespoon lemon juice
with the oil until both are used up.
Then beat in
  1 tablespoon hot water
Store in tightly covered jar in refrigerator.
Yield: 1½ cups.
NOTE: If the egg yolk-oil mixture separates, stop beating. Beat another egg yolk in a bowl and gradually add the curdled mixture to it. Continue as directed in the recipe.

VARIATIONS:

Mayonnaise blends well with many flavours and the variations are endless. Here are some suggestions for combinations of ingredients with mayonnaise to produce dressings for all types of salads. The ones which include French dressing can be used with tossed green and vegetable salads.

To ½ cup commercial or homemade mayonnaise, add the ingredients as listed below and adjust seasonings to taste:

(a) *Almond-Cucumber Mayonnaise*

2 tablespoons chopped toasted almonds and ¼ cup shredded cucumber, well drained.

(b)   *Curry Mayonnaise*

½ teaspoon curry powder, ½ teaspoon lemon juice and ⅛ teaspoon garlic powder.

(c)   *Sour Cream Mayonnaise*

½ cup commercial sour cream and ½ teaspoon seasoned salt.

(d)   *Italian Mayonnaise*

¼ cup French dressing and 2 tablespoons grated Parmesan cheese.

(e)   *Roquefort Mayonnaise*

¼ cup French dressing and 2 tablespoons crumbled Roquefort or blue cheese.

(f)   *Fluffy Lemon Mayonnaise*

3 tablespoons lemon juice, 3 tablespoons sifted icing sugar and ½ cup whipping cream, beaten stiff.

532   Thousand Island Dressing

To
- 1 cup mayonnaise

add
- 1 tablespoon vinegar
- ¼ cup chili sauce
- 1 teaspoon minced onion
- 2 tablespoons finely chopped green pepper
- 2 tablespoons finely diced celery
- 2 tablespoons finely chopped stuffed olives
- 1 coarsely chopped hard-cooked egg

Blend ingredients thoroughly. If desired, ¼ cup whipping cream, beaten stiff, may be folded in before serving.

Serve with head lettuce salads.

Yield: About 1½ cups.

533   Louis Dressing

To
- ⅓ cup mayonnaise

add
- 2 tablespoons French dressing
- ½ cup chili sauce
- 1 teaspoon horseradish
- 1 teaspoon Worcestershire sauce
- ½ teaspoon minced onion

Combine ingredients thoroughly. Chill.

Serve with seafood salads.

Yield: About ¾ cup.

534   Spiced Orange Cream Dressing

To
- 1 cup mayonnaise

add
- 1 teaspoon grated orange rind
- ¼ cup orange juice
- 3 tablespoons sifted icing sugar
- ½ teaspoon cinnamon
- ¼ teaspoon nutmeg

Blend thoroughly.

Gently fold in
- 1 cup whipping cream, beaten stiff

Chill.

Serve with fruit and dessert salads.

Yield: About 3 cups.

535   Coleslaw Dressing

Blend in a bowl
- ½ cup mayonnaise or salad dressing
- ½ teaspoon prepared mustard
- ¼ teaspoon salt
- 2 tablespoons cream or French dressing

Chill.

Yield: ½ cup.

536   French Dressing

Measure into a bowl or jar
- 1 tablespoon sugar
- 1 teaspoon salt
- ½ teaspoon dry mustard
- ½ teaspoon paprika
- Few grains freshly ground pepper
- ⅓ cup vinegar
- ⅔ cup salad oil

Beat together with rotary beater or shake well in tightly covered jar. Store in covered jar in refrigerator.

Shake well before using.

Yield: 1 cup.

VARIATIONS:

(a)   Celery Seed French Dressing

Combine 1 cup French Dressing with 2 tablespoons catsup, 1 tablespoon snipped chives and 1 teaspoon celery seeds.

(b)   Seafood French Dressing

To 1 cup French Dressing, add 1 cup chili sauce, 1 teaspoon horseradish and 1 teaspoon Worcestershire sauce.

(c)   India French Dressing

Combine 1 cup French Dressing with 2 tablespoons chutney, ½ teaspoon curry powder and 2 finely chopped hard-cooked eggs.

FOR ADDED FLAVOUR

Combine 1 cup French Dressing with 1 to 2 tablespoons of one of the following: anchovy paste, crumbled Roquefort or blue cheese, grated Parmesan cheese, prepared mustard, horseradish, Worcestershire sauce or other spicy meat sauces, finely chopped pickles or olives, fresh herbs.

---

537 Low Calorie French Dressing

Measure into a bowl
- **1 teaspoon dry mustard**
- **1 teaspoon salt**
- **1 teaspoon grated onion**
- **1 teaspoon Worcestershire sauce**
- **½ teaspoon non-caloric liquid sweetener**
- **2 tablespoons lemon juice**
- **1 cup tomato juice**
- **2 tablespoons salad oil**

Combine ingredients and beat until well blended. Chill. Shake well before using. About 15 calories per tablespoon.

Yield: About 1⅓ cups.

538 Sour Cream Dressing

Combine
- **1 cup commercial sour cream**
- **1 tablespoon sugar**
- **1 teaspoon salt**
- **2 tablespoons lemon juice or vinegar**

Chill.

Serve with cabbage, salad greens, sliced tomatoes or cucumbers.

Yield: 1 cup.

VARIATIONS:

Add one or two of the following:

1 tablespoon prepared mustard, horseradish or snipped chives; 1 teaspoon celery or dill seeds; ½ teaspoon curry powder or seasoned salt.

539 Quick Salad Dressing

Combine in a deep mixing bowl
- **1½ teaspoons salt**
- **1½ teaspoons dry mustard**
- **3 tablespoons sugar**

Gradually stir in
- **½ cup evaporated milk**

Beat until well blended.

Measure
- **1½ cups salad oil**

Add ¼ cup at a time, beating thoroughly after each addition. The mixture will be thick and smooth.

Add all at once
- **½ cup vinegar**

Beat until well blended.

Store in covered jar in refrigerator.

Use in salad mixtures, especially potato salad.

Yield: 2½ cups.

540 Cooked Salad Dressing

Combine in top of double boiler
- **3 tablespoons *Pre-Sifted* PURITY All-Purpose Flour**
- **3 tablespoons sugar**
- **1 teaspoon salt**
- **1 teaspoon mustard**

Blend in
- **2 tablespoons salad oil *or* melted butter**
- **4 well-beaten egg yolks *or* 2 well-beaten whole eggs**

Combine
- **⅓ cup vinegar**
- **1¼ cups water**

Gradually stir into egg mixture.

Place over rapidly boiling water and stir constantly until mixture begins to thicken (5 to 7 minutes). Reduce heat and continue to stir until mixture is thickened and smooth (about another 5 minutes).

Pour into a bowl or jar, cover and let cool.

Store in refrigerator.

Yield: 1¾ cups.

541 Coconut Cream Cheese Dressing

Gradually add
- **3 tablespoons orange juice**

to
- **1 (4-ounce) package soft cream cheese**

Blend until smooth.

Add
- **1 tablespoon liquid honey**
- **½ teaspoon grated orange rind**
- **½ cup flaked coconut**

Combine thoroughly. Chill.

Serve with fruit salads. Especially nice with fresh pineapple and strawberries.

Yield: ¾ cup.

Sandwiches

THINGS TO REMEMBER ABOUT SANDWICHES

Bread: A variety of breads will change the flavour and appearance of your sandwiches—try pumpernickel, French, Italian, rye, cracked wheat, crusty rolls, wiener and hamburg buns, as well as low calorie bread for dieters.

Use fresh or day-old bread for everyday sandwiches; very fresh sliced or unsliced bread for rolled and pinwheel sandwiches; day-old unsliced bread for party sandwiches.

If you wish to thinly slice fresh bread, first chill it in the refrigerator and then use a very sharp knife for cutting.

Frozen sliced bread is handy to use for lunch box and picnic sandwiches since it is easy to spread and will keep the filling fresh for hours.

Butter: Have butter or margarine at room temperature or cream well until soft and spreadable. Avoid using melted butter since it tends to soak into the bread.

Mayonnaise and salad dressing may be used as a spread for sandwiches, either alone or with butter.

Fillings: Choose fillings to suit personal taste and menu situation. Mixed fillings such as egg salad, ham and relish should be moist, with ingredients of contrasting colour and texture, and be well seasoned. Taste fillings as you make them and if necessary try a small amount with bread to be sure the flavour suits. Refrigerate all fillings until ready to use.

TO MAKE:

Use assembly line technique.

1. Line up bread slices two by two, pairing slices that are next to each other in the loaf.

2. Butter slices right to the edges, except for party sandwiches where crusts are to be cut off. A small flexible spatula is excellent for spreading.

3. Place fillings on every other slice and spread evenly to the edges. For accurate measurement, especially when preparing a large quantity of sandwiches, use a number 24 ice cream scoop. This holds ¼ cup.

TO STORE:

Leave crusts on all sandwiches to help retain moisture. Trim party sandwiches just before serving.

Cut lunch box and picnic sandwiches in thirds or halves as desired. Wrap individually in waxed paper or saran, using the "drugstore wrap". Refrigerate as long as possible and plan to use them within 4 hours.

Party sandwiches can be packed in waxed paper-lined bake pans, covered with waxed paper and a damp tea towel. Use clothes pegs to clip the towel to the edges of the pan and store in refrigerator. Sandwiches will keep fresh for 12 to 18 hours when packed this way.

WARNING

Completed sandwiches as well as sandwich fillings are perishable. To avoid the danger of food poisoning, keep sandwiches refrigerated until as close to serving time as possible.

---

542 Chicken Salad Filling

Combine
  1½ cups finely diced cooked chicken *or* turkey
  ½ cup finely diced celery
  1 tablespoon finely diced green pepper
  1 teaspoon grated onion
  ½ teaspoon salt
  ⅓ to ½ cup mayonnaise
Blend ingredients thoroughly.
Yield: 2 cups.

543 Egg Salad Filling

Combine
  6 hard-cooked eggs, chopped
  2 tablespoons diced celery
  2 tablespoons chopped stuffed olives
  2 tablespoons chopped parsley
  2 teaspoons grated onion
  ½ teaspoon salt
  ¼ to ⅓ cup mayonnaise
Blend all ingredients thoroughly.
Yield: 2 cups.

544 Tuna Salad Filling

Drain and flake
  1 (7-ounce) can tuna
Add
  ¼ cup finely diced celery
  ⅓ cup shredded Cheddar cheese
  1 teaspoon grated onion
  1 teaspoon lemon juice
  ¼ to ⅓ cup mayonnaise
Blend ingredients thoroughly.
Yield: 1¼ cups.

545 Salmon and Peanut Filling

Drain and flake
  1 (7¾-ounce) can salmon
Add
  1 tablespoon finely diced green pepper
  1 tablespoon chopped parsley
  1 teaspoon grated onion
  2 tablespoons finely chopped peanuts
  ¼ to ⅓ cup mayonnaise
Blend ingredients thoroughly.
Yield: 1¼ cups.

546 Ham and Relish Filling

Combine
  2 cups ground cooked ham
  ¼ cup sweet pickle relish
  1 teaspoon grated onion
  2 tablespoons prepared mustard
  1 teaspoon Worcestershire sauce
  ⅓ to ½ cup mayonnaise
Blend all ingredients thoroughly.
Yield: 2 cups.

547 Luncheon Meat and Dill Filling

Using a medium grater, shred the contents of
  1 (12-ounce) can luncheon meat
Combine with
  1 teaspoon grated onion
  ⅓ cup finely diced celery
  ¼ cup chopped dill pickles
  ¼ cup catsup
  ⅓ cup mayonnaise
Blend all ingredients thoroughly.
Yield: 2¼ cups.

548 Tongue and Horseradish Filling

Combine
  2 cups ground cooked tongue (fresh, smoked *or* pickled)
  1 tablespoon prepared mustard
  1 to 2 tablespoons horseradish
  2 teaspoons grated onion
  ½ cup mayonnaise
Blend all ingredients thoroughly. Season to taste.
Yield: 2 cups.
NOTE: Chopped canned corned beef may be substituted for the tongue.

549 Savoury Cheese Spread

Cream
  ½ pound process cheese
Have cheese at room temperature.
Add
  2 tablespoons catsup
  1 teaspoon Worcestershire sauce
Blend ingredients thoroughly.
Especially good in pinwheels, roll-ups and party sandwich loaf.
Yield: 1 cup.

For picnics or casual entertaining, a crisp Salad and tasty Sandwiches

550 French Toasted Sandwiches

Make up plain sandwiches as usual. *Suggested fillings:* thin slices of ham, chicken, corned beef; cheese spreads or slices; meat, chicken or fish sandwich fillings; devilled ham spread.

Prepare egg mixture as for French Toast (recipe No. 402). This is sufficient for 6 sandwiches.

Dip sandwiches in the egg mixture. Quickly brown both sides in butter in a hot frying pan. Cut in half and serve immediately.

The flavour of a mixed sandwich filling will improve if it is prepared a few hours before needed. Be sure to keep it refrigerated.

551 Club Sandwiches

Allow 3 slices of bread for each sandwich. Toast bread under broiler on one side only.

Trim crusts. Spread untoasted side with butter or mayonnaise.

Arrange a different filling on each layer (see below). Season as desired.

Cut sandwiches into triangles and fasten each triangle together with a toothpick.

Serve immediately, garnished with potato chips, olives and radish roses.

SUGGESTED COMBINATIONS:

1. Sliced chicken with lettuce; sliced tomatoes and crisp side bacon.

2. Sliced turkey with cranberry relish; lettuce and sliced tomatoes.

3. Sliced ham with lettuce and chili sauce; mustard and sliced cheese.

4. Tuna or salmon salad and hard-cooked egg slices; sliced tomatoes and cucumbers.

552 Hot Meat Sandwiches

For each sandwich, thinly slice meat or poultry and place several pieces on a slice of bread on a warm dinner plate. Ladle a small amount of hot gravy over the meat. Top with bread and cut in half diagonally. Cover with hot gravy. Serve with French fried potatoes and a cooked vegetable. Garnish with coleslaw or lettuce and tomatoes.

If desired, omit top slice of bread for an open-face type of hot sandwich.

1. Chicken or turkey with hot gravy, canned chicken gravy or diluted cream of chicken soup. Garnish with cranberry sauce.

2. Beef with hot gravy or barbecue sauce. Garnish with horseradish or pickled crab apples.

3. Cube steaks with Mushroom Sauce. Garnish with French fried onion rings.

4. Tongue with tomato or barbecue sauce. Garnish with horseradish.

5. Roast lamb with hot gravy (add some sautéed mushrooms). Garnish with mint jelly.

553 Broiled Open-Face Sandwiches

Almost any variety of bread, rolls, buns, tea biscuits or English muffins may be used as a base.

If using toast, trim crusts if desired and toast on one side only. Spread untoasted side with butter, margarine or mayonnaise. For rolls, buns, etc., split and then toast the split surface only.

Arrange fillings on top and place under broiler 5″ from heat until topping is melted and hot.

SUGGESTED COMBINATIONS:

1. **Tomato, Cheese and Bacon Broil:** Arrange thick slices of peeled tomato on toast. Cover each with a slice of process cheese and crisscross 2 slices partially broiled bacon on top. Broil.

2. **Zippy Wiener Broil:** Cut wieners in half lengthwise and broil. Arrange on split and toasted wiener buns. Spoon chili sauce across the wiener and cover each with slice of process cheese. Broil.

3. **Back Bacon and Pineapple Broil:** Cover one-half of toasted hamburg bun with slices of partially cooked back bacon. Cover other half of bun with well drained pineapple slice and sprinkle liberally with shredded old Cheddar cheese. Broil.

4. **Chicken Supreme:** Arrange toast on ovenware platter or baking dish. Cover toast with chicken slices and then with cooked asparagus tips. Ladle hot cheese sauce over each sandwich. Broil.

For additional filling recipes, see Canapés and Spreads.

554   Hot Ham Rolls

Preheat oven to 350°.

Combine and blend well
- ½ **pound cubed *or* shredded Cheddar cheese**
- 2 **cups finely diced cooked ham**
- ¼ **cup catsup**
- ¼ **cup sweet pickle relish**
- 2 **tablespoons mayonnaise**
- 1 **teaspoon grated onion**

Spoon mixture into 8 partially split wiener rolls. Wrap each roll in aluminum foil, filling side up. Fold the ends tightly to seal.

Arrange in baking pan and heat in preheated 350° oven for 20 minutes.

To serve, fold down aluminum foil around the rolls.

Yield: 8 servings.

555   Tuna T-V Special

Preheat oven to 350°.

Combine and blend well
- 1 **(7-ounce) can tuna, drained and flaked**
- 1 **cup shredded Cheddar cheese**
- 3 **tablespoons mayonnaise**
- 2 **tablespoons sweet pickle relish**
- 2 **tablespoons finely grated onion**
- 1 **tablespoon prepared mustard**

Spoon mixture into 6 partially split wiener rolls. Wrap each roll in aluminum foil, filling side up. Fold the ends tightly to seal. Arrange in a baking pan.

Place in preheated 350° oven for 20 minutes.

To serve, fold down aluminum foil around the rolls.

Yield: 6 servings.

Party Sandwiches

When you plan to serve sandwiches at a party, allow about 5 to 6 small sandwiches per person.

For variety, use 2 or 3 different kinds of breads and fillings. Allow about ¼ cup filling for each 2 slices of bread, then cut this large sandwich into 4 small ones. Recipes for special party sandwiches may be found on the following pages.

For additional information, see Cooking for a Crowd pages 193 to 197.

For stag parties, picnics and lunch box suppers, allow 2 full-sized sandwiches per person. Use ⅜″ to ½″ thick bread slices. Allow slightly more butter and filling than for the less hearty sandwiches.

556   Pinwheel Sandwiches

Trim crusts from the top and sides of a fresh 24-ounce loaf of unsliced sandwich bread. (Chill loaf for easier cutting.) With loaf of bread on side and bottom crust to your left, cut 8 to 10 lengthwise slices, ¼″ thick, using a ruler as a guide and a long thin sharp knife. To help reduce "cracking", roll each slice once with rolling pin, starting at the narrow edge. Spread bread slices with butter or margarine to the edges. Cover with a well seasoned sandwich filling which is not too moist.

Place a row of stuffed olives or gherkins at the narrow edge. Roll up tightly being careful to keep the sides in line. Wrap rolls individually in waxed paper, twisting the ends securely.

Chill for several hours or overnight.

Cut each roll into 6 slices.

Yield: 4 dozen pinwheels per loaf of bread.

VARIATIONS:

(a) Cheese and Wiener Pinwheels

Spread bread slices with Savoury Cheese Spread (recipe No. 549); place wiener at narrow edge and roll up as directed.
Wrap and chill.

(b) Egg and Gherkin Pinwheels

Spread bread slices with butter and then with egg salad filling. Place whole gherkins at narrow edge and roll up as directed.
Wrap and chill.

(c) Cheese and Cherry Pinwheels

Spread bread slices with soft plain or pineapple cream cheese. Place well drained whole red or green maraschino cherries in a row at narrow edge. Roll up as directed.
Wrap and chill.

557　Party Sandwich Loaf

FILLINGS:

Prepare Savoury Cheese Spread (recipe No. 549) plus three of the fillings given below. Cover and refrigerate until needed.

Chicken and Almond: Combine ⅔ cup ground chicken with 2 tablespoons each of finely chopped green pepper, finely chopped blanched almonds, pickle relish and mayonnaise. Season to taste with salt, pepper and curry powder.

Egg and Olive: Combine 2 finely chopped hard-cooked eggs with 2 tablespoons each of chopped ripe olives and mayonnaise, ½ teaspoon onion salt, ¾ teaspoon prepared mustard.

Ham and Pimiento: Combine ⅔ cup ground or finely chopped cooked ham with 2 tablespoons chopped pimiento, 1 tablespoon chopped green pepper, 1 teaspoon minced onion, 1 teaspoon prepared mustard and 2 tablespoons mayonnaise.

Other Fillings: Canned devilled ham, meat or fish pastes, pimiento cream cheese, tomato or cucumber slices. To make a seafood filling, follow Chicken and Almond recipe and substitute tuna, salmon or shrimp for chicken.

CREAM CHEESE ICING:

Combine 2 (8-ounce) packages soft cream cheese with 3 to 4 tablespoons cream. Set aside (not in refrigerator) until needed.

BREAD:

Trim all crusts from a 24-ounce loaf of day-old unsliced sandwich bread. Turn loaf of bread on side with bottom to your left. Measure and mark 5 even cuts about ½″ wide. With a ruler as a guide and using a long sharp thin knife, cut 5 lengthwise slices, keeping them in order of cutting so that the loaf can be re-assembled.

TO ASSEMBLE:

Spread each slice with butter.

Place bottom slice, buttered side up, on waxed paper-covered bread board or baking sheet. Spread to the edges with the Savoury Cheese Spread.

Place second slice on top of cheese spread and cover with Chicken and Almond Filling.

Add third slice of bread and spread with Egg and Olive Filling. Top with fourth slice of bread and spread with Ham and Pimiento Filling.

Place fifth slice of bread, buttered side down, on ham filling. Gently shape loaf so that the sides are even. Remove any excess fillings.

TO ICE:

Spread sides and then top with Cream Cheese Icing. Garnish top as desired with strips of green pepper, ripe olives and sliced radishes in design; or colour additional cream cheese and decorate using cake decorator. Chill at least 3 hours before serving.

TO SERVE:

Place Party Sandwich Loaf on large tray or platter. Cover remainder of tray with lettuce and arrange groups of sliced tomatoes, cucumbers and stuffed olives around the loaf. Garnish with parsley. Slice loaf into ten 1″ slices and serve on individual salad plates with lettuce and vegetable garnishes.

Yield: 10 servings.

558　Ribbon Sandwiches

Use day-old bread slices cut ½″ thick. For each stack, alternate 3 slices brown bread and 2 slices white.

Butter each slice and spread contrasting fillings between the layers.

Press firmly together. Cut off crusts from each stack with a sharp knife.

Wrap and chill several hours or overnight.

To Serve: Cut into ½″ slices, then cut each slice into thirds, halves or triangles.

Suggested Fillings: Use smooth textured moist fillings such as cream cheese spreads or any of the Party Sandwich Loaf Fillings (recipe No. 557).

559　Open-Face Sandwiches

Trim crusts and cut unsliced sandwich bread lengthwise into ¼″ to ⅜″ slices as directed for Pinwheel Sandwiches (recipe No. 556).

Use a variety of cookie cutters to cut out different shapes from each slice of bread.

Spread with butter or margarine and any desired fillings. Garnish with sliced stuffed olives, radishes, small whole shrimps, sardines, parsley, etc. If using fresh cucumber or tomato slices, cut bread ½″ thick and make up just before serving.

Cooking for a Crowd

THINGS TO REMEMBER WHEN COOKING FOR A CROWD

HOW TO PLAN:

In planning to serve a large number of people, one of two types of food preparation will be more suitable:

(a) When cooking facilities are limited, it is usually best to ask helpers to prepare the food at home and bring it at the required hour. For this, use regular recipes and calculate the number of salads, casseroles, pies, cakes, etc. you will need, based on the number of guests expected.

(b) When you have the facilities of a large functional kitchen from which to serve the meal, the food is prepared there. Some church and community halls have institutional type equipment, so that many servings can be prepared at one time. Lacking this large equipment, plan to prepare the food in home-size quantities and dishes. In either case, many problems are avoided with the convenience of *on the spot* cooking and baking.

HOW TO SERVE:

Buffet Style Service:—Arrange food in easy-to-serve portions on platters or dishes. Keep hot foods hot and cold foods cold. Carve meats ahead or have an expert carver in attendance to cut servings quickly. Allocate some of your committee to help serve from behind the table to keep everyone moving. Arrange platters in logical, comfortable sequence. Keep napkins, silver, glasses and beverage on side tables for the guests to pick up, or set the tables ahead of time.

Plate Service:—Adequate help is important here, with a smooth-running sequence of servers. Have a complete line of servers and two or three waitresses for each 25 people to be served. Plan the arrangement of the food on the plate ahead of time with the servers.

Quantity Servings for Fifty

BEVERAGES

Punch, Tomato Juice, etc.

4 ounce servings	5 quarts
6 ounce servings	7½ quarts

Coffee (allowing 2 cups per person)

Regular	1½ pounds
Instant	6 ounces

Tea (allowing 2 cups per person)

Tea bags	35
Loose tea	¾ pound

Cream—*Half and Half or 11.5% butterfat* (allowing 2 servings per person)

For coffee	1½ quarts
For tea	1 quart

Sugar	1½ pounds
Lemons, thinly sliced	6 - 8

SOUP

6 ounce servings	7½ quarts

BREAD

Sliced	5 loaves
Rolls	5 dozen

BUTTER

(1 pound cuts into 48 squares) 1-1½ pounds

SALAD DRESSINGS AND RELISHES

French Dressing (2 tablespoons per serving)	3 pints
Mayonnaise (1 tablespoon per serving)	1½ pints
Lettuce	8-9 heads
Celery	10 hearts
Pickles and Olives (2 per serving)	2 quarts
Chili Sauce, Cranberry Sauce (1 tablespoon per serving)	1½ pints

SANDWICHES (See recipes Nos. 565 & 566.)

MEAT AND POULTRY *Uncooked Weight*

Beef, minced (for patties) . .	15 pounds
Beef, roasted (boneless) . .	15-20 pounds
Beef, roasted (bone-in) . . .	25-30 pounds
Chicken or Turkey, roasted .	40-50 pounds
Ham, baked (boneless)	15 pounds
Ham, baked (bone-in) . . .	25-30 pounds
Cold Cooked Meat, sliced .	12-13 pounds

VEGETABLES

Canned	10 (20-ounce) cans
Frozen	5 (2-pound) bags
Fresh (carrots, beets, cabbage, etc.)	15 pounds
Tomatoes, sliced	8-10 pounds
Potatoes—	
Mashed, scalloped, creamed	15-20 pounds
Baked, boiled	20-25 pounds
Instant (see package directions)	

CAKES AND COOKIES

For tea or reception (3-4 per person)	18-20 dozen
To accompany dessert (2 per person)	9-10 dozen

ICE CREAM

Brick, sliced	10 bricks
Bulk, scoop #12	1½ gallons

IMPORTANT

All recipes are based on the Imperial 5 cup quart measure (40 ounces). Quantities given are for the *average*. You will have to adjust to suit your needs—teenagers will eat more than a women's group, for instance.

---

560 Tea

This quantity will allow for *seconds*.

In a large cheesecloth bag (about 20″ wide), place

¾ pound (4 cups) loose tea

Be sure that the bag is large enough to allow the tea to expand, and the water to circulate freely.

In a large pot or urn, bring to a boil

3 gallons water

Plunge tea bag into boiling water and immediately remove pot from heat. Cover pot and allow the tea to steep for 7 to 10 minutes.

Be sure to tie the top of the cheesecloth bag with string and attach to the handle of the pot. This will allow the bag to be removed easily.

After tea has steeped, stir with a wooden spoon and then remove the bag. Keep hot in a warm place but do not put over direct heat.

If the pot is covered, tea can be kept hot for 30 to 40 minutes.

Milk and sugar should not be added until after the tea has been served.

Yield: Tea for 50, with second servings.

NOTE: If desired, gauze tea bags may be used in place of the loose tea. For 3 gallons water, use 35 bags. Prepare as above (omitting large bag, of course). Use large sieve to scoop out tea bags after steeping.

561 Coffee

This quantity will allow for *seconds*.

In a large cheesecloth bag (about 24″ wide), place

1½ pounds coffee, coarse grind
Dash of salt and dry mustard

Be sure that the bag is large enough to allow the coffee to expand and the water to circulate.

In a large pot, bring to a boil

3 gallons water

Plunge coffee bag into boiling water. Cover pot and turn heat very low. Allow coffee to steep for 15 minutes.

Be sure to tie the top of the cheesecloth bag with string and attach to the handle of the pot. This will allow the bag to be removed easily. Plunge coffee bag up and down several times, then remove.

Keep coffee hot in a covered pot over very low heat. Do not boil.

Yield: Coffee for 50, with second servings.

562 Instant Coffee

This quantity will allow for *seconds*.

In a large pot, bring to a boil

3 gallons water

Reduce heat to very low and add

6 ounces (2½ cups) instant coffee powder

Stir until coffee is completely dissolved. Keep coffee hot over very low heat. Do not boil.

Yield: Coffee for 50, with second servings.

563   *Citrus Tea Punch*

Pour
> **6 cups boiling water**

over
> **8 teaspoons tea *or* 3 tea bags**

Brew tea for 5 minutes. Strain.
Add
> **3 cups sugar**

Stir until sugar is completely dissolved.
Add
> **6 cups orange juice**
> **3 cups lemon juice**
> **6 cups pineapple juice**

Just before serving, pour over ice in a punch bowl and add
> **2 large bottles ginger ale**

Garnish with slices of orange and lemon.
Yield: Approximately 50 (4-ounce) servings.

564   *Easy Party Punch*

Combine in a large punch bowl
> **1 (48-ounce) can pineapple juice, chilled**
> **1 (48-ounce) can orange juice, chilled**
> **1 (48-ounce) can apple juice, chilled**

Just before serving, add
> **2 large bottles ginger ale**

Top with scoops of firmly frozen sherbet (about 4 pints).
Yield: Approximately 50 (4-ounce) servings.

565   *Sandwiches*

FACTS AND FIGURES:

To estimate the number of sandwiches required to serve a group of people at receptions, teas, evening entertainments, etc., allow 3 or 4 small sandwiches and 2 open-face sandwiches per person.

For example:

To serve 50 people:—

Allow 50 whole sandwiches (200 small sandwiches).

This will require:
100 slices of bread ($\frac{1}{4}$″ or $\frac{3}{8}$″ thick)
$1\frac{1}{4}$ pounds butter or margarine
12-13 cups of filling ($\frac{1}{4}$ cup per sandwich)

Plus 8 dozen open-face sandwiches. (This will require 4 to 5 loaves of unsliced bread, cut lengthwise.)

BREAD:

Since the weight and shape of bakery bread is determined by provincial legislation, there is some variation in the number of slices per loaf and the diameter per slice. An average 24-ounce loaf of sandwich bread will cut into 20 to 24 slices which are $\frac{3}{8}$″ thick.

HEARTY SANDWICHES:

For stag parties, picnics and box lunch suppers, allow 2 whole sandwiches per person.

566   *Sandwich Fillings*

For 1 Loaf of Bread
OR
Approximately 10-12 Whole Sandwiches
NOTE: Allow $\frac{1}{4}$ pound softened, creamed butter or margarine per loaf. The following recipes provide $\frac{1}{4}$ cup filling per sandwich.

CHICKEN
> $1\frac{1}{2}$ **pounds, sliced**

CHICKEN SALAD
> $1\frac{1}{2}$ **cups (approximately $\frac{3}{4}$ pound) cooked cubed chicken**
> **1 cup diced celery**
> $\frac{1}{3}$ **cup chopped green peppers**
> $\frac{1}{4}$ **cup chopped pimiento**
> **Salt and pepper to taste**
> $\frac{1}{3}$ **cup salad dressing (approximately)**

EGG SALAD
> **6 hard-cooked eggs, chopped**
> $\frac{1}{2}$ **cup sweet pickle relish**
> $\frac{1}{4}$ **cup chopped onions**
> **1 teaspoon dry mustard**
> **Salt and pepper to taste**
> $\frac{1}{2}$ **cup salad dressing (approximately)**

FISH (tuna or salmon)
> **1 (1-pound) can salmon *or* 2 (7-ounce) cans tuna**
> **1 cup finely diced celery**
> **Salt and pepper to taste**
> **1 teaspoon lemon juice**
> $\frac{1}{3}$ **cup salad dressing (approximately)**

MINCED HAM
> $\frac{3}{4}$ **pound ham, minced**
> $\frac{1}{2}$ **cup sweet pickle relish**
> **2 teaspoons prepared mustard**
> $\frac{1}{2}$ **cup salad dressing (approximately)**

SLICED HAM
> **1 pound**

567   Baked Meat Loaf

Combine and beat together

    2 quarts (1 pound) dry bread, crumbled

    1 quart milk

    5 eggs

Then add

    10 pounds minced beef

    5 pounds minced pork

    1¼ cups chopped onions

    2½ cups coarsely shredded carrots

    5 tablespoons salt

    ½ teaspoon pepper

Combine thoroughly.

Shape into 5 loaves and place in roasting pans. Refrigerate until ready to bake.

Bake in preheated 350° oven for 2 hours or to an internal temperature of 185°.

Yield: 50 servings (one generous slice per serving).

568   Chicken à la King

Stew until tender

    12 pounds ready-to-cook stewing chickens

Remove meat from bones and dice.

There should be 12 cups of diced chicken.

Using a wire whisk, blend together

    8 cups chicken stock

    4 cups *Pre-Sifted* PURITY All-Purpose Flour

    3 tablespoons salt

Heat in a large double boiler or heavy pot

    16 cups milk

Add

    1 cup chicken fat, butter *or* margarine

Stir until butter is melted.

Add about half the hot milk to the flour mixture, beating with the wire whisk. Return to double boiler, continuing to beat. Cook until smoothly thickened, stirring frequently.

About ½ hour before serving, add

    Diced cooked chicken

    2 cups cooked frozen peas

    1½ cups sliced canned mushrooms

    ½ cup juice from mushrooms

    1 cup chopped canned pimiento

Heat thoroughly and season to taste. Serve hot on biscuits or patty shells.

Yield: 50 (⅔ cup) servings.

569   Barbecued Chicken

Wash and dry thoroughly

    50 chicken pieces (allowing about ¾ to 1 pound per person)

Place on racks over white-hot coals. Each time the chicken is turned baste with Barbecue Sauce (recipe No. 570). To test chicken for doneness, twist leg. If bone slips in meat or leg moves easily at joint it is cooked. Use tongs rather than a fork for turning chicken pieces to prevent loss of juices. Allow approximately ¾ to 1 hour cooking time depending on size of pieces.

Yield: 50 servings.

VARIATION:

(a)   Oven Barbecued Chicken

Brown chicken pieces, a few at a time, in hot fat (about 3 pounds fat will be needed). Drain and place skin side up in roasting pans. Pour Barbecue Sauce (recipe No. 570) over chicken pieces, being careful to coat each piece. Bake in preheated 325° oven for 1½ to 1¾ hours. Spoon sauce over chicken occasionally during baking.

570   Barbecue Sauce

The day before the sauce is to be used, combine

    5 cloves garlic, finely chopped

    1½ cups finely chopped onions

    7 cups lemon juice

    3¼ cups vegetable oil

    2 tablespoons salt

    2 tablespoons pepper

    2 tablespoons thyme

Cover and refrigerate.

Use as a sauce when barbecuing chicken.

Yield: 50 servings.

571   Roast Turkey

Two 20 to 25 pound ready-to-cook turkeys will serve 50 generously. If birds are frozen, plan on two days thawing time in the refrigerator with a final hour or two under running water to complete thawing. Simmer the necks and giblets in water for 2 to 3 hours. Grind the meat from these and store with the broth in the refrigerator to use in the gravy.

For large quantity service, turkey is best and faster roasted without stuffing. Sprinkle body cavity with salt and monosodium glutamate.

Add a slice or two of onion.

Roast stuffing separately in baking dish for about one hour.

Spread the surface of the turkey with fat, then cover loosely with foil or greased cheesecloth. Place the turkey on a rack in an open pan in preheated 325° oven. Roast for 7 hours or until the leg twists easily in the socket. Plan to have the turkey done at least one hour before serving time so there will be oven space for the pans of stuffing. This *resting period* will also make the turkey easier to carve.

Serve a slice of white and a slice of dark meat on a spoonful of hot stuffing. Serve gravy over this or separately. (Keep the carved slices covered with foil to prevent drying out before serving.)

572   Turkey Giblet Gravy

Combine in a large heavy kettle
   4 cups turkey drippings
   3 cups *Pre-Sifted* **PURITY**
   All-Purpose Flour
Cook together until bubbly, stirring constantly.
Gradually add
   4½ quarts hot giblet broth and water
Bring to a boil and cook for 15 minutes. Stir constantly until smoothly thickened. Add chopped or ground cooked giblets and season to taste with salt and pepper. Heat thoroughly before serving.

Yield: 50 servings.

573   Scalloped Potatoes

Preheat oven to 325°.
Combine
   2 cups *Pre-Sifted* **PURITY**
   All-Purpose Flour
   2 tablespoons salt
   ½ tablespoon pepper
Pare and slice
   15 pounds potatoes
Arrange alternate layers of sliced potatoes and flour mixture in greased baking pans.
Scald together
   3 quarts milk
   1 cup butter *or* **margarine**
Pour over potatoes in pans.

Cover pans and bake in preheated 325°oven for 1½ hours. Remove covers during last half hour of baking time.

Yield: 50 (½ cup) servings.

574   Potato Salad

Cook until tender
   15 pounds potatoes
Cut into cubes and while still warm, pour on
   1½ cups French Dressing
Stir gently to coat each piece of potato. Chill for at least 2 hours in refrigerator. **Do not allow to stand at room temperature.**

Add
   ¾ cup chopped onions
   4 cups diced celery
   1¾ cups stuffed olives, sliced
   3 cups sweet pickles, chopped
   20 hard-cooked eggs, chopped
   ¼ cup salt
Combine gently but thoroughly.

Mix together
   5 cups salad dressing
   ½ cup pickle juice
   ¼ cup prepared mustard
Pour over potato mixture and blend evenly.

Refrigerate until ready to serve.

Yield: Approximately 50 (⅔ cup) servings.

575   Tomato Aspic

Soften
   16 envelopes gelatine
in
   3 cups water
Simmer together for 20 minutes
   4 (48-ounce) cans tomato juice
   4 bay leaves
   3 whole cloves
   2 cups diced celery and leaves
   4 slices onion
Strain.

Add softened gelatine to tomato mixture. Stir until gelatine is dissolved, heating if necessary.
Add
   ⅓ cup sugar
   1 tablespoon salt
   ½ cup vinegar
   2 tablespoons lemon juice
Pour into large pans to a depth of about 2″.

Chill overnight. To serve, cut Tomato Aspic into squares, using a heated knife. Lift out with a wide spatula.

Yield: Approximately 50 (½ cup) servings.

Homemade Candies

THINGS TO REMEMBER ABOUT CANDY MAKING

It is always best to use a thermometer when making candy so the syrup is cooked to an exact temperature. However, if you do not have a thermometer it is possible to get satisfactory results with the "cold water test". To do this, fill a small bowl with cold water and allow candy to drop from a spoon into the water. The following chart explains what happens at each stage:

Temperature	Cold Water Test	Characteristics
230° to 234°	Thread	Mixture will spin a fine thread, about 2″ long, from a fork. This will disperse in water, sinking to bottom of the bowl.
235° to 240°	Soft Ball	Mixture forms a soft ball in water which gradually disappears when rubbed.
246° to 250°	Firm Ball	Mixture forms a firm ball in water which flattens when rubbed but will not disappear.
250° to 265°	Hard Ball	Mixture forms a hard ball in water which holds its shape when rubbed.
270° to 290°	Soft Crack	Mixture forms fine threads in water. These threads break when rubbed.
300° to 310°	Hard Crack	Mixture is very brittle in the air and in the water.

Always remove candy from the heat while doing the cold water test to prevent overcooking. When using a candy thermometer, make sure the bulb is completely immersed in the syrup.

Cooked fudges and fondants are made up of tiny crystals—the smaller the crystals the smoother the candy. If the crystals start to form early, they will be large and the candy will be "sugary". Therefore, avoid too much stirring while cooking the candy, and allow it to cool without stirring until it reaches the correct temperature for beating.

---

576 Chocolate Fudge

Combine in a saucepan
- **2 cups sugar**
- **¾ cup evaporated milk or cream**
- **2 squares unsweetened chocolate, cut-up**
- **2 tablespoons light corn syrup**
- **2 tablespoons butter or margarine**
- **¼ teaspoon salt**

Stir over medium heat until the sugar is dissolved and the chocolate melted. Continue cooking the mixture until it reaches the soft ball stage (236°). Stir occasionally to prevent sticking.

Remove from the heat and let stand, without stirring, until bottom of the pan is lukewarm (110°).

Beat until the candy loses its gloss.

Then quickly stir in
- **½ cup chopped nuts**
- **1 teaspoon vanilla**

Pour into a buttered 8″ or 9″ square pan.

When cool, cut into squares.

Yield: About 1¼ pounds.

NOTE: If desired, use ⅓ cup cocoa in place of the unsweetened chocolate. Increase the butter to 3 tablespoons.

Bake easier, bake better with Purity Pre-Sifted Flour

577 Maple Cream Fudge

Combine in a saucepan.

3 cups lightly-packed brown sugar
1 cup granulated sugar
½ teaspoon salt
1 cup evaporated milk *or* cream
2 tablespoons butter *or* margarine

Stir over medium heat until the sugar dissolves. Continue cooking the mixture until it reaches the soft ball stage (236°). Stir occasionally to prevent sticking.

Remove from heat and cool, without stirring, until bottom of the pan is lukewarm (110°).

Beat until the fudge loses its gloss.

Then quickly stir in

½ cup chopped nuts
1 teaspoon vanilla

Pour into a buttered 9″ square pan.

When cool, cut into squares.

Yield: About 1½ pounds.

578 Divinity Fudge

Combine in a saucepan

2⅔ cups sugar
⅔ cup light corn syrup
½ cup water

Stir over low heat until the sugar dissolves. Simmer until mixture reaches the hard ball stage (255°). Stir occasionally to prevent sticking.

Remove from the heat and cool slightly.

Meanwhile, beat until stiff but not dry

2 egg whites

Gradually add the syrup, beating until the mixture loses its gloss and will hold its shape.

Quickly add

½ cup chopped nuts
¼ cup chopped maraschino cherries
½ teaspoon vanilla

Pour into a buttered 9″ square pan.

When cool, cut into squares.

Yield: About 1½ pounds.

579 Peanut Brittle

Sprinkle

1 cup peanuts

over a cookie sheet which has sides.

Place in a heavy cast iron or cast aluminum frying pan

2 cups sugar

Cook over medium high heat, stirring constantly with a metal spoon until the sugar melts.

Then quickly pour over the peanuts.

Let stand until hard, then break into pieces.

Yield: About 1 pound.

580 Quick Fudge

Combine in a saucepan

1⅔ cups sugar
⅔ cup evaporated milk

Simmer together for 5 minutes, stirring constantly.

Remove from heat and blend in

1½ cups miniature marshmallows *or* 16 regular marshmallows, quartered
1½ cups chocolate chips
½ cup chopped nuts
1 teaspoon vanilla
¼ teaspoon salt

Stir until smooth.

Pour into a buttered 8″ or 9″ square pan.

When cool, cut into squares.

Yield: About 1¼ pounds.

581 Quick Fondant

Combine in a bowl

1 egg white
2 cups sifted icing sugar
2 teaspoons butter *or* margarine
½ teaspoon vanilla

Beat until creamy.

Tint as desired with a few drops of food colouring. Drop small spoonfuls on waxed paper and decorate with nuts, cherries, candied fruit, etc.

Let stand until firm enough to handle.

Yield: About 3 dozen pieces.

VARIATIONS:

(a) Mint Wafers

Prepare as for Quick Fondant, increasing the sifted icing sugar to 2¼ cups. Substitute 5 to 6 drops peppermint flavouring for the vanilla.

Roll into small balls and place on waxed paper.

Flatten with tines of a fork.

Let stand until firm enough to handle.

(b) Stuffed Dates

Prepare Quick Fondant as directed. Stuff whole dates with about a teaspoon of the fondant, then roll in granulated or fruit sugar.

Home Freezing

The complete and intelligent use of a home freezer can add pleasure to your labours as a cook, simplify menu planning and marketing, and enhance your reputation as a hostess.

Most foods can be frozen successfully, either cooked or uncooked, and in combination with other foods. The list of foods which cannot be frozen is very short and quite easy to remember.

FOODS NOT TO FREEZE

Lettuce, tomatoes, cucumbers, celery and radishes.

Whites of hard-cooked eggs.

Custard pies, cream fillings and puddings.

Gelatine salads and desserts unless whipped.

Mayonnaise.

Boiled potatoes, alone or used in potato salad, stews or meat pies.

Heavy cream. (It can be frozen after it has been whipped.)

Here are some suggestions to help insure success in the freezing of foods:

Select only foods of good quality: Freezing does retain the flavour, texture, colour and nutritive value of food, but it does not improve the quality.

Freeze foods promptly: Speed in preparing and packaging fresh produce from garden or grower is important. If immediate processing is impossible, refrigerate for a short time. This also applies to meat, fish and prepared foods.

Freeze suitable quantities of food: Consult your freezer instruction book to determine the quantities of food to prepare and freeze at a time to avoid overloading the machine.

Package and wrap foods carefully: Use only packaging materials designed for freezer use. See below.

Label and date all packages: It is important to include the type of food, weight or number of servings and date of freezing.

Freeze packages quickly: Do not let packages stand at room temperature before freezing. If a delay is necessary, refrigerate packages.

Use frozen foods regularly: Plan to use items from your freezer daily so that you have a complete yearly turnover.

Do not refreeze thawed foods: Once a food has been thawed completely, it should not be refrozen. Partially thawed food, which still has ice crystals and is quite firm, can be refrozen. This sometimes happens when there has been a power failure. Re-label and use as soon as possible. *The exception:* You can, of course, cook a completely thawed food and refreeze it.

Packaging

Proper packaging is necessary to protect the food from the cold dry air of the freezer.

Therefore, wrapping papers and containers suitable for freezing foods must be moisture and vapour resistant in order to keep the food from becoming dry, flavourless and unattractive. Proper wrapping and sealing is equally important.

FREEZER WRAPPING PAPERS

1. Plastic films — cellophane, polyethylene, pliofilm, etc.

2. Freezer aluminum foil.

3. Laminated papers, locker paper, or waxed freezer paper.

If using plastic films or foil on irregular shaped packages, it is sometimes necessary

Purity Pre-Sifted Flour — the All-Purpose Flour

to cover again with heavy paper to avoid puncturing.

To Wrap: Place food in centre of paper and bring two ends of paper together over the top of the food. Then fold over two or three times until tight, leaving as little air space as possible. Press out air at the ends and fold under the parcel. This is known as the "drugstore wrap".

Aluminum foil is shaped around the food and does not require the drugstore wrap.

To Seal: Secure wrappings with freezer tape, rubber or metal bands; or *heat-seal* using a hand iron set at "rayon" or "synthetic". If sealing plastic films, place some paper between the wrapping and the iron.

FREEZER BAGS

Assorted sizes of plastic bags are easy to use and are suitable for packaging poultry, dry pack fruits and vegetables, and some prepared foods such as bread, cake and cookies.

To seal, press out as much air as possible, then twist the top several times and secure tightly with paper or metal closures, or rubber bands.

After freezing foods in plastic bags, pack like foods in large paper or plastic bags. This will keep similar foods together.

FREEZER CONTAINERS

1. Folding Cartons: Wax or plastic lined, some with plastic-liner bags. Some liner bags require heat-sealing (see freezer wrappings), others are supplied with metal or elastic closures.

2. Rigid Containers: Made of plastic, glass, waxed cardboard, aluminum or aluminum foil. They are available in various shapes and sizes. Square shapes with flat tops and bottoms take up less space in the freezer since they stack easily.

3. Baking Dishes: Heat and freezer-proof glassware; aluminum pie, cake and roasting pans; special foil containers and pie plates.

> **Use only packaging material designed for freezer use.**

Headspace: When using a liquid or sugar pack, allow 1″ headspace for glass containers and ½″ headspace for others.

Freezing Fruits

Freeze only fresh high quality fruit of proper maturity. Choose varieties recommended for freezing, since some freeze better than others. Your Provincial Department of Agriculture will provide you with this information.

Fruits can be packaged in any leak-proof container or carton. Freezer bags can be used for dry packed fruit.

PACKING FRUITS

1. Dry Pack: Pack fruits such as blueberries, raspberries, currants and rhubarb without sugar or syrup. Drain prepared fruit thoroughly on towels, and fill containers or bags. Seal and freeze. Fruits packed in this way

can be used for jams, jellies, pies, desserts, or special diets.

2. Syrup Pack: Make syrup in advance, choosing the strength of syrup suited to tartness of fruit and personal taste. Recommended strengths are given with each fruit (Table below). Place prepared fruit in containers and cover with syrup, allowing headspace. To keep fruit under syrup, especially peaches and apricots, place crushed cellophane or waxed paper on top of the fruit.

3. Dry Sugar Pack: Sprinkle juicy fruits with the required amount of sugar in a shallow bowl or tray. Mix gently, coating each piece

SYRUPS:

Type	Sugar	Water	Yield (approximate)	To Make Syrup
Thin	1 cup	2 cups	2½ cups	Add sugar to water.
Moderately thin	1 cup	1½ cups	2 cups	Stir well to dissolve.
Medium	1 cup	1 cup	1½ cups	Chill.
Heavy	1 cup	¾ cup	1¼ cups	DO NOT HEAT

Allow ⅔ to 1 cup of syrup for each 16-ounce container.

with sugar. Spoon into leak-proof containers, allowing for headspace. Seal and freeze. The specific amount of sugar needed for each fruit is given in the Table below. The ratio of fruit to sugar is roughly 4 pounds fruit to 1 pound sugar.

To Prevent Discolouration of Fruits: Light coloured fruits, such as peaches, apricots and apples, will turn brown when exposed to air before completely frozen or while thawing in unopened package. To prevent this, powdered ascorbic acid is added to the fruit before freezing. For syrup pack: Add ½ teaspoon ascorbic acid for each quart of cold syrup and stir to dissolve. To use with dry sugar pack, mix ½ teaspoon ascorbic acid with each pound of sugar.

	PREPARATION OF FRUITS FOR FREEZING
APPLES	Use good tart cooking varieties as soon as they have ripened. Do not use storage apples. **Preparation:** To prevent discolouration while preparing apples, slice peeled, cored fruit into a brine solution made of 2 tablespoons salt to 1 gallon water. **Pack:** Drain off brine solution and pack using thin syrup with ascorbic acid added (see above).
APPLESAUCE	Prepare as usual. Chill thoroughly, package and freeze.
APRICOTS	Unpeeled frozen apricots are not satisfactory as a dessert fruit but are very nice when used in pies or puddings. **Preparation:** Wash but do not blanch apricots. Pit and cut into quarters. **Pack:** Use thin syrup with ascorbic acid added (see above).
BLUEBERRIES	**Preparation:** Sort, wash and drain. **Pack:** Dry Pack—for use in baking. OR Dry Sugar Pack—allow 5 pounds fruit to 1 pound sugar.
CHERRIES (Sour)	**Preparation:** Wash, stem and pit. **Pack:** Dry Sugar Pack—allow 4 pounds fruit to 1 pound sugar OR Syrup Pack—use medium syrup.
CRANBERRIES	**Preparation:** Sort, wash and drain. **Pack:** Dry Pack.
FRUIT COCKTAIL	Use 1 part each . . . . green grapes red grapes apples 2 parts . . . . cantaloupe 6 parts . . . . peaches **Preparation:** Prepare as for fruit cocktail or salad. **Pack:** Use thin syrup with ascorbic acid added (see above).
PEACHES	**Preparation:** Blanch, remove skins and pit. Slice fruit directly into syrup or dry sugar with ascorbic acid added (see above). **Pack:** Dry Sugar Pack—allow 4 pounds fruit to 1 pound sugar. OR Syrup Pack—use moderately thin syrup.

	PREPARATION OF FRUITS FOR FREEZING
PLUMS	**Preparation:** Wash, cut into halves and pit. **Pack:** Dry Sugar Pack—use 4 pounds prepared fruit to 1 pound sugar with ascorbic acid added (page 202). OR Syrup Pack—use moderately thin syrup with ascorbic acid added (page 202).
RASPBERRIES	**Preparation:** Sort, wash if necessary. **Pack:** Dry Sugar Pack—use 5 pounds prepared fruit to 1 pound sugar. OR Syrup Pack—use a thin syrup.
RHUBARB	**Preparation:** Wash, cut stalks into 1″ lengths. **Pack:** Dry Pack. OR Dry Sugar Pack—use 4 pounds prepared fruit to 1 pound sugar.
STRAWBERRIES	**Preparation:** Wash, sort and hull. **Pack:** Sliced Strawberries—Dry Sugar Pack using 4 pounds prepared fruit to 1 pound sugar. Whole Strawberries—Syrup Pack using a medium syrup.

STORAGE TIME:

Frozen fruits may be stored 8 to 12 months.

TO THAW:

Leave in unopened container. Allow 6 hours in refrigerator; 2 hours at room temperature; 1½ hours if container is placed in front of an electric fan; or 1 hour if container is placed in a bowl under cold running water.

Turn package over occasionally while defrosting to evenly distribute the syrup.

TO SERVE:

If using as a dessert fruit or in fruit cocktail, serve when partially thawed.

Dry packed fruits—can be used just as fresh fruit.

Dry sugar packed fruits—thaw only enough to separate. Add no more sugar unless desired. Use more thickening for pies made with frozen fruits than with fresh fruits.

Syrup packed fruits—should be drained if used in pies or puddings. Use amount of syrup necessary for recipe and save remainder for fruit drinks.

FOR BEST RESULTS

Prepare, pack and freeze small quantities of fruit at a time.

Wash fruit in ice cold water, working quickly, so fruit does not absorb excess water.

If freezing fruits for jams or jellies (dry pack), measure the desired amount of fruit *before* freezing as thawed fruits tend to collapse and are difficult to measure accurately. Use the same recipes for these pre-measured frozen fruits as you would for fresh fruits.

Freezing Vegetables

Freeze only good quality vegetables which have been freshly picked. Select the varieties recommended for freezing by your Provincial Department of Agriculture.

TO PREPARE:

Prepare vegetables as you would for table use. In addition, all vegetables must be blanched (scalded) to retard enzyme action and thus retain flavour, texture and colour. (See Table below).

TO BLANCH:

Heat two gallons of water in each of two large kettles, bringing them to a vigorous boil. Place about a pound of prepared vegetables in a wire basket, colander or cheesecloth bag. Immerse in first kettle of boiling water for 30 seconds. Transfer immediately to second kettle; start to count blanching time when the water returns to a boil after vegetables are added. For blanching times of various vegetables see Table below.

Carefully time the blanching process since over or under blanching can harm the quality of the vegetable. Do not attempt to blanch more than one pound of vegetables at a time.

Follow directions in the Table below when selecting, preparing and blanching vegetables. Then chill, drain, pack and freeze them as outlined on page 205.

	PREPARATION OF VEGETABLES FOR FREEZING
ASPARAGUS	Select young tender stalks. Remove tough ends and scales. Wash thoroughly. Cut into uniform lengths to fit containers or into 1″ pieces. **Blanch small stalks**............3 minutes **Blanch larger stalks**............4 minutes
BEANS **Green or Wax**	Select young tender beans. Wash, trim ends, string if necessary. Leave whole, slice crosswise or cut French-style. **Blanch**......................3 minutes
BROCCOLI	Select dark green compact heads. Trim off woody stalk. Cut through heads and stalk lengthwise leaving head about 1″ across. Immerse in brine solution (1 tablespoon salt to 5 cups water) for ½ hour; drain and rinse thoroughly. **Blanch**......................3 minutes
BRUSSELS **SPROUTS**	Select deep green compact sprouts. Trim and immerse in brine solution (1 tablespoon salt to 5 cups water) for ½ hour. Drain and rinse thoroughly. **Blanch**......................3 minutes
CARROTS	Wash and scrape. Slice or dice ¼″ thick. **Blanch**......................3 minutes **For tiny whole carrots blanch**...5 minutes
CAULIFLOWER	Select compact, white tender heads. Break into flowerets about 1″ in diameter. Immerse in brine solution (1 tablespoon salt to 5 cups water) for ½ hour. Drain and rinse thoroughly. **Blanch**......................3 minutes
CORN **on the cob**	Select freshly picked corn and prepare immediately. Remove husks and silk; trim cobs to even lengths. Wash. Blanch, allowing 2 quarts boiling water for each medium-sized ear. **Blanch large ears**............11 minutes **Blanch medium ears**...........9 minutes **Blanch small ears**.............7 minutes Chill very thoroughly, about 15 minutes in cold water so that the interior of the cob is **cold** before freezing. Freezer foil or wrappings may be used rather than trying to fit cobs into containers.

	PREPARATION OF VEGETABLES FOR FREEZING
CORN **whole kernel**	Choose corn as for corn on the cob. Remove husks and silk, then wash. Blanch........................3 minutes Chill and cut off kernels close to the cob.
PEAS	Select young tender peas. Shell, sort and wash. Blanch........................2 minutes
SPINACH **CHARD** **and other greens**	Use only tender green leaves. Discard tough stems and bruised portions. Wash very thoroughly. Blanch........................2 minutes NOTE: Drain well after chilling so that leaves do not mat.
SQUASH **PUMPKIN**	Cut or break apart, remove seeds and stringy portion. Cut into small pieces then steam or boil until tender. Cool quickly and remove from rind. Mash or sieve, then pack and freeze.

NOTE: Broccoli, brussels sprouts and cauliflower are immersed in a brine solution (1 tablespoon salt to 5 cups water) for ½ hour to remove any insects. Drain and rinse thoroughly before blanching.

TO CHILL:

Cool blanched vegetables quickly in ice water or cold running water. Remove as soon as vegetables are cold — do not leave in water any longer than necessary. Drain on a clean towel or paper towelling placed on a shallow pan or tray. Pack immediately in containers and then freeze.

TO PACK:

Select suitable size and type of container. A pint package will hold 3 to 4 servings. Since vegetables are dry packed, plastic bags are very popular and after freezing they can be packed in large paper bags for neater storage.

Exclude as much air as possible after filling bag and twist top nearly to vegetable, then seal with proper closure. If you use moulded plastic containers or glass jars, allow ½" headspace for expansion. Freeze packed vegetables at once.

TO PREPARE FOR SERVING:

Cook most vegetables while still frozen, allowing a shorter cooking period than for fresh vegetables because they have been partially cooked during blanching. However, corn on the cob should be completely thawed before cooking; spinach and greens should be partially thawed then broken apart before cooking. Pumpkin and squash can be completely thawed and used as you would cooked or canned.

TO COOK:

Allow ½ cup water and ½ teaspoon salt for 2 cups frozen vegetables. Bring quickly to a boil, reduce heat and boil gently, covered, until tender. Corn on the cob should be cooked in boiling water to cover.

Approximate Cooking Times:

Asparagus, broccoli, cauliflower, corn on the cob, peas and spinach, allow . .3 to 5 minutes Wax beans, brussels sprouts, whole kernel corn, allow.................4 to 6 minutes Green beans, allow.........5 to 7 minutes

Freezing Meats, Fish, Poultry

Take advantage of market specials by freezing meats, fish and poultry for year round enjoyment. Package individually in freezer wrapping, padding the bones to avoid puncturing the outer wrapping. Label each package clearly with date, cut and weight. An inventory is recommended.

Poultry and meats should be completely thawed in freezer wrapper for uniform cooking. Use the same cooking methods as for fresh. Fish may be cooked frozen or thawed, although partial thawing may be necessary if the pieces are to be separated. Never refreeze meats, fish or poultry that have been thawed.

Freezing Baked Foods

Freezing adds much to the joy of baking. It requires the same time to assemble utensils and ingredients, then clean up afterwards for one batch of cookies as it does for a double or triple batch. Therefore, with wise planning and little extra effort, you can stockpile a delightful variety of baked foods to take care of many occasions.

> It is especially important to package baked goods carefully. Exclude as much air as possible and seal securely.
>
> Wrap in foil those items you plan to heat and serve warm. Plastic bags or film will melt if heated.

YEAST BREADS AND ROLLS:

Prepare and bake breads, rolls and sweet breads as usual. Cool to room temperature, package and freeze.

To Package: Wrap in freezer wrappings or bags being careful to exclude as much air from package as possible. Small loaves of bread can be packaged in bags; pan rolls and coffee cakes in aluminum foil containers and covered with sheet wrappings. Package only amounts which will be used quickly. It is better to package bread cut in half or as many rolls as you need for a meal since they soon become stale.

To Thaw: Thaw in freezer wrappings at room temperature. Bread requires 2 hours, rolls and sweet breads less time depending upon size. If foil wrapped, place in preheated 300° oven for 15 to 30 minutes. Do not loosen wrappings.

Storage Time: 4 to 6 months for baked bread, rolls and sweet breads.

Commercially baked bread may be frozen in original wrapping and kept for 1 to 2 weeks. For longer storage, place wrapped loaf in a freezer bag. Storage time is 3 months.

QUICK BREADS:

All baked quick breads (muffins, biscuits, waffles, fruit and nut breads, and cornbread) can be frozen very successfully. Use any recipe you choose; bake, cool, package (see packaging directions for yeast breads above) and freeze.

To Thaw: Leave in freezer wrappings at room temperature. Muffins, tea biscuits, scones, etc. will require 1 hour. Loaves and square-shaped quick breads will require 2 hours or more depending upon size. If foil wrapped, place in preheated 300° oven for 15 to 30 minutes. Waffles and pancakes can be put in the toaster to thaw and warm.

Storage Time: 4 to 6 months for baked quick breads.

STEAMED PUDDINGS:

Prepare and steam as usual; chill, then remove from the mould if you wish. Wrap in freezer wrappings. If you usually allow a ripening period for rich fruit puddings, do so before freezing. If wrapped in foil, the puddings are ready for resteaming.

To Thaw: Thaw at room temperature then steam 30 minutes to 1 hour depending upon size of pudding.

Storage Time: 4 to 6 months.

CAKES:

All varieties of baked cakes may be frozen—sponge, chiffon, angel and fruit cakes; also butter cakes in any shape—loaves, layers or cupcakes. It is a good idea to make and bake two round or square cakes at a time, one for immediate use, the other to freeze. Cool baked cakes to room temperature before freezing.

To Package: Place cake on a piece of cardboard; wrap in freezer wrapping or bag, then freeze. Since cakes need extra protection during freezer storage, place frozen cake in an ordinary bakery carton, metal or plastic container; seal and return to freezer. Or, place unwrapped cake in container then wrap with freezer wrappings; seal and freeze. It is also convenient to cut cakes into halves, quarters or slices before freezing. Slices are handy for lunch boxes and thawed quarters of cake are excellent for one meal. You can also plan to have two or three varieties of cake halves for party use.

To Freeze Iced Cakes: Uncooked butter icings are best for freezing; boiled icings become sticky and fudge icings crumble. Do not use cream fillings in layer cakes.

Bake, cool, then ice the cake. Place unwrapped in freezer for 1 to 2 hours to set the icing.

Package as outlined above and return to freezer.

To Thaw: Leave in freezer wrappings at room temperature.

For uniced cakes allow 1 to 1½ hours for layers, and 2 to 3 hours for loaves and squares. In an emergency and if foil wrapped, thaw cake in preheated 300° oven for 15 to 20 minutes.

For iced cakes allow 2 to 3 hours. Reduce thawing time one-third by placing package in front of an electric fan.

For fruit cakes allow 1 hour per pound of cake.

Storage Time: Both iced and uniced cakes can be stored for 4 to 5 months; fruit cakes up to 1 year.

COOKIES:

Most cookies can be frozen baked or unbaked except macaroons and meringues which do not freeze well. It is best to freeze the dough as this saves space and gives cookies that fresh baked flavour.

However, it is convenient to have a package or so of the baked variety in the freezer. Doughs for drop, moulded or sliced cookies can be frozen successfully while bar cookies such as brownies should be baked before freezing.

To Package Cookie Doughs: Pack drop or moulded cookie dough in bulk in airtight freezer containers; or drop by teaspoonfuls on baking sheet ¼″ apart and freeze for 1 hour. Package these frozen cookie balls in containers with a double thickness of wax paper between layers. Refrigerator cookie dough can be shaped into rolls as usual and wrapped in freezer foil, plastic film or bags.

For Baked Cookies: Cool to room temperature; package in containers with crumpled wax paper between layers. Bakery cartons can be used if overwrapped tightly with freezer wrappings. If preparing for a party, decorated cookies can be arranged on trays or heavy cardboard with freezer paper between layers. Package with freezer wrappings.

To Thaw: Thaw cookie dough frozen in bulk in container at room temperature until it can be easily handled. Prepare and bake as usual. Frozen cookie balls can be placed unthawed on baking sheet and baked right away. Refrigerator cookie dough can be sliced as soon as the knife will go through the roll. Bake immediately. Return unused portion of roll to the freezer.

Thaw baked cookies in freezer wrappings at room temperature. The time will depend upon the number of cookies in the container and size of cookie. Bar cookies require longer than others.

Storage Time: Baked cookies of all varieties can be stored for 12 months, unbaked cookie doughs for 6 to 8 months.

PIES:

Pies and pastry freeze easily and with excellent results. In fact, pastry seems to improve with freezing, especially pies frozen before baking. The best pies to freeze are mince and double crust fruit or berry pies. Chiffon pies may also be frozen but never freeze cream or custard pies.

Unbaked Mince or Fruit Pies: Prepare as usual using regular pie plates or aluminum foil pie plates. For fruit filled pies allow one-third more flour in each recipe to keep extra juices from running out. Do not slit top crust before freezing. Quick-freeze pie first and then wrap. To protect pastry during storage, place in bakery carton or cover with inverted cardboard pie plate. Wrap with freezer wrappings or place in freezer bag.

To Thaw: Remove freezer wrappings, cut slits in top crust and place directly in preheated 425° oven and bake for 60 to 75 minutes.

Storage Time: 3 months.

> Double crust fruit or mince pies can be baked before freezing but the quality is not as good as the frozen unbaked product. Also, there is little time saved by doing it in this way.

Baked Pies: Chiffon pies are prepared as usual and the fillings allowed to set. Omit whipped cream topping. Quick-freeze pies for 1 hour, then remove for wrapping. Press a circle of foil or plastic film against the surface of the filling and wrap as directed for unbaked pies. Pecan and butter tarts may be prepared and frozen the same as chiffon pies. Wrap as directed, omitting the circle of foil over the filling.

To Thaw: Leave in freezer wrappings at room temperature for 20 to 30 minutes.

Storage Time: 2 months.

PASTRY:

Since frozen pastry dough requires a long thawing time, it is better to roll dough into rounds for pie shells, top and bottom crusts or tart shells.

Prepare pastry as usual; roll out and cut into rounds of the desired size. Cut a heavy cardboard circle larger than the pastry and cover with freezer wrapping. Place pastry rounds in layers on top with a double thickness of waxed paper between. Place in a freezer bag or wrap securely in freezer wrappings and freeze.

To Use: Thaw in freezer wrappings at room temperature until the rounds can be shaped in pie plate.

Storage Time: 6 months.

CREAM PUFFS AND ECLAIRS:

Freeze baked unfilled puffs and éclairs; package in containers or freezer bags. Thaw at room temperature in freezer wrappings 15 to 20 minutes. Fill and glaze as usual.

Storage Time: 3 months.

ICE CREAM PUFFS:

Cream puffs filled with ice cream can be frozen and then packaged. No thawing is required; serve frozen with ice cream sauce.

Storage Time: 1 month.

SANDWICHES:

Picnics, parties, teas and lunch boxes can be taken care of with dispatch when sandwiches are prepared ahead and frozen. Bread of any kind and most fillings freeze well. The ingredients which do not freeze satisfactorily are: Whites of hard-cooked eggs; mayonnaise; fresh celery, lettuce, tomatoes and cucumbers.

Jams and jellies are not suitable for freezing because they tend to soak into the bread.

Meats, poultry, fish, cheese, peanut butter and nuts are good fillings to freeze. Use them separately or in combination with each other or minced and mixed with cream cheese, salad dressing (small amount) or pickle relish. Sliced or chopped olives, dill and sweet pickles may be used with fillings or as garnishes on fancy sandwiches and canapés to be frozen.

Fresh lettuce, tomatoes and cucumbers may be added to the sandwiches when ready to serve.

Lunch Box Sandwiches: Spread bread slices (crusts on) with softened butter or margarine, any spread of the salad dressing type will soak into the bread. Fill, wrap and seal. Package sandwiches singly or in pairs in small

freezer bags or freezer wrappings. Be sure to label the package.

To Thaw: Leave in wrappings at room temperature for 3 to 4 hours. They will be ready for noon lunches if taken out in the morning.

Storage Time: 3 to 4 weeks.

DO NOT REFREEZE THAWED SANDWICHES

Picnic and Party Sandwiches: Prepare as for lunch box sandwiches. Arrange sandwiches together in loaf form (about 3 to 4 sandwiches) using crusts at each end for added protection. Use only one kind of filling for each package of sandwiches since flavours tend to intermingle. Wrap securely in freezer wrappings or bags.

Party sandwich loaves which are iced with cream cheese freeze well.

Ribbon, pinwheel, rolled and checkerboard sandwiches are best frozen unsliced. However, if it is desirable to have them sliced, place on tray or heavy cardboard covered with freezer paper; separate layers of sandwiches with the paper and overwrap the whole tray securely and seal.

Open-faced tea sandwiches may be made and spread with suitable filling and frozen on trays as described above. Or, slice and cut desired bread shapes for open-faced sandwiches. Stack and wrap in freezer wrappings. *To Use:* Spread while still cold and garnish as desired.

Canapés may be made as for open-faced sandwiches and packed in layers on trays and frozen. Garnish just before serving.

To Thaw: Leave sandwiches in wrappings at room temperature and plan so they will be ready just at serving time. If thawed too soon, store in refrigerator. Trim crusts and cut plain sandwiches; slice ribbon, pinwheel and checkerboard sandwiches; garnish open-faced sandwiches.

Allow ½ hour for thawing small fancy and open-faced sandwiches packed on trays; 2 to 3 hours for ½ loaf of sandwiches (3 to 4 sandwiches) packaged together and 4 to 6 hours for a whole loaf of sandwiches (6 to 8 sandwiches). Canapés thaw very quickly so place in refrigerator 2 hours before serving.

Storage Time for party type sandwiches is about 1 week.

Preserved Foods

Despite the variety of commercially made products on the grocer's shelves, homemade jams, jellies and pickles are still favourites with everyone. Nothing provides a greater feeling of pride for the homemaker than a colourful array of pickles and jams stored in the fruit cellar.

The use of canned vegetables for making zesty pickles and sauces in the "off season" period means that the homemaker need not be without the family's favourite.

Frozen, canned and dried fruits, and frozen and canned juices can all be used for jams, conserves and jellies in the same way. Commercial pectin in liquid or crystal form is used in many of these recipes with assured success.

For best results make small amounts of pickles, jams and jellies at a time.

For excellent information and detailed recipes for pickles, jams, jellies and canning, write for the Government publications. Address:

Information Division
Canada Department of Agriculture
Ottawa, Ontario.

PICKLES

General Directions

1. Containers: Pickles may be stored in clean glass jars, sealers or crocks.

Airtight sealers are best for some pickles and most relishes and sauces. Sealers are specifically mentioned in the following recipes when they are necessary.

Clean glass jars of any type, providing they have good lids, may be used in the following pickle recipes where sealers are not specified.

Crocks — Pickles stored in crocks should be kept in a cool place. An inverted plate on top of the pickles (inside the crock) with a weight added, will keep the pickle mixture covering the pickles.

2. Choose firm, fresh vegetables and slightly under-ripe fruits.

3. Salt: Coarse or pickling salt is recommended in most recipes. Iodized salt may be used, but "free running" salt will cause cloudiness in the pickle mixture.

4. Vinegars: Use good quality vinegar, full strength.

White vinegar is excellent for light coloured foods such as fruits, onions and cauliflower.

Cider or *malt vinegar* is used when a special flavour is desirable.

Blended vinegar or *pickling vinegar* is a mixture of white and cider vinegar and is a good general purpose vinegar.

5. Spices: These should be bought fresh each year since they lose flavour if stored. Whole spices give excellent flavour to pickles and should be tied loosely in a square of cheesecloth. The bag should be large enough for the syrup to boil through it.

When using ground spices and peppers, measure accurately since too much can cause an unpleasant bitter flavour.

582 Tomato Catsup

Wash, cut out green spots and remove stem ends from

**9 pounds ripe tomatoes
(about 36 medium)**

Cut tomatoes into pieces.

Peel, dice and measure

1 cup onions

Seed, dice and measure

¾ cup green peppers

Combine tomatoes, onions and green peppers and cook 20 minutes. Press pulp through fine sieve.

Put into preserving kettle.

Add

**1 cup sugar
3 tablespoons salt
1½ cups vinegar**

Tie in cheesecloth

**2 sticks cinnamon
1 teaspoon whole cloves
2 teaspoons whole allspice
1½ teaspoons mustard seeds
1 teaspoon celery seeds**

Add to ingredients in kettle.

Boil until thickened, about 1 hour. Stir to prevent sticking.

Remove spice bag and fill hot sterilized sealers and seal.

Yield: About 2 pints.

583 Chili Sauce

Blanch and peel

**7½ pounds ripe tomatoes
(about 30 medium)**

Chop or put through food chopper, and then measure

**2½ cups peeled onions (6 medium)
2½ cups seeded green and red peppers
(4 green and 2 red)**

Finely dice and measure

3 cups celery

Put these in large preserving kettle.

Add

**2½ cups sugar
2 tablespoons salt
4 cups cider vinegar**

Tie in cheesecloth

**1 tablespoon whole cloves
3 tablespoons whole allspice**

Add to ingredients; bring to a boil and cook

uncovered over moderate heat for 2 to 2½ hours, stirring frequently. The mixture should be fairly thick. Remove spice bag; ladle into sterilized sealers and seal immediately.

Yield: About 5 pints.

584 Gherkins

Wash and scrub 2″ to 3″ cucumbers to make

4 quarts

Rinse and drain.

Place in a clean dry crock.

Make a hot brine with

**1½ cups coarse salt
20 cups (4 quarts) boiling water**

Pour over cucumbers and let stand overnight, covered.

Drain cucumbers thoroughly and place in dry crock.

Combine

**8 cups blended vinegar
¼ cup salt
¼ cup sugar
¼ cup mustard seeds
½ cup mixed pickling spice**

Pour the cold pickling mixture over the cucumbers.

Each morning for the next 14 days add ½ cup sugar, stirring to dissolve. When last of sugar has been added, remove pickles from liquid and pack into clean jars.

Strain pickle mixture to remove spices. Pour over pickles and seal.

Yield: 7 to 8 pints.

585 Dill Pickles

Choose freshly picked cucumbers, 3″ to 5″ long. Scrub and soak overnight in cold water.

Place a piece of dill in each clean sterilized jar (either quarts or pints). The amount of dill used will depend upon individual tastes.

Pack cucumbers into jars whole or cut lengthwise in quarters.

For 4 quart sealers of pickles, prepare the following liquid:

Combine

**¾ cup coarse salt
2 cups white vinegar
6 cups water**

Bring to a boil and pour hot liquid over cucumbers. Seal. Let stand in a cool place for 6 weeks before using.

NOTE: A small piece of garlic may be added to each sealer of pickles.

586 Ice Water Pickles

Select, wash and cut 3 quarts firm cucumbers (4" to 5" in length) into quarters, lengthwise.

Soak in ice water for 3 hours.

Heat
4 cups vinegar
1½ cups sugar
⅓ cup salt
½ cup water

Boil for 5 minutes.

Keep liquid hot until needed.

Drain cucumbers well and pack into clean pint sealers.

To each sealer add
2 thin slices onion
½ teaspoon mustard seeds
½ teaspoon celery seeds

Pour hot liquid over cucumbers, filling sealers to the top. Seal immediately. Cool and store in cool dry place.

Yield: About 8 pints.

587 Bread and Butter Pickles

Wash and thinly slice sufficient medium-sized cucumbers to measure 16 cups, about 1 (6-quart) basket.

Peel and thinly slice
6 medium-sized onions

Wash, seed and cut into thin strips
1 green pepper
1 sweet red pepper

Combine the vegetables in a large preserving kettle, sprinkling ⅓ cup coarse salt between layers.

Mix a tray of ice cubes through the vegetables and cover with another tray of cubes. Let stand 3 hours.

Drain vegetables well.

Combine
3 cups white wine vinegar
5 cups sugar
1½ teaspoons turmeric
1½ teaspoons celery seeds
2 tablespoons mustard seeds

Pour over drained vegetables.

Heat to boiling point only. (This is all the cooking that is necessary.)

Pack in hot sterilized sealers, seal and store in a cool place for 1 month before using.

Yield: About 8 pints.

NOTE: For crisper and better coloured pickles, divide the batch in half and cook separately.

588 Spiced Pickled Beets

Select small young beets 1" to 1½" in diameter. Scrub thoroughly leaving root and 1" to 2" of stem.

Cook until just tender.

Dip in cold water and remove skins.

One 6-quart basket will yield about 12 cups prepared beets. For this quantity, prepare the following syrup:

Combine in saucepan
2 cups cider vinegar
2 cups sugar
2 cups water
1 tablespoon salt
1 teaspoon ground allspice
2 tablespoons whole cloves
(tied in cheesecloth)

Bring to a boil and boil for 5 minutes. Remove spice bag and keep syrup hot until needed.

Pack hot sterilized sealers with prepared beets.

Pour hot syrup over beets to completely cover them.

Seal, cool and store.

Yield: 6 pints.

589 Pickled Onions

Cover 2 quarts small white onions with boiling water. Let stand 3 minutes; drain and cover with cold water; then peel.

Make a brine with
8 cups boiling water
¾ cup coarse salt

Pour over onions and let stand overnight.

Drain, then rinse thoroughly with cold water.

Combine
4 cups white vinegar
1 cup sugar
1 stick cinnamon

Heat to boiling point, then boil 5 minutes, remove stick cinnamon.

Add onions and bring *just* to boiling point.

Pack into clean sealers; cover with boiling pickle mixture and seal.
Yield: About 4 pints.

590 Mustard Pickles

Wash and cut into pieces
2 cauliflowers
Wash cucumbers and cut into chunks to make
2 quarts
or use 2 quarts small whole cucumbers.
Peel and leave whole
2 quarts small silver skin onions
Wash, seed and cut into strips
3 green peppers
2 sweet red peppers
Combine vegetables in a large pan and add a brine made by combining
1 cup coarse salt
2½ quarts water
1 teaspoon alum
Let stand overnight.
In the morning drain off brine and rinse vegetables once.

MUSTARD SAUCE
Combine
½ cup dry mustard
1 cup *Pre-Sifted* PURITY All-Purpose Flour
2½ cups sugar
1 teaspoon turmeric
1 teaspoon cayenne pepper
These ingredients should be mixed in a preserving kettle large enough to hold the vegetables.
Blend in
2 cups water
Cook, stirring, until thickened and smooth.
Slowly add
7 cups cider vinegar
When sauce is hot, add vegetables and cook over medium heat about 15 minutes or until tender. Stir occasionally to prevent sticking.
Ladle into hot sterilized sealers and seal.
Yield: About 14 pints.
NOTE: 1. Allow the pickles to ripen 1 month before using.
2. The Mustard Sauce can be made the day before you make the pickles, if desired.

591 Mustard Bean Pickles

Wash and trim ends from
1 (6-quart) basket young yellow string beans
Cut into 1″ lengths. This amount will measure about 15 cups prepared beans.
Cook in boiling salted water until just tender.

MUSTARD SAUCE
Mix together in a large saucepan or kettle
2½ cups sugar
1 tablespoon turmeric
2 teaspoons salt
½ cup dry mustard
½ cup *Pre-Sifted* PURITY All-Purpose Flour
Blend in
½ cup vinegar
Heat to boiling point
2½ cups vinegar
1 tablespoon celery seeds
Stir hot liquid slowly into flour mixture.
Place over moderate heat, stirring until thickened and smooth (about 5 minutes).
Add drained beans; bring mixture to boiling point.
Ladle into hot sterilized sealers and seal.
Yield: About 6 pints.

VARIATION:

(a) Winter Mustard Bean Pickles
Substitute 4 (20-ounce) cans cut golden wax beans, drained, in above recipe. (10 cups drained beans.)
Yield: About 5 pints.

592 Corn Relish

Cook 6 to 7 ears corn for 5 minutes in boiling water. Dip in cold water. Cut corn from cob and measure
4 cups
Place corn in large saucepan or preserving kettle and add
½ cup chopped onions
½ cup chopped green peppers
½ cup chopped sweet red peppers
1 cup chopped celery
1½ cups white wine vinegar
½ cup water
2 cups sugar
1½ teaspoons coarse salt
1 teaspoon mustard seeds
1 teaspoon celery seeds

Mix well; bring to a boil, then simmer gently for 10 minutes.

Combine

1½ teaspoons dry mustard
½ teaspoon turmeric
¼ cup *Pre-Sifted* PURITY
All-Purpose Flour

with

½ cup water

Gradually stir paste into boiling relish. Allow mixture to cook for about 10 minutes or until thickened, stirring constantly. Fill hot sterilized sealers and seal.

Yield: About 4 pints.

NOTE: This recipe can be doubled with good results.

VARIATION:

(a) Winter Corn Relish

Substitute 4 cups canned whole kernel corn, drained, in the above recipe. Omit red sweet pepper and substitute ¼ cup diced pimiento, adding it to the relish 5 minutes before the mixture is finished cooking.

Yield: About 4 pints.

593 Hot Dog Relish

Wash, prepare and measure the following vegetables:

8 cups peeled, seeded, minced
cucumbers (8 to 10 large)
3 cups peeled, minced onions
(8 medium)
4 cups minced green tomatoes
(6 large)
1 hot red pepper, minced
½ cup minced green peppers
1 cup minced sweet red peppers
4 cups finely diced celery

Put vegetables in a large container; sprinkle with

⅓ cup coarse salt

Let stand overnight.

In the morning drain off liquid and add

4 cups white wine vinegar
3 cups sugar

Cook gently over medium heat for 15 minutes, stirring frequently.

Combine

½ cup *Pre-Sifted* PURITY
All-Purpose Flour
1 teaspoon turmeric
1 tablespoon celery seeds
1 tablespoon mustard seeds

Mix to a paste with

1 cup vinegar

Add to hot pickle mixture and stir until it is thickened and boiling.

Cook slowly for 10 minutes longer.

Ladle into sterilized sealers. Seal.

Yield: About 8 pints.

594 Spiced Watermelon Pickles

Slice watermelon in half horizontally, then cut into 1″ slices. Trim off hard green rind and pink flesh. The melon should be firm but not over-ripe.

Cut into 1″ cubes and place in large kettle. Cover with cold water mixed with

1 teaspoon baking soda

Let stand overnight at room temperature.

One medium-sized melon will yield 5 to 7 pounds raw rind or 6 to 8 pint jars of pickles.

Next morning drain rind and cover with cold water in which 2 tablespoons powdered alum has been dissolved. Bring to a boil quickly and boil 10 minutes.

Discard water. Cover rind with cold water in which 1 tablespoon ground ginger has been dissolved. Bring to a boil quickly and boil 15 minutes. Remove rind from ginger water with slotted spoon. Measure water and record the amount. Discard the water. Measure an amount of cider vinegar which is equal to the amount of discarded ginger water.

To each 4 cups of vinegar, add

3 pounds sugar

Tie in cheesecloth

¼ cup whole cloves
¼ cup cassia buds

Add to vinegar and sugar mixture, and heat to boiling point.

Add watermelon rind and cook 20 minutes, or until rind is clear and tender but not soft.

Pack rind into hot sterilized sealers.

Return syrup to heat and boil 15 minutes to reduce quantity and concentrate syrup. Remove spice bag.

Pour over pickles and seal.

Allow pickles to ripen 1 month before using.

To serve: If desired, cut cubes in half and spear with cocktail pick as an accompaniment for afternoon tea sandwiches or appetizer tray. Serve with hot or cold roast meats or poultry.

JAMS

General Directions

1. Jars: Almost any type of jar or jelly glass may be used for jams, conserves and marmalades. Use the size suitable for your family's needs.

Wash glasses and lids in soapy water; rinse, then sterilize in boiling water and leave in the water until needed. Drain well before using.

2. Paraffin: Use new paraffin since old or re-used paraffin can cause spoilage. Melt in a small pot placed over hot water.

3. Select firm ripe fruit and measure prepared fruit accurately. Follow directions given in recipes.

4. Jam Test: Recommended boiling times are approximate so a test should be made to check consistency. To test jam, remove kettle from heat, place a teaspoon of the jam on a cold saucer and chill rapidly. If jam does not set to required thickness, cook a few minutes longer and test again.

5. Carefully pour or ladle hot jam into scalded glasses leaving ½" space at top for paraffin. Avoid dribbling jam on the jars in this space.

6. Cover hot jam with a thin layer of hot melted paraffin. Leave until wax is hardened and jam cool, then add a second thin layer of hot paraffin, rotating the jar so the wax adheres to the glass. Cover with clean metal lids or paper covers secured with rubber bands. Label and store in a cool dry place.

NOTE: If using commercial pectin in either liquid or crystal form to make jams, follow exactly the manufacturer's directions. The booklet provided with the product includes recipes for practically all fruits used in making jams.

---

595 *July Jam*

(Cherry, Gooseberry, Red Currant and Raspberry)

Wash ripe cherries, pit and measure
4 cups

Wash gooseberries, top and tail, measure
4 cups

Wash and stem red currants, measure
4 cups

Wash and sort raspberries, measure
4 cups

Combine fruits in a large preserving kettle; crush, bring to a boil and precook uncovered for 15 minutes. Stir occasionally.

Add
8 cups sugar

Mix well; bring to a boil and boil uncovered to jam stage (see General Directions No. 4), about 10 to 12 minutes. Stir occasionally. Ladle into prepared glasses; seal, cool and cover as in General Directions No. 6.

Yield: About 14 (6-ounce) glasses.

A candy thermometer can be used to indicate the "jam stage" in making jam. Most fruits reach this point at 220° to 221°.

596 *Apricot Jam*

Wash fresh apricots, remove pits and cut into quarters.

Measure
12 cups of prepared apricots

Place in a preserving kettle, add
7 cups sugar

Let stand 1 hour.

Add
2 tablespoons lemon juice

Mix well and place over high heat. Bring to a boil and boil uncovered to jam stage (see General Directions No. 4), about 10 to 12 minutes, stirring occasionally. Ladle into prepared glasses; seal, cool and cover as in General Directions No. 6.

Yield: About 12 (6-ounce) glasses.

597 *Plum Jam*

Wash plums (any variety other than Damson plums); remove pits and cut into quarters.

Measure
12 cups of prepared plums

Place in a preserving kettle. If fruit is juicy,

add only ½ cup water; if using a dry variety of plum, add up to 1 cup water.

Precook plums, uncovered, for 10 minutes.

Add

7 cups sugar

Mix well and bring to a boil and boil uncovered to the jam stage (see General Directions No. 4), about 6 to 8 minutes, stirring occasionally. Ladle into prepared glasses; seal, cool and cover as in General Directions No. 6.

Yield: About 12 (6-ounce) glasses.

598 Peach Jam

Wash peaches and blanch in boiling water for 30 to 60 seconds (depending upon ripeness of fruit). Dip in cold water. Remove skins, pit and cut into pieces.

Measure

12 cups of prepared peaches

Place in preserving kettle and add

6 cups sugar

Let stand 1 hour.

Add

2 tablespoons lemon juice

Mix well and place over high heat. Bring to a boil and boil uncovered to jam stage (see General Directions No. 4), about 15 to 20 minutes, stirring occasionally. Ladle into prepared glasses; seal, cool and cover as in General Directions No. 6.

Yield: About 12 (6-ounce) glasses.

599 Damson Plum Jam

Wash plums. Measure

8 cups

Place in a preserving kettle and add

3½ cups water

Bring to a boil and cook, uncovered, for 15 minutes. Stir occasionally.

Add

7 cups sugar

Mix well; bring to a boil and boil uncovered to jam stage (see General Directions No. 4), about 6 to 8 minutes. Stir frequently, removing pits as they rise to the surface.

Ladle into prepared glasses; seal, cool and cover as in General Directions No. 6.

Yield: About 9 (6-ounce) glasses.

600 Rhubarb and Pineapple Jam

Wash, trim and cut in ½" pieces sufficient rhubarb to measure

8 cups

Pare, slice and dice in ¼" cubes fresh pineapple to measure

2 cups

Combine rhubarb and pineapple in preserving kettle; place over low heat and cook until juice begins to foam. (If rhubarb is not juicy add ¼ cup water.) Bring fruit to a boil and boil uncovered for 15 minutes, stirring frequently.

Add

4 cups sugar

Mix well; bring to a boil and boil uncovered to jam stage (see General Directions No. 4), about 25 minutes, stirring often.

Ladle or pour into prepared jars. Seal, cool and cover as in General Directions No. 6.

Yield: About 7 (6-ounce) glasses.

601 Strawberry Jam

Wash and hull sufficient ripe strawberries to measure

8 cups (about 4 quart boxes)

In a preserving kettle, alternate layers of the strawberries with

8 cups sugar

Let stand for 2 hours. Place over high heat and bring to a boil and boil uncovered for 5 minutes, stirring occasionally.

Add

½ cup lemon juice

Mix well and boil for 5 minutes longer or until mixture reaches the jam stage (see General Directions No. 4). Remove from heat, stir and skim by turns for 5 minutes. Ladle into prepared glasses. Seal, cool and cover as in General Directions No. 6.

Yield: About 9 (6-ounce) glasses.

602 Raspberry Jam

Wash, crush and measure

8 cups ripe raspberries (about 4 quart boxes)

Place in large saucepan; bring to a boil and cook uncovered for 15 minutes.

Add
  6 cups sugar

Mix well; bring to a boil and boil uncovered to jam stage (see General Directions No. 4), about 12 to 15 minutes, stirring occasionally.

Ladle into prepared glasses; seal, cool and cover as in General Directions No. 6.

Yield: About 9 (6-ounce) glasses.

603   Grape Jam

Wash and stem grapes. Press pulp from skins; cook the pulp 10 minutes. Then put through a sieve to remove the seeds.

Add skins to pulp and measure the mixture.

At this time measure the sugar to be added later, allowing ⅔ cup sugar for each cup of fruit. Bring fruit to a boil and boil uncovered about 10 minutes or until skins are tender.

Add sugar, mix well, bring to a boil and boil to jam stage (see General Directions No. 4), about 20 minutes, stirring frequently. Ladle into prepared glasses; seal, cool and cover as in General Directions No. 6.

604   Black Cherry Jam

Wash, stem and pit about 2 quarts ripe black cherries. Finely chop or put through food grinder.

Measure
  3¾ cups pulp and juice

Put in large saucepan and add
  ¼ cup lemon juice
  7 cups sugar

Mix well. Place over high heat and bring to a full rolling boil and boil hard for 1 minute, stirring constantly.

Remove from heat and stir in
  1 (6-ounce) bottle liquid pectin

Skim off foam with a metal spoon. Then stir and skim by turns for 5 minutes.

Ladle into prepared glasses. Seal, cool and cover as in General Directions No. 6.

Yield: About 11 (6-ounce) glasses.

NOTE: ½ teaspoon almond extract may be added after cooking the jam.

VARIATIONS:

(a)   Red Cherry Jam

Follow above recipe except use 4 cups of pre-

pared sour red cherries instead of 3¾ cups black cherries and omit the lemon juice.

(b)   Black Cherry Conserve

Prepare fruit as for Black Cherry Jam except measure 4 cups prepared black cherries and juice.

To prepared fruit add
  ¼ cup lemon juice
  1 tablespoon grated lemon rind
  ½ cup chopped seeded raisins
  1 cup finely chopped nuts

Proceed as directed for the Black Cherry Jam.

Yield: About 13 (6-ounce) glasses.

To prevent the fruit from coming to the top, cool jam for 5 minutes before ladling into prepared glasses. While cooling, alternately skim and stir the jam.

605   Orange Marmalade

To prepare the fruit; score and remove peel in quarters from
  3 medium-sized oranges
  2 lemons

Lay the peel flat, scrape off about half of the white membrane and discard. Slice the peel very finely with a sharp knife.

Put in a large saucepan and add
  1½ cups water
  ⅛ teaspoon baking soda

Bring to a boil and simmer, covered, for 20 minutes, stirring often.

Chop or finely dice the pulp of these fruits, removing any seeds. Add pulp and juice to peel mixture and simmer, covered, for 10 minutes.

Measure 3 cups of the peel, juice and pulp mixture into a large saucepan.

Add
  6 cups sugar

Mix thoroughly and bring to a full rolling boil. Boil hard for 1 minute, stirring constantly. Remove from heat.

Stir in
  ½ bottle liquid pectin (6-ounce size)

With a metal spoon, skim off foam, then stir and skim by turns for 7 minutes. Ladle into prepared glasses; seal, cool and cover as in General Directions No. 6.

Yield: About 8 (6-ounce) glasses.

VARIATIONS:

(a)   Christmas Conserve
To the 3 cups of fruit mixture in Orange Marmalade recipe, add ½ cup ground nuts, ¼ cup chopped light raisins and ¼ cup chopped maraschino cherries. Complete as directed.

(b)   Three Fruit Marmalade
Follow Orange Marmalade recipe exactly, substituting 1 medium orange, 1 small grapefruit and 1 medium lemon for the fruit.

606   Grape Conserve
Wash and stem 3 quarts ripe Concord grapes (about one-half 6-quart basket). Slip skins from pulp. Bring pulp to a boil, then simmer, covered, for 5 minutes, stirring occasionally. Press through a sieve to remove seeds. Put skins through food chopper. Combine pulp and skins then measure 4 cups into a large saucepan or preserving kettle.

Add

**¼ cup lemon juice
1 tablespoon grated lemon rind
½ cup raisins
1 cup finely chopped nuts (optional)
7 cups sugar**

Combine thoroughly and place over high heat and bring to a full rolling boil. Boil hard for 1 minute stirring constantly. Remove from heat.

Stir in at once

½ bottle liquid pectin (6-ounce size)

Skim off foam, using a metal spoon, then stir and skim by turns for 7 minutes. Ladle into prepared jars. Seal, cool and cover as in General Directions No. 6.

Yield: About 12 (6-ounce) glasses.

JELLIES
Jelly Making

Pectin, acid, water and sugar—in the correct proportions—are essential for jelly making. Some fruits are excellent for jelly since they are naturally rich in pectin and acid. These are:

Tart apples, Crab apples, Cranberries, Grapes, Red and Black currants, Gooseberries and Sour plums.
Other fruits such as raspberries, strawberries, cherries and rhubarb are low in pectin and high in acid. These can be combined with some of the fruits mentioned above to produce a good jelly.
The following table shows how to prepare the pectin rich fruits and the amount of water required for each:

Fruit	Preparation	Amount of Cold Water
Tart Apples	Wash, remove stem and blossom end. Cut into eighths.	Completely cover fruit.
Crab Apples	Wash, stem. Cut into quarters.	Completely cover fruit.
Red Currants	Wash, stem.	½ cup water for each cup of prepared fruit.
Black Currants	Wash, stem if necessary.	1 cup water for each cup of prepared fruit.
Gooseberries	Wash, stem.	¾ cup water for each cup of prepared fruit.
Grapes	Wash, stem.	Water level to be just below top layer of prepared fruit.
Sour Plums	Wash, stem, cut into quarters. Leave in pits.	Water level to be just below top layer of prepared fruit.

For the amount of sugar required see the General Directions No. 7 on next page.

General Directions

1. Select and sterilize jelly glasses or jars as for jam (page 214).

2. Select sound fruit using equal parts of ripe and slightly under-ripe fruit. Wash fruit; remove damaged spots and prepare following directions in table.

3. Add cold water to fruit according to directions in table. Cover and simmer until the fruit is soft, mashing it during cooking.

4. To extract the juice—Use a jelly bag, or several layers of 1-yard square, fine cheesecloth. Wet the cloth and spread over a colander in a bowl. Place cooked fruit in cloth, bring the corners together and twist while pressing down on the bag.

If a very clear jelly is desired, do not squeeze the bag. Suspend it over a bowl and let drain until dripping ceases.

5. Measure extracted juice carefully. Work with small amounts of juice at a time—about 8 cups.

6. Pectin Test—Boil juice uncovered for 3 minutes. Remove from heat; measure 1 teaspoon juice and 1 teaspoon rubbing alcohol into a small dish. Blend and let stand 30 seconds. If a jelly-like mass is formed, the juice contains sufficient pectin and requires no further boiling. If a heavy clot does not form, continue boiling, testing frequently.
Do not taste this mixture.

7. Measure sugar allowing 1 cup sugar for each cup of juice. If longer boiling has been required, allow ¾ cup sugar for each cup of juice. Add sugar slowly to hot juice. Quickly bring to a boil, removing scum as it forms. Boil from 3 to 10 minutes or until jellying point is reached.

8. Jelly Test—Dip up syrup in a large spoon and hold well above preserving kettle. Tilt spoon until syrup runs over the side. When jellying stage is reached, the liquid will stop flowing in a stream and divide into two distinct drops that run together and leave spoon in a "sheet".

9. Remove immediately from heat. Let stand 1 minute, while removing scum with a cold spoon.

10. Pour carefully into hot sterilized jelly glasses, leaving ¼" space at top.

11. Let stand until partially set; pour a thin layer of hot paraffin over the jelly. Let harden, then add a second thin layer, rotating the glass to insure a tight seal. Cover, label and store in a cool dry place.

Commercial Pectin:

Special directions are needed for jelly making when commercial pectin is used. These are included with each bottle or package and should be followed exactly.

If you would like to make some very special pectin jellies, try some of the following recipes.

---

607 *Four Fruit Jelly*

(Cherries, Red Currants, Strawberries and Raspberries)

Wash, stem and crush thoroughly (do not pit)
½ pound ripe sour cherries
Wash, stem and crush thoroughly
½ pound ripe red currants
Combine fruits and add
½ cup water
Bring to a boil, then simmer, covered, for 8 minutes.
Wash and hull
1½ quarts strawberries
Wash
1½ quarts red raspberries
Crush berries thoroughly and add to hot cherries and currants. Simmer for 2 minutes.

Place hot fruit in a jelly cloth or bag and squeeze out juice. Measure 4 cups of the juice into a large saucepan.
Add
7½ cups sugar
Mix well.
Place over high heat and bring to a boil, stirring constantly.
Stir in at once
1 (6-ounce) bottle liquid pectin
Bring to a full rolling boil and boil hard for 1 minute, stirring constantly.
Remove from heat, skim off foam with metal spoon. Pour into prepared glasses.
Cover jelly at once with hot paraffin. Cool, paraffin again, cover and store.
Yield: About 11 (6-ounce) glasses.

608 Apple Jelly
(Canned Juice)

Combine in a large saucepan
2 cups canned apple juice
3½ cups sugar
Mix well.
Place over heat and bring to a boil, stirring constantly.
Stir in at once
½ bottle liquid pectin (6-ounce size)
Bring to a full rolling boil and boil hard for 1 minute, continuing to stir.
Remove from heat, skim off foam with metal spoon. Pour into prepared jelly glasses. Cover with hot paraffin.
Cool, paraffin again, cover and store.
Yield: 5 (6-ounce) glasses.

VARIATIONS:

(a) Minted Apple Jelly

Make as directed for Apple Jelly above, adding a few drops green food colouring and ½ to ¾ teaspoon peppermint extract just before the liquid pectin is added.

(b) Grape Jelly
(Bottled or Canned Juice)

Make as directed for Apple Jelly above, substituting unsweetened bottled or canned grape juice for the canned apple juice.

609 Orange-Apricot Jelly
(Canned Sweetened Juice)

Combine in a large saucepan
2½ cups canned orange-apricot juice
4½ cups sugar
¼ cup lemon juice
Mix well and place over high heat.
Bring to a boil, stirring constantly.
Stir in
½ bottle liquid pectin (6-ounce size)
Bring to a full rolling boil and boil for 1 minute, stirring constantly.
Remove from heat, skim off foam with a metal spoon. Pour into prepared jelly glasses. Cover with hot paraffin.
Cool, paraffin again, cover and store.
Yield: 5 (6-ounce) glasses.
NOTE: Other canned fruit juices may be used for jelly making. If using a tart fruit juice such as grapefruit, omit the lemon juice.

610 Wine Jelly

Measure into top of double boiler
2 cups wine (port or sherry)
Add
3 cups sugar
Combine thoroughly and place over rapidly boiling water.
Stir to dissolve sugar, about 2 minutes.
Remove from heat and stir in
½ bottle liquid pectin (6-ounce size)
Skim off foam with metal spoon. Pour into prepared glasses and cover with hot paraffin.
Cool, paraffin again, cover and store.
Yield: About 5 (6-ounce) glasses.
NOTE: This jelly can be poured into inexpensive heavy wine glasses or small snifters and covered with fancy paper for gifts.

Always use standard 8-ounce measuring cups and level measures when making jams and jellies.

611 Fresh Mint Jelly

Wash 1 large bunch mint. Measure 1 cup leaves and stems, well packed. Place in a large saucepan and crush thoroughly with a wooden masher.
Add
2¼ cups water
Bring quickly to a boil.
Remove from heat, cover and let stand 10 minutes.
Strain and measure 1½ cups mint infusion into large saucepan.
Add
2 tablespoons strained lemon juice
Few drops green food colouring
3½ cups sugar
Mix well. Place over high heat and bring to a boil, stirring constantly.
Stir in
½ bottle liquid pectin (6-ounce size)
Bring to a full rolling boil and boil hard for 1 minute, stirring constantly.
Remove from heat, skim off foam with metal spoon. Pour into prepared glasses; cover at once with hot paraffin.
Cool, paraffin again, cover and store.
Yield: About 5 (6-ounce) glasses.

INDEX

PURITY COOK BOOK